D1154090

Saving Grand Canyon:
Dams, Deals, and a Noble Myth

A Bureau of Reclamation artist's depiction of Bridge Canyon/Hualapai Dam and reservoir. NAU.PH.96.4.68.39, Northern Arizona University, Cline Library, Bill Belknap Collection.

SAVING GRAND CANYON

Dams, Deals, and a Noble Myth

BYRON E. PEARSON

UNIVERSITY OF NEVADA PRESS

University of Nevada Press | Reno, Nevada 89557 USA
www.unpress.nevada.edu
Copyright © 2019 by University of Nevada Press
All rights reserved.

Cover design by Matt Strelecki
Cover photograph © Anton Foltin | Dreamstime.com

LIBRARY OF CONGRESS CATALOGING-IN-PUBLICATION DATA

Names: Pearson, Byron E., 1960- author.
Title: Saving Grand Canyon : dams, deals, and a noble myth / Byron Eugene Pearson.
Description: Reno, Nevada : University of Nevada Press, [2019] | Includes bibliographical references
    and index.
Identifiers: LCCN 2019011618 | ISBN 9781948908320 (pbk. : alk. paper)
Subjects: LCSH: Grand Canyon (Ariz.)--History. | Grand Canyon National Park (Ariz.)--History. |
    Dams--Political aspects--Arizona--Grand Canyon. | Sierra Club--Influence. | United States.
    National Environmental Policy Act of 1969.
Classification: LCC F788 .P37 2019 | DDC 979.1/32--dc23
LC record available at https://lccn.loc.gov/2019011618

The paper used in this book meets the requirements of American National
Standard for Information Sciences—Permanence of Paper for Printed Library Materials,
ANSI/NISO Z39.48-1992 (R2002).

FIRST PRINTING

Manufactured in the United States of America

For Kim

Contents

List of Figures   ix

Preface: Centennial Reflections   xi

Introduction   xv

1. "Something to be Skinned"   1

2. New Lines in the Sand   35

3. Dinosaurs and Rainbows   70

4. A Time for Water Statesmanship   100

5. A "Fjord-like Setting"   129

6. "A Little Closer to God"   153

7. "Permanent Massive Things"   181

8. Be Careful What You Wish For . . .   212

9. Alternative Realities   249

Notes   277

Selected Bibliography   311

Index   331

Acknowledgments   343

About the Author   345

Figures

Frontispiece: A Bureau of Reclamation artist's depiction
of Bridge Canyon/Hualapai Dam and reservoir. ii

1.1 President Theodore Roosevelt telling the people of Arizona
to "leave [Grand Canyon] as it is," on May 6, 1903. 2

1.2 John Wesley Powell, explorer and second director of
the United States Geological Survey, ca. 1869. 4

1.3 Arizona's Ralph Cameron, territorial representative,
US senator, and promoter of the first serious attempt to
build a dam on the Colorado River in Grand Canyon. 9

1.4 Map showing the location of the hydroelectric dam Ralph Cameron
sought to build in Grand Canyon National Monument. 12

1.5 Chief Forester Henry Graves who denied Ralph Cameron's
application to dam the Colorado River in Grand Canyon. 16

1.6 Map of the Colorado River Basin. 20

1.7 Map showing Fred Colter's proposed Arizona Highline
Canal and Colorado-Verde Project. 24

1.8 Nellie T. Bush, state legislator and Admiral of the
Arizona Navy in 1934. 28

1.9 Map of Grand Canyon National Park as it was created in 1919. 30

1.10 Lower Grand Canyon rim view just above the
Bridge Canyon Damsite looking upstream. 32

2.1 Newton B. Drury, director of the National Park Service
from 1940 to 1951. 37

2.2 Map of Grand Canyon National Park and Monument and various
proposals from the Bureau of Reclamation's 1946 report. 44

2.3 Department of Interior personnel inspecting the
Bridge Canyon Damsite in 1949 55

2.4 A construction camp on the Navajo Reservation above one of
the damsites in Marble Canyon located at river mile 32.7 just
downstream of Vasey's Paradise ca. 1950. 56

4.1 Sierra Club Executive Director David Brower in
Glen Canyon, 1963. 107

4.2   Environmentalist Martin Litton in 2013 holding the
      hand-drawn map he used to convince the Sierra Club's
      leadership to oppose the Grand Canyon dams in 1963.   114

4.3   Arizona Governor Sam Goddard, Representative Morris Udall,
      Interior Secretary Stewart Udall, and Senator Carl Hayden
      in December 1964 standing in front of a map of the proposed
      Pacific Southwest Water Plan.   122

5.1   Floyd Dominy, commissioner of the Bureau of Reclamation,
      in 1966.   132

6.1   Floyd Dominy's photo of Marble Canyon, with the proposed
      Marble Canyon Dam and Reservoir superimposed.   166

7.1   Physicist Richard Bradley and Representative Morris Udall
      with Floyd Dominy's scale model of Grand Canyon.   191

7.2   Sierra Club Executive Director David Brower and
      supporters at Grand Canyon in March 1966.   197

7.3   Representative John Rhodes, Hualapai Chief George Rocha,
      and Representative Morris Udall in front of an artist's
      depiction of the proposed Hualapai Dam , ca. 1966.   203

7.4   Map showing the proposed Bridge Canyon/Hualapai
      Dam and Marble Canyon Dam.   206

7.5   The first Grand Canyon Battle Ad commissioned by the Sierra
      Club and created by the advertising firm of Freeman, Mander
      & Gossage that ran in the New York Times and other national
      newspapers on June 9, 1966.   215

7.6   The fabled "Sistine Chapel" advertisement commissioned by
      the Sierra Club and created by the advertising firm of Freeman,
      Mander & Gossage, that ran in August 1966, still one of the
      most well-known examples of using the mass media to promote
      an environmental cause.   230

8.1   The committee that saved Grand Canyon: the 1967–1968
      Senate Committee on Interior and Insular Affairs.   242

8.2   President Lyndon Baines Johnson signs the "damless" Lower
      Colorado River Basin Project bill into law on Sept. 30, 1968.   245

8.3   A map of Grand Canyon National Park after the 1975
      park expansion.   246

9.1   Senator Henry Jackson and Bill Van Ness, special counsel
      to the Senate Committee on Interior and Insular Affairs and
      primary author of the National Environmental Policy Act.   275

Preface: Centennial Reflections

In the summer of 1997, while I was still in graduate school, I sat in David Brower's office at his home in Berkeley, California. Brower graciously let me interview him while I was examining the Sierra Club collections at the Bancroft Library. He patiently answered my questions about the Sierra Club's fight to save Grand Canyon for more than two hours. Afterwards, we discussed the future of the environmental movement.

Well into his eighties, and in frail health, he still fought battles from behind the same desk from where he led dozens of environmental crusades. Two things were uppermost on his mind: dam removal and growth—both economic and of population. "Zero-sum games," he called them. Shifting to dams for a moment, he reminisced about a series of debates he and his erstwhile nemesis Floyd Dominy had held recently in front of raucous audiences over the removal of Glen Canyon Dam. He then spoke of Hetch Hetchy. "We're gonna get that one back," he said, his voice filled with hope.[1]

Although Hetch Hetchy remains a reservoir, had Brower lived to celebrate the centennial of Grand Canyon National Park in 2019, he would have witnessed events unthinkable even to an unbridled optimist such as himself. Since the new millennium, more than one thousand dams have been removed from America's rivers. Fisheries have rebounded through the herculean efforts of ecologists, biologists, and nature's own ability to heal. Dam removal is accelerating, and it is being celebrated.

Transparency is now part of the process federal and state projects must go through before approval, thanks to the National Environmental Policy Act (NEPA). I think even Brower would have been astounded to read the book *Deadbeat Dams*, written by Dan Beard, former commissioner of the Bureau of Reclamation, in which he calls for the abolishment of the bureau and the decommissioning of Glen Canyon Dam.[2] Perhaps as we celebrate the centennial of Grand Canyon National Park (2019), and the fiftieth anniversary of the passage of the Central Arizona Project without dams in Grand Canyon (2018), there is reason to hope. And yet . . .

None of the recently decommissioned dams generated significant amounts of hydroelectric power. They were obsolete and, therefore, could be taken out with no impact upon energy production. Also,
population and economic development, the forces that drove Anglo
Americans to reduce the West's great rivers to a series of slack-water
reservoirs, continue to increase. We cannot remain on this path without
someday paying the cost. Because America lacks the foresight to realize
that any solution is merely temporary so long as it is wedded to growth,
Americans will demand that their lifestyles be sustained—perhaps the
only time "sustainability" will be a national issue.

China, inexorably, has risen as an economic colossus, in both
heavy-polluting industry and technology. To generate power for this
economy, hundreds of miles of scenic gorges have disappeared under reservoirs created by hydroelectric dams that dwarf anything Dominy ever
built. Little meaningful opposition to these dams has arisen—there are
no Chinese Browers to rally the troops, nor is the population of China
free to protest like its American counterpart. As long as America sub-
scribes to the growth model, we will have to compete with this rising
economic superpower, or be left behind, an unthinkable option in the
present political climate.

Water in the reservoirs behind Hoover and Glen Canyon Dams has
dropped dramatically since the dawn of the new millennium. Lake Mead
now stands only three feet above the level established to trigger an increasingly draconian series of emergency water conservation measures
in the lower Colorado Basin, which, if implemented, have the potential
to set off a western water war that will make the bitter conflicts of the
twentieth century pale in comparison. As drought grips the West, and
the US government continues to kowtow to the western agribusiness
lobby by subsidizing water-intensive crops such as corn for ethanol and
cotton in an area that averages four to six inches of rain a year, the need
for more water and power will continue to grow.

That water will have to come from somewhere—the Pacific Northwest
perhaps—and moving all of that water will require massive amounts of
power from all available sources, developed or not. Lying in the middle
of it all is almost two thousand feet of undeveloped hydroelectric potential in Grand Canyon, currently locked away in Grand Canyon National
Park. At some point, somebody will make a try for it and Grand Canyon
will be threatened once again.

The centennial of Grand Canyon National Park on February 26, 2019 came and went without much public fanfare. Most people who visit the canyon do not know that the government once seriously considered building dams there. Even those who do believe that that possibility is unthinkable today. However, there are still threats, grave threats looming over this most iconic of natural wonders just as there were five decades ago.

I do not believe the massive public outcry the Sierra Club and other environmental organizations generated during the 1960s saved Grand Canyon. Because I am a historian, I believe the Gordian Knot of events that resulted in the defeat of the Grand Canyon dams cannot be explained by a simple heroic narrative. As a result, my work has been criticized by people affiliated with environmental organizations, the Sierra Club in particular. One went so far as to say that my first book was an "ill-timed cheap shot," while another described my conclusions as "lurid" and my reasoning "slipshod."[3] But other people, including former Interior Secretary Stewart Udall and Dr. Stephen Jett, the cultural geographer who testified against the dams before Congress and worked closely with the Navajo Nation during this controversy, have affirmed for me the complexity of the events and the multiple reasons that the dams were defeated.

With the Grand Canyon National Park centennial year upon us, it is a good time to publish another book to remind people of how terribly close we came during the twentieth century to defacing the canyon with mountains of concrete and burying the river that carved it beneath reservoirs. Although by all outward appearances the environmental movement is richer and more popular than ever, there are signs of complacency. None other than Kenneth Brower, David's son, wrote recently that many environmental groups are now "run by MBAs," they are making deals "with the other side," and they "have much less fire in the belly."[4]

They are now part of the system. They *have* become complacent and perhaps even haughty. In the current political climate this attitude risks the loss of everything environmentalists have worked so hard to save for the last 150 years. Some of this smugness is reflected in recent widely-distributed documentaries that depart from the historical record. In a world where alternative facts are now a part of our vernacular, straying from what is documented risks discrediting the movement as a whole.

Although I do appreciate constructive criticism, I must admit to one exception. A reviewer once wrote that I lacked passion. Even though I always try to write from a detached perspective, nothing could be further from the truth. I am not without feelings and opinions. I am a native son of Arizona, the Grand Canyon State. I have backpacked hundreds of miles and spent dozens of nights in its namesake canyon, climbed—and been terrified—on some of its exposed perpendicular faces, and ridden the great river in a small boat. I am rooted deeply in its Redwall cliffs, Kaibab limestone walls, and the black Vishnu schist of the inner gorge. I too feel anger at the shortsighted environmental exploitation that has taken place on the Colorado Plateau. Although I currently teach in Texas, Arizona will always be home. Grand Canyon is still my place, and I love to tell its stories.

So let us celebrate the hundredth birthday of Grand Canyon National Park. But as we congratulate ourselves, let us be mindful that political, ideological, and environmental forces are building that may soon cause tectonic shifts in how Americans view their parks. I fear for the wild places America has set aside. I fear that in the not-so-distant future Americans will be forced to choose between providing the water and power for an exploding population and an artificial agricultural economy—and leaving two thousand vertical feet of hydroelectric potential untapped in the desert Southwest. Unless people tear themselves away from their cyberidentities and celebrity adulation and rise in wrathful protest, I am not optimistic about the choices that will be made.

In this centennial year, let us temper our celebration with a warning to others who love Grand Canyon that they cannot delude themselves into thinking that the battles to save it are over. I fear they have only begun.

—Angel Fire, New Mexico, 2019

Introduction

Grand Canyon has been saved from dams three times since President Theodore Roosevelt told the people of Arizona to "leave it as it is" in 1903.[1] That people mostly left it as it was, and the reasons why the canyon is free from dams today, are what this story is about. TR placed the canyon under the protection of the US Forest Service when he created Grand Canyon National Monument in 1908. However, those who assigned a higher value to profit than scenic grandeur ignored him and continued to pursue ways to harness the great river that carved it.

People had spoken of building hydroelectric projects on the Colorado River in Grand Canyon since the 1890s, but the first serious brush with a main-stream dam is a little-known episode that occurred immediately after the loss of Hetch Hetchy. In 1915, Chief Forester Henry Graves denied Arizona's Ralph Cameron the opportunity to build a massive hydroelectric dam at the bottom of Bright Angel Trail, in the heart of the modern-day Grand Canyon National Park. Had Graves decided otherwise, it is highly likely this dam would have been constructed as there was no unified environmental movement to oppose it or National Environmental Policy Act that could have been used to stop it.

The second near miss occurred after World War II when Arizona Senator Carl Hayden attempted to obtain the approval of the Central Arizona Project (CAP) in 1950 and 1951. His project included a dam 673 feet in height that would have backed water through the national monument and along the park boundary for thirteen miles. This proposal actually made it through the Senate . . . twice. California, Arizona's longtime antagonist, saved Grand Canyon by blocking Hayden's bills in the House of Representatives and threw the issue of dividing the water of the lower Colorado River Basin into the US Supreme Court where it remained for more than a decade.

The canyon was saved from dams a third time by a complicated series of events that involved an ambitious regional water proposal, numerous backroom political deals, and a massive public outcry led by environmental groups during the 1960s. All three of these episodes could have resulted in the desecration of America's most iconic natural wonder, and they serve as benchmarks that measure the state of American environmentalism at the time they occurred.

Although the last serious attempt to build dams in Grand Canyon was made more than fifty years ago, few people have written about it from a detached perspective. Historians, popular writers, bloggers, and producers of environmental documentaries have almost universally contended that the environmentalists, the Sierra Club in particular, are responsible for "saving" Grand Canyon. Most environmental historians who have written about the controversy have focused primarily upon the Sierra Club's successful mobilization of public opinion, which resulted in one of the most massive expressions of outrage in American history.

These historians argue that the tremendous outcry the Sierra Club generated translated into changes in policy, and that Interior Secretary Udall, who initially supported the dams, changed his mind as a result of this public reaction. The story that Udall and Congress capitulated to this pressure and eventually manipulated the political process to pass a Central Arizona Project bill without dams has been told and retold so often by so many people that through repetition alone it has gained such legitimacy that environmental historians and laypeople alike have scarcely questioned it.[2]

But policy is not made when people put bumper stickers on their cars that say, "Save Grand Canyon." This was particularly true in the mid-1960s when a national environmental policy that granted the public access to the process did not exist. Nor is it made when tens or even hundreds of thousands of angry letters arrive in congressional mailboxes. Laws are crafted in isolation, and at no time was this more the case than in the first six decades of the twentieth century, when the committee system lacked transparency and governmental agencies such as the Bureau of Reclamation ran amok. It was only after the National Environmental Policy Act became law in 1970 that environmental organizations and the American people became part of policymaking, and agencies seeking to build massive projects were finally required to evaluate alternatives and disclose the environmental consequences of their proposals.

Thus the fight to save Grand Canyon during the 1960s occurred on two levels: in the court of public opinion and within the political process. The most widely-believed version of these events does not give enough weight to the intricate and complex nature of the political aspects of the controversy. Although a romantic, feel-good account, it overstates the impact the Sierra Club, other environmental organizations, and public opinion had upon lawmaking in the late 1960s. With the passage of time, this widely published interpretation has become so embellished, and the Sierra Club's role in the controversy given so much emphasis, that recent environmental documentaries have taken such liberties with the historical record that some of them could aptly be described as historical fiction.

This book offers a more balanced account that remains true to documented events. It considers how the fight to save Grand Canyon played out in the context of shifting political agendas, technological advancements, and social unrest during the decade when the modern environmental movement arose. The controversy was so complicated and the committee process so byzantine, it is easy to lose sight of the human aspect of the story. People, both for and against the dams, are at the center of this narrative. Indeed, I have been privileged to meet, through my own interviews and interviews others have conducted, an amazingly eclectic cast of characters, such as: Arizona's shrewd representatives Morris Udall and John Rhodes; powerful Arizona Senator Carl Hayden; Wayne Aspinall of Colorado, the "prickly" House Interior Committee chairman; Washington's unyielding Senator Henry Jackson; Bureau of Reclamation Commissioner Floyd Dominy, the self-proclaimed "Messiah"[3] of western water development; California's brilliant legal strategist, Northcutt "Mike" Ely; David Brower, the Sierra Club's executive director and maybe the most important environmentalist since John Muir; the eminently quotable Martin Litton, who at times resembled an Old Testament prophet; Stewart Udall, the pragmatic interior secretary and former Arizona congressman; Bill Van Ness, the primary author of the National Environmental Policy Act; and thousands of ordinary citizens who were moved to write letters of protest, all of whom influenced the outcome of this struggle to save America's most famous natural wonder.

I will argue throughout this book that despite the preservationists' national publicity campaign, a bill containing the Grand Canyon dams would never have been passed after August 1966 because: (1) Senator Jackson, chair of the Senate Interior Committee, guaranteed that he would block any bill containing these dams because they would have been used to generate power sold to fund a diversion of water from the Columbia River; and (2) California water strategist Ely seized this opportunity to kill them in the House Rules Committee so California could continue using water that the Supreme Court had awarded to Arizona in 1963. Although inertia carried the process forward another two years and environmentalists gave passionate testimony in defense of the canyon before congressional committees in 1967, the dams had been dealt their death blow the previous fall. Stewart Udall did not remove the dams from the bill in 1967 because he felt pressured, as is so often claimed; he did so because he needed to gain Jackson's support to steer a CAP bill through Congress before he and Senator Hayden left office after the 1968 election.

But environmental groups did play an important role in the fight to save Grand Canyon, and none was as important as the Sierra Club. At the beginning of the controversy, the Sierra Club was but one of several environmental organizations that were attempting to change the nation's environmental consciousness. Groups such as the Wilderness Society, National Parks Association, Izaak Walton League, and others joined the Sierra Club during the successful battle to defeat dams proposed for Dinosaur National Monument in the 1950s. Thus several groups had attained enough public recognition to lead the cause of preservationism into the next decade. My analysis explains why the Sierra Club, instead of one of these other groups, emerged from the 1960s as the leading environmental organization in the world.

In a nutshell, the Sierra Club was willing to risk everything to keep dams out of Grand Canyon and the other groups were not. Influential club leaders who were also attorneys decided to defy court rulings and federal laws designed to prohibit lobbying by nonprofit organizations. Because it was the only group willing to challenge this governmental intrusion upon fundamental constitutional principles, the Sierra Club stood apart from all other organizations in terms of the lengths it was willing to go to defend the environment. Consequently, in 1963 when the greatest and most recent fight to save Grand Canyon from dams began, other organizations looked to the club for guidance, and it solidified its position of leadership as the controversy unfolded by making appeals to the American people through the mass media. When the IRS revoked the Sierra Club's tax-deductible status in June 1966 after David Brower placed ads condemning the proposed damming of Grand Canyon in national newspapers, it triggered a tsunami of sympathy from people concerned with civil liberties issues and created a broad constituency from which the club's leadership drew strength to push its environmental agenda after the controversy ended.

Most of the dams planned for Grand Canyon were part of various incarnations of the Central Arizona Project. However, this book is not a comprehensive discussion of the CAP. Rather, it examines dam proposals within the context of environmental policymaking, grassroots activism, and shifting public perceptions of land use in the twentieth century. Neither is it about conflicts over American Indian resources, even though American Indians play a pivotal role in this story. State and private schemes only enter the narrative when they interfered with federal projects. It is also a story that involves interesting people, but it is not biographical save when a brief sketch is needed to illuminate a person's ideas and actions. Finally, although the bitter water feud between Arizona and California plays a prominent role, this conflict within the conflict only enters the story when it interfered with the passage of regional schemes or became an obstacle that people who favored a regional project tried to overcome.

This book incorporates some of the articles I have published since 1994 and parts of my first book, *Still the Wild River Runs: Congress, the Sierra Club, and the Fight to Save Grand Canyon* (2002); however, this new study is not a simple rehashing or a second edition of anything I have written before. It is the first time I have had the opportunity to publish a work about the numerous issues related to various attempts to build dams in Grand Canyon in the entire context of the late nineteenth and twentieth centuries, rather than bits and pieces of the story that took place over the span of a few years. It is a chance for me to add eighteen years of research to what I wrote more than a decade ago, to reinterpret this evidence, and to assess and expand my previous conclusions. It also offers me the opportunity to situate the origin point of the National Environmental Policy Act within these events, a reinterpretation of the genesis of this landmark piece of legislation. The story is even more nuanced, complicated, frustrating, and outright fun to research than even I realized.

A clarification of some of the terms used in the text is appropriate here. In this discussion, "conservation," "preservation," and "environmentalism" are used interchangeably because their meanings have changed over the last century. For example, "conservation" organizations of the 1950s would describe themselves as environmentalists today. Advocates of early twentieth-century Progressive Conservation, or "wise use," also referred to themselves as "conservationists." Because the term "conservation(ist)" has held dual meanings for much of the twentieth century, I have used appropriate modifiers throughout this narrative to clarify the meaning of these words in context. Likewise, the meanings American society has associated with the term "wilderness" have also evolved since the British colonized the Virginia tidewater region in 1607. I have used this word to refer to places environmentalists believed were important to protect for scenic and psychological reasons, rather than to describe idealized pristine landscapes and roadless areas untouched by human development. Surprisingly, although the Wilderness Act of 1964 was one of the most important pieces of environmental legislation ever passed, relatively few connections existed between it and the fight to save Grand Canyon even though many people and environmental organizations supported both.

Also, dams of varying heights have been proposed over the years. For purposes of this discussion, a "low" dam at the Bridge Canyon Damsite refers to a dam topped out at 570 feet above the river (or lower), while a "high" dam would have measured at least 673 feet tall. A low dam would have backed water through Grand Canyon National Monument. The reservoir created by a high dam would have invaded the monument and also increased the depth of the river along thirteen miles of the national park boundary. No federal legislation included dams in between these two heights. The most frequent height proposed for Marble Canyon Dam located upstream of the park was 310 feet above the Colorado River. Both dams would have been of a "thin arch concrete design."[4]

This is an epic story, incredibly broad in scope. The struggles to keep dams out of Grand Canyon cannot be separated from other battles to save other canyons within the Colorado River watershed, particularly those that occurred over Glen Canyon and the canyons of the Green River in Dinosaur National Monument. Additionally, much of this chronicle is driven by the evolution of ideas, political and social transformations, and legal interpretations, all of which changed over time. From the beginning of the twentieth century, ideas and conflict over irrigation, reclamation, and preservation framed the parameters of the struggles that followed.

This book is written as events unfolded chronologically. Chapter one begins with late nineteenth-century evaluations of Grand Canyon and includes Arizona boosterism; the beginnings of western reclamation; the Hetch Hetchy dispute and how it framed battles to protect national parks for the rest of the century; how the US Forest Service saved Grand Canyon from a dam in 1915; the creation of Grand Canyon National Park in 1919; the importance, and consequences, of the Colorado River Compact of 1922; plus the Arizona-California water fight through World War II. Chapter two starts with National Park Service Director Newton Drury, who fought tenaciously against bureau proposals for Grand Canyon and other national parks, often without much help from conservation organizations. The Sierra Club's painful struggle to reinvent itself into an activist organization and the first attempt by Arizona politicians to obtain congressional passage of a massive hydroelectric dam in Grand Canyon as part of the Central Arizona Project are also discussed here.

Chapter three picks up with the Dinosaur controversy, the emergence of a vocal conservation movement, and the key political and environmentalist leaders who played important roles during the 1960s. Arizona's and California's "go it alone" attempts that affected subsequent events and the Rainbow Bridge National Monument fiasco are also covered. Chapter four focuses upon Stewart Udall's introduction of the Pacific Southwest Water Plan and how it gained the tentative blessing of California and Wayne Aspinall. Carl Hayden's renewed efforts to pass a bare-bones project in the wake of Arizona's victory in the Supreme Court in 1963 and the initiation of the environmentalists' opposition campaign are also discussed. Chapter five covers the rift between Hayden and Stewart Udall, the problems of presidential politics during the 1964 election year, Udall's agonizing decision to pursue a high Bridge Canyon Dam despite knowing it would incur opposition, the first serious mention of a Columbia River diversion since the 1940s and its ramifications, and the preservationists' attempts to publicize the growing threat to Grand Canyon.

Chapter six lays out the social and political context of the 1960s, particularly the public's concerns with threats to civil liberties, free speech, and civil rights, as well as the 1965 House hearings in the Subcommittee on Irrigation and Reclamation, and the preservationists' decision to target the national media when they realized that their legal and technical arguments were not powerful enough to change reclamation policy. Washington Senator Henry Jackson's upending of the bureau's well-established congressional approval process—the point of origin of NEPA—is also explained. Chapter seven shows how the environmentalists gained media coverage and the steps the pro-dam interests took to counter it, including the mobilization of the American Indians in the region. The unfolding drama in the House Subcommittee on Irrigation and Reclamation through June 1966 concludes this chapter.

Chapter eight analyzes the results of the Sierra Club's national media campaign, including the public reaction to its full-page ads in national newspapers and the IRS revocation of its tax-deductible status, as well as the complex political intrigue that caused the regional plan to unravel in the House Rules Committee when on the brink of success. Interior Secretary Udall's decision to change course and pursue a bill without dams in Grand Canyon, a strategy that led to the passage of CAP legislation in 1968, is also treated in this chapter, as are the hardball political maneuvers Carl Hayden used to gain the backing of a reluctant Wayne Aspinall in the House.

Chapter nine concludes the book with how historical interpretations, popular accounts, websites, and film have created and perpetuated the "noble myth" of how the Sierra Club saved Grand Canyon and how these interpretations, based upon "unintentional overstatements" by people closely associated with these events, have shaped public perceptions. The consequences for the Navajo people of a half century of using coal-fired power plants to generate electricity for the CAP are also discussed through the present. The chapter ends with how Henry Jackson's defense of the Columbia River evolved into the National Environmental Policy Act and how, after Congress passed this historic environmental legislation, the Sierra Club capitalized on the heroic myth of its having saved Grand Canyon to become the most influential environmental organization in the world.

One can argue that the mere preservation of natural curiosities such as Grand Canyon had become outdated by the close of the 1960s, and hence, that the fight to save Grand Canyon was merely the last major campaign of the twentieth-century conservation movement. However, it also represents an important transition, as environmental organizations such as the Sierra Club, having gained a large national audience during the Grand Canyon debate, began to change from being advocates of mere preservation to fighting for public health, environmental justice, and, eventually, sustainability. Perhaps this is the most important legacy of the fight to save Grand Canyon, for in leading the last great crusade of John Muir's style of preservation, the Sierra Club gained a reputation for environmental activism that enabled it to catch up to the portion of the American public that had left preservation behind, embraced the new environmentalism, and was waiting for an organization to step up and lead them to victory in future environmental crusades.

1

"Something to be Skinned"

"I have come here to see the Grand Canyon," Teddy Roosevelt told his audience of former Rough Riders, Arizona dignitaries, and ordinary citizens on May 6, 1903. Overcome by the "loneliness and beauty" of the chasm, the president asked Arizonans to not give in to the temptations of commercial and private development, and to leave the canyon alone. Be a good steward and preserve it for the entire country, he said, for it is a place of "unparalleled" grandeur, unique in all the world.[1]

Indeed it was, and still is today, despite the development of a massive tourist infrastructure on the south rim that TR would have undoubtedly viewed with distaste. Ironically, as he delivered the speech in which he told his audience not to "mar" the canyon with hotels, houses, or development of any kind and to refrain from treating it as "something to be skinned," he did so while standing on the porch of a hotel close to the brink of the abyss. That irony reflects the juxtaposition many people in the last half of the nineteenth and early twentieth centuries felt about the natural world. Although the Anglo Americans who first wrote about the canyon evaluated whether they could wring a profit from it, their words occasionally express the kind of awe that one typically finds in the writings of seventeenth-century enlightenment figures who struggled to find the language to describe the feelings of wonder—and terror—such landscapes evoked.

Thus we have the scribblings of Lieutenant Joseph Christmas Ives, who in 1857 wrote that the Colorado River would remain "forever undisturbed" along its "lonely and majestic way." Geologist John Wesley Powell reflected in 1875 that the canyon was so "awful, sublime, and

FIGURE 1.1. President Theodore Roosevelt telling the people of Arizona to "leave [Grand Canyon] as it is," on May 6, 1903. 560.51 1903 (olvgroup12374), Houghton Library, Harvard University.

glorious" that words and "graphic arts" combined could not capture it. Railroad builder Robert Brewster Stanton occasionally paused from his 1890 survey to lift his eyes upward and write of the "flaming scarlet sandstone cliffs" above the inner gorge. Indeed, as TR spoke about preservation, the nation struggled to reconcile conflicting ideas about protecting nature and developing it in the name of progress. TR's speech is best remembered for his admonition to protect Grand Canyon, but in the same talk he also extolled the virtues of western irrigation.[2] To place twentieth-century struggles over building dams in Grand Canyon into their proper historical context, it is with efforts to reclaim the West that we must begin.

Aridity, Shmaridity

Powell, a veteran of the American Civil War who lost his right arm at the battle of Shiloh, embarked upon his epic voyage down the Colorado in the spring of 1869. Despite reports of his party's demise, the expedition successfully navigated the river through Grand Canyon, and he made a second passage through the upper canyon to Kanab Creek in 1871. The fame that resulted propelled Powell into a tumultuous bureaucratic career that culminated in his becoming the second director of the US Geological Survey (USGS). Powell, an innovative and outspoken thinker, did not hesitate to air his views about how western settlement policies should take the region's aridity into consideration, much to the chagrin of his superiors and western land speculators.

During the 1870s, the wave of western migration reached beyond the ninety-eighth meridian. Lured by the promise of cheap land and spurred on by the mantra of "rain follows the plow," hordes of hopeful farmers poured into the virtually uncharted Southwest, an area so dry that it made the "Great American Desert" of the plains look like a verdant paradise. Fearing a disaster of biblical proportions, Powell published his landmark study, *Report on the Lands of the Arid Region of the United States*, in 1878 and tried to implement it as national policy upon becoming the director of the USGS in 1881.[3]

Powell advocated replacing the existing Homestead Acts and other laws designed to privatize land developed in the humid East with settlement policies designed for the West's arid environment. Specifically, Powell proposed a system of grazing and irrigation districts with irrigation farms of no more than eighty acres and pasturage farms of four sections. Powell's most revolutionary idea was to replace the rapidly emerging western water law doctrine of prior appropriation—which allows claimants to divert water great distances away from rivers and streams—with statutes tying water rights to land within a specific watershed. Water usage and regulation policy would be determined locally rather than at the state or federal levels. However, Powell also believed that

FIGURE 1.2. John Wesley Powell, explorer and second director of the United States Geological Survey, ca. 1869. National Park Service, 17227.

the federal government must assess the water resources of the West and he initiated a comprehensive irrigation survey he hoped would guide western settlement.

Powell did not advocate for centralized federal water development, but the very idea that the federal government should catalog and guide western settlement and water usage at all elicited bleats of protest from western politicians, cattle interests, real estate speculators, and government bureaucracies. The intensity of the opposition drove Powell from his position in the USGS in 1894, and he spent the rest of his life vigorously opposing uncontrolled western expansion until his death in 1902. Powell's survey, though incomplete, identified 147 potential reservoir sites located throughout the American West. Not one of these was in the Grand Canyon of the Colorado.[4]

With Powell out of the picture, individuals, promoters, and corporations tried to construct irrigation works to bring water to potentially rich western farmland. However, most sites where water could easily be diverted onto prospective farmland were settled by the late 1880s, while millions of acres of fertile soil lay uncultivated because farmers and small irrigation districts lacked the resources to construct large-scale water projects. As a result, several western states including California and Colorado attempted to construct irrigation works but most of these efforts ended in failure as well.

The lower Colorado River flows through one of the driest regions in the already arid American West. Although the soil is fertile, an annual mean rainfall of 2.4 inches prevented the development of a viable agricultural industry on either side of the Arizona-California border. Charles Rockwood, a Midwestern visionary, sought to irrigate these potentially rich farmlands with water from the Colorado by building a canal from the river to California's Imperial Valley. This project, the first attempt to divert water from the main stream of the Colorado on a large scale, resulted in one of the most spectacular failures of private irrigation in the history of western reclamation.

Rockwood and his partner George Chaffey constructed a canal that delivered water to California's Imperial Valley in 1901. They soon discovered why the river had been nicknamed "Big Red," for the canal quickly filled with silt. Undaunted, they dug another with the same result. Still determined to bring the Imperial Valley into cultivation, they constructed a temporary channel so they could clear the first canal during the spring rainy season of 1905. A major flood surged down the Colorado River, destroyed the headgate to the canal, and the rampaging waters flowed unimpeded into the Salton Sink, a natural depression within the valley that, when full of water, geologists called the Salton Sea. The river widened the fissure in its west bank to a half mile and washed away a vast amount of topsoil in addition to Rockwood's investment. The Southern Pacific Railroad took ownership of Rockwell's venture and finally, after two years of nonstop effort, sealed the breach in 1907 and returned the impetuous river to its former bed.[5]

Even as this private reclamation boondoggle was moving toward its epic failure, boosters and local politicians from California and Arizona already recognized that they needed federal assistance to construct a great dam to control the Colorado's flood peaks and provide a constant flow for downstream agriculture. Rockwood's debacle made it painfully clear that construction of projects of the scale necessary to stabilize the Colorado's flow and to channel the water was beyond the capability of individuals, corporations, or even states. Ironically, in the same year Powell died Congress passed the Newlands Reclamation Act of 1902, which created the US Reclamation Service and charged the new bureau with the task of opening vast areas of the West to agriculture through the construction of massive federally constructed water projects.[6]

As the new agency began to prioritize its potential projects, Arthur Powell Davis, Powell's nephew, a Progressive Republican and a strong supporter of federal water development, began to argue for federal development of the entire Colorado River Basin, including Grand Canyon.[7] Although Davis lobbied that his Colorado River scheme should receive the highest priority, the Reclamation Service kicked off its first comprehensive river basin development on a much smaller scale. Citing the need to provide water for agriculture in the Phoenix area, the service initiated the construction of several dams on the Salt River in central Arizona. The largest, Theodore Roosevelt Dam, was a majestic stone structure built by an astonishingly diverse labor force. It was assembled from hand-hewn blocks of native red granite and stood 280 feet tall when completed in 1911. The project also included a small hydroelectric generator that produced the first Reclamation Service electricity.[8] Thus from the very beginning, twentieth-century federal reclamation included both water storage and the production of hydroelectric power.

After it completed the Salt River Project, the Reclamation Service engaged in extensive water development throughout the West. Officials within the service began to view the sale of electricity as a potential source of revenue for *future projects,* an idea that eventually became a mainstay of reclamation policy. Although its primary focus remained the construction of irrigation works, the Reclamation Service expanded its hydroelectric capacity at Roosevelt Dam and built eighteen power plants across the West by 1923.[9] However, given the technological challenges of developing the water resources and hydroelectric potential of the Colorado River, Davis's dream of a large federally constructed dam in the canyon country of northern Arizona would not reach fruition until Congress approved the Boulder Dam project in 1928.[10]

Undaunted by the failures of private irrigation schemes and the obvious geological and technical obstacles, a few water developers believed Grand Canyon was an ideal place to build hydroelectric and water storage projects. They concocted some fantastic schemes and tried to implement them through the first two decades of the twentieth century. Engineer Robert Brewster Stanton led the second and third expeditions down the Colorado River through the entire length of Grand Canyon in 1889–1890 to assess the possibility of building a railroad through the canyon. Despite the remoteness and the difficulty of access, Stanton, in perhaps the first written reference to the hydroelectric potential of the Colorado River, wrote that the entire railroad line could be powered by "electricity generated by the power of the river tumbling down beside its tracks."[11]

In 1893 the *Salt Lake City Tribune* stated that the "supply of water in the Colorado is an unfailing one and sooner or later it will be the source of all great irrigation enterprises in Arizona." The *Tribune* advocated the construction of a steel-framed dam on the Colorado River in Grand Canyon at the same time that Utah was attempting to wrest all the land north of the Colorado River from Arizona Territory. Utah's attempted land grab failed, but this proposal is noteworthy because it was also conceived as a hydroelectric project rather than a dam for water storage alone.[12]

On the Arizona side of the river, boosters made extraordinary claims about the Colorado's potential, one going so far as to claim that its capacity to generate electricity was far greater than that of Niagara Falls. Despite this rhetoric, most early proposals focused upon the construction of small-scale projects on tributary streams within the canyon. A veterinarian, A. J. Chandler, attempted to obtain European capital to finance the construction of a power plant on Kanab Creek. A booster in every sense of the word, he argued that one plant built upon this relatively small stream could provide electricity for Prescott, Phoenix, and other Arizona communities. Although he ultimately failed to obtain the capital needed to begin construction, it would not be the last time Kanab Creek would be considered ideal for power generation.

In a rare triumph of private water development, David Babbitt of Flagstaff, Arizona, formed the Grand Canyon Electric Power Company in 1902 and constructed a modest generating plant on Bright Angel Creek, a tributary of the Colorado. Unlike many western water ventures, Babbitt's actually succeeded. His small hydroelectric plant supplied electricity to residences and hotels on the canyon's south rim until 1965.[13]

Still others sought to avoid the difficult task of dam construction and built waterwheels designed to generate power from the Colorado

River's main stem, but none of these schemes worked. Water developers were eventually forced to admit that the river's seasonal fluctuations were so extreme that a waterwheel would be rendered incapable of generating power during periods of low flow, while torrential spring floods would, in all likelihood, destroy it.[14] As in other parts of the West, it seemed as though efforts to develop the full hydroelectric power potential of the Colorado River could only succeed with federal backing. In 1910 it appeared that the Colorado River and Grand Canyon would prove Ives's bleak assessment correct by posing insurmountable obstacles to water development.

Hetch Hetchy and the Near Miss of 1915

Several events occurred before 1920 that brought construction of a dam on the Colorado River in Grand Canyon within the realm of possibility. The debates surrounding these proposals eerily foreshadowed the bitter dam fight of the 1960s.[15] In 1910 Ralph Cameron, the last congressional delegate from the territory of Arizona and a future US senator, held most of Arizona's political power. Cameron, a figure of some notoriety, had a reputation for advancing his varied interests through legal and extralegal means. He came to Grand Canyon in 1884; by 1900 he had staked more than thirty-five mineral claims in the canyon, built a hotel, and was charging tourists a dollar apiece to ride mules down the Bright Angel Trail he had constructed.[16]

Claiming that he "would make more money out of the Grand Canyon than any other man," Cameron moved forward with his plans for development even after President Roosevelt created Grand Canyon National Monument in 1908. Using the mechanism of patenting mining claims to tie up the best locations on and near the Colorado River for dams and power plants, by 1907 he had sold options for $175,000 to Warner, Tucker & Company, a Boston firm that intended to build a 230-foot-tall hydroelectric dam to supply power to northern Arizona's mines. The deal fell through when Cameron could not prove he held legal title to the land he was trying to sell. By the time Arizona become a state in 1912, the intrepid Cameron, unfazed by this temporary setback, had sold mineral rights to mining consortiums in Philadelphia and New York and promised to provide power for these and other mining interests by building his own massive hydroelectric

FIGURE 1.3. Arizona's Ralph Cameron, territorial representative, US senator, and promoter of the first serious attempt to build a dam on the Colorado River in Grand Canyon. Library of Congress. ggbain 32135.

dam near the bottom of Bright Angel Trail—in the heart of the new Grand Canyon National Monument.[17]

As Cameron framed his dam proposal for Grand Canyon, the struggle over the construction of a dam in Yosemite's Hetch Hetchy Valley reached its climax in 1913. John Muir and the Sierra Club had fought to preserve the scenic grandeur of Hetch Hetchy Valley while Gifford Pinchot, the father of Progressive Era resource management in the United States and the head of the new US Forest Service, contended that the valley should be used as a reservoir site even though it was located in Yosemite National Park. Pinchot preached the gospel of conservation and urged immediate development of the West's water resources. Pinchot and Muir, good friends at one point, parted over the issue of preservation versus conservation. After 1905, this break became more and more acute as preservationists and conservationists fought over Hetch Hetchy, the first important environmental battle of the twentieth century.[18]

Although the Sierra Club had battled wilderness exploiters since its creation in 1892 and successfully defended Yosemite and other national parks from various intrusions, its membership lacked political sophistication. Additionally, the process by which large federal projects were approved at the turn of the twentieth century did not require environmental assessments and public input as they do today. This lack of transparency allowed politicians allied with the city of San Francisco and its utility companies to quietly sponsor and pass a bill in 1901 that authorized the secretary of the interior to grant rights of way for water projects through the three national parks located in California. The Sierra Club, inexperienced in political subterfuge, did not become aware of this act until 1905. Thus when it joined the battle for Hetch Hetchy Valley, which many people viewed as a mirror image of Yosemite Valley itself, the groundwork for the defeat of the preservationists' opposition to a dam there had been already been laid.[19]

Even worse, a division emerged within the club between members who supported water development and those favoring preservation, a division that ran so deep that the club's board of directors asked the members to vote on the issue. Preservation out-polled conservation 3.6 to 1, and so Muir and the club continued to lobby vocally against the Hetch Hetchy dam. Muir even managed to convince a conflicted Roosevelt to qualify his initial support for the project despite the latter's advocacy of Progressive Conservation and close personal friendship with Pinchot.[20]

But Pinchot and the city of San Francisco gained the upper hand after the disastrous San Francisco earthquake and fire of 1906. Despite a national letter-writing campaign, the distribution of anti-dam pamphlets, and impassioned arguments from preservationists, the Hetch Hetchy bill passed both houses of Congress with substantial majorities in the fall of 1913. After twelve years of continuous struggle, politically outgunned and swamped by the rising tide of Progressive Conservation, Muir lost the greatest conservation battle of his life. On December 19, 1913, President Woodrow Wilson signed the Raker Act into law, granting San Francisco all water rights in the valley and the authority to build a dam.[21] According to Sierra Club lore, an embittered Muir died the following year of a broken heart caused by the loss of his beloved Hetch Hetchy, now condemned to become, in Muir's own words, "an open mountain sepulcher."[22]

The Hetch Hetchy debate gave rise to two opposing political agendas that had immediate effects upon Cameron's Grand Canyon project and continued to influence the development of water resources and the preservation of sublime landscapes for much of the twentieth century and beyond. First, by approving the construction of a dam in Yosemite National Park, Congress established the precedent that it would give resource development a higher priority over the preservation of nature *even within the national parks that had originally been created to protect areas of natural splendor from development.* However, in approving the destruction of Hetch Hetchy, Congress also gave the Sierra Club and other preservationists a lost cause that they would use effectively to generate support for the creation of the National Park Service in 1916 and to claim the moral high ground in future battles to preserve natural wonders.

Muir's rhetoric couched the Hetch Hetchy dispute in biblical terms. He described the valley as an "Eden," a "glorious mountain temple," and a "cathedral," that still bore the imprint of "the hand of the creator." Muir castigated the developers as "despoilers" akin to "Satan," and the progeny of the moneychangers whom Jesus drove from "Jerusalem's Temple," because they sought to "make everything dollarable." Muir would not live to see it, but his words would resonate throughout the twentieth century. His language framed the arguments raised by future environmental advocates such as David Brower, who wrote full-page newspaper advertisements and published oversized exhibit format books containing magnificent photographs and lovely poetic descriptions of what would soon be lost to development. Muir wrote a position of moral ascendency into being for the Sierra Club that it used as a foundation to persuade legions of Americans to join its fights to keep Dinosaur National Monument and Grand Canyon free of dams a half century later.[23]

Cameron and Arizona power interests kept a wary eye on these two congressional impulses and the possible ramifications for their own plans to develop the hydroelectric and reclamation potential of Grand Canyon. Despite increasing sentiment to protect the national parks in the wake of Hetch Hetchy, supporters of water projects appeared to have the upper hand, a position that the House of Representatives strengthened when it began to debate the Ferris Water-Power bill in April of 1914—a predecessor to the Federal Power Act of 1920— to promote federal water and power development. This legislation would have granted the secretary of the interior the discretionary

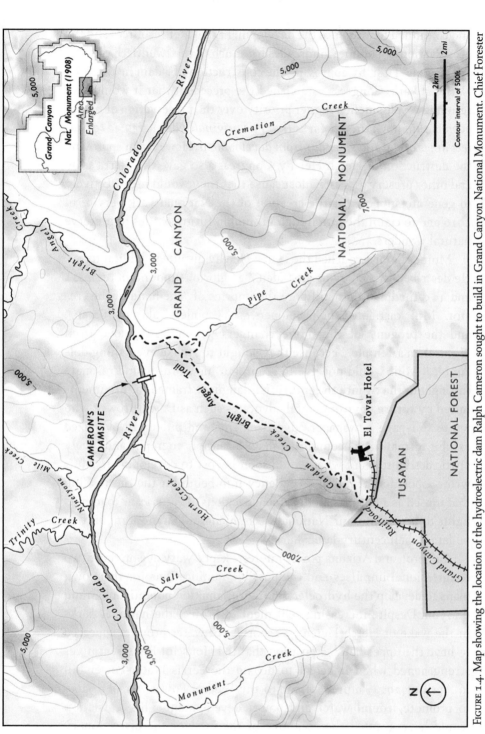

FIGURE 1.4. Map showing the location of the hydroelectric dam Ralph Cameron sought to build in Grand Canyon National Monument. Chief Forester Henry Graves denied Cameron's application to construct the project in 1915. Map by Nathaniel Douglass, ndcartography.com.

right to lease power sites on all public lands managed by the Interior Department *except* for national parks and monuments. But a relative newcomer to Arizona politics, Representative Carl Hayden, began his six decades of reclamation advocacy by inserting an amendment into the bill allowing water development in Grand Canyon and Mount Olympus National Monuments. Hayden argued, "The use of the water power in the Mount Olympus and Grand Canyon Monuments would not interfere with our enjoyment of any of the beauties of nature. That was the case in the Hetch Hetchy bill which we debated at great length in this house not long ago. This is a parallel one."[24]

Meanwhile, Cameron obtained financial backing from a New York firm and on November 14, 1914, made an informal application to the US Forest Service, the parent agency of Grand Canyon National Monument, to build a hydroelectric project just downstream from the terminus of Bright Angel Trail. Another developer, W. I. Johnson, hired Frank Baum, chief hydrological engineer for Pacific Gas and Electric Company and one of the most important proponents of the Hetch Hetchy dam, to submit a similar application and to design a power project for Havasu Creek in Cataract Canyon, which lay just inside the western boundary of the national monument.[25] Although Havasu Creek is only a tributary of the Colorado River, Cataract Canyon contains some of the most spectacular scenery in the Grand Canyon system, including the dramatic Havasupai and Mooney Falls, two of the most photographed places in the American West.

Thus less than a year after approving the Hetch Hetchy dam, Congress had taken additional steps that favored water development over the preservation of scenic resources even in the national parks and monuments. Furthermore, Franklin Lane, the former San Francisco city attorney who spearheaded his city's successful fight to build the dam in Hetch Hetchy Valley, had just been named secretary of the interior by President Wilson. Two proposals to construct dams in Grand Canyon National Monument, including one on the main stem of the Colorado River, now sat on the desk of the head of the Forest Service, the agency founded by Gifford Pinchot that was perhaps the most vigorous governmental advocate of Progressive Era resource conservation. The construction of a dam in the heart of Grand Canyon National Monument and the inundation of some of its most spectacular scenic features and archeological sites now seemed inevitable.[26]

Fortunately for preservationists, Pinchot was no longer the chief forester of the United States. By 1914 he had been replaced by his close friend Henry S. Graves. Graves was appointed to succeed him largely on the basis of the expectation that he would continue to carry out Pinchot's utilitarian policies but without Pinchot's political grandstanding. Indeed, since becoming chief in 1910, Graves had continued Pinchot's efforts to stop Congress from establishing a separate national parks bureau, declaring that the Forest Service should administer the national parks "because of the need to salvage the dead and down timber."[27] Preservationists and national park enthusiasts viewed Graves and his agency with mistrust and skepticism, especially after Hetch Hetchy. Initially Graves did nothing to dissuade these suspicions. At the same time he was weighing the construction of the two dams in Grand Canyon National Monument, he was also fighting efforts to transfer Forest Service land to the monument to control public access in case the latter should be incorporated into a new national park.

Graves, who had favored the Hetch Hetchy dam, moved cautiously; by the summer of 1914, it became apparent that the new chief forester was not going to approve the Cameron and Baum proposals without carefully considering all the ramifications of Hetch Hetchy. As historians Roderick Nash and Stephen Fox have argued, perhaps the most remarkable thing about the Hetch Hetchy debate is that it occurred at all, and that the construction of a dam at this location would not have been controversial had it been proposed fifty years previously.[28] The fierce congressional debates and the public outcry against the damming of Hetch Hetchy that culminated in 1913 gave Graves pause and forced him to balance the agenda of water development with that of the emerging preservation movement in the case of the Grand Canyon a year later.

As a result, Graves now found himself in a difficult dilemma because he knew that both houses of Congress were considering water-power legislation as well as bills to establish an agency to oversee the national parks. In addition, he was also aware of a growing sentiment within Congress to strengthen the protection given to Grand Canyon by incorporating the national monument into a new national park with or without an agency to oversee it. Knowing that their window of opportunity could potentially close, Cameron and Baum pressed Graves to approve their projects quickly before Congress enacted protective measures that would, in all likelihood, nullify their applications.

They also persuaded powerful politicians and influential citizens, including Representative Hayden, Arizona Senator Henry Ashurst, and Interior Secretary Lane, to pressure Graves to grant his approval. Lane contended that Graves should allow the permits because he anticipated that Grand Canyon would come under Interior's jurisdiction when it became a national park, thus making it eligible for power development because he believed it was highly likely Congress would eventually pass some form of the Ferris Bill that included Hayden's hydroelectric power amendment exception.

Graves refused to yield to this pressure and he denied the Cameron and Baum applications in January 1915 after weighing all of these factors. He wrote Lane, telling him he agreed that Grand Canyon National Monument would probably be transferred to the "Bureau of National Parks," which would become part of the Interior Department once the Senate approved impending legislation to that effect. But Graves also argued that because the House and Senate were far from agreement on federal water-power legislation, Lane's claim that Grand Canyon's hydroelectric potential should be developed immediately in anticipation of this legislation was without merit.[29]

Despite Graves's careful assessment of the status of both the water-power and national parks bills, since both were still pending before Congress, neither was applicable to the Cameron/Baum applications. Legally, federal policy governing water development in national parks and monuments had just been established in the Hetch Hetchy case and Graves could have easily justified approving the proposals based upon that recent precedent.

Instead, Graves based his decision upon the fact that the House had passed the national park service bill with a clause stating that no development could take place in a national park. Summing up he stated: "The bill [Cameron's Grand Canyon dam application] as it stands would, therefore, allow rights to be secured while action is being taken to create the park that would not be permitted if the creation of the park were an accomplished fact."[30] Graves weighed the *existing* year-old precedent of Hetch Hetchy against *potential* congressional protection of national parks and, despite tremendous pressure, he based his decision upon the possibility that the latter would soon become law.

Graves's letter to Secretary Lane demonstrates that he grasped the future implications of whatever decision he might make and the intensity of

FIGURE 1.5. Chief Forester Henry Graves who denied Ralph Cameron's application to dam the Colorado River in Grand Canyon. Photo courtesy of the Forest History Society, Durham, N.C.

the opposing forces focusing their energies upon potential park lands. What is even more remarkable is that, unlike Hetch Hetchy, preservationists did not protest the Cameron and Baum Grand Canyon dam proposals; in fact, it is highly probable that they did not even know of them. So Graves's decision must be read in this light—that it was made with virtually no pressure from environmental organizations such as the Sierra Club. His reasoning is particularly noteworthy when one considers that the precedent of Hetch Hetchy was barely one year old.

Although many environmental historians have portrayed the early twentieth century Forest Service as strictly a utilitarian agency, Chief Henry Graves assigned greater weight to the aesthetic values of Grand Canyon and its potential as a national park. He did so despite immense pressure from politicians, government bureaus, and pro-development interest groups, and despite the policy formed as a result of the Hetch Hetchy controversy that favored utilitarian and economic development within the boundaries of national parks and monuments—a policy he had strongly supported in the case of Yosemite National Park.[31]

The depth of Graves's convictions was shared by his subordinates within the Forest Service for the remainder of his term. Graves's chief engineer, Lyle A. Whitsit, echoed Graves's sentiments. After concluding that the power plant designed by Baum was feasible, he argued: "The writer believes that the scenic beauty of the canyon, the falls, and the rapids possess greater value and is [sic] one of the important features of Grand Canyon National Monument. . . . Should this hydro-electric development be made, all the scenic beauty of the falls and rapids that makes the trip to this country worthwhile would be destroyed. Therefore, the writer believes that the Service is perfectly justified in refusing an application for water power [sic] permit for these resources and would so recommend."[32]

Even while Graves was absent from the Forest Service because of his military service during World War I and while on medical leave in 1919, the agency continued to rebuff inquiries from other parties interested in constructing hydroelectric projects in Grand Canyon. Faced with these forcefully stated positions, Baum notified his employer that it would be "useless to carry the matter further," while Cameron's claims remained in limbo until 1920 when the US Supreme Court invalidated them.[33]

Federal Water Development and the Law of the River

Although preservationists lost a magnificent scenic wonder in Hetch Hetchy, they gained a national constituency and a federal agency, the National Park Service, by the end of 1916. Because of the careful reasoning of Chief Forester Graves, the Colorado River in Grand Canyon remained free of hydroelectric projects when Carl Hayden began to push for the establishment of Grand Canyon National Park. However, after the National Park Service was created in 1916, it was not given jurisdiction over Grand Canyon National Monument; the monument remained under the management of the Forest Service.[34] Three years after the creation of the park service, Hayden and Ashurst sponsored bills to convert Grand Canyon National Monument into a national park.

The boundaries for the proposed park included approximately one hundred miles of river but they did not encompass the entire Grand Canyon system, which geologists defined as extending from Lee's Ferry to the Grand Wash Cliffs, a distance of 277 miles. Thus park protection did not extend to all, or even most, of Grand Canyon. Since the national park act of 1916 prohibited water development in parks and monuments, the wily Hayden inserted a special provision granting the secretary of the interior the power to authorize reclamation projects within the park. Hayden's action not only provided the legal foundation necessary for the future utilization of both the power and water resources within Grand Canyon for his native state, but it also gave the federal government the upper hand with respect to potential water development within it.[35]

Hayden's language from the Grand Canyon National Park Establishment Act of 1919 reads: "That whenever consistent with the primary purpose of said park, the Secretary of the Interior [sic] is authorized to permit the utilization of areas therein which may be necessary for the development and maintenance of a Government [sic] reclamation project." The ensuing congressional discussion pitted Hayden against Representative William Henry Stafford of Wisconsin, who questioned him about this reclamation provision. Hayden responded, stating that future reservoirs for the storage of water for irrigation purposes would be built only when "consistent with the primary purposes of the park—that is, not to impair its scenic beauty." Stafford, apparently satisfied, did not pursue the matter further, and the bill passed the House unanimously.[36]

Scarcely debated at the time, this reclamation clause constituted an almost insurmountable legal obstacle for environmentalists defending the canyon in subsequent disputes because it established congressional endorsement of federal water projects within Grand Canyon National Park itself, and the park service was powerless to do anything about it. Fifty years later when environmentalists attempted to strictly construct the measure, they found that Hayden had stated clearly that, in his opinion, a reclamation project within Grand Canyon—which by 1919 was understood to encompass both water storage and the generation of hydroelectric power—would not impair the canyon's scenic beauty and thus would not violate the "primary purpose" of the park's establishment.

When denying the Cameron and Baum hydroelectric proposals in 1915, Chief Graves had argued that, since Grand Canyon National Monument would soon be established as a park, it should be managed as though it already was one because he assumed that hydroelectric development would not be permitted. But he had not anticipated congressional assent to Hayden's reclamation provision.

Ironically, in creating Grand Canyon National Park and transferring it to the National Park Service, a subsidiary agency of the Interior

Department, Congress reduced the protection Grand Canyon enjoyed as a national monument administered by the US Forest Service. And because the Colorado River dropped 950 feet in elevation within the park, and 1,930 feet within the canyon as a whole, all of Grand Canyon would remain the subject of intense interest as westerners seeking to use its water prepared to divide the waters of the Colorado among the seven states of the Colorado River Basin and initiate comprehensive federal development of the river.[37] It is these fights over Colorado River water that would bring the debate of development versus preservation of the West's rivers to a head in the mid-twentieth century, and force environmental organizations to enter the political arena to fight for the protection of scenic values within the boundaries of national parks and monuments such as Dinosaur and Grand Canyon a half century later.

While Graves deliberated and Hayden and Ashurst lobbied for national park protection for Grand Canyon, federal agencies moved forward with plans for the development of the lower Colorado River for reclamation and irrigation. The USGS sponsored a basin-wide damsite study in 1916 conducted by its chief hydrologist, E. C. La Rue. La Rue identified several damsites from the rims of Marble and Grand Canyons, but he did not render a comprehensive analysis at river level because of the difficulty of access. Despite this incomplete data, he suggested that the power potential of the river could be utilized by constructing thirteen dams in the canyon, writing that "foundations suitable for high masonry dams can probably be found."[38]

Because it was the only large metropolis in the Pacific Southwest, the City of Los Angeles, having already requisitioned the entire flow from the Owens River, also began to eye the Colorado as a future water source. Farmers from the Imperial Valley continued to seek a dam to control the river's flood peaks and to store water as a hedge against drought. Because California alone among the Colorado Basin states had an immediate need for water, it attempted to obtain congressional authorization to build the dam. These efforts failed, much to the relief of the other six states in the basin. However, the federal government did recommend the construction of such a dam in the future.[39]

It soon became apparent that some sort of agreement among the seven Colorado River Basin states had to be reached before orderly development of the river could proceed. The aridity of the American West had necessitated the creation of a new water law doctrine in the mining

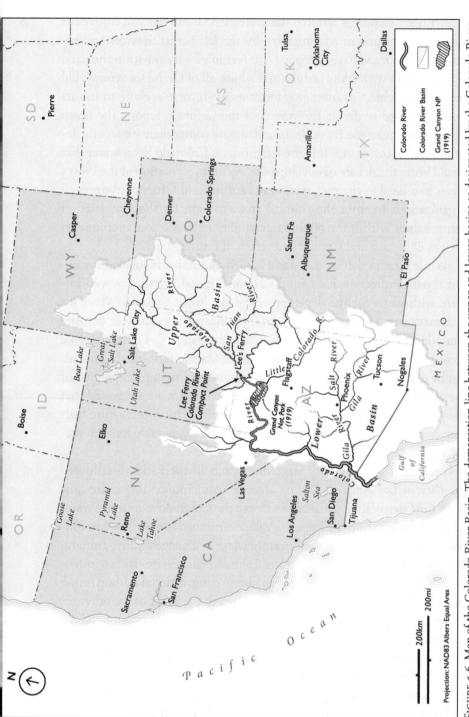

FIGURE 1.6. Map of the Colorado River Basin. The demarcation line between the upper and lower basins as designated by the Colorado River Compact of 1922 crosses the Colorado River at a point called "Lee Ferry," just downstream from where the Paria River joins the Colorado River about a mile below the old Lee's Ferry crossing. Map by Nathaniel Douglass, ndcartography.com.

camps of California and Colorado that addressed the need to divert water long distances to use for mining and agriculture. Departing significantly from the principle of riparian water rights that governed surface water use in the East, this new doctrine, called "prior appropriation," was not based upon the water's proximity to the land but upon when people began diverting it and putting it to a "beneficial use." Under the eastern law of riparian water rights, landowners could claim a right only if their land touched surface water of some kind. The water right could not be severed from the land. John Wesley Powell favored a variation of this doctrine for the West and incurred the wrath of many westerners for his troubles.

In 1922, the US Supreme Court ruled that prior appropriation would govern water disputes between western states, inducing panic in the six Colorado River Basin states not named California. If southern California had succeeded in gaining congressional approval of a dam and diversion works, it could have legally perfected water rights for as much of the Colorado as it could put to a beneficial use *to the exclusion of the other six states in the basin.* Under prior appropriation doctrine, this held true even though these states lay upstream and contributed most of the river's flow. Its preemptive efforts having failed, California agreed to negotiate a division of the Colorado's water with the other basin states in exchange for their support of a large dam. Secretary of Commerce Herbert Hoover summoned representatives of the seven basin states to Santa Fe, New Mexico, in 1922 to sort it out and, after much haggling, they signed the Colorado River Compact, which created the legal foundation for all future Colorado River water development.[40] Arizona governor George W. P. Hunt and state senator Fred Colter opposed the compact and so the state legislature refused to ratify it, setting the stage for more than a half century of legal battles over the lower river's apportionment between Arizona and California.

The compact arbitrarily divided the river into upper and lower basins at Lee Ferry, a point about one mile downstream from where the Paria River meets the Colorado, just south of the Arizona-Utah border.[41] Based upon an annual estimated flow of 17.5 million acre-feet, it allocated 7.5 million to the upper basin states of Wyoming, Colorado, Utah, and New Mexico and 7.5 million to the three lower basin states of Arizona, Nevada, and California. Mexico was allotted 1.5 million acre-feet and the surplus of one million was given, albeit reluctantly, to the lower basin in years of excess flow. The compact did not include agreements between the individual states of each basin; they were left to argue among themselves. Prior appropriation would determine the water rights within each basin in cases of conflicting claims. Nor did the agreement address the potential water claims of American Indian nations.[42]

Schemes and Schemers

Water developers in Arizona and California immediately began to draw up plans for the lower Colorado River. Californians argued over whether the first big dam should be constructed at Diamond Creek, Glen Canyon, or in Black Canyon on the Arizona-Nevada border.[43] Meanwhile, private Arizona developers with political connections concocted several creative schemes designed to circumvent the compact and gain a senior water right over California by putting Colorado River water to a beneficial use first. Prior to the signing of the compact, Arizona State Senator Fred Colter filed claims upon lower Colorado River water on Arizona's behalf and founded the Highline Reclamation Association, a group of influential state leaders dedicated to bringing Colorado River water to central Arizona. The organization studied several plans for water storage, transport, and hydroelectric power generation, all of which involved the diversion of water through lengthy canals and tunnels. The most important proposals were the Arizona Highline Canal and the Colorado-Verde Project. Although different in many respects, these two projects both called for the construction of dams in Grand Canyon even though a comprehensive USGS damsite survey did not exist.

Between 1922 and 1923 Arizona Governor George W. P. Hunt hired La Rue to assist with a survey conducted by the Arizona State Engineering Commission to ascertain the feasibility of the Highline Canal proposal. Although outvoted 2-1, La Rue wrote a favorable minority report and submitted it to Hunt who then released it amid much fanfare in July 1923, creating the impression that the commission had approved the project. Engineer Porter Preston, dumbfounded with the conduct of La Rue and Governor Hunt, wrote his superior within the Reclamation Service and surmised that La Rue's actions were intended as a "slap at the Colorado River Compact."[44]

However, La Rue was hedging his bets, for he also was on the payroll of Southern California Edison and at its behest he organized the first comprehensive USGS damsite survey of the canyon in 1923.

This time La Rue actually floated the entire length of the canyon downstream from Lee's Ferry. Topographical engineer Colonel Claude Birdseye led the voyage. The national media covered the expedition as though it were a death-defying adventure and the October 1925 cover of *Scientific American* featured a painting of an expedition surveyor dangling precariously from a rope above the raging river. Birdseye hired Emery Kolb, the famous Grand Canyon photographer and river runner, as a guide and regretted it almost immediately, for apparently they almost came to blows on several occasions. For his part, La Rue managed to alienate virtually everyone on the trip with his abrasive personality.

Despite the threat of hostilities, La Rue obtained geological data confirming his earlier conclusion that rock formations of suitable strength and hardness for the construction of high dams existed in the canyon. He investigated sites, including two that would become the focus of preservationists and water developers alike for the next several decades: Marble and Bridge Canyons. Bridge Canyon was located about seventy-eight miles below the western boundary of the national park while Marble Canyon, initially referred to as the Red-Wall site, lay twelve miles upstream of it.[45] This comprehensive damsite survey has been the basis of every analysis of hydroelectric power potential within Grand Canyon since its publication in 1925.

LaRue's stubborn public advocacy of his findings brought to a head a dispute between the USGS and the Reclamation Service (renamed the Bureau of Reclamation in 1928), the two federal agencies charged with mapping and developing the West's water resources. While California pushed for the bureau's proposal, which involved the construction of a dam in Boulder Canyon, advocates of the Arizona Highline Canal and the Colorado-Verde Project immediately drew up plans that included dams upstream at Glen Canyon and several of La Rue's sites in Grand Canyon. The Highline proposal would have diverted water from a reservoir created by a dam at the Bridge Canyon site, southeast through a tunnel sixty miles long, then into a canal that meandered for more than 300 miles through the desert, eventually ending southwest of Phoenix. All tunnels and channels would have been lined with concrete and had a channel depth of twelve feet. This design, intended to accommodate boat and barge traffic, was an apparent attempt to create an intra-Arizona water transportation network.

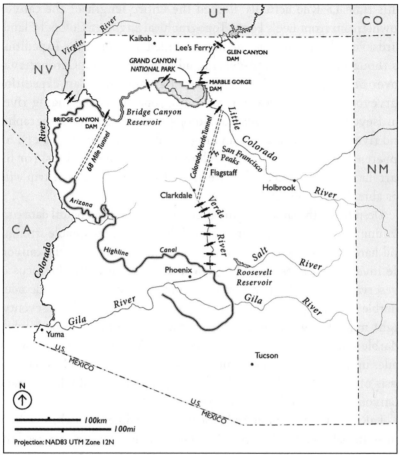

FIGURE 1.7. Map showing Fred Colter's proposed Arizona Highline Canal and Colorado-Verde Project. Map by Nathaniel Douglass, ndcartography.com.

The Colorado-Verde scheme was even more imaginative. It entailed the construction of a dam in Marble Canyon just downstream of Lee's Ferry, which would divert water into a tunnel 46.4 miles in length to a reservoir on the Little Colorado River, ten miles above its mouth. Because the grade of the riverbed is relatively flat, the designers of this project contended that a shallow reservoir would raise the water level enough so that it could be drawn into a second tunnel nine miles farther *upstream*, in effect reversing the Little Colorado's flow over that distance. This tunnel would have traversed deep beneath the Colorado Plateau and the San Francisco Peaks to the confluence of Oak Creek and the Verde River, a distance of 97.8 miles. Eight dams on the now-swollen

Verde River would have generated power, and the water, after passing through these power plants, would have been diverted into irrigation canals in the Salt River Valley.[46]

Advocates of these proposals contended that Arizona would become the most prosperous state in the union if it constructed just one of these projects. They also argued that if one were to include return flows, the Colorado River would have an effective use of one hundred million acre-feet each year, a striking figure when one considers that even the most optimistic hydrologists estimated the total annual flow at 17.5 million acre-feet, an amount that most experts now agree is grossly overestimated. It is in this context of virtually unlimited optimism that the Bureau of Reclamation was about to embark upon the greatest dam building program in human history, and that people who spoke in favor of preservation were drowned out by the cacophony of voices clamoring for federal water projects.[47]

Although Arizona had not signed the Colorado River Compact, Arizona, California, and Nevada attempted to negotiate an equitable division of the 7.5 million acre-feet allocated to the lower basin. Negotiations continued for six years but ultimately failed. California finally agreed to compromise in exchange for congressional approval of a high Colorado River dam. As a result, Congress inserted two key provisions into the bill that authorized Boulder Dam: First, approval would be contingent upon California's agreement to limit its annual use to 4.4 million acre-feet, and second, only six of the seven basin states needed to ratify the Colorado River Compact for construction to begin.

The first provision reassured the rest of the basin states that water would remain in the river for their future use, while the second nullified Arizona's obstinacy. The California legislature, desperate to win congressional approval of the project, enacted a self-imposed annual limitation of 4.4 million acre-feet, prompting Congress to pass the Swing-Johnson bill authorizing the construction of Boulder Dam in 1928. When Utah became the sixth state to ratify the Colorado River Compact in March 1929, Arizona could do nothing to prevent the construction of the world's tallest dam, half of which would be anchored to its side of the river.[48]

Despite Arizona's opposition, the erection of Boulder Dam commenced in 1931, initiating a thirty-year period of unprecedented water project construction in the American West and settling the issue of federal water development in favor of the Bureau of Reclamation. While

Arizona politicians and water developers chafed, the rest of the nation, mired in the depths of the Great Depression, watched the unfolding drama with a mixture of awe and pride as a mountain of shimmering white concrete rose from the depths of Black Canyon. Scarcely four and a half years later, President Franklin Delano Roosevelt dedicated the gigantic edifice, proclaiming: "This morning I came, I saw, and I was conquered as everyone will be who sees for the first time this great feat of mankind." Boulder Dam, perhaps the most important structure ever built in the United States, had tamed the untamable Colorado at a cost of $48,890,955 and the lives of ninety-six men.[49]

The significance of Boulder Dam to twentieth-century American history cannot be overstated. It was by far the largest dam built up to that time, and its engineers pioneered construction processes that were used later on other enormous projects such as Grand Coulee Dam on the Columbia River. When completed, Boulder Dam provided power for the great defense industry of southern California that played such an important role in the Allied victory in World War II. Finally, by stabilizing the river's unpredictable flow, it ensured a dependable water supply for farmers and ranchers and safeguarded downstream irrigation works.

Prior to the completion of Boulder Dam, FDR encouraged the bureau to expand its efforts in conjunction with the New Deal. Roosevelt approved the Columbia Basin Project after his inauguration in 1933, and construction began the following year. The bureau completed Grand Coulee Dam, the cornerstone of the project, in 1941, just in time to power the wartime industries of the Pacific Northwest. Additional great ventures were initiated simultaneously, including California's Central Valley Project, the Big Thompson Project in Colorado, and a host of others. Further development of the lower Colorado was also planned and seen as inevitable by many people.

Even before the completion of Boulder Dam, the bureau began building Parker Dam 155 miles downstream. This low diversion structure was designed to create a reservoir from which water could be transferred via a 245-mile aqueduct to Los Angeles. Construction began in 1934 without congressional approval, and Arizona leaders watched nervously as California attempted to appropriate still more of the river. California viewed the construction of the new dam and aqueduct as inevitable; the Metropolitan Water District of Southern Californian (MWD) even celebrated by sponsoring a Colorado River-themed float in the

1934 Tournament of Roses Parade (and it would do so again in 1935).[50] But on the other side of the river, having twice been defeated in the Supreme Court in his attempts to block Boulder Dam, Arizona's flamboyant Governor Benjamin. B. Moeur weighed his remaining options and decided it was time to go to war.

In spring of 1934, Governor Mouer declared war on the state of California. He dispatched a small force of five national guardsmen to the Parker Dam site where they were ordered to monitor the bureau's activities and tell him specifically about trespasses on the Arizona shore. Led by Major F. I. Pomeroy of the 158th Infantry Regiment, Arizona National Guard, the unit commandeered two dilapidated ferryboats owned and operated by erstwhile lawyer and Arizona State Representative Nellie T. Bush, whom the governor soon commissioned "Admiral of the Arizona Navy." The unlikely flotilla chugged upriver to inspect a cable that the bureau had anchored on the Arizona shore to secure a drilling barge. One ancient craft capsized after becoming entangled in the cable and Pomeroy and his men were rescued by an "enemy" vessel, a motorboat belonging to the MWD. This Arizona expeditionary force maintained daily radio contact with Governor Moeur for seven months and endured sandstorms, poisonous snakes, and temperatures in excess of 120 degrees.[51]

When the bureau began to construct a trestle bridge from the California shore, Moeur issued a proclamation in November 1934, titled "To Repel an Invasion," and placed the entire Arizona side of the river under martial law. Moeur dispatched eighty more national guardsmen to the site. This incident, which actually resulted in a casualty when one of the guardsmen caught pneumonia and died, became a national embarrassment for Interior Secretary Harold Ickes and forced him to suspend construction of the dam while the Supreme Court decided the dispute. To the astonishment of all parties, the court ruled in favor of Arizona because the bureau had not received congressional approval to build the dam. Arizona's victory was short-lived, however, for a few months later, California's delegation rammed a bill through Congress authorizing Parker Dam. Arizona was now without any recourse unless, according to historian Marc Reisner, it wanted to declare war on the United States.[52] Although humorous in the light of eighty years of hindsight, this episode illustrates the enmity between Arizona and California, a resentment so deep that it would prove a decisive factor during the battles

Figure 1.8. Nellie T. Bush, state legislator and Admiral of the Arizona Navy in 1934. Arizona Historical Society, SSL-018.

over the Central Arizona Project and the Grand Canyon dams that occurred during the 1950s and 1960s.

Staking Legal and Political Claims

As Arizona and California contemplated military operations, competing agencies within the Interior Department began to solidify their positions regarding future dam construction on the Colorado River in Grand Canyon. By 1930 the Bureau of Reclamation considered Bridge Canyon one of the most desirable power sites on the Colorado River, now that Boulder Dam had been authorized, and it proposed to construct a 570-

foot "low" dam that would back water to the western boundary of the national park. President Herbert Hoover's proclamation of a new Grand Canyon National Monument downstream of the park on December 22, 1932 caused immediate concern within the bureau because any dam constructed to maximize the power potential of the Bridge Canyon site would back water through the new monument. Although it appeared that legally the monument did not pose an obstacle to the construction of a dam at Bridge Canyon, the bureau wished to avoid a conflict with the National Park Service.[53]

In anticipation of Hoover's action, Elwood Mead, the commissioner of the Bureau of Reclamation, wrote Park Service Director Horace Albright during the summer of 1932, asking whether he would object to a dam at Bridge Canyon that would back water through the proposed monument. Albright, in turn, polled his subordinates; Roger Toll, superintendent of Yellowstone National Park, who had previously undertaken a comprehensive study of the lower reaches of Grand Canyon, responded, arguing that the "only objection would be one of precedent" and stated further that a lake would make the lower reaches of the canyon more accessible to tourists. Albright wrote Mead on January 11, 1933, after Hoover's proclamation, outlining the park service position:

> As I see it, the Bridge Canyon Project is in no way affected by the Grand Canyon National Monument proclamation and the area insofar as power development is concerned is under the jurisdiction of the Federal Power Commission, so far as the granting of power license is concerned. The power withdrawals are intact. *We have had in mind all the time the Bridge Canyon Project.... As a matter of fact ... there can be no necessity for the Reclamation Service [sic] seeking the approval of the Park Service on this project* [emphasis mine].[54]

This exchange reveals much about intra-agency relations within the Department of the Interior when the Bureau of Reclamation first began to consider the construction of dams in Grand Canyon. A feeling of cordiality existed between Mead and Albright, unlike the conflicts that occurred after 1940 when different people held these positions. It also reveals the pervasiveness of the Hetch Hetchy precedent well into the 1930s. Even had Toll and Albright objected to a reservoir backing water into Grand Canyon National Monument, Hetch Hetchy and subsequent

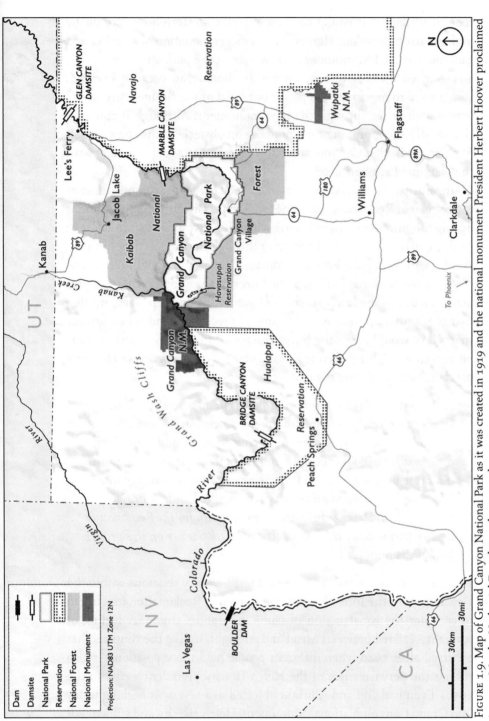

FIGURE 1.9. Map of Grand Canyon National Park as it was created in 1919 and the national monument President Herbert Hoover proclaimed in 1932. Map by Nathaniel Douglass, ndcartography.com.

legislation already demonstrated that Congress supported water development in *national parks*. Since only the national monument would have been affected, and given that the monuments were chronically underfunded and viewed as less scenic by most park service personnel, Albright's letter demonstrates that the service had become resigned to this type of intrusion into national monuments by the 1930s.[55]

Albright's argument that a lake would improve accessibility to the lower reach of the canyon is consistent with the arguments he made before Congress during the debate over whether to establish the National Park Service twenty years earlier. This perspective is also similar to the bureau's arguments in favor of the Grand Canyon dams; the bureau would use this park service correspondence to great effect against environmentalists during the 1960s.

What may be more astounding in light of subsequent events is that the Bureau of Reclamation appeared sympathetic to preservationist views in the case of Grand Canyon. M. T. Tillotson, superintendent of Grand Canyon National Park, attended a meeting of the Colorado River Commission on June 27, 1938, where he listened to a speech given by E. B. Debler, assistant commissioner of the Bureau of Reclamation. Debler spoke of utilizing the hydroelectric potential of the West's free-flowing rivers; however, he also argued that Grand Canyon—or at least the one hundred miles of it located within the national park—was a special case. "Although there are a number of such dam sites within Grand Canyon National Park, *it should be generally agreed that Grand Canyon is more valuable to the State of Arizona and the nation as a recreational and scenic feature, than as a source of power and water development*" [emphasis mine], he said.[56]

Relations between the two agencies grew so warm that when Arizona filed applications with the Federal Power Commission to build Bridge Canyon Dam as a state-constructed project in 1938, park service personnel asked Interior Secretary Ickes to intervene. They preferred that Bridge Canyon Dam be constructed as a federal project by the bureau, "because of the background of experience and cooperation between the Bureau of Reclamation and this Service."[57] This civility is remarkable in light of subsequent events, for relations between the two agencies were soon to become very strained.

The entry of the United States into World War II, after the December 7, 1941 attack on Pearl Harbor, temporarily ended serious consideration of

FIGURE 1.10. Lower Grand Canyon rim view just above the Bridge Canyon Damsite looking upstream. NAU.PH.96.4.68.4, Northern Arizona University, Cline Library, Bill Belknap Collection.

new water development proposals for the American Southwest. Although the Bureau of Reclamation continued to build irrigation and hydroelectric projects, it only did so in areas directly linked to the war effort. Thus the bureau completed the massive dams on the Columbia River to provide power to the aircraft and shipping industries of the Pacific Northwest. It also finished California's Central Valley Project to supply water to Los Angeles and San Diego where key military installations and a growing number of manufacturing plants were located. Although Arizona was an ideal location for Army Air Corps bases, as well as a desert training ground for General George Patton's tank crews, it did not have a sufficient industrial base to warrant further power development of the Colorado River.

Consequently, both federal and state plans to construct a dam at the Bridge Canyon site remained stymied for the duration of the war.[58]

But the war years 1941–1945, seemingly a period of inactivity for Arizona reclamation interests, are important because Arizona's politicians began to gain political influence and develop strategies to obtain federal approval and funding for a water project for central Arizona despite wartime political constraints. By 1940 Hayden was an ascending force in the US Senate, having moved over from the House in 1927. Because of the seniority system and the continuing dominance of the Democratic Party, Hayden gained power and influence throughout the decade. He did not become the chairman of the all-important Appropriations Committee until 1955, but by the early 1940s he had already acquired a reputation as a friend of western reclamation whose support was indispensable. Hayden began to position himself as a coalition builder in the Senate, a role that was to prove vital for supporters of the Central Arizona Project (CAP) in the years ahead.

Ernest McFarland joined Hayden in the Senate after defeating incumbent Senator Henry Ashurst, who had served since 1912, in the Democratic primary and beating his Republican opponent in the 1940 general election. McFarland immediately made his presence felt in the upper chamber as he acquired a seat on the Senate Subcommittee on Irrigation and Reclamation, a key appointment because all reclamation projects had to pass through it before the full Senate Interior and Insular Affairs Committee would consider them. Hayden and McFarland recognized that Arizona had become its own worst enemy and that its intransigence had resulted in delay and frustration for the state's water developers. They began lobbying influential state leaders to persuade the Arizona legislature to reconsider ratifying the Colorado River Compact.

California's self-imposed limitation effectively guaranteed Arizona 2.8 million acre-feet per year from the Colorado, an amount stipulated within the Boulder Canyon Act of 1928. However, Arizona had refused to put this water to the beneficial use required to perfect water rights under the doctrine of prior appropriation. Consequently, when California completed yet another aqueduct from Lake Mead in 1939, swelling its total use to more than five million acre-feet per year, it placed Arizona's water rights in jeopardy. To make matters worse, the federal government had also begun to negotiate a treaty with Mexico over the amount and quality of water it should receive from the Colorado. Since Arizona had not perfected its own rights in the river as defined by federal law, it stood in a very tenuous legal position.

In early 1944 Hayden and McFarland's efforts proved successful. The Arizona legislature ratified the compact on February 24 and authorized the state to sign a contract with the Interior Department for the delivery of the 2.8 million acre-feet of Colorado River water guaranteed by the Boulder Canyon Act. Arizona's actions resulted in three important consequences. First, the state now recognized the supremacy of the Interior Department's authority to allocate the water from the Colorado, a position that for all intents and purposes invalidated Colter's filings, to the dismay of advocates of the Highline Canal and Colorado-Verde Projects. Second, after recognizing federal authority over the Colorado, the state legislature was much more amenable to allocating funds for feasibility studies by the bureau. Indeed, the same day that the state ratified the Colorado River Compact, it also appropriated $200,000 for the bureau to initiate a study of a possible central Arizona water diversion. Finally by recognizing federal supremacy, Arizona removed the obstacles that had blocked congressional consideration of a reclamation project. Now with the end of the war in sight, the Colorado River Compact ratified, and the political chess pieces in place, Hayden and McFarland were poised to make their move.[59]

2

New Lines in the Sand

Although the 1930s ended with Grand Canyon still free of dams, the delusions of boosters who dreamed of irrigating central Arizona by boring tunnels one hundred miles in length had given way to rational discussions and unprecedented cooperation between the Bureau of Reclamation and the National Park Service. Both agencies had accepted the idea of building a 570-foot low dam at Bridge Canyon, even though it would back water through Grand Canyon National Monument. Environmental organizations, most of which had been formed to promote outdoor activities or to protect specific areas of natural beauty, had rarely engaged in public protests since the Hetch Hetchy defeat and it is unlikely they were even aware of these plans. The issue of water development with respect to Grand Canyon appeared to be settled, at least for the moment.[1]

But as America entered World War II, forces of personality and intellect had begun to stir that would contest and ultimately redefine America's environmental ideology for the next three decades. Sierra Club member and aspiring mountaineer David Brower trained with the US Army's Tenth Mountain Division for eventual deployment in Italy. A single-minded heavy equipment operator, Floyd Dominy, created hundreds of earthen dams, first in Wyoming and later with the Seabees in the South Pacific. In the skies over western Europe, B-24 gunner Stewart L. Udall fended off enemy fighters and hoped he would live to see another dawn. Aldo Leopold, ex-forester and professor of game management at the University of Wisconsin, struggled to put into words the ethical duty he believed humanity owed the natural world. An introspective US Fish and Wildlife Service marine biologist, Rachel Carson, published her first book and submitted an article about the dangers of the pesticide DDT to *Reader's Digest*, only to have it rejected because, according to the editors, the subject was "unpleasant."[2] And FDR appointed Newton Drury, an erudite, soft-spoken, preservation-minded graduate of the University of California and former head of the Save the Redwoods League, as director of the National Park Service.

During the war years, the warm relationship between the Bureau of Reclamation and the National Park Service quickly deteriorated, largely because the bureau tried to use the wartime emergency to impose its will upon Interior Department policy. Since many of the remaining damsites in the West lay within national parks and monuments, the bureau's efforts to develop these sites created a dilemma for the park service, which had begun accommodating reservoir projects prior to Drury's tenure as director.

While Horace Albright and his successor, Arno Cammerer, had cooperated with bureau plans to build a dam at Bridge Canyon, they had done so during Elwood Mead's tenure as commissioner. Mead, a tactful person interested in maintaining good relations with other bureaus within the Interior Department, sought out park service officials and compromised with them over water projects that would intrude upon park lands. Despite his strong preservationist leanings, Drury initially attempted to cooperate with the bureau in the manner of his predecessors. Exiled to Chicago for the duration of the war, the park service was besieged by interests that sought to develop its natural resources to further the war effort. His funding greatly depleted, Drury fought to maintain the status quo and resisted these incursions as best he could.[3]

Some park service historians have written disparagingly of Drury, and they are especially critical of his allowing Bureau of Reclamation surveyors to study damsites in Dinosaur National Monument in 1941.[4] However, the leading historian of the Echo Park controversy, Mark Harvey, writes that the park service agreed to the construction of dams in the Green and Yampa River Canyons in the early 1930s so long as Congress consented. As was the case with the Albright-Mead arrangement, Drury inherited this agreement when he became director in 1940. Although Dinosaur National Monument was created in 1915, it initially did not include these dam and reservoir sites. They became part of the monument and subject to park service protection

FIGURE 2.1. Newton B. Drury, director of the National Park Service from 1940 to 1951 and staunch defender of Grand Canyon National Park. The Denver Public Library, Western History Collections, CONS225.

when FDR enlarged the monument in 1938.[5] Thus Drury was not in a position to effectively oppose dams that would affect Dinosaur and Grand Canyon national monuments because he was bound by agreements the Interior Department and his predecessors in the park service had already approved.

Building a Legal Defense

His agency stripped of funding, the scenic resources he was sworn to protect under siege, and handcuffed by his predecessors' agreements with other agencies, Newton Drury believed that only through the establishment of a legal defense could he successfully resist the increasing pressure from those who sought to use the war as an excuse to invade the national parks. As Drury developed his strategy, a young attorney had been laying the groundwork for monumental changes in the area of civil rights. Both would ultimately succeed in overturning harmful, well-established legal precedents and in both cases, the people who conceived of and built these legal foundations for change would be largely forgotten by history.

In 1954 the US Supreme Court ruled in *Brown v. Board of Education* that race-based segregation in public schools violated the equal protection clause of the Fourteenth Amendment to the US Constitution. This holding overturned the noxious *Plessy v. Ferguson* decision of 1896 that had imbedded racial segregation into American constitutional law. NAACP attorney Thurgood Marshall argued the case before the high court and, after winning this and other landmark civil rights victories, he would eventually be appointed a Supreme Court justice by President Lyndon Johnson. Most people who have even a casual interest in twentieth-century American history have heard of Thurgood Marshall. However, Marshall had lots of help.

The unsung hero of the civil rights era is a little-known African American attorney named Charles Houston. A World War I veteran and a graduate of Harvard Law School, Houston mobilized an army of attorneys who began to challenge Plessy's "separate but equal" doctrine one local ordinance, one hearing, one state-level trial at a time. Throughout the 1930s until he died in 1950, Houston and his cohorts battled to kill the insidious tumor of state-sponsored racial discrimination in America. When Marshall, one of his protégées, finally brought *Plessy* down, he was standing on Houston's shoulders when he did it.

Just as Houston crafted many of the arguments that demolished the most virulent portions of the *Plessy v. Ferguson* decision, Drury did the same when he laid the legal foundation environmental leaders such as David Brower and Martin Litton would use to defend the national parks and monuments against water development in places such as Dinosaur National Monument and Grand Canyon National Park. He was not an attorney, but Drury soon proved to be an astute legal tactician. His goal was nothing less than to reverse the harmful precedent of allowing developers to violate the boundaries of national parks that began with the 1913 approval of the dam in Hetch Hetchy Valley. The only question in 1942 was, where would Drury would draw his legal line in the sand?[6]

Although no dams or reservoirs had encroached upon an established park since the Hetch Hetchy project, this precedent still constituted the controlling federal policy governing the construction of water projects in national *parks*. If, in 1942, national parks could be legally invaded for water development, it is beyond dispute that national monuments enjoyed a lesser degree of protection, making it even more difficult to defend them from exploitation.

That Drury distinguished between the relative status, and thus the defensibility, of parks and monuments became apparent in early 1942. Past discussions between the Bureau of Reclamation and Drury's predecessors only concerned the construction of a dam at the Bridge Canyon site 570 feet tall with a maximum reservoir surface elevation of 1,772 feet above sea level. Such a dam, located 53.5 miles downstream from Grand Canyon National Monument, would back water through the monument, but not threaten the park. Although E. C. La Rue, in his 1925 report, determined that rock formations at the Bridge Canyon site could support dams in excess of 800 feet—despite the lack of funding to conduct foundation studies—no bureau or state proposal had included a dam approaching that height.[7]

In 1942 Drury received a new bureau proposal that argued Bridge Canyon Dam would only be economically feasible if it were constructed at least seventy-five feet taller than any dam previously considered, a height that would back water through the entire length of the monument and along the western border of the national park for several miles. Because Grand Canyon in its entirety fell under the jurisdiction of several government agencies, the boundaries had been drawn haphazardly. The river separated the park to the south from the monument and national forest land directly north of it. The position of these boundaries is crucial because it greatly weakened Drury's case that the reservoir created by the high dam would invade the national park.

When Drury contended that this "high" Bridge Canyon Dam would create an intrusion into the park, bureau personnel pounced on this weakness and argued that a reservoir would only raise the water level *along* the park's northern boundary at that point. By the time the water touched national park land, it would only be eighty-five feet deeper than at normal stream flow, an increase that would be hardly discernable in a canyon a mile deep. Drury consulted with Grand Canyon National Park Superintendent Harold Bryant, who also argued against the higher dam. In addition, in a last attempt at finding common ground, the park service and the bureau commissioned Edwin McKee, a University of Arizona geology professor, and Frederick Law Olmsted Jr., the noted landscape architect, to undertake studies of the geological and natural values that would be affected by the flooding of the lower reach of Grand Canyon.

Both experts concluded that a significant loss of scenic values would occur if the high Bridge Canyon Dam were built. Olmsted elaborated upon the problems of driftwood deposition that frequently occurred at the head of Lake Mead, stating that he found it to be an impenetrable barrier to upriver navigation at certain times of the year. "Fortunately," he wrote, "most of the corpses of dead animals carried into Lake Mead sink quickly to the bottom." Olmsted added that if the high Bridge Canyon Dam were built, this "rather gruesome procession" would be deposited at the western end of Grand Canyon National Park as a result. The grandeur of the lower canyon so impressed McKee that he proposed an enlargement of the park downstream all the way to Lake Mead.[8] Bureau personnel, however, contended that the minute loss of scenic values that would occur within the park would be more than offset by new recreational opportunities.

Drury now began to ponder how to successfully advance his two arguments: (1) that the high Bridge Canyon Dam reservoir would invade the park; and (2) whether the park could be defended against such an admittedly minuscule encroachment. After reading McKee's and Olmsted's reports, Drury consulted important preservationists such as Dr. John Merriam, former president of the Carnegie Institute, and began to reconceptualize the park service's relationship with the bureau that, he believed, had resulted in his predecessors agreeing to allow water development and other intrusions in national parks and monuments.

Writing Merriam in October 1942, Drury asked for his views about the proposed Bridge Canyon Dam and ended his letter stating: "The important question is whether this Service should take a stand resisting the flooding of 8 [sic] miles of the inner gorge in the western portion of Grand Canyon National Park." In response to a letter from Superintendent Bryant, Drury was even more definitive:

> It is imperative that the Service obtain complete and reliable data on the exact damage that would be done within the park by backing water 8 [sic] miles up the Colorado and one-half mile up Havasu Creek. *In replying to the Bureau of Reclamation I want to state clearly the sacrifice of park values that will be involved in order that they may be weighed against the immediate and potential economic advantages* [emphasis mine].[9]

Drury decided to challenge the bureau's economic arguments with the intangible value of preserved wilderness, a radical position in 1942. In Drury's opinion, *any* encroachment upon a national park, even if it were just along a park boundary, was no longer acceptable. Believing he could not defend Grand Canyon National Monument, Drury drew his legal line of defense at the boundary of Grand Canyon National Park.

The very next year, Drury faced yet another threat to the National Park System, this time in a remote area of Montana just south of the Canadian border. The Army Corps of Engineers applied for permission to build a dam at the Glacier View damsite on the North Fork of the Flathead River just outside of Glacier National Park. This dam and reservoir would have inundated almost twenty thousand acres of that park, including much of its winter elk and moose habitat. Interior Secretary Harold Ickes opposed this development, but he also recognized that the exigency of World War II had given the corps a free hand with respect to park service resources. The secretary approved of the corps' site tests and reservoir assessments while instructing his subordinates to drag their feet. Drury applied his new Grand Canyon strategy to the Glacier View proposal and began to mobilize opposition to this project as well.[10]

The Bureau Tips Its Hand

On June 6, 1944, D-Day in the European theater of World War II, another D-Day of sorts took place in the American West, a day that would chart the course of Arizona's struggle to obtain water for its central valleys for the next three decades. On this date, the Bureau of Reclamation presented its preliminary development report for the Colorado River Basin, which included a high dam at Bridge Canyon. Senator Ernest McFarland immediately received permission to convene his subcommittee in Phoenix to discuss the bureau's plans for the "Central Arizona Diversion" as it was now called. These hearings, the first on what was to become the Central Arizona Project, began on July 31 and continued until August 4. The bureau's E. B. Debler, having repudiated his earlier support for the preservation of Grand Canyon National Park, described the status of the project and presented three proposals: (1) a modified version of Colter's Colorado-Verde plan that called for a high dam in Marble Canyon upstream of the national park; (2) a high dam at Bridge Canyon that would back water into the park; and (3) a diversion to central Arizona from Lake Havasu farther downstream.

These options were ominous from the perspective of the park service because now the high Bridge Canyon Dam was imbedded in an official bureau publication. However, the report also included a scheme that did not involve the diversion of water to Central Arizona at all. Perhaps anticipating the public outcry that would result if it sought to build dams on the main stem of the Colorado within Grand Canyon National Park, the bureau drew up a plan designed to tap the hydroelectric potential of the Colorado in what its leaders believed was a less invasive manner, a project it referred to as the Kanab Creek Power Development. Bureau engineers proposed to divert water around and *underneath* Grand Canyon National Park through a tunnel under the north rim and through a hydroelectric generating station at the mouth of Kanab Creek where it would reenter the Colorado River at that point.

The park service did not react to this proposition, probably because the report was only preliminary and was not publicly released. However, with the end of the war and the appointment of the ambitious Michael Straus as Reclamation Commissioner in 1945, all semblance of civility between the bureau and the park service soon dissolved in the wake of the former's postwar dam-building agenda.[11]

The conclusion of World War II also ended the wartime constraints upon western water development. After the war the population of the United States began a second westward migration as millions of people moved to the Southwest, placing an unprecedented strain upon existing municipal infrastructures. Between 1940 and 1960, Arizona gained almost one million new residents while Phoenix alone grew from 65,000 to 439,000, a figure that is even more astonishing when one considers that most of this growth occurred after 1949. In that year, Motorola Inc. moved its research and development lab to Phoenix, the vanguard of a wave of high-tech industries to relocate their facilities there. California's wartime growth also continued in the postwar period, and its population grew from nine million in 1945 to nineteen million by 1964. Faced with exploding desert populations and without feasible alternatives, Arizona and California once again looked to the Colorado River to provide the water and power to sustain them. The Bureau of Reclamation, freed from wartime restrictions and with the aggressive Straus at the helm, now embarked upon an extraordinary period of dam building.[12]

The bureau released its official plans to develop the Colorado River to the public in a March 1946 publication titled *The Colorado River, a*

Natural Menace Becomes a National Resource, in which it outlined its comprehensive plan for the development of the Colorado River Basin. The analysis included the three proposals from its 1944 report, including a high Bridge Canyon Dam, and several earlier schemes such as the Colorado-Verde project. It also recommended the construction of dams on the Little Colorado and Paria Rivers to prolong the useful life of Bridge Canyon Dam, which it estimated at thirty-seven years. The Coconino silt-retention dam proposed for the Little Colorado River would not have been located in Grand Canyon National Park; however, its reservoir would have inundated two miles of the Little Colorado River gorge in Wupatki National Monument. The bureau also quoted selectively from Olmsted's 1942 report and used it to argue that a high dam at Bridge Canyon would destroy few scenic values, when in fact Olmsted stated conclusively that just the opposite would occur.

The report also included a description of the Kanab Creek Power Development, now called the Marble Canyon–Kanab Creek Project (MCKC). Specifically, this plan contemplated the construction of a dam in Marble Canyon that could stand alone as a separate project, twelve miles upstream of Grand Canyon National Park. The primary feature of this proposal was the forty-five-mile-long tunnel from the Marble Canyon Reservoir, underneath the north rim of the canyon, to Kanab Creek.[13]

This plan also included a dam, reservoir, and a power plant at the mouth of Kanab Creek. The tunnel was designed to carry ninety percent of the Colorado's flow to Kanab Creek reservoir, where the water would have been stored before being discharged through the power plant. The plant, located in the heart of Grand Canyon, would have been built on the Forest Service land on the north side of the Colorado River across from the national park. From there the water would have flowed into the new reservoir created by the high Bridge Canyon Dam. The plan also called for the release of a meager flow of one thousand cubic feet per second from Marble Canyon Dam through the park for "scenic purposes" after it first passed through the turbines of a power plant at Marble Canyon Dam.[14]

Unlikely as it may seem, the bureau conceived of this project to avoid conflict with the park service and other groups interested in the preservation of Grand Canyon. None of these features would have been visible from the popular tourist viewpoints on the south rim, and Marble Canyon and Bridge Canyon dams would have been built outside of the park and monument. This proposal was designed to utilize all of the

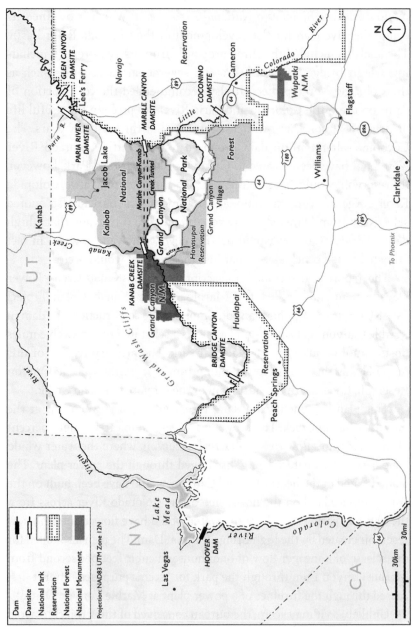

FIGURE 2.2. Map of Grand Canyon National Park and Monument and various proposals from the Bureau of Reclamation's 1946 report including the high Bridge Canyon Dam, the Marble Canyon–Kanab Creek Project, and the Coconino and Paria silt-control dams. The Coconino Dam would have created a reservoir on the Little Colorado River that would have encroached upon Wupatki National Monument. Map by Nathaniel Douglass, ndcartography.com.

water and the entire 950-foot drop of the river within the park for power generation. The bureau estimated its power output at more than 6.6 billion kilowatts per year.[15]

Thus by 1946 Drury confronted three threats looming over the Colorado River and its tributaries that imperiled two national monuments as well as Grand Canyon National Park. Although geologists included Marble Canyon as a part of the Grand Canyon system, because this spectacular gorge remained unprotected Drury believed he could not successfully oppose a dam there. He also believed he stood little chance of defeating the long-contemplated low Bridge Canyon Dam that would be built downstream of the monument because his predecessors had already acquiesced to it.

However, no park service official had ever agreed to an invasion of the park itself, so Drury remained adamantly against a high Bridge Canyon Dam despite the friction he knew it would create within the Interior Department. Drury also opposed the Marble Canyon–Kanab Creek project because he feared that the Kanab Creek power plant and its transmission lines would be visible from the south rim, and that the reduction in flow through the park below Marble Canyon Dam would result in a great loss of scenic values. At a time when the bureau seemed to be gaining political support for its projects, and politicians such as Arizona Representative John Murdock were arguing that the bureau should build a one-thousand-foot-tall Bridge Canyon Dam, Drury was forced to fight battles where he believed he had a reasonable chance to prevail.[16]

Drury Asks for Help

As the park service struggled to reestablish itself in Washington, DC, after the war and knowing that he needed allies to combat the mounting threats to the park system, Drury began to look outside of his agency for support. In May 1947 he sent letters to the leaders of more than forty environmental organizations and societies outlining the most critical of these threats, and he asked for their help in opposing them. The first threat on his list was the proposed Glacier View Dam, and he began to build a coalition of conservation leaders willing to testify at the public hearings he anticipated would soon occur.[17]

He also began to apprise these same organizations of the threats to Grand Canyon. No major environmental organization had yet gone on record as opposing either the high Bridge Canyon Dam or the MCKC project. But as Americans reveled in their postwar prosperity and began to engage in outdoor recreation in ever increasing numbers, these groups began to stir from complacency. People began to visit the national parks in record numbers, and this quickly created a national constituency for conservation issues that would ultimately be reflected in increasing membership and activism on the part of these organizations. Still, Drury fought the first phase of this battle virtually alone; it was not until 1948 that he began receiving correspondence from the leaders of the Sierra Club and other organizations about developing a strategy to defeat the high Bridge Canyon Dam and the Marble Canyon–Kanab Creek project.

In 1947 Carl Hayden and Ernest McFarland introduced Senate Bill 1175 attempting to gain authorization for the CAP, and they scheduled hearings for June. Although their bill stood little chance of passage because new Interior Secretary Julius Krug had not officially approved the bureau's 1946 studies, these hearings set the tone for the CAP debates that would occur over the next two decades. During the hearings Arizona's delegation argued that without the project, the state's agricultural economy would be ruined. Senator Sheridan Downey of California contended that because California was now using more than 4.4 million acre-feet annually, the water allotments of the lower basin states should be determined by the US Supreme Court before congressional consideration of the CAP.

Californians also invoked Cold War rhetoric, arguing that Commissioner Straus had become a "western Stalin," and reclamation projects like the CAP were "formidable weapons" in the hands of those who wished to transform the United States into a "socialist utopia." Arizona's opposition to a Supreme Court adjudication of water rights was, according to California representatives Harry R. Sheppard and Norris Poulson, "dangerously imperiling national defense" by threatening California's water supply. Indeed, Cold War fears extended into the War Department, which communicated to Drury in September that it was considering construction of a power dam and "subterranean defense works" within Grand Canyon in case of a nuclear war—this before the Soviet Union had even exploded an atomic device! The War Department viewed Grand Canyon as an ideal spot for the dam because the depth of the canyon would make it difficult for bombers to attack it.[18]

Meanwhile, Arizona water advocates accused California of conspiring to obtain the diversion of Columbia River water to supplement the over-allocated Colorado. California denied these allegations; however, it was later revealed that the bureau had initiated a preliminary study of a Pacific Northwest diversion at the behest of California water officials. The bureau's studies were very speculative, but the mere fact that this issue had been broached raised suspicions in the Pacific Northwest that California was going to attempt a water grab sometime in the future.[19]

The threat of a Columbia diversion would loom above debates over Bridge Canyon Dam for the next two decades, pitting powerful politicians from the states of Oregon and Washington against those of the Colorado River Basin. The bureau's cavalier assumptions that it could study a diversion of water from the Columbia River without first gaining the approval of the Pacific Northwest's senators and representatives would eventually motivate politicians from that region to write the most sweeping environmental legislation in the history of the United States.[20]

Conservation organizations remained conspicuously absent from these hearings. These proceedings served notice that the federal government now considered development of the water and power resources of the Colorado a top priority. It seemed only a matter of time before the secretary of the interior gave his approval to the bureau's CAP study, which would throw the weight of the department behind the proposal, including a high Bridge Canyon Dam that would back water thirteen miles into the park.

Although he had laid the groundwork for his opposition, Drury had refrained from discussing these projects with his new boss, Interior Secretary Julius Krug—who had replaced Ickes after the latter's resignation in February 1946—because he believed the bitter disputes between the basin states over Colorado River water would delay them indefinitely. Now the release of the bureau's report and the Hayden-McFarland bill spurred him into action.[21] Drury began conferring with the secretary over how to reconcile the conflicting positions of the Bureau of Reclamation and the National Park Service. As he had done with respect to Glacier View Dam, he also wrote the leaders of several leading conservation organizations to determine how to meet the emerging threat.

Ominous as a high Bridge Canyon Dam must have seemed, Drury also had to contend with the possibility that the bureau would try to obtain authorization for the Marble Canyon–Kanab Creek project. This proposal had an almost hypnotic effect upon just about everyone, from the bureau engineers who conceived of it, to Los Angeles city officials who wanted to build it, and conservation leaders, some of whom were willing to pay almost any price to kill it.

Drury wrote Krug on March 22, 1948, and eloquently objected to both the high Bridge Canyon Dam and the MCKC project. The director indicated that he realized Interior was under severe political pressure to construct the Bridge Canyon project and hinted that he would not object to a low dam. But he also argued that his agency would not agree to a high dam because it would be "inconsistent with our duty, under the basic statutes which established the National Park Service, to preserve natural phenomenon [sic] unimpaired." Drury acknowledged that he recognized the vast majority of the park would not be affected by the reservoir, but he still refused to compromise the park. Sensing the potential public reaction to such an intrusion, he stated: "Repercussions . . . will be long and loud when the general public learns that one of its best known and most spectacular national parks might someday be partially sacrificed to permit an alien use." Drury advised Krug to confer with the new Interior Department advisory committee on conservation, made up of eight representatives from prominent conservation organizations, hoping that they might help sway the secretary in favor of a low dam.[22]

Despite Drury's efforts, Secretary Krug approved the bureau's proposal in February 1948 and released it to water officials from the states of the Colorado Basin for review.[23] Perhaps as an afterthought, he then met with the advisory committee in May to discuss the Bridge Canyon project as Drury had suggested. Bestor Robinson, representing the Sierra Club, voted in favor of the project while the other seven members, including Fred Packard of the National Parks Association, voted against it.[24] Robinson, a lawyer from the San Francisco Bay area, viewed Bridge Canyon Dam and its relatively slight encroachment upon the park as the lesser of two potential evils when compared with the destruction that would occur if the bureau gained approval to build the MCKC project.

Whither the Sierra Club

Robinson also believed the conservation organizations should focus upon convincing Congress to repeal the reclamation language in the 1919 law that created Grand Canyon National Park. Convinced that his colleagues on the advisory committee did not understand the legal ramifications of this language, Robinson drafted an argument designed to convince conservationists to support a high Bridge Canyon Dam in exchange for this repeal and the elimination of the MCKC project from further consideration.

Not all Sierra Club leaders agreed with Robinson's assessment. Richard Leonard, a tax attorney and Sierra Club board member who served with Drury in the Save the Redwoods League, wrote the park service director in June, seeking to coordinate a strategy in opposition to a high Bridge Canyon Dam. Leonard indicated that although Robinson seemed "resigned to the construction of a high dam," the rest of the board of directors still thought that it could be stopped.

But a dejected Drury, weary of campaigning alone, considered giving up the fight because he was discouraged by Krug's approval of the high dam. While he "deplored" the construction of a dam that would invade the park, Drury thought Krug's approval made construction virtually inevitable. Drury believed that he had done all he could and the service had no choice but to go along. In his correspondence with Leonard throughout the summer of 1948, Drury indicated that he substantially agreed with Robinson's position.

Instead of resisting a high Bridge Canyon Dam, Drury decided to focus his energy on defeating the MCKC project because the secretary had not yet approved it. He insisted that he had only shifted his focus because his boss's decision had effectively rendered his own opinion moot.[25] With Drury seemingly sidelined, the question remained whether conservation organizations not restricted by the Interior Department's internal mandate would carry on the fight to defeat a high Bridge Canyon Dam.

Drury did not remain out of the conflict for long. Sensing the explosive potential of the MCKC proposal, in 1946 Commissioner Straus had agreed, in a rare moment of interagency cooperation, that the bureau would not undertake studies of projects affecting parks and monuments without first consulting with the director of the National Park Service. Yet as the bureau continued to lobby for political support of a high dam at Bridge Canyon in the summer of 1948, Drury began to suspect that this effort was an attempt to conceal its actual goal of obtaining approval for the construction of the MCKC project.

The prospect that the Interior Department would give even more than a passing glance at this scheme horrified preservationists both inside and outside of the park service. Writing to Leonard, Drury called the bureau's suggested flow rate of one thousand cubic feet per second for "scenic purposes," an amount that constituted one-tenth of the river's average normal flow, "a sham and mockery in comparison to the once great force that carved the canyon."[26] Reducing the river to a veritable trickle would, in Drury's opinion, also have a physical impact on the canyon because, he contended, river and canyon were both components of a single natural phenomenon and thus harming one would hurt them both.

By emphasizing the organic relationship between river and canyon in his opposition to the MCKC project, Drury conceived of the holistic argument that environmentalists would use to great effect against Bridge and Marble Canyon Dams during the climactic battles of the 1960s. He used it to construct a legal argument as well, contending that since the river and canyon were inextricably intertwined, a project that detrimentally affected the river's flow through the canyon would violate the language in the park establishment act, which stated that the "primary purpose" of the park was to preserve the canyon's scenic beauty. And though Drury's contentions were designed to combat the MCKC diversion, they became especially important to environmentalists who lacked the means to oppose Marble Canyon Dam as a separate project during the 1960s, because this dam and reservoir would have been located twelve miles upstream of the park in what at that time was a completely unprotected section of the canyon.

While Drury fought to defend Grand Canyon National Park, two other threats to national parks were reaching their respective climaxes. By midsummer public hearings had been held on the proposed Glacier View Dam, and both Los Angeles and the bureau were seeking permission to build hydroelectric and water storage dams in Kings Canyon National Park. Park service personnel, conservation groups, local residents, businesses, and even the Montana Power Company all united against the Glacier View Dam and testified at public hearings in June 1948 in Spokane, Washington. In the face of this opposition and already under fire from the Truman administration, the corps of engineers dropped the proposal to build Glacier View Dam in 1949.[27] The threats to Kings Canyon were also defeated by a similar coalition. The park service played an active oppositional role in both controversies and in the case of Glacier, Drury had taken the lead in organizing the conservationist opposition against these dams.[28]

Drury continued his covert offensive against the high Bridge Canyon Dam and in August he mailed copies of the bureau's publication *The Colorado River*, along with Olmsted's report, to Leonard, who had requested more information about these projects for the Sierra Club's September 1948 board of directors meeting. On a spectacular autumn day, the Sierra Club's leaders gathered outside at Tuolumne Meadows in Yosemite National Park to discuss these threats to the National Park System and what, if anything, the club should do about them.[29]

Robinson skillfully argued his case and reiterated the reasons why he believed the club should compromise on Bridge Canyon Dam in exchange for an amendment to the establishment act and the elimination of the MCKC project. Several directors objected, echoing another of Drury's contentions that to allow an intrusion into Grand Canyon National Park would greatly weaken opposition to dams that threatened other national parks. But director Alex Hildebrand argued that the club must allow Bridge Canyon Dam to be built because if it were not, then Los Angeles would pressure the Interior Department to develop power sites in Kings Canyon National Park, a site it had long coveted for power development. Hildebrand's idea, to trade saving a known area of scenic beauty for the flooding of a canyon few had seen, is eerily suggestive of the Sierra Club's agreement to allow the height of Glen Canyon Dam to be raised in exchange for the removal of the dams planned for Dinosaur National Monument almost a decade later.

The directors were split and so the board voted to oppose the MCKC proposal and to defer action on a Bridge Canyon Dam strategy until its November meeting. After voting to send Olmsted's report—forwarded by Drury—to the Natural Resources Council, composed of leaders from twenty-six conservation organizations, the board adjourned. Robinson went home to craft his arguments, and at the end of October he outlined his strategy and sent it to Drury and other leading conservationists not affiliated with the Sierra Club. Robinson's memo, when read in conjunction with Olmsted's report, demonstrated to conservationists that significant divisions existed among them. These differences needed to be reconciled if they were going to present unified opposition to the increasing pressure to open the national parks to development.

In the late winter of 1948, the Interior Department reviewed preliminary drafts of the CAP bill. Either by design or inadvertence, the secretary neglected to forward a copy to Drury for his review. When his agency finally obtained a copy of the bill, Drury was dumbfounded. The legislation Arizona's delegation was about to introduce called for the construction of a Bridge Canyon Dam with a crest of *not less than 1,877* feet above sea level. He sensed a ploy to allow the bureau to construct a dam that could possibly be much higher than the *maximum* elevation of 1,876 to which he had agreed earlier. He drafted an amendment to limit the height of the dam and hoped that Secretary Krug would insert it. But he was too late; the secretary approved the bill as originally submitted, leaving Drury without any more opportunities to shape it.

His boss had now taken an official position, but Drury continued to work behind the scenes. He bombarded Commissioner Straus with letters throughout 1949 in which he demolished the bureau's economic justification for the high dam.[30] Short of resigning, Drury had done everything possible to derail the legislation. Now all he could do was watch as Congress prepared for the upcoming hearings.

In March 1949 Arizona Senators Hayden and McFarland and Arizona Representative John Murdock simultaneously introduced CAP bills in both houses of Congress. It quickly became apparent that California would be Arizona's chief opponent once again. California's delegation continued to argue that the US Supreme Court needed to determine the water rights of the lower basin states before the authorization of any more projects on the lower Colorado River.

After twenty intense sessions at the subcommittee level, the House hearings adjourned without any action being taken. No conservation organization had sent representatives to testify against the bill; most of the opposition came from private utility companies and California water interests. The Senate Committee on Interior and Insular Affairs approved the bill with little discussion and on July 1 sent it to the floor, where it was scheduled for debate in January 1950.[31] The CAP legislation, though temporarily stalled, remained unchanged in both houses, with the language calling for the construction of a Bridge Canyon Dam to a *minimum* elevation of 1,877 feet remaining intact.

At almost the same time, conservationists were debating whether to support Robinson's Bridge Canyon Dam strategy. In January 1949 Robinson convinced the interior secretary's conservation committee to endorse a shift in park boundaries, the abolishment of Grand Canyon National Monument, and a high Bridge Canyon Dam. Then, in a shocking development, he somehow persuaded them to approve the construction of a dam with a reservoir elevation of two thousand feet above sea level. Robinson contended that if the dam were built to this height, it would nullify the MCKC project and create a water highway into the "heart of the Grand Canyon area" in exchange for a relatively small loss of scenic values.[32]

That Robinson could convince leading conservationists to endorse these arguments demonstrates that environmentalists believed the bureau could obtain authorization for its proposals virtually at will. It also reveals that many conservation organizations had not yet experienced the ideological transformation that would make them such formidable opponents of reclamation during future controversies involving Dinosaur National Monument and Grand Canyon National Park. A significant number of members belonging to these societies still supported recreational development within national parks and monuments. Finally, it shows that Drury stood at the forefront of the emerging preservation movement in the spring of 1949 without reliable support from leading conservation organizations. Although Drury convinced conservationists to oppose the Glacier View Dam, he would soon discover that obtaining their support to protect Grand Canyon would be a much more arduous task.

After the disastrous conservation committee meeting, Drury's correspondence with leading conservationists assumed an angry tone. He argued vehemently that to move the park boundary and abolish the national monument would establish a "dangerous precedent" that could have only one end result—the destruction of the National Park System. In May, he completely repudiated his earlier consideration of Robinson's first Bridge Canyon Dam compromise. Perhaps he was buoyed by a memo from Olmsted that urged him to continue his policy of "uncompromising adherence" to the national park ideal and to resist all proposals that would intrude upon Grand Canyon National Park. Still alone in his opposition, Drury again began to fight against the high Bridge Canyon Dam within the Interior Department while he attempted to mobilize support from environmental organizations outside of it.[33]

The Bureau Goes Rogue

Although stymied in Congress, preparations to construct the Bridge Canyon project continued to move forward on other fronts. By July 1949 the Bureau of Reclamation had studied several townsite locations for construction workers and their families and the possibility of constructing a 2,270-foot elevator shaft to provide access from the south rim to the damsite for personnel and supplies. After touring these sites on the rim and river with Grand Canyon National Park Superintendent Harold Bryant and several bureau officials, Lake Mead National Recreation Area Superintendent George F. Baggley concluded in amazement that the bureau was pursuing its own agenda without congressional or Interior Department approval and had ignored the sovereign rights of the Hualapai Nation by conducting these damsite preparations on reservation land without obtaining their permission.[34]

This bureau's seeming omnipotence caused great distress within the park service because it was becoming readily apparent that Commissioner Straus's agency was now only nominally under the control of the Interior Department. Drury, reminiscing about his tenure as park service director in a 1972 interview, described the relationship between the interior secretary and the bureau at the height of the dam-building era:

> Secretary Chapman, who doubtless meant well, was utterly impotent in the hands of his subordinates. He was very much in the position of the mahout who rides the elephant and thinks he is guiding it but really is being carried along. That wasn't true of men like Ickes but it surely was true of Chapman as Secretary of the Interior. The Great Bureau of Reclamation was the—well it was like Prussia in the German Empire where everything was weighted in its favor. That's about the essence of the situation.[35]

Although the events at the Bridge Canyon Damsite occurred a few months before the beginning of Oscar Chapman's service, Drury's description is applicable to Krug's tenure as well. The bureau had become so powerful within the Interior Department by 1949 that it was able to appropriate funds, trespass upon Native American lands, and make preliminary preparations for the construction of Bridge Canyon Dam without obtaining permission from the secretary of the interior.

As though this display of hubris was not enough, the bureau also began to investigate studies of Marble Canyon Dam and the MCKC project in May 1949 without the approval of Drury or the interior secretary, a direct violation of the interagency agreement Commissioner Straus had made with the park service in 1946. Soon after he learned of the bureau's intent, Drury and his chief of land and recreational planning, Conrad Wirth, met with Straus on June 14 to discuss the situation. A testy meeting followed where Straus breezily admitted that he intended to ignore the 1946 agreement. He challenged Drury to ask

FIGURE 2.3. Department of Interior personnel inspecting the Bridge Canyon Damsite in 1949, including George Baggley, superintendent of Lake Mead National Recreation Area (*left rear*), M. R. Tillotson, superintendent of Grand Canyon National Park (*front center*), and Michael Straus, commissioner, Bureau of Reclamation (*far right*). NAU. PH.96.4.85.19, Northern Arizona University, Cline Library, Bill Belknap Collection.

Secretary Krug to decide which should have the higher priority, the power that could be produced by the MCKC project or the preservation of scenery in Grand Canyon National Park.

During this stormy session, the agreement was read aloud to Straus without any visible effect whatsoever.[36] Then Straus also revealed that in addition to the activity at the Bridge Canyon site, he had also contracted with a construction firm to build a cableway for men and materials from the rim to the river at the Marble Canyon damsite and that after the completion of the cableway the bureau intended to bore test shafts into the canyon walls. When Drury asked Straus to wait until the matter could be discussed with Krug, Straus refused, saying that he would only stop if ordered by the interior secretary himself.

The bureau built its cableway and started boring into the walls of Marble Canyon later that summer. But Drury won a partial victory because the Interior Department abandoned the Kanab Creek tunnel, as it

FIGURE 2.4. A construction camp on the Navajo Reservation above one of the damsites in Marble Canyon located at river mile 32.7 just downstream of Vasey's Paradise ca. 1950. NAU.PH.2003.11.2.B-4737, Northern Arizona University, Cline Library, Josef Muench Collection.

turned out, for good.[37] Although the MCKC project would lay dormant for almost ten years until it was briefly resurrected by Los Angeles as a state project, the specter of it still hung over the park and influenced the actions of people trying to defend it.

Conservationists Weigh In . . . and Out

Drury gained his first steadfast ally in the struggle against the high Bridge Canyon Dam in May 1949 when the National Parks Association (NPA) began publishing a series of articles written by field secretary Fred Packard opposing the Bridge Canyon and MCKC projects in *National Parks* magazine. Historically, the association had been one of the park service's most vocal critics since its founder, Robert Sterling Yard, and the first director of the National Park Service, Stephen Mather, had parted ways over the service's promotion of the "firefall" and other carnival-like attractions at Yosemite and other national parks. Now the NPA became the first environmental organization to try to gain support for Drury's campaign to return the park service back to its founding principles by publicly opposing reclamation projects in Grand Canyon.

Packard attacked the economic feasibility of the projects first, explaining that all of the bureau's recent proposals for the Colorado River added up to a staggering sum of almost $3.5 trillion—by comparison, the Marshall Plan to rebuild western Europe cost $12–15 billion. Only after making this economic argument did he echo Olmsted's assertions of 1942, that at some point the American people were going to have to decide where to draw the line between the preservation of scenery and water development. NPA executive secretary Devereux Butcher wrote Robinson of the Sierra Club in June and chastised him for trying to convince people that "a great national monument [should] be abolished to accommodate an engineering project."[38]

Work continued at the Bridge Canyon site in the fall of 1949 while Drury hounded Interior Secretary Krug to amend the language in the bills pending before Congress to limit the height of Bridge Canyon Dam to a maximum of 1,877 feet in elevation. When Krug asked for the bureau's position, the obdurate Straus refused to compromise and so the language remained. However, in October Drury discovered that the bureau had studied proposals to build a dam with a normal high-water elevation up to 1,930 feet, concluding that a reservoir with a maximum surface elevation of 1,876 feet was the best economic alternative.[39]

Drury had now done all he could from within the Interior Department and his unceasing efforts were finally beginning to bear fruit. He had already gained the support of the National Parks Association. In the fall both Ira Gabrielson of the Wildlife Management Institute and Harlean

James of the American Planning and Civic Association repudiated their earlier support of Robinson's proposal. They wrote letters to key politicians, asking them to fight against the CAP unless the elevation of Bridge Canyon Dam was capped at 1,877 feet. In July, the Wilderness Society's executive council held its annual meeting at Olympic National Park and passed a resolution calling for the interior secretary to order new studies and to reconsider the entire project.[40]

By late autumn of 1949, it was becoming apparent that the leaders of several important conservation organizations were finally angry enough at the Interior Department to take a public stand against a dam and reservoir that would intrude upon Grand Canyon National Park. Hoping to gain another important ally, Drury anxiously awaited the November meeting of the Sierra Club's board of directors when the club's leadership planned to discuss the merits of Robinson's proposal of the previous year and finally take a definitive position on the height of Bridge Canyon Dam.

On November 12, 1949, the Sierra Club directors met. Leonard read a letter from Krug that assured Leonard that he had cancelled the MCKC project and pledged to limit the elevation of Bridge Canyon Dam to 1,877 feet above sea level. After some discussion, Robinson took the floor and reiterated his compromise of the previous spring:

1. Bridge Canyon Dam should not be authorized unless the bureau constructed silt-retention dams on the Little Colorado and upstream on the main stem of the Colorado River first.

2. The reclamation provision within the Grand Canyon National Park Establishment Act should be repealed before the authorization of Bridge Canyon Dam.

3. The boundaries of the park should be moved east to exclude the reservoir, and Grand Canyon National Monument should be abolished.

4. Bridge Canyon Dam should be constructed so as not to *impound water above Tapeats Creek, two thousand feet above sea level.* [emphasis mine].

5. The water level in the reservoir should be maintained at a stable level to avoid scarring of the canyon walls between the high and low water marks.

After discussing these recommendations thoroughly, Robinson called for a vote. The Sierra Club's board of directors, including Leonard and Brower, unanimously adopted them as the club's official position on Bridge Canyon Dam.[41]

Improbable as it may seem today, the Sierra Club's leadership in November 1949 *unanimously* approved proposals that would: eliminate Grand Canyon National Monument; flood part of Wupatki National Monument on the Little Colorado River; shift the boundaries of Grand Canyon National Park to accommodate a reservoir project; and allow Bridge Canyon Dam to be constructed to an elevation of almost two thousand feet, *seventy feet higher than any dam the bureau had studied and more than 120 feet taller than the dam it was most likely to build*. Although the Sierra Club leadership now believed that they had staved off the MCKC project and set the stage to remove the reclamation provision from the park's enabling act, they had only done so by compromising the canyon and the club's own founding principles to an almost unimaginable degree. Other environmental organizations quickly condemned the Sierra Club's actions.

An outraged Drury fired off a letter to Leonard in February 1950 and expressed his anger with the Sierra Club's leadership in no uncertain terms:

> That the Sierra Club, founded by John Muir for the protection of the national parks, should adopt a resolution approving of a reservoir which would back water more than 30 [sic] miles into Grand Canyon National Park is somewhat of a shock. *Administrators sometimes have to reconcile themselves to something less than the ideal, but conservation organizations are under no such necessity.* This action of the club greatly weakens our defense of the park and is confusing to many other conservation organizations [emphasis mine].

As to the suggested boundary shift, Drury continued:

> I feel sure you will agree that it would be establishing a very dangerous precedent to embark upon a program of shifting national park boundaries to accommodate reservoir projects. If that were undertaken, it would be only a matter of a few years before there wouldn't be any national parks worthy of the name.[42]

Drury's disillusionment and anger with the Sierra Club leadership are obvious, even though filtered by the bureaucratic language of his letter. And no wonder! Since 1942, Drury had fought almost single-handedly to uphold the national park ideal, retreating when it made tactical sense but never losing sight of his ultimate objective of protecting Grand Canyon National Park from reclamation projects. Possessing a keen legal mind and a willingness to confront bureau and Interior Department officials, Drury knew supporters of western water development would use the Sierra Club's position to undercut other conservation organizations fighting against it. Despite long odds, Drury was willing to risk his career to fight against the high Bridge Dam and the reinforcement of the Hetch Hetchy precedent it represented. The Sierra Club's leadership, on the other hand, had completely surrendered.

Drury has not received enough recognition for his role in keeping Grand Canyon and other national parks free of dams and for goading environmental groups into action.[43] When these organizations finally weighed in on dams planned for Dinosaur National Monument in the 1950s, it was with a vengeance. They have been rightly credited with forcing politicians and the American public to think about weighing the intangible values of preservation against the economic value of water development, and they deserve credit for reinventing themselves and becoming steadfast defenders of the national parks.

But Drury got there first. By drawing his last line of defense at the boundary of Grand Canyon National Park in 1942 and Glacier National Park a year later, Drury became the first conservationist inside or outside of the federal government to fight against the policy of reservoir accommodation begun at Hetch Hetchy. Drury's relentless opposition to the high Bridge Canyon Dam is the origin of the legal strategy of defending national parks and monuments at their boundaries that environmentalists have used to fight and win subsequent battles against dams and other intrusions into the park system ever since.

Drury's actions also renewed the park service's credibility in the eyes of many conservation organizations for a short time in between the pro-development tenures of Albright/Cammerer and Conrad Wirth. Briefly forced to make a tactical retreat in the face of insurmountable opposition with respect to the high Bridge Canyon Dam, Drury fought tenaciously behind the scenes to defend the borders of the National Park System, and until 1948 he fought this battle virtually alone. Although Drury had convinced the leadership of several important conservation organizations to oppose the high Bridge Canyon Dam by 1949, the Sierra Club still favored compromise, guaranteeing that the conservation front would remain fragmented in February 1950 when Carl Hayden and Ernest McFarland once again brought legislation to the Senate floor calling for the construction of Bridge Canyon Dam.

Unity at Last

When the Senate CAP hearings began on February 6, 1950, California's senators made a futile attempt to derail the Hayden-McFarland bill. So sure were the two Arizonans of victory that they did not even bother to attend the sessions in the interior committee. On the same day, Anthony Wayne Smith, future executive secretary of the National Parks Association, sent a telegram to every member of the Senate. It stated that his organization opposed the high Bridge Canyon Dam because the reservoir would encroach upon Grand Canyon National Park and Monument and that it also would violate the property rights of the Hualapai and Havasupai tribes, who had not consented to the flooding of parts of their reservations. Drury, still fighting for a height limitation for Bridge Canyon Dam, spoke with Senator McFarland on February 7 and 15, and McFarland assured him that he and Senator Hayden would sponsor an amendment limiting the dam's height to 1,877 feet above seal level. To Drury's astonishment, McFarland revealed that he had not considered the effects that a high Bridge Canyon Dam would have on the national park.

Packard of the National Parks Association tried to gain permission to testify at these hearings but his requests were repeatedly denied. However, he managed to enter a statement into the hearing record in support of Drury's amendment, the only opposition from a conservationist to make it into the official proceedings. Hayden's prestige and political power overcame California's opposition and the committee reported the bill to the Senate floor, but without Drury's amendment limiting the height because the senators felt that it would be better to insert it in conference committee after the House passed the bill. On February 21, 1950, the US Senate voted 55–28 in favor of the Central Arizona Project with a high Bridge Canyon Dam.[44]

As these CAP hearings took place, conservationists started to mobilize against this danger to Grand Canyon and other threats to the park system. Packard began corresponding with congressmen and stated that the NPA now opposed even a low Bridge Canyon Dam that would intrude upon the monument because of the precedent it would create. To emphasize his point, Packard listed several areas threatened by reservoir projects, including Glacier and Mammoth Cave National Parks and Dinosaur National Monument. James, executive secretary of the American Planning and Civic Association, wrote Leonard and argued that the Sierra Club should: (1) join with her organization in supporting Drury's opposition to a dam greater than 1,877 feet in elevation; and (2) repudiate the resolution it passed in December 1949. Both the National Parks Association and the American Planning and Civic Association still looked to the National Park Service for "guidance," and indeed, Drury continued his campaign against the higher dam even after Senate passage of the bill.[45]

Threats to the National Park System soon became more acute as the bureau framed additional proposals calling for dams that would encroach upon western national parks and monuments. As Congress discussed and conservationists debated how to respond, and how to proceed in the case of Bridge Canyon Dam, politicians from the upper Colorado River Basin states were also lobbying for more federal water development. In response, by 1949 the bureau had conducted watershed studies of the upper basin and was close to obtaining Interior Department approval of a scheme it called the Colorado River Storage Project.

Breathtaking in scope, this plan called for the construction of ten major dams on the Colorado River and its tributaries within the upper basin. The bureau argued that revenues from hydroelectric power would pay for this massive development, whose total storage capacity of 48.5 million acre-feet was greater than that of all the river's existing reservoirs. The most important features of the plan were dams in Flaming Gorge in Wyoming, Echo Park in Colorado, and Glen Canyon in northern Arizona.[46] The dam at Echo Park, planned for the confluence of the Green and Yampa Rivers, and the Split Mountain Dam downstream, were slated for construction within Dinosaur National Monument.

As the bureau moved forward with this latest massive upper basin development, Packard of the NPA and Howard Zahniser of the Wilderness Society began calling for a reappraisal of the entire CAP and they now questioned any intrusions into Grand Canyon National *Monument.* With threats mounting at Glacier and Mammoth Cave National Parks, in addition to Dinosaur National Monument, some leading conservationists now took the position that intrusions into any and all park service lands for purposes of development were no longer acceptable. When the Phoenix Chamber of Commerce published an article blasting Fred Packard's statement against Bridge Canyon Dam during the 1950 Senate CAP hearings, he quickly responded. Succinctly capturing the angry mood of conservationists in scorching Cold War vernacular, he wrote:

> Should one national park or monument be subjected to invasion by a major engineering project or to any sort of exploitation, the door will be open to similar desecration of other such reservations. Many are under attack at this moment. No matter how impressive the immediate local argument for this exploitation may be, the national interest demands that a 38th parallel be established around our national parks and monuments beyond which such projects will not encroach.[47]

Meanwhile the Sierra Club's leadership was rethinking its support of the high Bridge Canyon Dam. The club had adopted Robinson's Grand Canyon compromise on the contingency that the Interior Department would agree to build silt-retention structures before starting construction of Bridge Canyon Dam. However, the secretary had not agreed to this proposition, and his recent approval of dams in Dinosaur National Monument reinforced a growing suspicion among conservationists that the Bureau of Reclamation would always have the last word when it came to water development.

Although the bill authorized the construction of silt-control dams, the language did not stipulate the priority of construction, so in all likelihood Bridge Canyon Dam would be built first. The Sierra Club leadership believed that the bureau should build the silt-control dams first to reduce deposition within the park and monument. Additionally, the full House Interior Committee took up the CAP question in closed sessions in August and, in the interest of expediting the proceedings, it chose to debate the Senate bill, so it also ignored the Sierra Club proposal. The House committee adjourned without taking action in early September because of the upcoming congressional elections, thus sealing the fate of the CAP in the Eighty-First Congress.[48]

Even though the bill had died in committee, Leonard felt trepidation because politicians and the Interior Department alike had ignored the concerns of conservationists since obtaining their assent to a high Bridge Canyon Dam. As a result, Leonard wrote the leaders of other conservation organizations. He told them he would bring the issue before a meeting of the Western Federation of Outdoor Clubs in early September to see if these groups would adopt a unified position in opposition to a Bridge Canyon Dam of any height until Congress and Interior agreed that the silt-retention dams would be constructed beforehand.

The Sierra Club board discussed Dinosaur and Bridge Canyon Dam in September and resolved to vigorously oppose a dam in Dinosaur National Monument and to coordinate with other conservation societies in doing so. Sensing that their bargaining efforts had gone unrequited, the Sierra Club's leaders then voted unanimously to repudiate their earlier approval of the Robinson compromise. The meeting ended with the Sierra Club having taken the official position of being against any intrusion into Grand Canyon National Monument.[49] Now all of the major conservation organizations stood united against a high Bridge Canyon Dam, and many had decided to extend Drury's last line of defense to include the boundaries of national monuments.

Ironically, as conservationists outside of the Interior Department began to take a more active role in opposing intrusions into Grand Canyon National Park and Monument, officials within the park service began to disassociate themselves from outright opposition to Bridge Canyon Dam and the positions they had held previously. Since the Interior Department had incorporated a high Bridge Canyon Dam into its CAP proposal of 1949, Drury no longer communicated his opposition to anyone outside the government. Newspapers, however, particularly in the western states, gave widespread coverage to the congressional debates over the CAP and also, usually in rebuttal, discussed conservationist opposition, particularly that of the NPA. This publicity resulted in a trickle of protest letters to the National Park Service from private citizens inquiring as to what, if anything, could be done about the Bridge Canyon Dam.

In response to a letter from Robert C. Stebbins, the vice president of the American Society of Ichthyologists and Herpetologists, Lemuel Garrison, the acting superintendent of Grand Canyon National Park, wrote in August 1950 that he "dread[ed] the construction of this dam and the consequent flooding of the lower end of Grand Canyon." This prompted a terse response from his boss, Tillotson, now a regional park service director, who instructed Garrison and other park service personnel to limit their responses to such letters to "factual data" and "known

Service policies or decisions." Tillotson also ordered Garrison to write Stebbins and ask him not to publicize his earlier letter, a request to which Garrison, fearing for his job, complied.[50]

The muzzling of Garrison and other park service personnel occurred as the tension between Drury and Interior Secretary Chapman reached its peak. Infuriated by a scathing article by Bernard DeVoto titled "Shall We Let Them Ruin Our National Parks" published in the July 22 edition of *The Saturday Evening Post*, Bureau of Reclamation Commissioner Michael Straus claimed that Drury, a close friend of the impetuous *Harper's* columnist, had coauthored the piece, a charge Drury denied. Chapman, having approved of the dam at Echo Park, and weary of the constant sniping between his park service director and commissioner of reclamation, forced Drury out of his position by asking him to relinquish his directorship for an advisory position without any authority at a lower salary. Drury refused and resigned, effective April 1, 1951.[51]

While Echo Park may have been the final straw, Drury had been a thorn in the bureau's side for the better part of a decade with his opposition to the high Bridge Canyon Dam. Preservationists would miss this erudite, relentless defender of the national parks, and his removal heightened their resolve to continue the struggle he had begun. The National Park Service under Drury's successors Conrad Wirth and George Hartzog would never again publicly oppose federal water development proposals that would intrude upon national parks and monuments.[52]

California Saves Grand Canyon

The congressional elections of November 1950 appeared to strengthen Arizona's position in the House of Representatives. Democrat John Murdock ascended to the chairmanship of the Committee on Interior and Insular Affairs, increasing the already disproportionate amount of political power Arizona enjoyed. With the powerful Hayden and McFarland entrenched in the Senate, the prospects for passage of a CAP bill seemed bright in the Eighty-Second Congress.

Arizona politicians introduced CAP bills in both houses in January 1951. The proposals were essentially the same as those debated during the previous year with one notable difference—the bills now included Drury's height limitation of 1,877 feet in elevation, a fitting tribute to the outgoing director who had lobbied for it for so long. Hayden and McFarland reintroduced the bill in the Senate Interior Committee and on January 30 the committee reported it favorably. Because the 1950 House Interior Committee debates had been conducted in such an acrimonious tone, the two senators decided to wait and see what would happen in the House before scheduling the bill for floor debate in the Senate.[53]

The House debate began in February 1951 in the Interior Committee, and it soon became apparent that the animosity between California and Arizona still existed. California had also gained strength in the 1950 election and now held three seats on the committee to Arizona's one. Furious verbal exchanges occurred in February and March, and though several peripheral issues intruded into the proceedings, most of the discussion centered upon the question of whether the Supreme Court should adjudicate the water rights of the lower basin states.

Arizona argued that no justiciable issue existed because the bill had not been passed and that, consequently, House approval must occur before a Supreme Court review. California contended that the court needed to resolve the dispute because the three lower basin states of Arizona, California, and Nevada had not divided their 7.5 million acre-feet of water as required by the Compact of 1922. California argued that it did not make sense to approve a water project while water rights were still in doubt.

After twenty-three stormy sessions during which accusations of water stealing flew across geographical and party lines, Republican Congressman John Saylor from Pennsylvania introduced a motion on March 18 endorsing the California position, and called for a moratorium upon CAP legislation until the Supreme Court determined the water rights of California, Arizona, and Nevada. A dejected Murdock brought Saylor's motion to a vote and it carried with sixteen ayes, eight nays, and three abstentions. Federal construction of Bridge Canyon Dam as a part of the CAP was now indefinitely delayed.[54]

It was a bitter, bitter, defeat. How could Arizona, with two powerful, strategically-placed senators and a representative as the chair of the all-important House interior committee—arguably the most powerful political position Arizona would ever have during its long struggle to obtain the CAP—have lost this political battle? Future Arizona politicians, frustrated over dealing with the intractable Wayne Aspinall as interior committee chair during the 1960s, would write critically of Murdock's inability to obtain a favorable report from his committee in 1950 and 1951.[55]

In light of the ferocious environmentalist offensive that occurred during the CAP debates of the 1960s, the question becomes even more intriguing: Aside from Drury's efforts from within the Interior Department and Packard's statement entered into the 1950 hearing record, *no preservationists testified or took part in the political process* that led to this defeat of Bridge Canyon Dam. With Senate passage virtually assured, and Murdock's chairmanship of the House committee that oversaw all bills related to reclamation, how could Arizona have fumbled away this opportunity?

Supporters of the CAP blamed California for the defeat, arguing that its congressional delegation had frightened the other basin states with claims that the CAP would preclude the construction of anymore water projects on the Colorado. That California and Arizona were implacable foes with regard to the Colorado River is beyond dispute, and the Golden State certainly had a tremendous numerical advantage in the House with twenty-three representatives to Arizona's two. Arizona's increased political influence in the House proved illusory because it did not run much deeper than Murdock's new committee chairmanship. On the surface it appears as though California was able to defeat Arizona's bid for the CAP because of the sheer magnitude of its numerical advantage.

However, an examination of the committee vote reveals that a switch of five votes would have defeated the California position. Of the six representatives from Colorado Basin states other than California and Arizona, four voted in favor of Saylor's motion, one opposed, and a relative newcomer to congressional politics from Colorado, Representative Wayne Aspinall, abstained. So California's tactics, while effective in swaying votes from basin representatives, were not necessarily decisive, because nine of the sixteen votes in favor of the Saylor motion came from outside the basin.[56]

It appears as though broader social and political trends had a far greater influence upon the outcome than Arizona's water advocates realized. When analyzing the CAP defeat, one must consider the political issues that influenced the election of 1950, a time of increasing fiscal conservatism. Even President Truman, a Democrat, had created a bipartisan commission, headed by former president Herbert Hoover, a Republican, to investigate the economic viability of water projects proposed by the Bureau of Reclamation and the Army Corps of Engineers. Budgetary constraints became even more acute in June 1950 when

North Korea's invasion of South Korea embroiled the United States in a major overseas conflict.

Further, politicians from east of the Mississippi River, suspicious of the reclamation program, had begun to question why their constituents' tax dollars were being spent to bring desert land into cultivation at a time that farmers in the Midwest were being subsidized for taking cropland out of production. Finally, though the Democrats had controlled the White House since 1933 and retained Congress every year except for a brief period from 1947–1949, Republicans made significant gains during the midterm elections of 1950. This was the start of a trend that, in a final repudiation of the New Deal, would sweep Dwight D. Eisenhower into the presidency in the election of 1952. Many of these new legislators had been elected on pledges of fiscal conservatism and opposed expensive water projects.

An examination of the committee vote also reveals that it separated along party lines. Of the twelve Republican committee members, eleven voted aye (against the CAP). The vote also broke geographically, with only three of twelve representatives from non-reclamation states voting with Murdock. All three of these were Democrats, and they most likely supported Murdock out of party loyalty.[57]

California certainly played an important role in the defeat of the CAP; however, it received a great deal of gratuitous assistance from representatives who voted either along party lines or out of anti-reclamation sentiments during a period of reduced federal spending. These obstacles were far too great for Murdock, a committee chairman from a sparsely populated state, to overcome. Conservationists, knowing that they did not have the power to stop Bridge Canyon Dam if it had passed in the House, applauded these fortuitous circumstances. The Sierra Club's Robinson called Saylor's motion and the resulting Supreme Court litigation "manna from heaven."[58]

Hayden made a last-ditch effort in the Senate and secured passage of a CAP bill in June 1951 in the hope that the House would reconsider, but for all intents and purposes, Bridge Canyon Dam had been defeated in the House interior committee during the spring. Hayden's efforts elicited a blast from the editors of the *Chicago Daily News* who, in an article entitled "Dam Foolishness," vigorously opposed the Senate action in light of increasing international tensions and tightening fiscal policy, a position also publicly endorsed by William Voigt of the Izaak Walton

League.[59] Preservationists could breathe a collective sigh of relief because Congress was now barred from authorizing the construction of Bridge Canyon Dam until the Supreme Court ruled upon the water rights of the lower basin. This process would require several years of litigation at the very least. Despite Hayden's influence, his project had been defeated by backroom congressional maneuvers and shifting political winds during an era of increasing fiscal restraint.

But the water and power needs of Arizona were not going away, and Hayden would bide his time until the Supreme Court settled the issue of lower basin water rights. All eyes now turned toward the Colorado River Storage Project. Although the CAP and Bridge Canyon Dam had been defeated with virtually no input from conservationists, just a couple of years later a unified environmental coalition would emerge and implement a strategy to protect Dinosaur National Monument. Time would tell whether these conservationists, having embraced environmental activism at last and with their public influence growing, would be able to wield enough power within the political process to defeat other dams planned for other great canyons in the American West.

3

Dinosaurs and Rainbows

It is a popular misconception that most environmental societies were founded to promote wilderness preservation. The Sierra Club's position in spring of 1950 is typical of the dilemma most prominent conservation organizations faced at the start of the decade. Future leaders of the preservation movement such as Richard Leonard and David Brower approved of the bureau's plan to create a reservoir that would intrude into Grand Canyon National Park and Monument. This was entirely in line with the attitudes many Americans held toward their natural environment in 1950. Why not build a water highway that would open up the lower reaches of the canyon to sightseers? Why not believe that humans could improve upon nature? Indeed, the club's leaders would find themselves in the embarrassing situation of having their own arguments used against them in hearings over Bridge Canyon Dam a decade later by none other than reclamation commissioner Floyd Dominy.

By the early 1960s, the idea that building dams could improve upon nature would be repugnant to environmentalists fighting to preserve Grand Canyon. The 1950s were a time of great ideological change, a period when, at least in the minds of many environmental advocates, encouraging the development of recreation in parks and monuments was to give way to the belief that the primary purpose of the parks and monuments was to protect wilderness and scenic beauty. The modern environmental movement would emerge largely as the result of important environmental controversies and social and political transformations that occurred during this critical decade.

Toward the end of the 1930s, Interior Secretary Harold Ickes had briefly considered protecting the spectacular canyons of the upper Colorado River by creating an Escalante National Monument. This enormous reserve would have stretched more than two hundred miles from north of the confluence of the Green and Colorado Rivers to Lee's Ferry in Arizona and brought all of Glen Canyon under the protection of the National Park Service.[1] Ickes failed to gain FDR's approval, and so this lovely, red-sandstone gorge and its magical slot canyons tragically remained unprotected.

As a result, Glen Canyon would become an important subject of debate in the struggle over the Colorado River between preservationists and water developers because both sides would come to view a dam at the Glen Canyon site as acceptable, at least initially. California had long argued that the first big Colorado River dam should be constructed there, and it still contended that it should be built before a dam at Bridge Canyon because the immense Glen Canyon Reservoir would trap silt from the upper basin and extend the useful life of dams planned later for Grand Canyon. The Sierra Club agreed with this position, although it had since withdrawn its support of Bridge Canyon Dam. The upper basin states also pushed for the construction of Glen Canyon Dam because it would allow them to build irrigation projects in the upper reaches of the river without impeding their responsibility under the Colorado River Compact to deliver 7.5 million acre-feet each year to the lower basin states. Glen Canyon Dam was the keystone for the entire Colorado River Storage Project (CRSP) or, in Brower's words, "that was the big one, that was the moneymaker."[2]

In hindsight it is interesting to speculate about what might have happened had Glen Canyon been protected in a national monument. Because it was not protected at all, it eventually became a place that environmentalists were willing to sacrifice as part of compromises designed to thwart proposals to build two dams in a little-known national monument called Dinosaur that straddled the Utah-Colorado border. Many environmental historians point to the Dinosaur controversy as the most important battle between the emerging preservation movement and the developmental interests of the 1950s, some arguing that it represents a reversal of the harmful precedent established at Hetch Hetchy.[3] If Glen Canyon had been given even the nominal protection of a national monument, perhaps the pivotal struggle to protect the National Park System that took place during the 1950s would have involved saving Glen Canyon rather than Dinosaur.

The 1950s would close as they began, with water developers seeking to build dams for power generation in Grand Canyon, but only after several important changes had occurred. The leadership of the preservation movement would pass from Newton Drury and the park service to the environmental organizations at the outset of the Dinosaur controversy, and these groups would extend Drury's last line of defense to include national monuments. However, as their activism increased and they became more politically astute, conservationists would soon find that their newfound power and influence would result in increased federal scrutiny of their activities at the height of the Cold War that threatened their constitutional rights of free speech and petition. As new perils to Grand Canyon emerged in the wake of Dinosaur, one organization would defy the government's suppression of civil liberties and in so doing, emerge from the 1950s and its repressive social environment prepared to do battle for the soul of Grand Canyon and perhaps of America itself.

The defeat of the Central Arizona Project in 1951 had removed the threat of Bridge Canyon Dam for the foreseeable future. Now conservationists began to focus upon the impending threat the Colorado River Storage Project posed to Dinosaur National Monument. Park Service Director Drury was so adamant in his opposition to the Dinosaur dams that he pressured new Interior Secretary Oscar Chapman into scheduling public hearings so that all views could be aired. On April 3, 1950, representatives of conservation organizations, the Bureau of Reclamation, and members of Congress all testified at these Interior Department hearings, an important event simply because it is indicative that opposition to proposed violations of the National Park System had now risen to such a level that the interior secretary believed it necessary to air these views in a public forum.

Environmentalists argued that the dams would irreparably harm the canyons of the Green and Yampa Rivers within the monument, that the bureau had not adequately considered alternative sites, and that it was Chapman's duty as interior secretary to defend the National Park System from intrusions. They also tried to take advantage of Congress's increasing reluctance to allocate funds for large public works by arguing that the dams were not economically viable. Western congressmen and the bureau countered that: (1) the power generated by these dams would ensure Utah's continued economic prosperity; and (2) since the flow estimates upon which the Compact of 1922 had been based were too high, upper basin storage was more necessary than ever in order for these states to fulfill their delivery obligations to the lower basin. Although the issue was not discussed at the hearings, President Truman had also approved the development of the hydrogen bomb, and since the Department of Defense planned to conduct tests in Utah and Nevada, Chapman believed that it was the Interior Department's duty to provide power for this program. Ultimately the arguments of the water interests, especially those citing national defense issues, swayed Interior Secretary Chapman, and he approved the controversial Echo Park and Split Mountain Dams in June of 1950.[4]

After Drury resigned in April 1951, conservationists intensified their protests about the Dinosaur situation to Interior Secretary Chapman who, after considering strong arguments from the Army Corps of Engineers attacking the project's economic feasibility, reversed his earlier endorsement of the dams in December 1952. This respite was short-lived because after the Eisenhower administration assumed office in January 1953, senators from the upper basin states began to lobby Douglas McKay, Ike's new interior secretary, to reinstate the Dinosaur dams into the CRSP. In December 1953, McKay assented, and the conservation organizations began to prepare for what turned out to be an epic series of congressional hearings scheduled to begin in January 1954.

Environmentalists Take the Field

The year 1954 was a watershed in the history of American environmentalism because it was during this year that conservation organizations formed a coalition to fight the Dinosaur dams and developed strategies to influence future legislation. Their assault consisted of two thrusts: (1) a publicity drive designed to stimulate public opposition, which they hoped would result in large numbers of people writing letters to Congress; and (2) testimony at congressional hearings in which expert witnesses would attack the dams on both aesthetic and technical grounds. In January conservation leaders including Ira Gabrielson of the Emergency Committee on Natural Resources, Fred Packard of the NPA, David Brower of the Sierra Club, and General Ulysses Grant III of the American Planning and Civic Association and formerly of the Army Corps of Engineers, testified before the Senate Interior Committee.

During the hearings Grant and Brower attacked the evaporation figures that the bureau had used to discredit arguments that dams built at alternate sites could produce the same amount of power generation and water storage by discovering fundamental errors in the bureau's arithmetic. Brower contended that if the dam planned for Glen Canyon were raised, it would create a reservoir with the same storage capacity as the impoundments behind the Echo Park and Split Mountain Dams planned for Dinosaur. The bureau's experts challenged these arguments by stating that the enlarged Glen Canyon Reservoir would result in much greater evaporation losses than those created by the Dinosaur dams.

However, Richard Bradley, a Cornell University physics professor whom Brower enlisted in the fight, received a letter in response to a query from assistant reclamation commissioner Floyd Dominy in April 1954 that substantiated Brower's claims. Brower then issued a press release that was picked up by national newspapers, and the resulting publicity shattered the myth of the bureau's expertise in water engineering. By the end of 1954 the battle had not yet been won, but environmentalists had made significant gains.[5] This two-pronged approach of generating public support to apply pressure from the outside and using expert opinions to challenge the technical and economic justification of reclamation projects at congressional hearings, first developed during the Echo Park campaign, would provide a blueprint for environmentalists fighting to save Grand Canyon in the years ahead.

The Dinosaur controversy entered its climactic phase during 1955 as a parade of opposition witnesses testified against the dams. The Sierra Club raised the level of its public appeal even further by publishing the first of its exhibit format books, *This Is Dinosaur*, filled with stunning color photographs of the monument's canyons and essays by prominent environmental writers. The book was intended to influence Congress to vote against the Dinosaur dams, and thus it signaled the entry of conservation organizations into the lobbying arena, which would soon have consequences for the environmental movement as a whole.

As the CRSP came before the interior committees of both houses in 1955, opponents testified not only against the dams planned for the Echo Park and Split Mountain sites but they also addressed the broader question of how the construction of these dams would affect the

National Park System. Packard of the NPA testified during the Senate committee hearings in March that at least sixteen dam proposals currently threatened national parks and monuments, and he argued that reclamation interests would use congressional permission to construct dams in Dinosaur as "the entering wedge" to open the rest of the park system to resource exploitation.[6]

More than twenty conservation organizations now stood united against a dam in any national park or monument and, under rigorous questioning from Senator Clinton Anderson of New Mexico, Packard served notice that these same organizations would oppose any new proposals to construct a dam at Bridge Canyon. Anderson asked why he had not testified at the Central Arizona Project (CAP) hearings, and Packard replied that he had "on six separate occasions" attempted to get on the schedule but that he had been prevented from testifying by Senate staff and Senate Interior Committee member Joseph O'Mahoney of Wyoming. When Anderson questioned him about the height of Bridge Canyon Dam, Packard stated that it would be 1,877 feet high, confusing the dam's height as measured from streambed to crest with its maximum elevation above sea level.

The crusty Anderson seized this opportunity to belittle Packard and he mockingly asked, "If we built a dam in New Mexico at 9,000 feet, would you call it a 9,000-foot dam?" Packard, embarrassed, was forced to admit his mistake, whereupon Anderson used the situation to call attention to the importance of presenting factually correct information, a slap at the conservationists' prior testimony and publicity campaign against the Dinosaur dams.[7]

Representative Stewart Udall of Arizona, who had just been elected to Congress during the 1954 midterm elections, closely watched these Senate hearings and paid particular attention to both the content of the conservationists' testimony and the treatment the witnesses received from committee members. Udall managed to land a seat on the key House Committee on Interior and Insular Affairs, and he, like most Arizona politicians, viewed the CAP as essential for the state's economy. He had followed the CAP debates of 1950–1951 and was aware that the record contained no evidence of conservationists' opposition. Surprised by Packard's testimony against Bridge Canyon Dam, Udall prepared to question him further about the conservationists' position on the CAP when the CRSP came before the House.

Hearings before the House Subcommittee on Irrigation and Reclamation began in March 1955, and conservationists once again argued that if Congress approved of a reclamation project in Dinosaur National Monument it would set a precedent that would threaten the entire National Park System. Under questioning from Udall and subcommittee chairman Wayne Aspinall, four prominent conservationists—Packard, Grant, Howard Zahniser of the Wilderness Society, and Brower of the Sierra Club—all testified that their organizations would oppose Bridge Canyon Dam the next time it came before Congress. A "thunderstruck" Udall pressed Brower further, and asked if his organization would be willing to compromise and accept a dam that would not affect the national park. Brower apparently misspoke and replied affirmatively, even though he and the Sierra Club had voted to resist intrusions into both national park and monument three years previously. Udall, anticipating future CAP hearings, then stated prophetically: "That is something I know both of us will be interested in and might have a collision of our own on some day."[8]

A few days later, Udall raised the issue of compromise once again, this time with Packard, trying to discern whether the NPA would object to a small invasion of a national monument. Basing his argument on the legal doctrine of *de minimis*, where the law overlooks "trifling" violations, Udall asked Packard whether his organization would object to an intrusion of only a "few feet." Packard responded that while the NPA opposed all invasions of the National Park System, including national monuments, one also had to use "common sense" in these matters. Udall appeared to be satisfied and left the hearings with the mistaken belief that conservationists would be willing to compromise in the case of Grand Canyon National Park and Monument.[9]

Even at this early stage in his career, Udall had already shown the practical qualities that made him such a successful politician. Always seeking compromise, Udall had become aware of the growing political power that preservationists had gained during the Echo Park Dam controversy. Arizona's federal representatives communicated regularly with state organizations, such as the Central Arizona Project Association (CAPA) and the Arizona Interstate Stream Commission (AISC), to coordinate efforts to obtain the CAP, and Udall was a key member of the team.

Udall presented his measured opinion of the conservationists' growing strength and how CAP supporters should deal with it immediately after the conclusion of the spring House hearings on Dinosaur. Having kept abreast of the Senate Interior Committee hearings, Udall was appalled at how upper basin senators harangued the opposition witnesses. Udall himself remained very tactful during the House hearings, telling witness after witness that he believed in their sincerity and that he would listen to their arguments so long as they did not attack the reclamation program as a whole. In his opinion, the upper basin states had "badly mishandled" the opponents of the Dinosaur projects, and he feared that these same people would also fight Bridge Canyon Dam. Cutting to the crux of the matter Udall argued that he now believed the conservationists had enough influence to turn the votes of 75–100 representatives against future CAP legislation.[10]

In Udall's opinion, the best way to deal with the conservationists was to convince them that Bridge Canyon Dam would not create a major invasion of Grand Canyon National Monument. Udall felt that he had gained Packard's assent to a minor intrusion; however, it is highly unlikely that Packard and other preservationists would have viewed a reservoir through the length of Grand Canyon National Monument as a *de minimis* infringement. Still, it appears that with the Dinosaur campaign undecided, Udall was among the first of the CAP supporters to understand the political influence that the conservation organizations had gained, and that compromises would have to be made if the CAP was to avoid the pitfalls that he believed would likely doom the Echo Park and Split Mountain Dams.

Udall had another purpose in attempting to discern the conservationists' position with regard to Bridge Canyon Dam. California had indefatigably opposed the CRSP, much to the annoyance of representatives of the upper basin states. In June 1955 after convincing Arizona's CAP leaders and Arizona's other representative, Republican Congressman John Rhodes, of the validity of his plan, Udall proposed an amendment to the CRSP bill before the House Interior Committee. The measure, if approved, would have granted the state of Arizona the right to construct dams at the Marble and Bridge Canyon sites, and it guaranteed that no federal money would be solicited to build these projects. Although he was just a freshman congressman, Udall adroitly sought to take advantage of the Interior Committee's favorable disposition toward the CRSP and gain the upper basin support that had been lacking during Arizona's fight to obtain the CAP four years previously. Even the *Arizona Republic,*

a Phoenix newspaper that would prove highly critical of Udall throughout his years of public service, called the move the "shrewdest piece
of political work" on the part of Arizona's congressional delegation "in
many years." Udall's end run failed, but his amendment put the upper
basin states on notice that Arizona expected them to support future CAP
legislation in exchange for Arizona's support for the CRSP.[11]

At What Price, Victory?

In 1956, after passage by both houses of Congress, President
Eisenhower signed the Colorado River Storage Project bill into law
without the controversial Dinosaur dams. For the first time in the history of American environmental advocacy, a water project had been deleted from a reclamation proposal because it would have intruded upon a
unit of the National Park System. It was at the boundaries of national
monuments that the conservationists had defended Packard's 38th parallel—and Drury's last line of defense—successfully. Unfortunately for
preservationists, they defended Dinosaur by pressing for an alternative
they had not investigated thoroughly. Split Mountain and Echo Park
Dams had been removed from the Colorado River Storage Project in
favor of raising Glen Canyon Dam by thirty-five feet, making it the
largest and most important part of the project in terms of water storage
and power production.

Glen Canyon lay outside of the National Park System, and few environmentalists had ever visited it. Only after agreeing to withdraw opposition for the CRSP with a high Glen Canyon Dam did conservationists
begin to visit the area in significant numbers. They discovered, to their
horror, that Glen Canyon was arguably more spectacular than the canyons for which it had been sacrificed. Brower and other environmentalists soon realized the terrible cost of their bargain to save Echo Park,
but it was too late for them to oppose Glen Canyon Dam with a realistic chance of stopping it.

The high Glen Canyon Dam posed another problem in addition to
flooding a canyon that was worthy of national park status. Its reservoir
would back water into Rainbow Bridge National Monument just north
of the Arizona-Utah border. Drury voiced alarm about this possibility as
early as 1949, and environmentalists feared that the water would undermine the sandstone foundation of the arch, the largest freestanding natural bridge in the world. Bowing to these environmentalists' concerns,

Congress inserted a provision within the CRSP act calling for the construction of a small dam to protect this monument from encroachment.[12] Time would tell whether this promise to protect Rainbow Bridge National Monument would be fulfilled.

The increasing activism of the conservation organizations also attracted attention from federal agencies, most notably the Internal Revenue Service (IRS), which had established code provisions governing the political activities of nonprofit organizations. Based upon the Federal Regulation of Lobbying Act of 1946, the relevant provisions of the tax code stated that so long as an organization's "primary purpose" was not to engage in "substantial" efforts to influence legislation, contributions made to that organization would be tax deductible for individual contributors. Further, the act specified, persons and organizations that lobbied without first registering with Congress would be held criminally liable.[13]

Historian Stephen Fox argues that postwar conservation issues and the rise of new leadership forced environmental organizations to change and become more professional. The Sierra Club created the position of executive director in 1952 and hired Brower to fill it, just in time for the Dinosaur campaign.[14] With this professionalization came tactical changes as well as changes in the fundamental purposes for which these organizations existed.

Brower's new tactics included exhorting private citizens to write their congressional representatives directly to communicate their opposition to the Dinosaur dams. In addition to *This Is Dinosaur*, the Sierra Club and other preservation advocates published pamphlets, distributed leaflets, and produced a movie, all designed to sway public and congressional opinion. By entering the public arena for the purpose of influencing legislation, conservation organizations now found themselves coming dangerously close to the vague limits of Internal Revenue Code section 501(c)(3), which stated that contributions would remain tax deductible so long as "no substantial part of the activities [of the recipient organization involved] is . . . carrying on propaganda or otherwise attempting to influence legislation."[15] What constituted "substantial" in the case of conservation organizations had not yet been clarified.

Most conservationists were not aware that their increased advocacy could potentially trigger an IRS investigation. However, even as the Dinosaur protests were generating a massive public response, two constitutional issues collided in the US Supreme Court: the people's rights of free speech and

petition guaranteed by the First Amendment and the government's enu-
merated power to guard against the manipulation of the legislative process by special interest groups. In *United States v. Harriss*, decided in
June 1954, the Supreme Court in a 5–3 decision upheld the constitu-
tionality of the Federal Lobbying Act of 1946 because it was intended
to limit the ability of special interest groups to influence Congress. The
court specifically referenced "artificial letter-writing campaigns" as well
as IRS code provisions governing the tax deductibility of contributions
to nonprofit organizations to support its decision.[16]

The Sierra Club and other organizations had encouraged the public
to write their congressional representatives, used membership dues to
print propaganda, and participated in hearings while trying to defeat the
Dinosaur dams—actions that the court specifically cited as "substantial"
attempts to influence legislation. As a result, the Supreme Court's decision threw these organizations into a panic. There was nothing confusing about the *Harriss* decision in the opinion of the Sierra Club's
Leonard, a tax attorney and person to whom other conservation organizations turned for legal advice. Leonard consulted with other attorneys
who urged that the Sierra Club retreat from public activism. Fearing an
IRS action, Leonard began to discuss with other conservation leaders the
problem of how to continue the club's advocacy without risking the tax
deductibility of funds needed to finance lobbying efforts.[17]

Leonard's solution was to create a new organization, the Trustees
for Conservation, registered with Congress and the IRS, to solicit funds
to be specifically used to lobby against the Dinosaur dams. But David
Brower of the Sierra Club and Zahniser of the Wilderness Society believed that even though this provided legal protection, it detrimentally
affected their ability to raise money. The American people looked to the
Sierra Club, Wilderness Society, National Parks Association, and other
groups as the standard-bearers for the preservation movement. Brower
and Zahniser feared the public would not understand the legal necessity
for this move and believed it would create the perception that the long-
established organizations were too cowardly to lead the fight to protect
the National Park System.[18]

Ironically, as the Dinosaur victory was being won, most conservation
leaders, fearful of losing the large gifts and bequests that kept them afloat,
began to pull their organizations back from the legislative arena in light of
the *Harriss* decision. However, after debating the merits of continuing to try

to influence legislative activity, the Sierra Club decided to adopt a policy of "calculated risk," as its directors felt that the statute did not clearly outline the extent of permissible legislative activity.[19] Even while Leonard advised other conservationists to curtail their legislative efforts, the Sierra Club strove to remain a "fighting organization" and it continued to lobby for wilderness preservation and the protection of the National Park System.[20]

Arizona and California: Alone Together Again

Although the 1951 House moratorium on CAP legislation prevented federal consideration of this project until the Supreme Court adjudicated the water rights of the lower basin, it did not prevent states from applying with the Federal Power Commission (FPC) for permission to construct dams in Grand Canyon themselves. With some conservation organizations once again retreating from the legislative arena, for the first time since the 1920s Arizona and California began to push their own plans to build hydroelectric dams in Grand Canyon. Los Angeles even tried to breathe new life into the MCKC project.[21]

Congressman Udall reminded his Arizona constituents that the conservationists still constituted a powerful political force that could endanger the CAP. He suggested to state water leaders that a lower Bridge Canyon Dam would possibly be a compromise that these groups might find acceptable. Chastened by the political influence the conservationists had wielded during the Echo Park fight, he now believed that federal reclamation projects could not gain House approval without their support. He also felt that environmentalists would fight against any state project that intruded upon the National Park System.[22]

The National Park Service was aware of these state efforts to investigate the construction of Bridge Canyon Dam without federal support, even as the Dinosaur controversy raged. Director Conrad Wirth wrote his superiors and reminded them that the park service would oppose any future Bridge Canyon proposals. Wirth also contended that the 1935 Federal Power Act nullified all previous power site withdrawals within lands under the jurisdiction of the National Park Service. Finally, in response to Los Angeles, he reiterated the park service's unyielding opposition to the MCKC project.[23]

Grand Canyon National Park Superintendent John McLaughlin, after reading the public notices filed by the FPC in the Flagstaff, Arizona, local paper, called upon his superiors to oppose the projects, and these objections soon caught Wirth's attention. The outspoken Wirth, whom McLaughlin's successor characterized as being as "independent as a hog on ice," demanded that the interior secretary file an official complaint. New Interior Secretary Fred Aandahl wrote the FPC and told the commissioners it was highly doubtful that they had the authority to issue a license for a high Bridge Canyon Dam that would encroach upon Grand Canyon National Park and Monument. But the FPC ignored him and scheduled hearings in 1958 on the Arizona and California applications anyway.[24]

Of all the conservation organizations, only the Sierra Club and National Parks Association publicly opposed these proposals. The NPA published articles critical of the high Bridge Canyon Dam in its March–April 1956 and April 1957 editions of *National Parks* magazine. Meanwhile, the Sierra Club directors still debated how far the club should go in trying to influence legislation, and what position it should take with regard to water projects. In January 1957 the Sierra Club leadership met to discuss these issues and adopted as a matter of policy a unanimous resolution to oppose hydroelectric projects in any area dedicated for scenic resource preservation. Then the directors went even further and voted to "oppose in principle the sacrifice . . . of any high quality scenic resource area *which has not been dedicated but whose need as a dedicated area has not yet been thoroughly considered* [emphasis mine]." The Sierra Club had now taken the position that dams in any portion of Grand Canyon were unacceptable, and issued a press release in June 1957 condemning the Los Angeles Bridge Canyon application.[25] The club's position also set the stage for a conflict with Arizona, even though state water interests agreed to construct a low Bridge Canyon Dam, while hastening the day that Udall and Brower would confront each other over future CAP proposals.

The Sierra Club now stood alone at the cutting edge of the preservation movement. While other conservation organizations backed away from activism in the face of IRS threats to their tax-deductible status, only the National Parks Association had joined with the Sierra Club in opposing these latest threats to Grand Canyon, and the NPA only objected to intrusions upon the national park and monument. Emboldened by the victory at Dinosaur, in which conservationists had moved beyond Drury's defense of national parks and successfully defended a national monument from encroachment, the club's leaders now believed, despite the chilling effect of the

Supreme Court's holding in *Harriss,* that preservationists should strive to save unprotected scenic areas in addition to those under park service jurisdiction. Having adopted a policy of calculated risk in the face of these threats and by advocating the preservation of scenic resources not protected within the National Park System, the club assumed the role as the leading environmental advocate in the political arena, and would now reap the benefits as well as the consequences of taking this stand as Arizona and California once again squared off over building dams in Grand Canyon.

Arizona's state water leaders recognized the growing power of the conservationists and they conceived of a plan to deal with it. Because the Sierra Club was the only environmental group to have taken a position against *all* dams in Grand Canyon by the summer of 1957, they believed it was possible to isolate the club by proposing to build dams in unprotected areas that would not infringe upon the park or monument. The Arizona Power Authority (APA) hired Harza Engineering Company of Chicago to conduct a detailed analysis of the Bridge and Marble Canyon damsites in August 1957. The firm concluded that both projects were economically feasible and that low dams and reservoirs at these two sites—including a Bridge Canyon reservoir low enough that it would not intrude upon the monument—would produce enough electricity to power a large-scale water diversion to central Arizona. As a result, the APA amended its application in 1958 to include only low dams at the Marble and Bridge Canyon sites.[26]

However, the APA had not suddenly become "green"; rather it had become pragmatic. Harza's proposed low Bridge Canyon Dam was only 359 feet in height. However, unbeknownst to California, the study also recommended the construction of a third low dam on the Colorado River at the mouth of Prospect Canyon, 276 feet tall, six miles downstream of the monument. This reservoir would have the same surface elevation as one created by the high Bridge Canyon Dam California was trying to build. The study concluded that Arizona could begin construction much earlier on this two-stage development and avoid the legal entanglements and environmentalist opposition that, in light of Echo Park, a high dam would undoubtedly cause. Once the low Bridge and Marble Canyon Dams were completed, the APA could apply for a license to build Prospect Dam to develop the hydroelectric potential within the monument and westernmost thirteen miles of the park.[27]

Harza also recommended the construction of a 276-foot-tall silt-control dam on the Little Colorado River, even though the reservoir would flood the town of Cameron, Arizona, encroach upon Wupatki National Monument, and inundate open-pit uranium mines recently established in the area as a result of the "uranium rush" of the early 1950s. The Harza plan guaranteed that even if Arizona was unsuccessful at gaining the approval of Prospect Dam, the APA would still have succeeded in obtaining power for the CAP while avoiding the ire of most of the conservation organizations—a solution brilliant in its pragmatism. In the summer of 1958 the APA submitted the Harza proposal without Prospect Dam in its amended license application before the FPC.[28]

A New "Indian Problem"

Although the APA and Harza Engineering Company had conceived of a way to split the conservationists and avoid an Echo Park type of fight, they soon confronted another, unanticipated legal complication.[29] The northeast abutment of Bridge Canyon Dam would rest within Lake Mead Recreation Area, a subunit of the National Park System; however, its southwest abutment would be located upon the Hualapai Reservation. Likewise, although the west abutment of Marble Canyon Dam would rest on lands under the jurisdiction of the Forest Service, its east abutment would lie within the Navajo Reservation. During the late 1940s and early 1950s, the Bureau of Reclamation had begun preliminary studies of both sites at a time when Congress was attempting to end the "trust" relationship between Native Americans and the federal government. Congressional advocates of this policy of "termination" in many cases sought to gain access to American Indian resources. In the case of Bridge and Marble Canyon Dams, the bureau did not even bother to obtain permission before invading Native American land to build cableways and construction camps.[30]

By 1958 the National Congress of American Indians had begun to effectively reassert the argument that tribal governments were separate and independent of states within the federal constitutional framework as affirmed by early nineteenth-century US Supreme Court interpretations of Article I of the Constitution. Beginning in 1960 the Supreme Court began to issue new holdings in support of American Indian sovereignty, creating a body of case law during the next two decades that greatly strengthened the legal position of Native Americans.[31] Even though the APA possessed a legal right to seek a license to develop power sites on reservation lands in accordance with the Federal Power Acts of 1920 and 1935, these statutes also stated that the authority could only do so if it agreed to pay an appropriate amount of compensation as determined by the FPC for the use of the sites. In 1958 it appeared as though the Navajo and Hualapai Nations were in a favorable bargaining position as a result of increasing Native American nationalism and successful legal challenges.[32]

Lawyers for the APA began negotiating with the Hualapai and Navajo Nations, which retained savvy legal counsel to negotiate on their behalf. The attorneys from each side confronted a bewildering morass of legal issues and conflicting statutes. In the case of the Hualapai Nation, the Federal Power Acts appeared to support the APA's assertion that the authority should be allowed to construct Bridge Canyon Dam if it agreed to give the Hualapai a nominal payment for the use of the site. However, attorneys Arthur Lazarus and Royal Marks who represented the Hualapai Nation asserted that its constitution, adopted in accordance with the Indian Reorganization Act of 1934, gave them sovereign rights over all of their territory and negated the effect of the Federal Power Acts entirely.

After more than a year of negotiations, the APA's attorneys reluctantly concluded that the Hualapai had a very strong legal position. Finally, perhaps frightened by effective Hualapai objections to a proposal advanced by Nevada Senator Alan Bible that called for federal construction of Bridge Canyon Dam for the benefit of his own state, the APA agreed to grant the Hualapai, whose population at the time numbered considerably less than one thousand people, a contract promising annual payments that would vary between $550,000 and $620,000 for the life of the project. On August 30, 1960, representatives from the APA and Hualapai Nation signed the contract, eliminating the possibility that Native Americans would object to the construction of Bridge Canyon Dam by the state of Arizona.[33]

The APA also negotiated with attorneys from the Navajo Nation over the rights to the Marble Canyon damsite, and the legal muddle in this case was even more confusing than that in the Hualapai situation. The Navajo Reservation had been created by a combination of presidential proclamations and acts of Congress, and the Navajo people had rejected Commissioner of Indian Affairs John Collier's attempt to have them adopt a constitution under the provisions of the Indian Reorganization Act during the 1930s. Congress, as a condition of statehood, granted Arizona a five-year window beginning with its admission to the Union in 1912 during which the state had the right to reserve power sites along the Colorado River for future use. Arizona filed a power withdrawal on the Marble Canyon site prior to the 1917 deadline; the site at that time was located within the Tusayan National Forest outside of the reservation boundaries.

But as part of the Indian Reorganization Act, Congress also transferred parts of the Tusayan National Forest, including the damsite, to the Navajo Nation while preserving "all valid rights and claims of individuals initiated prior to approval of the Act." In 1934, Congress enlarged the reservation further but specifically preserved Arizona's power site withdrawals and nullified the provisions of the Federal Power Act of 1920 that would have given the Navajo Nation a claim against the state. Even though the APA sought to construct a state project, constitutionally it appeared as though it would prevail against Navajo claims of sovereignty under the Indian Reorganization and Federal Power Acts because Congress had granted—and preserved—Arizona's right to utilize this reach of the Colorado River for hydroelectric projects.[34]

Attorneys for the authority did not offer the Navajo Nation, which numbered just under seventy-four thousand people, any compensation because the APA believed that the Navajo did not have any legal rights to the Marble Canyon site.[35] So long as the APA acted in accordance with authority granted to it by the Arizona state legislature, the Navajo Nation could not prevent state construction of Marble Canyon Dam, and was not entitled to revenue from the power it would produce, even though half of it would be on Navajo land.

By the summer of 1960, as attorneys for Los Angeles and the APA prepared for hearings before the FPC, it looked as though the APA had eliminated any potential conflicts with Native Americans. However, as future events would soon prove, they had not. Offering generous compensation to the Hualapai while at the same time denying the Navajo claims might have been legally justifiable, but alienating one of the largest Native American groups in the United States at the height of the civil rights movement was a colossal blunder that would soon have a dramatic effect upon the project's ultimate fate.

Shifting Political Winds

As water interests within the states of Arizona and California once again focused upon Grand Canyon, a seismic shift in the national political landscape was about to occur. Republican President Eisenhower's administration, though supportive of the Colorado River Storage Project, had imposed a policy of "no new starts" with regard to reclamation projects for most of the 1950s. Both John F. Kennedy and Lyndon Johnson campaigned for the 1960 Democratic presidential nomination promising to reverse this policy. Although Kennedy entered the campaign's final weeks with a relatively large lead in state delegates, Democratic Party strategists still questioned Kennedy's inexperience and some predicted that he would not win the nomination on the first ballot at the Democratic National Convention. The calculating Johnson tailored his tactics to that effect and intensified his attacks on Kennedy during the days leading up to the convention where, he believed, his close relations with House Speaker Sam Rayburn and Senator Carl Hayden would help him to capture a second ballot nomination.[36]

But Congressman Udall maneuvered behind the scenes and convinced Arizona's delegation to support Kennedy unanimously rather than split its vote between the two candidates. This strategy worked, and Kennedy stole all of Arizona's votes from beneath the nose of Hayden, the senior member of the Senate and a strong Johnson supporter. Although Kennedy later won in a landslide, he claimed afterward that because Arizona's delegation was one of the first to record its vote, Udall's ploy initiated a shift of support away from Johnson that swept the Massachusetts senator to a first-ballot nomination.

After his razor-thin victory over Richard Nixon during the November presidential election, Kennedy rewarded the Arizona congressman by naming him secretary of the interior. Udall's ideas about conservation impressed the president-elect and Kennedy's first conservation message to Congress, delivered on February 23, 1961, reflected Udall's philosophy. Handsome, athletic, and an outdoor enthusiast, Udall exuded the youthful aura of the new administration and he soon became a great favorite of the president.[37]

At first blush it appeared that Arizona was now in a strong political position to obtain authorization to build the Central Arizona Project, with Udall as the head of the Interior Department. However, Udall's triumph also came at a cost, for not only did he antagonize Senator

Hayden with his pre-election antics, he also created two new powerful enemies: Lyndon Johnson who, as the former Senate majority leader, understood the nature of practical politics better than perhaps any politician on Capitol Hill, and Wayne Aspinall, the House Interior Committee Chairman, who had also aspired to become interior secretary and believed himself the best available candidate.[38] But in the afterglow of the election of 1960, with Johnson banished to the vice presidency, Udall, basking in Kennedy's support, contemplated how to solve the political infighting that had thus far prevented Arizona from obtaining authorization of the Central Arizona Project.

Environmental advocates viewed Udall's appointment as interior secretary with great optimism. Wallace Stegner, author and Sierra Club member, writing for the Outdoor Recreation Resources Review Commission in 1961, articulated what many preservationists were trying to grasp—a response to the charges of elitism that were often used to argue against wilderness preservation. Stegner wrote that wilderness as an idea—just the knowledge that it existed somewhere—provided comfort and reassurance to people unable to experience it, and that it constituted a "geography of hope," for millions of Americans.

Udall became entranced with the idea and the phrase, and he asked Stegner and Sharon Francis, an expatriate from the Wilderness Society, to collaborate with him in writing a book in the spirit of the new style of environmentalism that was beginning to crystalize in the early 1960s.[39] The Quiet Crisis, published in late 1963, established Udall as a leader in the emerging environmental movement. Artfully written with a ringing introduction by President Kennedy, The Quiet Crisis called upon Americans to reassess their industrial materialistic society in light of the environmental depredations it had caused. Udall ultimately argued that scientific and technological advances would enable Americans to both achieve harmony with the natural world and allow them to retain their high standard of living.[40]

Yet despite his lofty rhetoric, Udall remained a political pragmatist at heart, and this is also evidenced in The Quiet Crisis. Although he strongly favored wilderness preservation, Udall also believed in Gifford Pinchot's tradition of efficiency, and he called for "regional planning . . . and transmountain diversions of water" to arid lands. Environmental leaders who initially hailed his appointment with great optimism soon found themselves disillusioned as Udall acquiesced to the flooding of

Glen Canyon and the invasion of Rainbow Bridge by the rising waters of Lake Powell. But Udall had cut his teeth as a politician in Arizona, where to oppose reclamation projects was political suicide. Buoyed by the release of Special Master Simon H. Rifkind's preliminary opinion in December 1960, in which he recommended that the US Supreme Court find in favor of Arizona in its lawsuit against California, Udall began to conceive of a strategy designed to obtain federal approval of the CAP even while the states of Arizona and California battled to obtain licenses from the FPC in the spring of 1961.[41]

As these forces began to converge upon Grand Canyon, conservation organizations still struggled over how active a role they should take in the face of IRS threats. In December 1959 the Sierra Club board voted to place strict curbs upon the activities of its executive director despite its previous approval of a policy of "calculated risk" with respect to lobbying. Although the Sierra Club continued to advocate in the public arena, especially in favor of a national wilderness system, it did so cautiously, keeping its twenty-five thousand members apprised of Grand Canyon developments in its monthly publication, the *Sierra Club Bulletin*. Unlike the Echo Park fight, the club did not encourage its members to write to their congressional representatives nor did it print literature designed to influence legislation. Brower chafed under these restrictions and feared that the club would no longer be able to face the environmental challenges he felt sure it would have to confront during the next decade.[42]

Brower became exasperated as the Trustees for Conservation and other lobbying organizations failed to generate the funding and publicity needed for major campaigns. In the spring of 1960, with threats looming over Rainbow Bridge and the North Cascades, and with the Wilderness Bill in trouble, Brower once again appealed to the club's executive committee and suggested that the club form a "Sierra Club Foundation" to carry on the club's scientific and educational work. The Foundation would free the club to lobby, while shielding the majority of the club's assets in the event that the IRS revoked its tax-deductible status. Brower had made this suggestion previously, only to have Leonard and Bestor Robinson reject it with legal arguments that he lacked the expertise to contest.

However, Brower had conferred with Philip Berry, a Stanford law student, who in turn consulted with Phil Neal, the Stanford Law School dean. Berry and Neal crafted arguments for Brower to use before the executive committee. As Brower passionately argued his case, Leonard became convinced that a Sierra Club Foundation was the best alternative and he agreed to draft the paperwork to create it. With Leonard now in support, the rest of the board acquiesced and agreed to "let Dave lobby as effectively as he wanted to." Now the Sierra Club was free to enter the political arena with a contingency plan in place should its lobbying efforts evoke a response from the IRS. Even if that occurred, Leonard believed that the club would have a good chance of defeating the IRS in court on First Amendment grounds.[43]

Dam Lies: Intrigue Before the FPC

The Marble Canyon Project hearings before the Federal Power Commission finally opened in the spring of 1961. Although at first glance these hearings would appear to be nothing more than sterile administrative proceedings, just below the surface lay a seething cauldron of half-truths and deception. Despite a myriad of unresolved legal issues, Arizona and California were attempting to obtain FPC approval for dams that would be partially constructed on the soil of American Indian reservations. Arizona viewed all Grand Canyon damsites and the water and power they represented as its birthright and, now that the federal government was out of the picture, it was willing to use almost any means to fend off the California threat. Fortunately for Grand Canyon—and unfortunately for water leaders from its namesake state—squabbling soon erupted within their ranks that essentially destroyed any realistic chance of Arizona building the CAP as a state project.

In the light of some of its past legal shenanigans, California was quite forthcoming at these hearings, for its water leaders openly desired the MCKC project and made no bones about it. When the proceedings began, Arizona immediately attacked, arguing that the MCKC project would be devastating to Grand Canyon National Park while emphasizing that its own proposal would not intrude upon the park and monument at all. The APA even acknowledged environmentalists' concerns about unprotected reaches of Grand Canyon. It assured the FPC that its low Marble Canyon Dam would have a far lesser impact on Marble Canyon because it was planned as a "run of the river" generating plant that would not produce the dramatic reservoir fluctuations caused by "peaking plants" like the one planned for Glen Canyon Dam. The constant water level would eliminate the possibility of scarring the canyon walls—one of the arguments conservationists had used effectively against Echo Park Dam during the Dinosaur controversy. California countered, stating that the Southwest was one of the fastest-growing regions of the country and that a peaking plant promised the most comprehensive development of the badly needed power potential of this reach of the river.[44]

Despite claiming that they were trying to balance necessary water development with preserving national park values, Arizona water leaders engaged in what can only be described as skullduggery behind closed doors. Outwardly Arizona appeared united, but deep divisions existed within the coalition of state agencies pushing for the Central Arizona Project. By the time the FPC hearings commenced, CAPA, the Arizona Interstate Stream Commission, and the APA were fighting "like cats and dogs." Although it had adopted the Harza low-dam scheme, attorneys for the APA revealed during these hearings that they were negotiating with California and Nevada over building a high Bridge Canyon Dam as a three-state project that would intrude on the park.[45]

Arizona Governor Paul Fannin also divulged to a few close confidants that despite the APA's rhetoric about the harmful nature of the Los Angeles MCKC proposal, Arizona also wanted to build the controversial tunnel and power plant. Just as they had publicly endorsed the Harza two-stage development at Bridge Canyon, some Arizona water leaders thought the MCKC project could also be developed in two stages. They believed they had fragmented the conservationists by isolating the Sierra Club from the rest of the environmental organizations, and that the latter would not oppose a low Marble Canyon Dam because this stretch of the river was not protected.

This Arizona strategy was discussed in utmost secrecy and relied upon deceiving the park service and environmentalists into thinking that Arizona sincerely wanted to avoid damaging the park and monument. In reality, Arizona leaders from Governor Fannin on down wanted to use the environmentalists to help them defeat the Los Angeles case before the FPC and obtain the license to build Marble Canyon Dam. After accomplishing these two objectives, they planned to abandon the conservationists and fight to gain FPC approval of the very project they had opposed.[46]

In an attempt to implement this strategy, the APA tried to obtain National Park Service Director Conrad Wirth's support of Marble Canyon Dam. Now that the Los Angles proposal was out in the open,

Reclamation Commissioner Floyd Dominy asked his new boss, Udall, whether he could initiate feasibility studies of the MCKC—which, unbeknownst to the secretary, Dominy had already completed the previous summer.[47] Udall asked Wirth for the position of the National Park Service and the director indicated that while the service did not object to Marble Canyon Dam, it still opposed the Kanab Creek tunnel proposal.

Wirth even showed Udall a legislative history that demonstrated how the bureau had engaged in a little trickery of its own and prevented the park service from obtaining the strip of Forest Service land between Tapeats and Kanab Creeks—which happened to be where the bureau planned to build the MCKC power plant—even though Interior Secretary Krug had supposedly killed the project in 1949! The pugnacious director then scolded Udall and told him to live up to his preservationist rhetoric, saying in effect that if he did not fight against this new threat to Grand Canyon National Park, all of his eloquent expressions in favor of the national park ideal would be "undercut."[48]

Stewart Udall's Albatross

Just six months into his tenure, Udall already found himself being forced to choose from among several conflicting ideas. Should he listen to environmentalists who looked to him as an advocate of park values and wilderness preservation, or should he remain true to his Arizona political roots and act in what he thought would best ensure the ultimate construction of the CAP? Although Udall did not favor the MCKC project, neither was he enamored with the APA's attempt to "go it alone." Torn between his Interior Department responsibilities and loyalty to his native state, Udall would struggle for the rest of his political career to make peace with both federal and state water advocates and to reconcile his preservationist instincts with his belief in modernity. He would never lose his soul to "Life in Death" as did Samuel Coleridge's ancient mariner, but it took retirement from politics, adopting New Mexico as his new home, and publishing thoughtful books about the perils of modern technology before he would be truly free from his unsolvable dilemma.

Physically strong, optimistic, and a hardheaded political pragmatist, Udall spent years in Congress, which had shown him the futility of direct confrontation with California. As a result, Udall made it one of his highest priorities as interior secretary to end the Arizona-California water fight so lower Colorado River development could move forward. Almost immediately after his own appointment, Udall named James Carr, a former legislative assistant to California Senator Clair Engle, as his undersecretary, a move widely criticized in Arizona, especially in the conservative Phoenix newspapers. Believing that the House of Representatives would once again become the battleground when the Supreme Court handed down its final opinion in *Arizona v. California*, Udall needed more time to conceive a strategy designed to gain California's support for a federal CAP. Believing that the FPC hearings could be used to buy that time, Udall agreed to allow Dominy's study of the MCKC proposal to proceed and he instructed Wirth to stop criticizing the bureau.[49]

The National Parks Association soon got wind of the bureau's studies and its executive secretary, Anthony Wayne Smith, sent Udall a bluntly phrased telegram in late June. Udall responded that although he had "grave reservations" about the wisdom of the project, he could not withhold the information that the bureau had gathered during its previous studies. Smith, an aggressive former labor lawyer whose vociferous opposition to water projects and legal sorcery would soon earn him the nickname of "Mad Anthony Wayne Smith" from the Army Corps of Engineers, began to contemplate intervening in the FPC proceedings on behalf of the National Park Service in opposition to the Los Angeles proposal.[50]

Despite Udall's attempt to keep the unpredictable "Connie" Wirth under wraps, Dale Doty, attorney for the APA, asked the director in late October if he would testify during the hearings as part of Arizona's response to California's case. After reading a copy of the bureau's study, an angry Wirth agreed and the FPC scheduled his testimony for December. The director then fired off an angry memo to his boss imploring him to use his authority as interior secretary to stop the project. "Park supporters and other conservationists the Country [sic] over," he penned, "would be outraged if the Interior Department were to sponsor or support this measure."[51]

Ignoring Wirth's latest blast—or perhaps because of it—Udall tried to intervene with the FPC to keep the director from testifying, even though Wirth was only scheduled to speak against the MCKC proposal. But the secretary feared that Wirth might also oppose Marble Canyon Dam, a project Udall viewed as essential to a viable CAP. He was new to his office, but Udall already knew that one could never predict what his outspoken park service director might say or do.

As Udall contemplated how to obtain passage of the CAP, he closely studied Arizona's failed attempts in 1950 and 1951. Hayden's previous proposals had not included a dam at Marble Canyon and much had changed in the years since he had obtained Senate passage of the high Bridge Canyon Dam. Now a relatively unified conservation movement existed that had recently proven powerful enough to defeat the Dinosaur dams. Udall feared these environmentalists' ability to sway votes in Congress. But Udall's concern was based upon his experience during the contentious congressional debates of 1954–1956 over Dinosaur. He did not consider how these organizations had reacted to the Supreme Court's *Harriss* decision and the potential IRS threat to their lobbying efforts.

Udall wrote his brother Morris—who had recently been elected to his old congressional seat—that he believed the conservationists were in "an ugly mood" as a result of the recent Rainbow Bridge "fiasco" and were "spoiling for a fight." The one positive development that had arisen out of the new controversy over the MCKC was that it might now be possible to enlist the conservationists' support for a federal CAP and give him a powerful new ally against California.[52]

The Rainbow Bridge situation enraged many conservationists who believed that the sanctity of this unit of the park system had been guaranteed by the Colorado River Storage Project Act. However, these promises, approved both by Congress and Udall's predecessor, were in the process of being subverted by Dominy, who had convinced Congress to deny funds for the protective works. Although he was demonized by environmentalists for these actions, Dominy argued that he was trying to protect the monument. "I am the environmentalist who saved Rainbow Bridge," Dominy thundered while rapidly sketching a diagram of the protective works, when I interviewed him almost forty years later. "It was," he exclaimed, "the damndest thing I ever saw!" Indeed, the structures, which included earthen dams above and below the natural bridge, a diversion tunnel upstream of the monument, and two diesel pumping units to siphon away runoff from under the arch, would have been incredibly invasive from almost any point of view.[53]

Dominy believed that the protective measures would be even more intrusive than the potential threat from Lake Powell, and in April 1961 he organized an "invasion" of Rainbow Bridge National Monument— complete with US Navy helicopters—for fifty-seven people including members of the press, conservation leaders Anthony Smith and Brower, and several bureau chiefs including Udall and Wirth. After ridiculing Wirth and Smith, neither of whom had visited the monument before, the commissioner pointed out how destructive the protective measures would be as the group walked around the site. Yet the conservationists remained adamant that the promise Congress made in the Colorado River Storage Project must be kept even if it required intrusive measures they would normally oppose to fulfill it. Appalled, Dominy convinced the House Appropriations Committee to withhold funding for the protective works and incurred the wrath of preservationists as a result. Because Udall was his boss, some environmentalists began to have doubts about the secretary's true intentions as well.[54]

Meanwhile the FPC hearings continued, and Connie Wirth prepared to testify. Oddly enough, he now found himself courted by both the APA and the National Parks Association, both of which planned to subpoena him. Udall debated whether he should invoke executive privilege to override the subpoena, but he decided to allow Wirth to testify on the condition that he restrict himself to factual responses that lined up with previous statements of departmental policy. On December 6, 1961, the park service director testified against the MCKC proposal, saying that it would "dewater" the Colorado River in Grand Canyon, leaving it unable to carry an adequate silt load. Wirth also questioned how the bureau intended to dispose of the vast amount of debris that would result from the tunnel and power plant excavations. To the delight of the APA, Wirth stated that the park service had no objection to Marble Canyon Dam because that damsite was not in the park.[55]

The FPC adjourned until the new year, and when testimony resumed Anthony Wayne Smith and Smith Brookhart of the NPA filed a brief in opposition to the Los Angeles application, attacking the project on both statutory and aesthetic grounds. Smith and Brookhart were the only conservationists to participate in these proceedings. Edward Marsh, chief FPC hearing examiner, concluded the hearings after considering a recommendation by FPC counsel Joseph Hobbs that Arizona receive the license. On September 10, 1962, Marsh ruled that Los Angeles had failed to prove that the MCKC project was the best option, and he awarded a license to the APA authorizing construction of a low Marble Canyon Dam and power plant over the objections of the Navajo Nation.[56] Although Bridge Canyon Dam was still in limbo, Arizona was now free to begin construction of the Marble Canyon project . . . and to fight for the MCKC tunnel and power plant at a later date.

Opposition Old and New

Even as the FPC hearing examiners deliberated, the National Parks Association launched an opposition campaign against the proposals. "Mad Anthony Wayne Smith" authored a polemical article published in the June 1962 issue of *National Parks* magazine that was essentially a call to arms. Smith wrote:

> The battle for Grand Canyon has long been smoldering; it has now burst into flames. The integrity of the entire National Park System is at stake. The enemies of the parks are callous and ruthless; they have nothing but contempt for the values of the defenders of the parks. This battle may be just the beginning of a long war. Our prediction is that by the time this war is over, the American people will have made it plain that they will not tolerate the ruination of one of their greatest national shrines, nor the destruction of the National Park System.[57]

Strong as these words may seem, they reached only the thirty thousand members of the NPA. The caution with which Smith wrote this article demonstrates the impact of the *Harriss* decision upon the leadership of the NPA. Nowhere did Smith exhort his readers to write their congressional representatives, and though the inference is clear that he would like to have seen the American public respond to these threats, he did not suggest that the NPA take a leadership role in generating this response. Although the NPA did intervene in the FPC hearings, it did little to bring this crisis to the attention of the public, in all probability because it feared reprisals from the IRS. In the autumn of 1962, with the most serious threat of dam construction to date hanging over Grand Canyon, conservation organizations had yet to make a plea for public action.

The Sierra Club's absence from the FPC hearings is somewhat of a mystery. While it is true that the club voted to restrict its lobbying efforts in 1959, the board repudiated this position in 1960, giving Brower the freedom to lobby as vocally as he wanted. Since *Arizona v. California* had yet to be decided, possibly the club refrained from opposing the Los Angeles proposal because its leadership, consisting primarily of attorneys, believed that no major developments would occur on the river until after the court determined the respective water rights of the lower basin states. It is also possible that this legal expertise determined that the club lacked standing to intervene. Unlike the NPA, the club did not speak in behalf of a specific entity such as the park service, and the landmark Storm King case, which created the opportunity for environmentalists to intervene in behalf of *nature*, had not yet been decided.[58] So, for reasons that are not entirely clear, the Sierra Club failed to take a position or actively participate in the 1961–1962 Marble Canyon hearings before the Federal Power Commission.

But the APA was not entirely without opposition. The Navajo Tribal Council passed a resolution in May 1961 opposing the APA license application. After voting to oppose the state project, the council then agreed to ask the federal government to build the dam because it believed that Congress would be more sympathetic to its demands. Accordingly, Navajo Tribal Chairman Paul Jones informed Representative Morris Udall of the Navajo position in the fall of 1961.[59]

The Navajo resolution placed "Mo" Udall in a most uncomfortable situation because two separate elements of his constituency now directly opposed each other over water, arguably Arizona's most hot-button issue. The fact that his brother Stewart now held the position of interior secretary only complicated matters, because Stewart's opposition to the highly popular state proposal was well known. For Morris Udall, a freshman congressman, to oppose the APA plan in favor of the Navajo Nation would have been difficult; for him to be accused of doing so in support of the Interior Department position probably would have ended his political career. Yet Udall represented both groups and so he began to communicate with his House colleagues about the possibility of someone else sponsoring the Navajo bill.[60]

Perhaps only one Arizona politician could have openly opposed the APA proposal in favor of a federal project in the fall of 1962 without causing severe damage to his political career—Senator Carl Hayden. Hayden was deeply suspicious of it privately but he had not yet taken a public position. Mo Udall and Dominy met with representatives from the various Arizona agencies in Denver shortly after the FPC granted the APA license and tried to convince them that Marble Canyon should be reserved for federal development. Rich Johnson of CAPA wrote that Dominy "bluntly told us that the high dam in Bridge Canyon . . . could not be authorized in face of opposition by the Sierra Club and other organizations of its type," an astonishing admission from Dominy who in subsequent interviews denigrated the power of the conservationists.⁶¹ Both Dominy and Udall believed that the threat was so serious that they tried to persuade the representatives of state water agencies to rein in the APA for fear of losing the CAP.

Stewart Udall's aides feared that he would further antagonize the powerful Phoenix press and Arizona water interests by continuing to warn against taking the conservationists lightly. Udall took these warnings seriously because he intended to resume his Arizona political career after his tenure with the Interior Department. As early as November of 1960, Dominy had told him that if he accepted the post of interior secretary he would most likely destroy his political future in Arizona, because as a federal official he would be forced to make decisions about the lower Colorado River that would be highly unpopular with influential Arizona water leaders. After enduring merciless criticism from the Phoenix press during the APA hearings, Udall told Dominy in the fall of 1961, "by God you're right, I couldn't even be elected dogcatcher in Arizona."⁶²

Despite the criticism within his native state, Stewart Udall believed the time was right for Arizona to make an all-out effort to obtain the CAP and that he was the man with the right strategy to spearhead it. Arizona's influence at the federal level was already strong, and it appeared that the US Supreme Court was about to rule in Arizona's favor. But Udall also identified several obstacles that could derail congressional passage of the CAP that needed to be overcome or negotiated away. First, California's congressional bloc had now swollen to thirty-eight representatives. Overcoming this "California elephant" as he called it, would be difficult, and Arizona's victory in the recently concluded Marble Canyon hearings certainly would not enhance this prospect.⁶³

Second, the frequently irascible Wayne Aspinall from Colorado now chaired the key House Interior Committee at a time when the upper basin states were becoming increasingly apprehensive about the possibility of new lower basin projects preempting their entitlements under the 1922 Compact. Although some of Arizona's CAP supporters, most notably Senator Hayden, wanted to introduce bills virtually identical to those that had been defeated in 1950–1951, the CAP by itself offered nothing for either California or Colorado. Udall decided that the support of these two states was the key to obtaining a federal project. He might come under fire for opposing the APA license and the reintroduction of the old CAP proposals, but Udall believed that he would also reap the rewards if his strategy succeeded.[64]

Udall's first move was to convince the FPC to set aside its ruling in the recent hearings, and he filed a motion to that effect three weeks after the hearings ended. Udall contended that it was his public duty to ensure that all the basin states benefitted from the development of the Colorado River. Licensing an individual hydroelectric project for a single state would negate its contribution to the Southwest as a region. The FPC granted Udall's motion on November 2, 1962, and over the APA's withering objections it nullified the license it had just granted to Arizona.[65]

How ironic the situation must have seemed from the perspective of the APA leadership! After fighting for years to obtain permission to build a hydroelectric project on the lower Colorado River, the authority had finally succeeded in wringing approval from one federal agency only to have the Interior Department, led by a native Arizonan of all people, preempt it. Udall's actions set off a storm of protest in Arizona's newspapers, which published letters to the editor from incensed people who could not understand why the Arizona-born Udall would betray his native state.[66]

But Udall chose to oppose the APA proposal despite the known political risk because he felt he could fashion a regional solution to the Southwest's water problems and gain California's support for the CAP. As he surveyed the federal political landscape, he believed that Arizona was in a strong position with himself as interior secretary and Hayden who was the senior member of the Senate. In addition, two of the state's representatives, Republican John Rhodes, a quiet but effective coalition builder, and Udall's brother Morris, a Democrat and shrewd political strategist, carried the CAP banner in the House.

However, this strong position rested primarily upon Hayden's diminutive shoulders. With the Arizona FPC license now on hold, Udall had bought enough time to build unity among all the states of the Colorado River Basin including California. Arizona would take the lead in the House and Senate, and Udall would coordinate the effort from the Interior Department. But Udall knew this political strength would crumble if Arizona's increasingly frail senior senator died or was forced to retire.[67] Although he had only been in office for two years, Stewart Udall already knew he was running out of time.

4

A Time for Water Statesmanship

In his 1963 book *The Quiet Crisis*, Stewart Udall wrote that the scientific developments of the twentieth century held the key to overcoming the paradox of maintaining a high economic standard of living while degrading the natural world, a problem with which Americans had struggled since the first European settlers carved out a tenuous toehold in the Virginia Tidewater more than 350 years previously. A great civilization with a national identity firmly grounded in its natural splendor had arisen, yet, ironically, it had left wanton environmental destruction in its wake as an unfortunate consequence of progress. In Udall's book, written in the optimistic tone of the early 1960s, no dream seemed too far-fetched, including maintaining the upward arc of American progress while protecting its environment at the same time.

And why not? The Soviet Union and the United States had both sent men into orbit and, perhaps even more remarkably, had brought them safely home. President Kennedy had challenged the nation to conquer the "New Frontier" of space and to take the first step toward that objective by executing a successful moon landing by the end of the decade. American nuclear chemist Glenn Seaborg, winner of the 1951 Nobel Prize for his discovery of plutonium, predicted that clean power generated by fusion reactors would be a reality by 1970. US Atomic Energy Commissioner John von Neumann prophesied that by 1980 energy would be so plentiful and cheap to produce there would be no need to charge a fee for it. With the world's leading scientists sharing such visions, it is not hard to imagine how the promises of modern science captured the nation's imagination—and that of its young interior secretary.

Udall wanted his department to be on the cutting edge of scientific advances, especially those that could potentially solve the water shortages
of the American Southwest.[1]

Already the secretary had created the new position of science advisor within his department so he could be kept informed of the latest scientific developments and determine how they might benefit Interior
Department programs. He directed Commissioner Floyd Dominy to
open a dialogue with the Atomic Energy Commission about developing nuclear-powered desalinization plants and adding them to the federal reclamation program. Udall also pushed for an enormous expansion
of the federal saline water program and, at the beginning of his tenure
in 1961, he had asked Congress to appropriate $100 million for it over
the next five years.[2]

Despite his belief in the possibilities of big science, Udall knew that
the Southwest's water problems could only be solved within the existing political system. Udall would have to persuade people who held the
levers of political power that science, combined with cooperation, could
remedy the consequences of the Colorado River Compact's overalloca-
tion of water and solve the mounting crisis. If he could convince key politicians to work together for the benefit of the entire Southwest rather
than fighting tooth and nail to obtain water for their individual states,
Udall believed that the inefficiencies and obstacles within the political
system could be overcome. If long-simmering interstate rivalries could
be set aside, eventually there would be enough water for everyone. In
order to eliminate the barriers that had doomed Arizona's previous efforts, Udall began thinking about regional alternatives—"transmountain"
diversions he called them in his book—to move water from places where
it was plentiful to regions where it was lacking. And moving this amount
of water would require enormous amounts of power.[3]

The Pragmatics of Water Politics

Power of a different sort was the key to moving the political process
and, in the early 1960s, it lay mostly in the hands of the senior members of Congress who chaired important committees. In 1962 nobody
held as much power and influence as Carl Hayden, now in his mid-
eighties and the ranking member of the Senate, who now chaired the
Senate Appropriations Committee. With the ability to block any bill
that required federal funding, Hayden's influence in the upper chamber

was unrivaled. Although his relations with the senator were sometimes strained, Udall believed Hayden would eventually support him when he realized that Udall's regional strategy would result in Arizona obtaining the CAP.

Arizona's position in the House of Representatives was much weaker. Udall knew he would have to use all of his charm and political acumen to finesse a project through that chamber. Udall did not have many allies in the House, but he did have many potential enemies there. Cobbling together a political coalition to obtain a majority would be a daunting proposition to say the least.

The most important vote of all, Udall knew, had to come from a man from the upper basin whose interests directly conflicted with those of Arizona. Somehow the secretary would have to gain the blessing of Colorado Representative Wayne Aspinall, the chair of the House Committee on Interior and Insular Affairs, whose power to stop water projects was almost as great as that possessed by Hayden in the Senate. Udall knew from the outset that without this "one-man committee" on board, his idea would never get off the ground. Udall knew that these committee chairs held in their powerful hands the success or failure of anything he might propose. Antagonizing just one strategically-placed committee chair in either house would doom any proposal no matter how promising and well-supported.[4]

Undaunted and excited about the possibility of solving the Southwest's water crisis, in the autumn of 1962 Udall asked Aspinall what he would require for his committee to report a CAP bill favorably to the House floor for debate. Aspinall wrote Udall in November and emphasized that only through "thoughtful discussion" between states could the problems of the lower basin be resolved. Aspinall suggested that Udall use the upper basin's Colorado River Storage Project as a model for lower basin legislation, and he asked to see a summary of the Interior Department's basin studies and a preliminary outline of a comprehensive lower basin plan.

Most importantly, although Aspinall understood that representatives from the southwestern states intended to introduce water project legislation immediately after the Supreme Court handed down its ruling, the chairman emphasized that only legislation based upon mutual cooperation among the lower basin states would receive his blessing. To Udall the ramifications were clear—projects that served only local interests, such as the CAP, stood virtually no chance of making it out of the House Interior Committee. Aspinall, unlike John Murdock a decade before, ruled his committee with an iron fist, and members who hoped to obtain favors from the occasionally "prickly" chairman dared not oppose him, particularly on legislation that could potentially affect the water rights of his home state of Colorado.[5]

Stewart Udall responded to Aspinall's letter in January 1963 and outlined his first ideas about basin-wide water resource planning. Udall viewed the Colorado River Compact of 1922 as a straitjacket because its allocations were based upon a great overestimation of the Colorado's annual flow. Thus projects based upon this estimate would inherently overdevelop the river. Udall even told Aspinall that he believed the impending Supreme Court decision was of secondary importance because he understood that no matter what the ruling, the lower Colorado did not contain enough water to meet the Southwest's needs.

The solution lay in more efficient usage of water still available in the river for the short term and in "developing additional supplies" to meet the inevitable shortages caused by utilization of all available surface water and groundwater overdrafts. The Phoenix area faced an imminent crisis, the secretary wrote, because the city pumped four million acre-feet of groundwater each year while its sustaining aquifer only regained half that amount in annual recharge.

Udall suggested that more water for the Colorado River Basin could be obtained from nuclear-powered desalinization plants and interbasin water transfers, particularly from rivers in northern California. Although this idea might fly with Aspinall, it was sure to anger representatives from northern California, a region whose running feud over water with southern California predated even the Golden State's enmity towards Arizona. Attempting to get Hayden and other Arizona water leaders behind the regional plan, he insisted that the CAP be incorporated into it and that it be one of the first projects constructed.

Although existing hydroelectric plants at Hoover and Parker Dams would be integrated into the regional proposal, they alone would not provide enough power. Despite the threat from conservationists, Udall called for new hydroelectric dams "to be constructed on the Colorado River at Marble Canyon, Bridge Canyon and *wherever else such plants on the Colorado may prove feasible* [emphasis mine]." As the only remaining stretch of the lower Colorado River (apart from the Bridge and

Marble Canyon dam sites) lay within Grand Canyon National Park and Monument, it appears that in addition to the two Grand Canyon dams, Udall was also, at least initially, considering the possibility of including the MCKC project in his plan.[6]

Udall continued to hone his ideas during the first few months of 1963, attempting to piece together a proposal that would bring additional water to the Southwest and cut across regional and political differences. Although an ominous development from the perspective of environmental organizations concerned with keeping Grand Canyon free of hydroelectric projects, given the IRS threat, the willingness of the conservationists to lobby Congress as they had during the Dinosaur controversy was very much in doubt.

Indeed in 1958, shortly after President Eisenhower signed the CRSP into law, the IRS launched an investigation into the lobbying activities of the National Parks Association and the organization had avoided losing its tax-deductible status by a whisker. Chastened, the NPA's executive secretary, Anthony Wayne Smith, convinced its board of directors in 1959 that it would doom the organization to lose its tax status because individual members would stop making contributions if they were not tax deductible. The mere threat of an IRS revocation was enough to render the NPA, in the words of one incensed board member, "supine and apparently spineless."[7]

Other environmental societies looked to the NPA as an example, figuring that if the brash, outspoken Smith recommended the NPA curtail its lobbying they should follow suit. With the single exception of the National Parks Association, conservationists had not attempted to influence the outcome of the recently concluded Marble Canyon project hearings, and the NPA was very careful to "educate" instead of "advocate," only publishing articles opposed to the project within the pages of its in-house magazine with the caveat that the opinions of the author did not reflect the opinions of the association.[8]

The Sierra Club had even retreated from its bold stance of 1957 when its board decided to oppose all further water development in the lower Colorado River, and it had not participated in the 1962 Marble Canyon Dam hearings at all. It appeared as though the conservationists no longer possessed the hard-won political influence they wielded during the Dinosaur controversy because of the chilling effect of the IRS investigation of the NPA. This potential resistance was of little concern to Udall because he believed the overwhelming political support he was building would crush any opposition these organizations might mount.

However, 1963 would see important developments that would shape the struggle over dams in Grand Canyon for years to come. Unbeknownst to Udall, the Sierra Club finally decided to enact remedial measures to protect the majority of its income should its future lobbying efforts run afoul of IRS regulations. The Hualapai and Navajo Nations also participated in the discussions about utilizing sites located on their reservations, serving notice that advocates of projects for the lower Colorado River would now have to consider how these schemes would affect Native Americans or face opposition during a time of increasing Indian nationalism and public sensitivity to civil rights issues.

Yet the legal position of the two groups most likely to be affected by dams in Grand Canyon differed significantly—as did their strategy. In the decade since the bureau had trespassed onto the Hualapai Reservation to study the Bridge Canyon site, the Hualapai had gone from having their rights virtually ignored to negotiating from a position of strength as a result of increasing awareness of civil rights issues and the realization by both state and federal agencies that the law strongly supported the Hualapai claims. On the other hand, advocates for the Navajo Nation could not rely upon a strong legal foundation and, as a result, the Navajo lost in the hearings before the FPC. Only then did they seek federal development as a last-ditch alternative. While the Navajo position remained clouded, it appeared as though the Hualapai could be induced to support the Bridge Canyon Dam.

In early 1963, the US Supreme Court stood on the verge of ruling on the water rights of the lower basin states after almost twelve years of litigation. Senator Hayden and his allies planned to introduce CAP bills that were essentially the same as those debated in 1950–1951, believing that a holding favorable to Arizona would create enough momentum that they could drive a bill quickly through the House. But Udall knew that potentially fatal obstacles, some old and some new, had arisen since the CAP debates of the early 1950s. A powerful conservationist lobby, dormant but still dangerous, California's growing congressional delegation, and Aspinall would in all likelihood pose grave threats to Hayden's proposal.

Secretary Udall believed that in nuclear power and desalinization, along with intra-basin cooperation, lay the means to solve the present water crisis and heal the bitter wounds of conflicts past. "The hour for a water statesman in the Pacific Southwest has arrived," Udall wrote to the governors of Arizona, California, and Nevada in June 1963. Idealistic, vigorous, and with absolute faith in scientific progress, the secretary eagerly anticipated taking the lead in implementing a new framework for conservation, based upon maximum efficiency and technological advances he believed were just over the horizon.

The secretary understood that political differences brought about by short sightedness could prevent the implementation of these bold new solutions. The ideas of the past, and the politicians who promoted them, had already been given a chance, and they had failed. Both, he believed, would fail again if they tried to follow the strategy of the 1950s, even if the Supreme Court rendered a favorable decision, because California still stood in the way of House approval. Arizona still held a strong political position because of the influence of its senior senator, but this position was growing ever more precarious with each passing year.

Udall believed there was only one way for Arizona to gain authorization of the project of which it had long dreamed, and that was to formulate a revolutionary new proposal designed to break the political logjam and gain the support of California, the upper basin, and, if possible, the conservationists. While most of Arizona's federal water advocates planned to introduce bare-bones CAP legislation in the wake of a favorable Supreme Court ruling, Udall had already concluded, based upon his assessment of the political landscape, that these renewed efforts would be in vain. An innovative approach was needed, one that reflected the persona and philosophy of the Kennedy administration. This was not a time for archaic ideas that had already been proven unsuccessful in the harsh realm of western water politics. It was time, Udall believed, to "think big!"[9]

Udall Unveils His Regional Proposal

On the morning of January 21, 1963, David Brower of the Sierra Club waited nervously in Secretary Udall's outer office. Brower's mood was one of urgency as he hoped that he could convince the secretary to refrain from closing the gates of the recently completed Glen Canyon Dam. Although the high Glen Canyon Dam was the product of a complex political agreement brokered during the Dinosaur controversy a few years previously, Brower blamed himself for the impending loss of Glen Canyon, which contained some of the most spectacular scenery in the world.

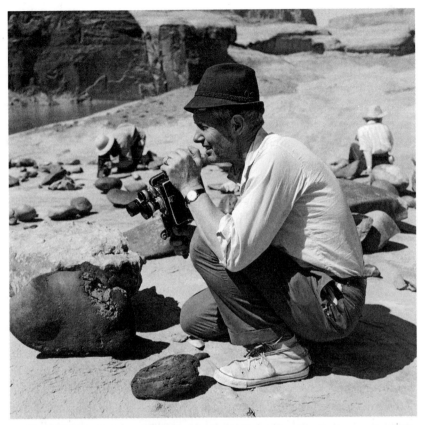

FIGURE 4.1. Sierra Club Executive Director David Brower in Glen Canyon, 1963. NAU. PH.99.3.1.28.54, Northern Arizona University, Cline Library, Tad Nichols Collection.

Convinced that his suggestion to raise the height of Glen Canyon Dam in exchange for the deletion of the Dinosaur dams had been an egregious mistake, Brower appealed to Udall's preservationist instincts, seeking to persuade him to intervene and delay the filling of Lake Powell. Brower hoped to convince the interior secretary that the dam was not needed in the twentieth century and that it should only be utilized after Lake Mead filled with silt. By the time that occurred, Brower believed, alternative energy sources would be available and Glen Canyon could be spared. As Brower waited in vain, Udall gave his assent, Reclamation Commissioner Floyd Dominy ordered his personnel at the site to close the gates, and the Colorado River began to create Lake Powell—water playground for millions, pride of the Bureau of Reclamation, and a source of revulsion in the minds of many environmentalists.[10]

The loss of Glen Canyon haunted conservationists once they realized that their efforts at Echo Park resulted in the destruction of a canyon more beautiful than the one they had saved. They viewed it as a tragic mistake, but Brower and his followers learned a hard lesson from the Echo Park compromise, one equally as important as what preservationists had learned from the Hetch Hetchy dispute. In agreeing not to oppose the construction of a high Glen Canyon Dam in exchange for the deletion of the dams at Dinosaur, environmentalists left themselves without recourse when they discovered that Glen Canyon should also be protected.

Rendered powerless by his own compromise, Brower agonized as construction neared completion, and he pleaded eloquently with Udall to spare this spectacular canyon he believed was worthy of national park status. When Glen Canyon Dam's steel gates slammed shut in 1963, Brower cried over what would soon be destroyed. When I interviewed him thirty-five years later, he could barely speak of it, still despondent over the loss of the magnificent canyon he believed he could have saved.[11]

The controversies over Glen Canyon and Hetch Hetchy closely parallel one another, though separated by more than sixty years. Both involved the destruction of indescribable beauty by dams whose opponents claimed were not necessary because, in both instances, other sources of water and power were available. The Hetch Hetchy and Glen Canyon defeats devastated the leaders of the Sierra Club—the heartbroken Muir dying the year after Congress gave San Francisco the authorization to flood Hetch Hetchy Valley, while Brower's friends feared he might take his own life in the wake of losing Glen Canyon.[12]

Both controversies awakened the Sierra Club from relatively lengthy periods of complacency and spurred it into public activism. And, most importantly, each contest taught tactics needed for future conflicts: Hetch Hetchy—the necessity of political awareness; Glen Canyon—that entering into compromises to protect wilderness without fully investigating the ramifications can endanger other areas of equal or greater scenic beauty. The bitter fruits of the Echo Park compromise, and the belief that the interior secretary had abdicated his responsibility to preserve Rainbow Bridge National Monument, strengthened the resolve of many environmentalists to prevent a similar situation from occurring downstream in Grand Canyon.

The same day he authorized the filling of Lake Powell, Stewart Udall held a press conference, which Brower attended, to reveal that the Interior Department was studying a massive regional water plan for the southwestern United States, combining the importation of water with the construction of desalinization plants to meet the needs of the lower Colorado River Basin. "Piecemeal development cannot do the job," the secretary said, and he stressed that both nuclear and conventional generating plants would provide power for the immense proposal—including hydroelectric projects at the Bridge and Marble Canyon sites in Grand Canyon.

The interior secretary had lobbied for congressional authorization of the construction of the world's largest nuclear power plant at Hanford, Washington, for the regional plan he was now beginning to conceptualize. He stressed that revenue from existing hydroelectric projects such as Hoover and Parker Dams combined with the sales of power from Bridge, Marble, and other feasible Colorado River developments would finance the rest of the plan, including the trans-basin water diversions to augment the Colorado River upon which the success of the entire proposal hinged.[13]

Udall argued that the hydroelectric generating plants must be constructed as the first phase of the proposal because the revenue generated from the power they would produce would be used to create a basin account to fund the rest of the project. According to the secretary's plan, this development account constituted the key to gaining the political support of California and the other basin states because it represented tangible evidence that these states also stood to gain from the proposal. Obtaining this trust was of utmost importance because Udall contemplated the construction of the CAP as the major portion of the first phase, both to put the revenue-generating dams in place as quickly as possible and to gain the support of Arizona's water leaders. The regional plan offered something for virtually everyone in the Pacific Southwest, and California's representatives initially reacted positively to the scheme. Encouraged, Udall pressed forward.[14]

Udall conceived of the regional proposal after touring hydroelectric facilities in the Soviet Union in the summer of 1962. At one point during the secretary's trip, Premier Khrushchev promised Udall that the Soviet Union would "overtake" the United States in an "energy race," a contest Udall enthusiastically supported, because it offered the United States an opportunity to showcase its technological prowess before the rest of the world. In January 1963 the United States needed such an opportunity:

despite President Kennedy's bold challenge of a lunar mission by the end of the decade, the Soviets held the lead in the space race and used it to argue the superiority of communism before a global audience. As Udall later recalled, the early 1960s were a time of "the space program, atomic power, big technologies. We [the Interior Department] are left out of the big picture except for our program, water desalting."[15]

But in 1962 President Kennedy declared that the desalinization of seawater was even more important than the moon mission because the rest of the world would "look to the nation" that developed it. As an enthusiastic disciple of Kennedy's New Frontier, Udall believed that conservation of water resources and the development of desalinization offered the Interior Department the chance to develop peaceful technology that the United States could share with the rest of the world.[16] While the secretary grappled with the complexities of reconciling reclamation and preservation in the context of the Cold War and scientific advances, a disheartened Brower, defeated in his attempt to save Glen Canyon and discouraged by the new Interior Department proposal, returned to California, unsure of the effect that Udall's regional plan would have upon Grand Canyon.

Ever the practical politician, Udall hedged his bets in January 1963 and did not specify the height of the latest dams proposed for the Colorado River gorge.[17] However, the political support of California and the rest of the basin states rested upon the promised lower basin account. Contractual agreements controlled the revenues from Parker and Hoover Dams, thus these generating plants would not be available to contribute revenue to the account for several decades. Hoover Dam, the largest existing hydroelectric producer in the Southwest, could not be utilized to contribute revenue to the basin fund until 1990.[18]

Desalinization and nuclear power, while attractive, would not be practical alternatives for at least another decade by even the most optimistic estimates. Whether Udall wanted to admit it or not, California's support hinged upon the rapid construction of the hydroelectric dams at the Bridge and Marble Canyon sites because they were the only way to generate immediate revenue for the basin account and the rest of the project for the foreseeable future.

According to a 1962 Bureau of Reclamation analysis of three possible heights for the Bridge Canyon project, the agency found that a dam sufficiently low to avoid backing water into the national monument would

not be justifiable from an economic standpoint. Next, the bureau compared a low dam that would back water through the length of the monument to the long-debated high dam that would back water through
the monument and encroach upon the park. Although it found both to
be feasible, bureau engineers estimated that the high dam would generate 250,000 more kilowatts annually than the low dam, while the
best option to maximize revenues, according to Commissioner Dominy,
would be to construct a high Bridge Canyon Dam in conjunction with a
dam at Marble Canyon.[19]

Udall wrestled with his dilemma of having to decide between kilowatts and wilderness preservation as he tried to drum up support for his
regional proposal. He briefly flirted with the MCKC project and the high
Bridge Canyon Dam, but Udall decided initially to pursue the construction of a low Bridge Canyon Dam and Marble together to avoid conservationist opposition. Dominy's proposal, however, suggested a way
to maximize revenue generation that would, in all likelihood, appeal
to water interests throughout the region including the indispensable
California voting bloc and Aspinall, the all-important House Interior
Committee chairman. Capital generated by a high Bridge Canyon Dam
in concert with Marble Canyon Dam promised a much greater and more
rapid increase in the basin development fund than any other option and
would allow the bureau to build the water-importation phase of the project that much sooner.

If his new political allies from California and the rest of the
Colorado Basin states insisted upon maximum power and revenue
production, Udall would be forced to choose between their support,
which could be measured in actual votes gained in the House, and the
support of conservation organizations whose influence, though potentially powerful as demonstrated by their tenacious defense of Dinosaur
National Monument, could not be assessed in conventional political
terms. Conservationists had not initiated a national opposition campaign other than Dinosaur since the Supreme Court's affirmation of
the Federal Lobbying Act in its 1954 *Harriss* decision, creating the appearance that the holding had caused them to withdraw from the political arena in light of potential IRS threats. The secretary bought
some time by not revealing publicly which proposition he favored;
soon a day would come when he would no longer have that luxury.
Udall would then have to decide whose political support he could afford

to lose—and overcome—and whose he would deem indispensable and openly court.

The Environmentalists Mobilize

The Sierra Club began a crash opposition effort in the spring of 1963. Angry at Interior Secretary Udall for refusing to reconsider filling Lake Powell, and at himself for agreeing to raise Glen Canyon Dam to save Dinosaur, Brower began to contemplate ways to increase public awareness of the threats the bureau's plans posed to Grand Canyon and other western wilderness. He knew that stunning visual imagery would resonate with people, and he had already dispatched Eliot Porter, a skilled photographer, to capture Glen Canyon on film in 1961 and 1962 before it disappeared under the rising waters of Lake Powell. Brower himself filmed Glen Canyon for a forthcoming movie. Porter compiled his own gorgeous color photos and the words of wilderness advocates including Brower into a large, magnificently crafted exhibit-format book titled *The Place No One Knew: Glen Canyon on the Colorado*. Designed to form an image of Glen Canyon in the minds of people who now would never have the chance to see it, the book was such an elegant symphony of haunting prose and stunning photographs that Aspinall, the crusty House Interior Committee chairman who had supported the construction of Glen Canyon Dam, is said to have wept when he read it.[20]

Published as a requiem for Glen Canyon, *The Place No One Knew* also warned of future proposals that were "well underway to eradicate the finest miracles left on the Colorado" and that alternative energy sources such as fossil fuel or nuclear power could be used in the place of hydroelectric power. Brower wrote in his foreword:

> Glen Canyon died in 1963 and I was partly responsible for its needless death. So were you. Neither you nor I, nor anyone else, knew it well enough to insist that at all costs it should endure....The rest will go the way Glen Canyon did unless enough people begin to feel uneasy about the current interpretation of what progress consists of—unless they are willing to ask if progress has really served good purpose if it wipes out so many of the things that make life worthwhile.[21]

Although the book argued against future development of the Colorado River, *The Place No One Knew* was also remarkably restrained, for the Sierra Club had yet to adopt an official response to

Udall's regional water plan. Other than exhorting people to become aware that important decisions about wilderness preservation were being made without public input, the book did not appeal for an out- pouring of letters or other public efforts to try to influence Congress. Exquisitely photographed and skillfully edited, *The Place No One Knew* is also notable for what it did not include. Nowhere are Grand Canyon or the proposed dams mentioned by name. In a very real sense, the book reflects the Sierra Club's continuing uncertainty about how politically active it should be in the face of the potential threat to its tax status. It was one thing to mourn what was already lost, it was quite another to enter the legislative arena to try to prevent it from happening again.

The Sierra Club now stood at an important crossroads in its evolu- tion as an environmental organization. In 1957 it had taken an official position against anymore water development between Glen Canyon and Lake Mead—park service boundaries be damned—but the club's leader- ship had walked that position back by 1959, probably as a result of the IRS investigation of the NPA. Yet the next year it reversed course again and voted to allow Brower to lobby at his discretion. Despite giving Brower the green light, however, the club had been conspicuously absent from the 1962 FPC hearings. Now, with Glen Canyon going under, the Interior Department developing a regional water plan that included dams in Grand Canyon that would threaten the national park and mon- ument, and the Supreme Court's ruling in *Arizona v. California* immi- nent, the club could no longer avoid taking a public stand.

The Sierra Club board of directors met on May 4, 1963, to discuss what position the club should take concerning these latest Grand Canyon dam proposals. Bestor Robinson, now the Sierra Club vice president, still wielded great influence among the leadership. He argued, just as he had in 1949, that the club should meet the bureau halfway. Robinson made a strong case for the recreation potential of Marble Canyon Dam and even contended that because the dam would create a wonderful tail-water trout fishery downstream, the club should urge the bureau to build ele- vators for fishermen. Somehow these ideas gained traction, and with the board on the verge of approving yet another disastrous Robinson com- promise, it was time for Brower to pull an ace out of his sleeve. Brower, having anticipated that Robinson would favor appeasement, had asked Martin Litton, Sierra Club member, travel editor of *Sunset* magazine, and staunch Grand Canyon advocate, to prepare a few remarks beforehand.

FIGURE 4.2. Environmentalist Martin Litton in 2013 holding the hand-drawn map he used to convince the Sierra Club's leadership to oppose the Grand Canyon dams in 1963. Photo courtesy of Robert Wyss.

Litton rose, and hurling verbal lightning bolts like an Old Testament prophet he castigated the board for its hand-wringing and for even considering such a ridiculous idea while the bureau was drawing up plans to build dams in Grand Canyon. Emphatically pointing at a map of Grand Canyon he had sketched on a piece of cardboard to drive his points home, Litton showed the board how dams above and below the park would hurt the park itself, and he argued that all of Grand Canyon, whether it lay within the artificial boundaries of park service jurisdiction or not, was worth fighting for. As David Brower recalled later, Litton "devastated" Robinson's arguments, and when he finished his fiery oration he received a spontaneous round of applause from those in attendance.

After an hour and a half of additional debate, board member Pauline Dyer moved that the club should oppose all further dams and diversions in Grand Canyon and that it should press for the enlargement of Grand Canyon National Park. By now the board had seen the light and it approved, essentially returning to the position it adopted in 1957. Those who favored environmental advocacy had won the day and, because its leadership had already taken steps to shield most of its assets from the IRS, the Sierra Club was ready to fight against the Grand Canyon dams. Never again, no matter what the potential consequences, would the Sierra Club retreat from challenging those who were trying to destroy Grand Canyon.[22]

Twelve Years On

As environmental organizations reinvented themselves, and Udall plotted his regional water strategy, the Supreme Court struggled to find a way out of the legal quagmire created by the competing water claims of seven states, two nations, and numerous American Indian groups. The Compact of 1922, based upon a great overestimation of the river's flow, divided the river into two artificial basins, each of which was given a guaranteed amount of 7.5 million acre-feet of water each year. Because it allocated water that did not exist, it practically guaranteed that the basin states would be engaged in continuous conflict over water use.

The compact set aside the western water law doctrine of prior appropriation with respect to competition between the upper and lower basins. However, prior appropriation still governed water rights *within* each basin. As a result the water rights of the lower basin states of Arizona, California, and Nevada had never been legally determined—save for California's annual use of 4.4 million acre-feet each year, a self-imposed restriction to which it had agreed in exchange for the approval of Boulder Dam. After the great dam was authorized, California went back on its agreement, built additional aqueducts, and by the 1950s it was using more than five million acre-feet of water each year, while at the same time wielding its political muscle to block Arizona's attempt to build water projects of its own.

It had even succeeded in having the issue of lower basin water rights thrown into the Supreme Court in 1951, resulting in more than a decade of delay. As the court deliberated, California established more and more perfected water rights under prior appropriation by putting its water to the "beneficial use" the doctrine requires while preventing Arizona from doing the same. For twelve long years Arizona could only watch and wait. Carl Hayden bided his time, increased his senatorial power through seniority and committee chairmanships, and shepherded water projects for many other western states through the congressional maze of approval. But the quiet Arizonan, highly respected because he chose actions over words, expected his senatorial colleagues to return the favors he had granted them once the issue of lower basin water rights had been settled once and for all.

All eyes now turned to the highest court in the United States. Would it apply the doctrine of prior appropriation strictly and grant California a permanent water right of 5.2 million acre-feet? It could have easily done so; prior appropriation dictated such an outcome, and the court itself ruled in 1922 that this doctrine would govern all water disputes between western states in the absence of a binding agreement. The stakes couldn't have been higher for all parties concerned,a as the visions of glittering cities and making the desert bloom that Arizona developers had long desired depended entirely upon access to water. And the Colorado River was the only water available, at least for the time being.

Although numerous issues divided the three lower basin states, the status of the Gila River was probably the most controversial and certainly had the most bearing with regard to the CAP. California contended that the Gila's flow should be deducted from Arizona's Colorado River entitlement because it was a tributary. Attorney Mark Wilmer argued persuasively that since the Gila's watershed lay almost entirely within the Grand Canyon State, its annual flow should not be considered a part of Arizona's allotment because the Compact of 1922 measured the Colorado River's annual flow at Lee's Ferry, several hundred miles *upstream* from where the Gila joins it. The difference represented by the Gila River amounted to about a million acre-feet. Arizona feared that if the Supreme Court upheld California's position on the Gila River, it would reduce its allotment so drastically that in all likelihood, the CAP could never be built.[23]

The Supreme Court handed down its opinion on June 3, 1963. In a divided 5–3 decision with Chief Justice Earl Warren, who was from California, abstaining, the court held that in a year of average flow, California was entitled to 4.4 million acre-feet, Arizona to 2.8 million, and Nevada to 300,000. Furthermore, it ruled that the flow of the Gila River was a separate issue and would not be counted as part of Arizona's Colorado River entitlement, effectively granting the Grand Canyon State an annual allotment of 3.8 million acre-feet.[24] The decision was a monumental victory for the state of Arizona. Finally, pending congressional approval, construction of the CAP could begin. The next day, Carl Hayden and Barry Goldwater in the Senate, and Morris Udall, John Rhodes, and George Senner in the House of Representatives, introduced CAP legislation in both houses of Congress calling for a high Bridge Canyon Dam.

Although Stewart Udall tried unrelentingly to convince Arizona's congressional delegation that a regional proposal was the best approach, they disregarded this advice and followed Hayden's lead. Arizona's political influence at the federal level was thus divided when it should have been united in the immediate aftermath of the Supreme Court decision. Arizona's political leaders were aware that water attorney Northcutt Ely, California's brilliant lower Colorado River strategist, intended to use his influence to negate the Supreme Court decision through political action. The failure of Arizona water leaders to present a united front played right into the wily Ely's hands. CAP task force member J. A. Riggins expressed the frustration many Arizonans felt in a biting piece of satire about Ely's role in the Arizona-California controversy:

"The law of the West," my lawyer said, "is Prior Appropriation."
And on this point we'll stand or fall in the High Court of the Nation.
For ten long years we tried our case and never did give in—
Just kept on using water which belonged to you and him.
The day we lost, my lawyer spoke — sans fear or trepidation.
"What you have lost in Court today, regain!—by legislation!"[25]

Udall's regional proposal was designed to avoid this exact situation. The secretary, frustrated with his colleagues' shortsightedness, knew that the Supreme Court victory, though important, would not change the existing political situation. Arizona might now have its water rights clarified legally, but without the means to use them the court case might as well have not even been tried. Only legislation with California's approval could be guided through the House of Representatives, and Hayden's introduction of a standalone CAP, in Udall's measured opinion, only guaranteed California's continuing obstruction. Why then, did Arizona's water leaders, his own brother included, take such a course of action?

The answer lies in the reverence with which Hayden was held by Arizona's CAP proponents, the public at large, and in Hayden's own perceptions of the proper congressional strategy. Why should Hayden, whose own legislative experience dated back to 1912, defer to a former representative with only six years of legislative experience, when he, as the Senate's ranking member, had built political coalitions that fostered the passage of dozens of reclamation bills, including many of great benefit to the states of California and Colorado, for nearly a quarter century?

As chairman of the Senate Appropriations Committee, Hayden was well acquainted with the practical side of politics and the influence he held, yet Hayden seldom used his position to force others to bend to his will.

Hayden believed that the major obstacle to the passage of the CAP had been removed now that the Supreme Court had adjudicated the water rights of the lower Colorado River Basin. "Ordinary principles of fair play are bound to operate to our advantage," Hayden wrote to the rest of the Arizona delegation shortly before the Supreme Court decision. Hayden expected that his colleagues in both the House and Senate, many of whom he had aided in obtaining benefits for their home districts, would now help him realize his lifelong dream for Arizona even if California refused to get on board.[26]

Hayden feared also that a bill radically different from his previous legislation, such as a regional project along the lines suggested by Stewart Udall, would require more in-depth studies by the Bureau of Reclamation and result in additional lengthy delays. The senator also believed that if the CAP tied to a basin account along with Hoover, Parker, and Davis Dams, it would give the opponents of a high dam at Bridge Canyon ammunition to demonstrate that the CAP was feasible with a low dam and power revenues from Hoover.

Finally, Hayden sensed that Congress was in a fiscally conservative mood in the summer of 1963 and that it would be reluctant to pass a multi-billion-dollar regional proposal; hence, the senator believed that to tie the CAP in with a more ambitious plan would jeopardize the CAP unnecessarily.[27] Hayden, calling upon his fifty-one years of congressional experience, convinced the Arizona delegation of the practicality of his approach. United behind their senior senator, they supported the reintroduction of the CAP proposal of 1950–1951, which included a high dam at Bridge Canyon with no mention of a dam in Marble Canyon—although Hayden reserved Marble Canyon Dam as an option should the high Bridge Canyon Dam meet insurmountable opposition . . . wherever it came from.

Undaunted, Stewart Udall continued to try to convince Hayden to back the regional approach. Citing practical reasons of his own, Udall appealed to Hayden's bitter memories of past CAP failures, writing to the senator that he had consulted several congressmen in "strategic" positions on the House Interior Committee who not only backed the regional proposal, but argued that the old CAP legislation would create such controversy in the House, that it would probably go down to defeat despite the respect in which Hayden was held.

Mindful of Hayden's great political influence and the important role the senator had played in Arizona's quest for the CAP, Udall pleaded with Hayden to "give the regional approach a chance," arguing that if Hayden pushed for CAP hearings in 1963 it would undercut his own negotiations with California Governor Edmund "Pat" Brown and Senator Thomas Kuchel. Udall contended that only by tying the CAP to the larger proposal would California's congressional representatives be convinced to support it and that to strive for a separate CAP authorization would be "disastrous."[28] But the secretary failed to convince the senator to support his regional plan, and Hayden obtained Senate approval to convene CAP hearings in the fall of 1963.

Udall now came under withering attack from Arizona Republicans who invoked his recent trip to the Soviet Union and subsequent positive comments about hydroelectric developments in the USSR as evidence that the interior secretary desired to "socialize" power production in the United States. On July 21 Arizona Republican Party Chairman Keith Brown accused Udall of being "a hatchet man for the New Frontier [who is] doing everything in his power to block Arizona from obtaining its long-fought-for goal." Brown invoked New Deal imagery that played well before the conservative Arizona electorate, calling Udall's regional proposal an "international Colorado Valley Authority," an obvious shot at the Tennessee Valley Authority, an enormous New Deal regional project Senator Goldwater loathed. Brown also accused Udall of stalling the CAP in order to placate California to assure that state's forty electoral votes would go to Kennedy in the 1964 presidential election.[29]

Indeed, despite the vituperative Republican rhetoric, it appears as though Udall was doing exactly that. California supported favorite son Richard Nixon in 1960 and Kennedy's advisors viewed its electoral bloc as pivotal because, in the light of JFK's razor-thin margin of victory, they wanted to guarantee a mandate for JFK in 1964. In addition, Senator Goldwater was already being mentioned as a possible presidential candidate for the election of 1964; in the event that he won the nomination, it would be highly unlikely that Arizona would vote to keep Kennedy— and Udall—in office.[30] Ironically, Udall, who believed that the best chance of obtaining the CAP for Arizona in any form was to gain California's support, was now forced into the position of having to oppose Senator

Hayden of his own state and party because Udall feared the effect that Hayden's CAP strategy would have on the California electorate and ultimately upon his own ability to use the power of his office to influence the congressional debate.

"Are We Resigned?"

With Hayden and Udall at loggerheads, Arizona's CAP camp remained divided as conservationists now began their campaign to oppose these latest Grand Canyon dam proposals. Brower wrote Udall in late June 1963 attempting to open a dialogue about Grand Canyon and expressed concerns environmentalists held about Hayden's CAP bill, the regional plan, and the APA's attempt to build Marble Canyon Dam.

In light of the Glen Canyon debacle, Brower was most worried about the APA's proposal because the FPC was empowered to authorize water projects in unprotected reaches of the canyon without having to obtain congressional approval. But because the APA proposal did not infringe upon the national park or monument, he also realized that there was little he could do to stop it.

Brower, attempting to carve a niche for aesthetic arguments in the existing policymaking process, urged Udall to try to persuade President Kennedy to use the Antiquities Act of 1906 to enlarge Grand Canyon National Monument so that all 277 miles of the canyon from Lee's Ferry downstream to the Grand Wash Cliffs would be under park service protection. Then, with the entire canyon removed from the jurisdiction of the FPC, proponents of water development and conservationists could air their respective views before Congress.

Brower sent Udall a copy of *The Place No One Knew*, with its persuasive pictorial and philosophical arguments. He also cited some quantitative evidence of his own, a 1958 USGS report compiled by hydrologist Luna Leopold that concluded Glen Canyon Dam would be an unnecessary development on the already overallocated Colorado River. Arguing that the American people should have had a chance to publicly debate the fate of Glen Canyon, Brower contended that it was Udall's duty as the chief guardian of the public lands to ensure that the people were not denied this opportunity in the case of Grand Canyon.[31]

Evidently, Brower was unaware that Udall also opposed the APA project, and that the secretary had taken action to suspend the FPC's jurisdiction over the damsites. But Udall brushed aside Brower's other arguments, and the Interior Department moved forward with its plans for a regional development plan. In early July the department released a preliminary draft of what it called "The Lower Colorado River Project," which included a high dam at Bridge Canyon, and in early August the final draft of the project was ready for distribution. Udall stumped the western states trying to gain support for the regional proposal and, in doing so, he incurred the ire of Senator Goldwater who, together with Hayden, had cosponsored the CAP bill introduced in June.

Udall carefully avoided attacking Hayden, but on August 22, 1963, the secretary struck back at his antagonists during a town hall meeting in Los Angeles, calling Goldwater a "bitterender" who sought to "reactivate the competition among western states for water rather than work toward a regional solution." While Goldwater's office declined to comment, Eugene Pulliam, the publisher of the *Arizona Republic*, declared that "Udall's grandiose scheme is . . . nothing except a grab for personal power."[32] Despite this opposition within his own state, on August 26, 1963, Stewart Udall released the regional proposal his departmental task force had framed, one day before the CAP Senate hearings were scheduled to begin. Udall called this massive regional scheme the Pacific Southwest Water Plan (PSWP) and anticipated bringing it before Congress in early 1964.[33]

Udall modeled the PSWP after the Colorado River Storage Project, as Chairman Aspinall suggested in November 1962, but on a much larger scale. In addition to the CAP, it included projects in California, Nevada, Utah, and New Mexico. Recognizing that the Colorado River Compact of 1922 was based on a grossly overestimated flow of 17.5 million acre-feet annually, this scheme called for development in two phases. The construction of these water projects within several western states would commence first, followed by water augmentation of the Colorado Basin from northern California rivers and desalinization plants up to a total of 7.5 million acre-feet per year.[34]

The importation of this much water would require the construction of aqueducts with huge lifting capacities to transport the water over mountain ranges and would need an immense amount of power to drive the pumps and produce enough capital to build the projects. To finance the plan, enormous "cash register dams," solely for the generation of hydroelectric power twenty-four hours a day, were planned for many of the West's great rivers. Consequently, the PSWP included dams at the Bridge and Marble Canyon sites to help pay for the project,

Figure 4.3. Left to right: Arizona Governor Sam Goddard, Representative Morris Udall, Interior Secretary Stewart Udall, and Senator Carl Hayden in December 1964 standing in front of a map of the proposed Pacific Southwest Water Plan. Morris K. Udall Papers, box 735, folder 42, courtesy of University of Arizona Libraries, Special Collections.

which, according to initial estimates, would cost a staggering $4 billion and take thirty years to build.

Phase one alone, including Bridge and Marble Canyon Dams, would cost $1.9 billion. Udall released the proposal to the five governors of the states affected by the plan, as required by the Flood Control Act of 1944, for their comments and suggestions. Although the draft the governors received included a high dam at Bridge Canyon, Udall refrained from endorsing it publicly, stating only that he supported the general concept of regional water development. Consequently Udall was able to obtain favorable publicity for the PSWP from the *New York Times*, even though John Oakes, a Sierra Club member and the paper's editorial page editor, opposed a high Bridge Canyon Dam.[35]

In the summer of 1963, agencies within the Interior Department submitted their respective positions to Udall's PSWP task force, including the

National Park Service, which voiced opposition to the high dam. Preliminary versions of the park service statement also included a strong protest against the MCKC project. Its final statement did not include this opposition, presumably because the draft of the PSWP released publicly on August 26 did not include the MCKC project. But in July Merrill Beal, park naturalist at Grand Canyon, began compiling data for Udall's "crash study" about the detrimental effects that a high Bridge Canyon Dam and the MCKC project would have upon the park, and Wirth reiterated the opposition of his agency toward both projects in August, shortly before Udall released the PSWP to the public.[36]

For Udall, who was seeking to generate every possible kilowatt to fund his massive scheme, the MCKC project must have looked enticing. The bureau estimated in 1961 that the project would be capable of generating 2.53 million kilowatts per year, almost twice the estimated capacity of a high Bridge Canyon Dam.[37] The proposal also promised a massive infusion of funds into the basin development fund that Udall hoped would entice California into supporting the CAP. Although it is impossible to determine with certainty when Udall decided against the MCKC project, evidence suggests that as late as August 1963 the secretary contemplated including it in his regional water plan and discarded it only after considering either the public outcry the proposal would generate or the political impossibility of passing it.

The National Park Service also weighed in at this preliminary phase of the discussion. In response to the growing influence of the conservationists, the APA had applied for a license to build a Bridge Canyon Dam so low that it would not invade the park or monument. Ironically, the park service, despite the environmentalists' recent success in stopping dams planned for Dinosaur National Monument, recommended that the PSWP include a low Bridge Canyon Dam that would invade Grand Canyon National Monument. At no time did the service suggest that the dam be lowered further to keep water out of the monument, and it even reminded Udall that it had acquiesced to the creation of a reservoir in Grand Canyon National Monument years before.[38]

In the mid-1950s Wirth had supported the Echo Park Dams only when the Interior Department approved them as a matter of policy; at all other times he opposed their construction. Although viewed suspiciously by preservationists as being pro-development, especially after he instituted the controversial Mission 66 Program and advocated for the improvement of the Tioga Road in Yosemite National Park, Wirth had been so outspoken in his opposition to encroachments upon national parks and monuments that Hayden had singled him out as someone who needed to "get in line."[39]

Wirth's tenure under Stewart Udall was marked by controversy as the old park service veteran and the young secretary clashed repeatedly over philosophy and policy. By the time Udall ordered the PSWP studies in June, Wirth was on his way out; indeed, he would resign on October 18, four days after undersecretary John Carver delivered a scathing speech at the annual National Park Service Superintendents' Conference in which he compared the "private mystique" of park service philosophy to the "quasi-religious" nature of the "Hitler Youth Movement"![40]

Park service officials faced this latest threat to Grand Canyon at a time of great uncertainty, when both the Interior Department and Carl Hayden promoted various plans for the construction of hydroelectric dams in Grand Canyon. Hayden wielded tremendous power over the service because as chairman of the Senate Appropriations Committee he controlled the flow of funds to the agency. Thus the park service could not actively oppose Hayden on Bridge Canyon Dam without inviting fiscal retribution.

Some service officials at the superintendent and regional director levels opposed invasions of the national monument, but they apparently were unable to convince director Wirth to risk the consequences of combating both Hayden and the interior secretary.[41] Aware of the momentum and political pressure behind proposals to build Bridge Canyon Dam, Wirth focused upon limiting the height of the dam to keep the reservoir confined to the monument. Failing that, he favored shifting the park boundary eastward to the high water line of the proposed reservoir so that it would not intrude into the park, a retreat from Drury's position of more than a decade before.

The Sierra Club and National Parks Association reacted to the PSWP with dismay. Both organizations devoted large sections of the October 1963 issues of their respective publications to the plan, condemning it in the strongest terms. Two articles in National Parks magazine mourned the continuing destruction of the Colorado's canyons and argued that this process could only be arrested by "concerted and determined action." Although evidently its leaders wanted the public to weigh in, the NPA did not suggest or endorse specific action for its members to take. The association confined its efforts to educating the readership of its magazine so that they could "decide for themselves" what to do.[42] By limiting itself to an educational role, the NPA, with attorney Anthony Smith as its president, stayed in compliance with the IRS lobbying regulations affirmed by the Supreme Court in *Harriss*.

The Sierra Club also published articles in the *Sierra Club Bulletin*. In marked contrast to the NPA, the club took a confrontational stance and urged that its twenty-two thousand members write their political representatives. In a blistering essay, Martin Litton attacked the dams by accusing the bureau of manipulating its figures to make the dams appear economically feasible. He also argued that it was ludicrous to partition Grand Canyon into separate pieces. Echoing the arguments Drury advanced thirteen years previously, Litton contended that just because the dams were planned for outside of the national park did not mean that they would not injure the canyon, for how could one flood one part of it without damaging the whole?

Although he acknowledged that the club faced threats on several fronts, Litton pointed out that it did not have the luxury of picking and choosing its battles. Then, in a resounding call to arms to the membership, he outlined the position and tactics that the Sierra Club would take into its fight to save Grand Canyon for the duration of the struggle:

> The men in government who might be induced to oppose the dams and who once did appear resigned to the loss of the canyon. But are we resigned? Shall we fail to go into battle because it is hard to win? . . . Could not 22,000 Sierra Club members, without strain, turn out 22,000 letters a day for a week? . . . There has never been a Congress, a President, a Secretary of the Interior, a governor or a newspaper editor who would not sit up and take notice of that kind of mail. . . . three letters each . . . and more to follow . . . could assure the Canyon's interim survival and rescue the opportunity for reason to prevail.[43]

After Litton's article, the magazine listed the addresses of Interior Secretary Udall, senators, representatives, and the president of the United States. By urging that its members write to their political representatives, the Sierra Club had now clearly crossed over the Rubicon and chosen to engage in "substantial lobbying" activity as defined by the Supreme Court. How long the IRS would remain tolerant of the club's expanded attempts to influence legislation remained to be seen. For the Sierra Club there would be no turning back.

Stewart's Folly?

People who backed Hayden's CAP bill opposed Udall's introduction of the PSWP because they believed that the regional plan would confuse Congress. Hayden set hearings on the bill for August 27–28 and again for October 1–2. However, real progress on the Hayden CAP proposal could not be made until the Interior Department issued a new CAP report, and despite Senator Hayden's urgings, the secretary refused to issue a CAP report separate from the PSWP. As a result, Hayden's bill stalled, and the already high tensions between Udall and members of Arizona's congressional delegation began to reach the breaking point. Although Udall believed his plan was the only way Arizona could prevail in the current political environment, Hayden's allies viewed him as a big-government obstructionist who had betrayed his native state. Without the Interior Department report, CAPA lobbyist and attorney Rich Johnson argued, the "meaningless" Senate hearings were held only because Hayden's "Senatorial friends" [sic] would not deny Arizona's senior senator his desire to hold them.[44]

As though Udall's troubles with Arizona were not enough, officials in California had also begun to question the PSWP. The planned diversion of water from the northern part of the state to the Colorado Basin so angered representatives from that region that Governor Pat Brown told Udall that he could no longer support the PSWP without drastic modifications. Udall gave his undersecretary James Carr, a Californian, the task of rewriting the proposal to California's satisfaction, a move that in turn angered Senator Hayden, who feared even more delays.

But Hayden was engaging in a little gamesmanship of his own. Unbeknownst to Udall, the senator secretly negotiated with Governor Brown and Senator Kuchel, who hinted that they might be willing to compromise on the CAP if the bill was amended to grant California's 4.4 million acre-feet of water priority over all other water interests in the lower Colorado River. But even while Hayden was trying to cut his own deal with California, he learned that the APA had somehow managed to convince the mercurial Goldwater to make public statements supporting a state-funded project, even though Goldwater had just cosponsored Hayden's federal bill, a development California would surely oppose.[45]

With Arizona's water interests at each other's throats in the autumn of 1963, House Interior Committee Chairman Aspinall stepped into the fray. Aspinall was tired of the bickering and he reiterated that he would only approve of a regional water plan for the Southwest modeled on the CRSP. If the various state factions would cooperate with the interior secretary and present the House Interior Committee with such a plan, he assured them it would "receive the earliest possible consideration." Aspinall, acting the part of an old schoolmaster disciplining a class of unruly adolescents, then declared that his committee would refuse to act on any CAP legislation unless unity existed: (1) within Arizona's political delegation; (2) between the seven basin states; and (3) unless all parties supported a regional development. Aspinall's pronouncement shocked Arizona's warring factions back to reality and laid the ground-work for future cooperation among the basin states. Everyone now understood that Aspinall's approval was indispensable to the House passage of any CAP or regional proposal and that the only way they would receive it is if they put aside their differences.[46]

In November 1963, supporters and opponents of dams in Grand Canyon could look back at a year of mixed successes and failures. Environmentalists viewed Hayden's CAP proposals and Udall's PSWP, and the momentum building behind them, with trepidation. Perhaps initially encouraged by Udall's pro-environmental rhetoric, many preservationists now viewed him cynically. They were angry about the loss of Glen Canyon and the threat the rising waters of Lake Powell posed to Rainbow Bridge, and they believed he should have intervened to prevent these tragedies.

As new threats to Grand Canyon emerged, conservation organizations had begun to lay the groundwork for opposition campaigns; the National Parks Association and the Sierra Club both publicized the latest dam proposals, while the Sierra Club had gone a step further and initiated a public letter-writing campaign designed to influence CAP legislation, clearly crossing the line of permissible activity defined by the Supreme Court. Its leadership now believed that only through generating a public outcry large enough to influence policymaking could environmentalists gain the legal protection necessary to defend the National Park System. The club now prepared for its first national campaign since the Echo Park controversy, having made a measured decision to try to sway public opinion despite the known risk of an IRS revocation.

Supporters of the CAP could take encouragement from the landmark Supreme Court decision in *Arizona v. California*, which finally awarded Arizona the water rights it had long claimed. One faction, led by Senator Carl Hayden, believed that the barrier that prevented the passage of the CAP in 1950–1951 had been removed, and they had introduced new CAP legislation in the summer of 1963. Hayden was also exasperated enough with the APA that he had introduced a bill to remove the lower Colorado River from the jurisdiction of the FPC to eliminate this potential obstacle to a federally constructed project. Hayden and his supporters believed that the senior senator could call in enough favors from his colleagues to finally put the CAP within their grasp.

Udall's regional water plan, though it received mixed reviews, promised at least the potential for compromise between Arizona and the other basin states, particularly California. Northern California objected strongly to the idea of using its water to augment the water of the Colorado Basin, but Governor Brown had endorsed the regional proposal as a concept, albeit with some alterations. Remarkably, it now appeared that California's representatives might be induced to support a major Arizona diversion of the Colorado River, a possibility that had never existed before.

Udall could also be heartened by the fact that Aspinall, the cantankerous House Interior Committee chairman, endorsed his regional plan and had sent a clear message to the squabbling factions that they need only cooperate and he would move it forward. In this era of seemingly limitless scientific advancement, the secretary also served a president who was enamored of big technology and who assigned the highest priority to desalinization, a major component of Udall's regional plan.

Although Kennedy did not endorse the PSWP publicly and evidently did not plan to until after he secured California's electoral support in 1964, Udall claimed that the president had given him his tacit approval of the project in the summer of 1963.[47] Udall looked forward to bringing the proposal before Congress in early 1964 and gaining the president's public backing after the election. Major obstacles lay ahead but Udall believed that through further negotiation with the basin states, technological advancements, and the support of the popular young president, that Congress would approve his PSWP and finally resolve the water disputes that had plagued the Colorado River Basin once and for all.

5

"A Fjord-Like Setting"

Stewart Udall's hopes of gaining President Kennedy's support ended with an assassin's bullet on November 22, 1963. On that date, the interior secretary and five other members of JFK's cabinet were flying to Japan to prepare for a presidential visit tentatively scheduled for the following spring. High above the Pacific, Udall learned the dreadful news that Kennedy had been slain in Dallas, Texas. Shocked into stunned silence, the secretary stared out at the ocean, and as the plane banked to the east and headed back to Washington, DC, he hurriedly scribbled down his thoughts and feelings about Kennedy, whom he had served for almost three years, on an Interior Department notepad. Udall also took written measure of Lyndon Baines Johnson, the man who—even as he wrote—was already grasping the reins of presidential power.

To Udall, Kennedy had been a "modern president," blessed with a keen intellect that "could catch up and deal with the most complex problems of the age," a president who had endorsed technological advances such as desalinization and nuclear power, as well as Udall's philosophy of resource conservation. As he fought to understand the day's events, the secretary conjectured that LBJ would fail if he did not carry on "the President's Civil Rights program," unconsciously expressing his own struggle to comprehend the transition of power that had already taken place.

Turning his thoughts to the new chief executive, Udall wrote of Johnson's "ruthless[ness] with people" and numbered among his strengths his "skill as a politician" and "Johnson's roots in rural America."[1] Perhaps even then, Udall was pondering whether Johnson, raised in the Texas hill country and so intimately acquainted with the struggles of farmers trying to scratch out a living out in an arid environment, would embrace the Pacific Southwest Water Plan, designed to aid agricultural interests in the parched Southwest.

Johnson was more than just an ordinary politician; he was, in Udall's estimation, "easily the best Senate leader of the age" because of his ability to move the legislative process and forge coalitions to obtain his objectives. To a great extent, LBJ's political career had been built upon his support of reclamation, first in Texas and later the Far West. Indeed, as a senator Johnson backed the CAP and Bridge Canyon Dam strongly when the Senate debated the proposal in 1950 and 1951, twice voting in favor of the project.

As a result, LBJ forged ties with Arizona politicians such as Carl Hayden and former Senate majority leader Ernest McFarland, soon-to-be justice of the Arizona Supreme Court.[2] Given the new president's relationship with these and other western politicians and his previous endorsement of the CAP, Udall believed LBJ would back his regional scheme. Hayden and others who sought passage of a bare-bones CAP had reason to be optimistic about gaining Johnson's support as well.

But Udall also had reason to worry, for he now served the very man whom he had opposed during the Democratic primary race of 1960. Johnson had not forgotten that Udall worked behind the scenes at the 1960 Democratic convention to deny him the nomination. LBJ also posed a potential threat to the PSWP and CAP because of his own sense of political pragmatism and need for acceptance. According to Johnson biographer Robert Caro, LBJ's latent insecurities drove him to great lengths to gain the affection of people, even as he ascended to the heights of power. Johnson proved adept at attracting support from conservatives and liberals alike, because he would keep his negotiating options open for as long as possible when discussing controversial issues. For example, as a young congressman LBJ gained and maintained favor with President Franklin Roosevelt, while only a few years later he condemned the New Deal during his campaign for the Senate in 1948.[3] The enigmatic Johnson successfully appealed to both sides of the political spectrum during his twelve years in the Senate.

Because he became president as a result of Kennedy's assassination, LBJ looked forward to the 1964 presidential election with even greater anticipation than had Kennedy, because it offered him the chance to be elected on his own terms and to be legitimized by a mandate from the electorate. As badly as Udall and Hayden wanted his support, with eleven months to go until the presidential race Johnson was too politically astute to risk antagonizing a state that controlled an Electoral College voting bloc the size of California's by backing a water project that would benefit Arizona. LBJ viewed California's electoral vote as essential to his own place in history; consequently, though Udall and Hayden would try to gain presidential endorsement for their water projects for the rest of the year, their efforts were in vain.

Udall made his first appeal to President Johnson on November 27, two days after the majestic funeral procession for Kennedy. In a memo to Bill Moyers, a member of Johnson's staff, the secretary emphasized the importance of his regional plan to the Southwest, and he also urged LBJ to authorize a dramatic increase in the saline water conversion program. Udall also recommended that the president read *The Quiet Crisis*, especially the chapter about the resource policies of Theodore and Franklin Roosevelt, to gain "inspiration" and insights into his own philosophy of resource conservation.[4]

As Udall struggled with the transition from Kennedy to Johnson, he also came under increasing fire from Hayden and his allies because the secretary continued to withhold the separate CAP report they needed to pursue their "bare-bones" strategy. However, Udall believed California Governor Pat Brown would view a separate report as a breach of faith as he had gone to great lengths to assure Brown that the project would benefit California. The governor had responded by taking a great political risk by endorsing Udall's regional concept even though the CAP would be built long before any benefits would accrue to California. In turn, Hayden and Arizona Governor Paul Fannin accused Udall of favoring California over Arizona and demanded that he give the Grand Canyon State an "equal opportunity" to put its share of the Colorado River to beneficial use. Attempting to limit the fallout, Udall dispatched Commissioner Floyd Dominy, whom Hayden respected, to Arizona to try to persuade state leaders that a regional plan promised the best solution to the Southwest's water problems.[5]

Dominy spoke to Arizona water leaders in Tucson on December 11. He said he believed Arizona was justified in seeking the CAP in light of its decisive Supreme Court victory, but he emphasized that state leaders consider the overall situation in the Pacific Southwest before pressing forward. Explosive population growth had caused the current water crisis

FIGURE 5.1. Floyd, Dominy, commissioner of the Bureau of Reclamation, in 1966.
Floyd E. Dominy Collection, Box 8A, American Heritage Center, University of Wyoming.

in the region and there simply was not enough water in the Colorado
River to go around. Only through massive imports into the basin from
northern California and the desalinization of seawater through the use
of "mammoth nuclear power plants along the West coast" could future
water supplies be assured.

Dominy also reminded them that House Interior Committee
Chairman Wayne Aspinall wanted the CAP to be part of a regional
plan, and that passage of any bill without Aspinall's endorsement would
be virtually impossible. Any plan acceptable to Aspinall would largely
depend upon creating a development fund from the sale of hydroelectric
power. It would be foolhardy to "partially utilize" the Bridge Canyon
Damsite by building a low dam because a high dam would create this
fund far more quickly. Invoking the imagery of the vanished Hohokam
civilization, the commissioner closed by saying that "additional water
must come to the State [sic] before the faucets in Tucson and other cities

dribble dust." Although he later vehemently denied that he had ever supported augmentation from northern California or the nuclear desalinization of seawater, Dominy publicly advocated for both with great enthusiasm at the end of 1963.[6]

The source of Dominy's additional water, however, had yet to be determined. Northern California's opposition to augmenting the Colorado River with water from its rivers and streams caused Governor Brown to have second thoughts, threatening to unravel the entire regional plan. But if water could not be imported from northern California, then from where would it come? Desalinization, though it appeared promising, still was years away from becoming a reality. The technological breakthroughs needed to make it competitive with other water sources had not yet occurred and, despite the optimism of leading scientists and the interior secretary, there was no guarantee that they ever would.

New Water, New Risks

With northern California water off of the table and desalinization an unrealistic alternative, in December 1963 Udall's staff began to secretly study a diversion from the Pacific Northwest. Assistant Commissioner of Reclamation Bill Palmer specified that the importation should come from the Columbia River, which annually discharged 140 million acre-feet of fresh water into the Pacific Ocean, a "waste" of water equivalent to ten times the flow of the Colorado in an average year.[7] However, even to contemplate this alternative risked incurring the wrath of Washington Senator Henry Jackson, who became the chair of the Senate Committee on Interior and Insular Affairs earlier that year.

Udall did not initially include Jackson on his list of people whose support he deemed indispensable when he first began to think about the PSWP. California, Aspinall, and the conservationists were his three main obstacles, and his regional strategy had gained the support of all but the latter. However, any discussion about taking water from the Columbia River would surely raise the hackles of Jackson. Along with other politicians from the Northwest, Jackson had feared California's designs upon their water since the late 1940s. As chair of the Senate Interior Committee, Jackson's Senate power with respect to water diversions was as great as that of the mighty Hayden; an angry Jackson could stop the PSWP or any other reclamation proposal in its tracks. Still, a Pacific Northwest water diversion seemed to be the only way to keep California on board even at the risk of alienating Jackson. Perhaps, Udall thought, Jackson's support could be bought with economic incentives/assurance for his Pacific Northwest constituents.

Udall sent a revised PSWP to western governors and other interested parties on December 26, 1963. Despite Hayden's "vigorous protests" because it did not include the CAP as a separate project, Udall released it to the press on February 15, 1964. This latest version changed the northern California importation proposal to a "feasibility study," an attempt to delay the portion of the plan most objectionable to the Golden State. The secretary slashed almost a billion dollars in projects from the initial plan, which now had an estimated cost of $3.1 billion. The scheme still included the Coconino Dam on the Little Colorado River, even though it would create a reservoir encroaching upon Wupatkai National Monument. It also still called for the construction of an additional silt-retention dam in the spectacular chasm of the Paria River just downstream from Lee's Ferry. The savings were largely attributable to: (1) a redesign of the Bridge Canyon Dam; and (2) the elimination of desalinization plants, making California's support more dependent than ever upon water augmentation. The plan did not include any provision for the importation of water from a specific source, thereby avoiding Jackson's ire, but the final draft included a potentially explosive issue: In early 1964, after months of indecision and despite the threat posed by the environmentalists, Udall finally committed to a high Bridge Canyon Dam.[8]

National Park Service personnel had done their best to dissuade Udall from choosing the high dam during the months leading up to this decision. John S. McLaughlin, the superintendent of Grand Canyon National Park, blasted the proposed high dam in a December 1963 letter to new park service director, George B. Hartzog Jr. McLaughlin lamented the loss of the unique igneous geological features that would be inundated by Bridge Canyon reservoir, stating, "To cover up a large part of this evidence of the Canyon's fiery past will obscure the primary interpretive story at Grand Canyon National Monument. Such volcanic activity did not occur in the park proper—if it is not preserved at Grand Canyon National Monument, it will not be preserved at all!" A few weeks later, McLaughlin wrote Hartzog again, citing evidence from an article written by Harold Myers, dean of the College of Agriculture at the University of Arizona, who concluded that the PSWP would also be feasible with a low dam.[9]

Hartzog asked Udall whether a high dam would be included in the revised PSWP. The director reminded the secretary that under the reclamation provision in the 1919 act that created Grand Canyon National Park, invasive projects could only be authorized "when consistent with the primary purposes of the park—that is, to not impair the scenic beauty." Hartzog also pointed out that when park service personnel had discussed the Bridge Canyon project during the 1930s with the bureau, they had only agreed to the construction of a low dam that would back water through the monument.[10] Udall did not respond to Hartzog immediately, but Senator Hayden, author of the Grand Canyon National Park Establishment Act, did.

Citing park service literature that endorsed the recreational values a high dam would create, Hayden wrote Hartzog on February 19, 1964, demanding a clarification of his agency's position. The next day several newspapers published articles about the dispute, and soon afterward a chastened McLaughlin issued orders to his staff at Grand Canyon that his and their official response would be "no comment" if reporters asked for an opinion about the PSWP. The final word on the park service's position was given by assistant secretary Carver, who wrote the senator assuring him that the Interior Department favored the high dam. Carver penned, "The National Park Service, having discharged its responsibilities in advising the Secretary [sic] as it saw fit, is now bound to the departmental position approved by the Secretary [sic]. I have every confidence that all of its actions will be in strict conformity with this decision."

This correspondence with Hayden was distributed throughout the park service, eventually finding its way to McLaughlin and his staff. Udall had now adopted the high Bridge Canyon Dam as official policy and the park service director, having made his case, was now obligated to support Udall's decision as a matter of propriety. For the duration of the struggle, the National Park Service would not oppose the high dam publicly, although the disparaging margin notes written on some park service archival documents suggest that it remained a festering wound within the agency.[11]

Leading preservationists, appalled at Director Hartzog's seeming acquiescence to a reservoir in Grand Canyon National Park and Monument, quickly criticized him for not fighting against the dam. Relations between the park service and conservationists, which had been warm during Newton Drury's tenure, had grown tepid during Conrad Wirth's administration (largely because of his pro-development policies such as Mission 66) and degenerated further under Hartzog.

The hostile tone that permeated letters between Hartzog and David Brower suggests that they developed what can only be described as a mutual dislike for one another. Brower, in a 1978 interview, gave this assessment of Hartzog: "He was always a hale and hearty man. He had a powerful handshake. He'd look you in the eye—and forget about wilderness." Hartzog, for his part, also had strong feelings and told me later that "you were just a no good son of a bitch if you didn't agree with everything [Brower] said."[12]

Occasionally profane and a courtly southern gentleman to his core, Hartzog prided himself on his ability to work with people such as Dominy, whom others found difficult. He was the first to admit that he was not the same caliber of preservationist as Drury. However, Drury was not a practical politician, and Director Hartzog believed that dealing with the PSWP required a pragmatic approach. Hartzog appreciated the difficulty of Udall's situation and recognized that the PSWP was going to include either a high or low dam at Bridge Canyon; he opposed the high dam forcefully so long as it appeared prudent but retreated when tact and good sense required it because he did not want to endanger other park service programs by being intransigent.[13]

Udall's desperate attempts to find a politically acceptable solution impaled him on the horns of an impossible dilemma. If he favored the low dam, he would most certainly face opposition from California, and possibly Aspinall who by now had become enamored with the possibility of water importation. If he chose the high dam option, he was likely to be opposed by conservationists still smarting over the Rainbow Bridge and Glen Canyon fiascos, possibly united with Native Americans during a time of increasing public sensitivity to civil rights issues. Director Hartzog felt great empathy for Udall, and he later reflected that it was the "most painful decision that [he] ever witnessed the secretary having to make."[14]

Having to decide upon the high dam as a matter of policy forced Udall to interpret the language in the park's establishment act and decide just what constituted an "interference" with its scenic beauty. Clearly in 1919 Hayden believed that reservoirs and even dams within the park would not violate this provision, and in 1964 the senator still felt the same way. Judging by the congressional and public support of the Hetch Hetchy reservoir, despite John Muir's campaign against it, a significant majority of politicians and the public agreed with his views at that time. But by 1964, public perceptions had changed. Not even the Bureau of

Reclamation proposed to construct dams within the park proper, and its most intrusive proposal—the MCKC project—although scorned by environmentalists and the park service—was actually an attempt to utilize the hydroelectric potential of the river's 950 foot change in elevation within the park boundaries without scarring the park with dams.

The objections of some conservationist organizations to the high dam had only surfaced recently. Many others were still undecided and where they would ultimately stand on the issue was difficult to predict. Boating and fishing enthusiasts, for example, might welcome more desert reservoirs in the canyons of the Colorado River. Even the park service, though it opposed the high dam, recognized in its appendix to the PSWP that it would create new recreational opportunities, including improved fishing and boating in a spectacular "fjord-like setting."[15]

In the spring of 1964, Udall realized he could no longer avoid making a decision, and he believed that an acceptable compromise lay in the vast gulf that existed between what the reclamation provision permitted and what the American public would accept. A narrow reservoir that raised the water level along thirteen miles of the boundary in the most remote section of the park seemed a small price to pay when compared to the benefits that the Pacific Southwest would receive. Ultimately Udall chose the pragmatic route in both the court of public opinion and the political arena, and he believed reasonable people would not view this small intrusion as damaging to the scenic beauty of Grand Canyon National Park.

Politically, Udall was convinced he had to have the support of California and Aspinall if the project was to gain approval from the House, and that this support would overcome the potential opposition of conservationists and Native Americans. The secretary made his decision based upon that political reality. The final version of the Pacific Southwest Water Plan would now include a high Bridge Canyon Dam, and he would throw the weight of his department behind it to ensure the continued backing of California and Aspinall and do whatever it took to overwhelm any opposition that might stand against it.

Cracks in the Conservationists' Front

Conservationists felt betrayed by Udall's decision and intensified their opposition efforts against both dams. Brower believed that it might be possible to attack the PSWP on legal grounds and asked Robert Jasperson of the Conservation Law Society to analyze the reclamation provision of the Grand Canyon National Park Establishment Act in the light of subsequent statutes and cases. The reclamation provision reads, "Whenever consistent with the primary purpose of said park, the Secretary of the Interior is authorized to permit the utilization of areas therein which may be necessary for the development and maintenance of a government reclamation project."

Jasperson based his analysis upon what he believed were the two most vulnerable sections of the provision: (1) how courts had defined "necessary" park invasions for reclamation; and (2) what Congress had meant by "consistent with the primary purposes" of the park. Jasperson found that even though the national park act of 1916 stipulated that the primary purpose of the parks was to leave them "unimpaired for the enjoyment of future generations," it did not appear as though Congress intended to conflate the term "unimpaired" with the term "untouched."[16]

Citing numerous park establishment acts that included similar reclamation provisions and a 1935 opinion rendered by the US attorney general, Jasperson concluded the preservationists' argument—that the amended Federal Power Act of 1921 superseded the reclamation provision—was invalid. Congress conferred "specific authority" upon the secretary of the interior in the act of 1919—authority that was not expressly withdrawn by the 1921 amendment.

Further, he argued, even though one federal court had distinguished between reclamation and hydroelectric projects, the bureau linked revenues from power dams such as those included in the PSWP to irrigation diversions. That policy made an attack upon the high Bridge Canyon Dam, based upon the contention that it was not "necessary for reclamation," highly problematic.[17] If preservationists sued to prevent the construction of the high dam, as a matter of law they would not prevail, Jasperson concluded.

Environmentalists began to confer about other strategies and the possibility of mounting a coordinated anti-dam effort. In addition to the Sierra Club and the National Parks Association, the Western Federation of Outdoor Clubs, comprised of thirty-five thousand members of mostly small western conservation organizations, adopted a resolution against the PSWP at its Labor Day conference in 1963.[18]

Now, at the March 1964 annual meeting of the National Wildlife Federation (NWF), an enormous organization with a total membership of more than two million people, representatives of the Izaak Walton

League (IWL) scheduled a special conclave to discuss the Grand Canyon situation. Leaders from prominent conservation associations attended, and Udall sent Henry Caulfield of the Interior Department's resource planning staff to try to convince these environmentalists how important the high Bridge Canyon Dam was to gaining congressional approval of the PSWP.

After Caulfield's presentation, Brower and Anthony Smith stood up and rebutted his statements, both leaders saying that their organizations would oppose the dams with everything they could bring to the fight. Smith also stated that the NPA had hired an expert in resource management to develop a plan based upon alternative energy sources, demonstrating that coal-fired steam plants and atomic power were viable alternatives. This study, Smith revealed, was scheduled for publication in a forthcoming issue of *National Parks* magazine.[19]

Conservation organizations that favored the Grand Canyon dams also used the National Wildlife Federation conference as a forum to present a pro-dam view. The Arizona Game and Fish Department (AZGF) emphasized the recreational benefits that would result from the PSWP, including the planned construction of fifty small reservoirs in Arizona alone during its latter phases. The state of Arizona financed the Game and Fish Department offensive, which was designed to counter the anti-dam factions at the NWF conference.

The AZGF, supported by two Arizona conservation organizations, the Arizona Game Protective Association and the Arizona Council of Conservationists, sponsored a series of "aerial safaris" over the dam and reservoir sites for conservation leaders, to demonstrate that the high dam would not hurt Grand Canyon National Park and Monument. The flights were so popular that Bureau of Reclamation officials loaned the AZGF their own aircraft to supplement the single plane the AZGF had chartered. AZGF officials believed that emphasizing the recreational aspects of the PSWP was an effective counterargument to the preservationists' opposition that would gain support from fish and wildlife organizations.[20]

The National Wildlife Federation was the largest conservation organization in the world in 1964, and its member societies represented many different conservation viewpoints. Even more encouraging from a pro-dam perspective, the NWF executive director, Thomas L. Kimball, had previously held posts in the state game and fish departments of both

Arizona and Colorado and would probably be sympathetic to arguments based upon increased recreational benefits for hunters and fishers. By targeting the NWF, the AZGF, Interior Department, and other recreational enthusiasts hoped to prevent the National Wildlife Federation from joining with the Sierra Club, Izaak Walton League, and National Parks Association against the Grand Canyon dams as it had during the Echo Park controversy. If successful, this strategy would isolate these smaller anti-dam organizations by portraying them as extremist and show Congress and the public that outspoken preservationists such as Brower and Smith did not speak for all conservationists.

Indeed, the Sierra Club, Izaak Walton League, Wilderness Society, and the National Parks Association combined, only totaled about one hundred and forty thousand members, fifty thousand of whom belonged to the IWL, which itself was an advocate of sportfishing.[21] Thus, the supporters of the PSWP unleashed a potentially devastating counterattack against the anti-dam organizations in the first quarter of 1964. If they could split the conservationists, supporters of the PSWP thought they could appeal to people who loved the outdoors, who believed in balancing development and preservation, and would resent the anti-dam organizations' attempt to appropriate the term "conservationist" for their own exclusive use.

Fudging the Facts and Unexpected Pitfalls

Supporters of the Grand Canyon dams pursued their objectives in the political arena in addition to taking on the preservationists. On April 9, 1964, Udall appeared before Senator Jackson's Interior Committee to present the Interior Department's position during the latest round of CAP hearings on the Hayden-Goldwater bare-bones CAP bill. Udall argued in favor of the regional plan and was subjected to intense questioning by Hayden, who had recently accepted a position as a junior member of the committee in order to promote his own bill.

During the course of the hearings, Hayden gave a little ground and congratulated Udall for proposing the regional approach, although he made it clear that he would insist that the CAP be constructed first. However, the senator also approved the idea of a basin account similar to the PSWP development fund for the first time. This was one of the major sticking points that had kept Udall and Hayden from joining forces after the 1963 Supreme Court decision.[22]

Udall also described his dilemma in having to decide between a high and low Bridge Canyon Dam, and he echoed David Brower's arguments of the previous summer in which Brower urged him to allow Congress to decide the issue. Udall testified that, although he favored the high dam for its revenue potential and believed encroachment upon the park to be "peripheral," ultimately Congress must "balance scenic values against critical water needs." He argued that Congress previously anticipated its construction by inserting the reclamation provision into the national park establishment act, and that the park service personnel, who helped write President Hoover's December 1932 executive order proclaiming Grand Canyon National Monument, had agreed to the construction of either "a high or a low dam" that would, at the very least, create a reservoir in the national monument. To support this contention, Udall cited the letter from Park Service Director Horace Albright to Reclamation Commissioner Elwood Mead in which Albright assented to the construction of the Bridge Canyon Dam in January 1933.[23]

However, the secretary misinterpreted this evidence. If one looks closely at the correspondence, it is clear that Albright and Mead only agreed upon a reservoir that would encroach upon the monument—by definition a low dam. That a low dam would not affect the park was a common understanding among dam supporters and opponents alike since the first CAP debates of the late 1940s, and this meaning was reaffirmed within the language of the interior secretary's PSWP itself.

Although Udall's assertion that the park service agreed to the construction of a high dam could be easily disproved by his own evidence, his statement nevertheless had the potential to sway congressional opinion. Director Albright recognized this in his January 1933 letter when he stated that the secretary's approval of the Bridge Canyon project would carry with it the weight of both the park service and the reclamation bureau. Shortly thereafter, Albright took a definitive position against the high dam in February 1934 when he wrote that the park service did not intend to "interfere with the Reclamation Service's work on the Colorado River *west* of Grand Canyon National Park [emphasis mine]." At no time did he agree to the invasion of the park, and the larger intrusion into the monument, that a high dam would create.[24]

From that point forward, even bureau officials refrained from seeking a dam that would encroach upon the park, a position the agency did not repudiate until it included a high dam in its 1944 CAP report. Despite this document, Udall did not inform the committee that the park service had long opposed a high dam, and a reading of the testimony suggests that Udall invoked the Albright-Mead correspondence to show that the park service approved of the construction of a dam of either height.[25] But no one present challenged Udall's erroneous testimony about the park service position, and the committee simply adjourned after two days of testimony without deciding when it would report the bill to the Senate floor.

The secretary also forwarded the PSWP to the Bureau of the Budget in January 1964. The Budget Bureau completed its financial feasibility analysis by April, and the news was not promising. Budget Director Elmer Staats reported that the Department of the Army objected to the importation studies because the rivers of northern California lay within the purview of the Army Corps of Engineers, which had already obtained congressional authorization to study the potential utilization of these watersheds. Staats was even more concerned about a provision Udall included at the behest of California guaranteeing that the consumer cost of future water imports into the Colorado River *would not exceed the cost of water already available in the river*, and that the difference would be subsidized by the federal government.

Staats was also alarmed that the drafters of the PSWP had not adequately studied alternative proposals to the high Bridge Canyon Dam to avoid conflict with the preservationists. But the most difficult question the Budget Bureau raised was that of necessity. Noting that future lower basin water shortfalls would be caused by the construction of new projects in the upper basin, particularly in Colorado, Staats questioned the PSWP's inclusion of upper basin water projects and the desirability of expanding its irrigated agriculture at a time when the nation produced annual agricultural surpluses of eight to nine percent. Staats recommended that the Interior Department "take the lead" in creating a task force to study the problem.[26]

Staats' pronouncement constituted a bombshell of the highest magnitude for CAP proponents: To question the necessity of Colorado's irrigated agriculture would not only assure the undying enmity of Aspinall, but it would open the CAP to the same criticism. Udall and other western politicians attempted to steer clear of the Budget Bureau's recommendation, and they appealed to President Johnson to help break the bill loose. LBJ adamantly refused to commit himself during this election year despite his long record of supporting reclamation and a personal appeal from his old Senate ally Hayden. Udall later reflected that he believed Johnson viewed the Pacific Southwest water controversy as a nasty, "sticky," and ultimately unsolvable problem and that LBJ, mindful of the potential political fallout, had no intention of getting involved in it.[27]

When the Senate Interior Committee reconvened in the summer of 1964, its members debated three amendments to Hayden's bill that would prove crucial to the next four years of debate over the CAP. Senator Hayden now approved of the secretary's idea of establishing a development account and inserted it into the legislation without opposition. In addition, Hayden and Senator Thomas Kuchel of California had been negotiating behind the scenes about prioritizing the water rights among the lower basin states. Kuchel told Hayden that California would support the CAP but only if its annual 4.4 million acre-foot allotment was given priority over all other rights in the river, a position first advanced in 1961 by the California water strategist, Northcutt Ely.

Hayden balked initially, but the secret negotiations continued. By the summer of 1964 they entered a critical phase, for Hayden now seemed amenable to a California guarantee in some form. Utah Senator Frank Moss proposed an amendment assigning first priority to California's 4.4 million acre-foot allocation for twenty-five years, after which enough water would be imported into the basin to make the priority unnecessary. Hayden and Governor Brown accepted the provision and the committee voted to include the amendment, the only dissent coming from Kuchel who continued to seek the guarantee in perpetuity.[28] This "California guarantee," as it would later be called, would resurface during the months and years of negotiations ahead.

Senator Jackson also inserted an amendment into the bill limiting the water augmentation studies to potential water sources in California, putting all parties on notice about where he stood on the idea of a water diversion from the Pacific Northwest. Even though the Hayden bill and the PSWP did not include mention of the subject of a diversion from the Columbia or Snake Rivers, Jackson suspected that bureau personnel were already studying the idea in secret. At Jackson's prodding, the Senate Interior Committee approved the amendment and on July 31 reported the bill, now called the Lower Colorado River Basin Project Act (LCRBP), favorably to the Senate floor. The first inkling of trouble to come emerged when Governor Brown immediately withdrew his support for the measure in the wake of Jackson's amendment.[29]

Hayden understood that without the support of LBJ, the bill could not run the gauntlet of a Senate floor debate in the brief time remaining before the 1964 elections. So Hayden advised Arizona water leaders to look ahead to 1965 when, he felt, real progress could be made.[30] From Udall's perspective, the 1964 congressional session yielded mixed results. Perhaps most importantly, Udall had convinced Senator Hayden to add some regional elements to his CAP measure, including the vital development fund, creating the possibility of a future alliance. Once again the specter of California opposition had raised its head, and Udall believed he could use it to his advantage to convince Hayden to get behind his regional proposal.

Hayden aside, Udall realized that after a year and a half of negotiations, his attempt to implement a regional water plan had become bogged down in the morass of presidential politics and continued bickering among the various water interests of the lower basin. Despite some encouraging progress, Udall knew Chairman Aspinall's grand accord had not yet materialized. All congressional debate over the CAP and the PSWP would remain at a standstill until Congress reconvened in 1965.

"Informed and Militant"

The National Parks Association published its study of alternatives to the PSWP in April of 1964. Ironically, Stephen Raushenbush, the expert in natural resources management the NPA hired, based his study upon some of the same assumptions that underlay Udall's environmental philosophy, namely, that alternative energy sources such as hydrogen-based nuclear fusion would soon be available, according to many leading scientists. "It [fusion] is expected to separate out the salts and minerals in a flash, producing vast amounts of completely fresh water and energy at the same time, both at very low costs indeed," Raushenbush wrote optimistically.

He also proposed that in the event scientists could not perfect fusion, the fossil fuel resources of the Four Corners region or atomic fission plants should be utilized instead of hydroelectric dams. Analyzing the figures given in the PSWP, Raushenbush argued the proposal was feasible without the Bridge Canyon Dam, that Marble Canyon Dam alone could provide enough pumping power, and that by altering the scale and order of the construction of the projects included within the plan, a development fund could still be created.[31]

Anthony Smith wrote in his introduction to Raushenbush's proposal that Bridge Canyon Dam must be stopped because it would open the way to either the construction of dams in the park itself or the MCKC project. Smith reiterated his argument that the controversy would generate public protests against the dam. However, nowhere did he exhort people to write their congressional representatives or take any action to encourage this reaction. Carefully tiptoeing up to the IRS line of permissible action, Smith emphasized that the NPA existed "strictly for educational and scientific" purposes and that Rauschenbush's alternatives were simply developed to advance those objectives.[32]

By enlisting an expert to pose alternatives to Bridge Canyon Dam, the NPA became the first conservation organization to propose a substitute plan based upon quantifiable data. However, the NPA refused to join the Sierra Club in trying to provoke a public outcry against Bridge Canyon Dam, and it limited its defense of the canyon to what was already under the jurisdiction of the National Park Service. Indeed, Marble Canyon Dam, upstream of the park and monument, would constitute the major source of power generation for the Raushenbush proposal until other sources of electricity could be brought on line.

As other organizations debated strategy, the Sierra Club began to shift its plans to enlist the public in its fight against the Grand Canyon dams into high gear. In February, Brower created a special "Grand Canyon Task Force" to coordinate the Sierra Club's efforts, and he also proposed that the club publish a new exhibit book similar to *The Place No One Knew* to be used in the Grand Canyon campaign. The task force consisted of conservationists such as USGS hydrologist Luna Leopold, who began to secretly share USGS data with Brower and others to use against the bureau.

The book moved forward quickly as well. All during the spring and summer of 1964, writer François Leydet, Sierra Club board member Martin Litton, and others rafted, hiked, and camped in Grand Canyon, taking photos and gathering information for the Sierra Club's latest publication. Meanwhile Brower and his associates prepared to take on the supporters of the dams in what Brower accurately forecast would be the major environmental battle of the sixties, "one requiring that all conservationists keep themselves informed and militant."[33]

In early November the Sierra Club published its Grand Canyon book titled *Time and the River Flowing: Grand Canyon*. Its format was modeled after *The Place No One Knew* and it featured stunning photos of Grand Canyon, including some rare color images taken by famed black-and-white photographer Ansel Adams. In the foreword, Brower argued that with alternative energy sources such as atomic power and fossil fuel available, it was not necessary for the bureau to create reservoirs that would increase salinity through evaporation and decrease the total amount of water available for downstream uses. With these energy sources just over the horizon, he asked, why destroy a significant stretch of the free-flowing Colorado in Grand Canyon? The club intended *Time and the River Flowing* to be a tool to sway public opinion while the issue was still in doubt, rather than a pictorial record of what would be lost as was the case with *The Place No One Knew*.

In addition to the book, Brower's Grand Canyon Task Force also developed traveling photo exhibits and a movie about Grand Canyon, mailed copies of *Time and the River Flowing* to every member of Congress, and dusted off a film called *Two Yosemites* that Howard Zahniser used effectively during the Echo Park campaign almost a decade earlier.[34] *Two Yosemites* offered striking footage of Hetch Hetchy Valley before and after the construction of the dam. It showed how reservoir fluctuations had scarred its granite walls with mineral deposits, a stark pictorial rebuttal of the bureau's claim that a reservoir would enhance the beauty of the canyon.

One member of the Sierra Club Grand Canyon Task Force, Richard Bradley, a physics professor at Colorado College, took on Dominy himself. This tenacious academic hailed from a large family of western river and outdoor enthusiasts who played an important role during the Echo Park controversy. His father, Harold Bradley, who became president of the Sierra Club in the late 1950s, took the family on rafting trips down the Green River and filmed his sons as they shot the rapids. In so doing, Harold Bradley exploded the bureau's myth that river running was a hazardous undertaking and his film helped publicize the sport for the generation of Americans taking to the outdoors in the postwar period.

David Brower credited Harold Bradley with raising his own awareness of the spectacular beauty of Dinosaur's canyons and for convincing members of the Sierra Club that this unique wilderness, though far different from the California mountains and redwoods the club had originally been formed to protect, was worth saving. Richard and his brother David also testified against the Dinosaur dams during the CRSP hearings and they had attacked the bureau on both technical and aesthetic grounds.[35]

Richard Bradley's involvement in the Grand Canyon campaign started innocuously enough when he delivered a lecture in opposition to the PSWP during a campus guest speaker series at Colorado College in early September 1964. In his speech, Bradley told the story of the triumph at Echo Park, the loss of Glen Canyon, and concluded with an overview of his opposition to the dams now proposed for Grand Canyon. He condemned the bureau's Grand Canyon proposal as unnecessary and self-perpetuating. Alternative energy sources, including thermal and nuclear power, would soon be available to generate electricity far more cheaply without destroying more spectacular canyon country with dams. Professor Bradley urged his audience to break this cycle, and he blasted the Interior Department's policy of imposing its will upon its subagencies, declaring that as with Echo Park and Glen Canyon, "once again we find the Park Service pathetically silent, unable to speak in its own defense."[36]

The *Denver Post* picked up the story and soon Bradley received a letter from Dominy himself, in which the commissioner not only countered his arguments but questioned his integrity by accusing Bradley of "hoodwink[ing]" his audience. Dominy's letter also received play in the *Post*, and Bradley became embroiled in an exchange of sharply worded letters with the pugnacious commissioner. Bradley soon received another reply from Dominy that, although it emphasized the necessity of hydropower for peaking purposes, did not refute Bradley's contention that other forms of energy that were currently—or would soon be—available were cheaper to produce. Acting on confidential advice from hydrologist Leopold, Bradley wrote to Representative John Saylor of Pennsylvania, a strong anti-dam conservation advocate, about the possibility of having Congress force the bureau to do cost comparisons between hydroelectric power and other forms of energy.[37]

The Sierra Club printed Bradley's lecture in the December issue of the *Sierra Club Bulletin*. Bradley also wrote an article for the December issue of the Wilderness Society publication *Living Wilderness*, in which he questioned the dams' necessity by quoting a provision within the PSWP itself, which stated that the power produced by Bridge and Marble Canyon Dams would "Provide only a small increment of the projected future demand of the area. . . . The major portion of the future electrical energy demand of the area in the Pacific Southwest will be generated by thermo-electric plants. . . . Reserves of fossil fuels are more than adequate to meet foreseeable power needs."

After citing this language Bradley then questioned why, with the availability of feasible alternative energy sources, would the Interior Department insist upon desecrating an area of such scenic grandeur to produce a relatively small amount of power? The Interior Department's own Office of Science and Technology estimated that within ten years nuclear power plants would be able to produce electricity for about forty percent of the cost of hydropower, while Senator Clinton Anderson of New Mexico argued that coal-fired steam plants in the Four Corners region could produce power for two-thirds, the cost of additional hydropower immediately.

Taking up Litton's challenge from the previous year, Bradley called for an extensive letter-writing campaign of "one million letters to congressmen," stating that only an "aroused public" can save the canyon from destruction.[38] By publishing Bradley's article, the Wilderness Society now joined the Sierra Club in trying to generate a national outcry against the dams and became the second national conservation organization willing to risk its tax-deductible status by challenging the IRS prohibitions against lobbying to influence the legislative process.

Schmoozing Congress

No IRS regulations prohibited legislators themselves from lobbying their peers in Congress, and dam supporters soon launched an all-out effort to do just that. In November, the Arizona congressional delegation and the CAPA held a carefully orchestrated series of "field" hearings and social functions for members of the House Committee on Interior and Insular Affairs. According to Arizona Representative John Rhodes, the sole purpose of these hearings was to "impress the Committee."

No Californians or conservationists were invited to testify; the only adverse witnesses included were water interests from the state of Arizona who felt they had been left out of the plan. Feting the committee at Phoenix's finest restaurants and hotels, the CAPA footed most of the bill so that these congressmen would experience "the full Arizona red-carpet treatment." After a shopping trip for the committee members' wives to the toney suburb of Scottsdale, the hearings' grand finale consisted of an aerial tour of Lake Powell and the Bridge and Marble Canyon Dam sites, followed by a stop in the town of Florence, just south of Phoenix, where members viewed withered fields overgrown with cacti and other desert plants that could no longer be farmed because of groundwater depletion.[39]

As these Arizona water promoters wined and dined the House Interior Committee, the Interior Department, just as it had during the Echo Park controversy, tried to sway public opinion with publications of its own. In late 1964, it printed a pamphlet titled *Bridge and Marble Canyon Dams and Their Relationship to Grand Canyon National Park and Monument*, in which it explained the necessity of damming the Colorado to create reservoirs that would flood half of the canyon, including Lava Falls, its most spectacular whitewater.

In an aside to river running, the pamphlet stated: "Below Kanab Creek, this recreational opportunity would be replaced by the usual reservoir boating type of experience." As for the dams themselves, the pamphlet described the department's position as favoring the regional and national economic opportunities the dams would create over the slight "impact on the scenic grandeur of the Grand Canyon."[40] Dominy, a skilled photographer, was also in the process of creating a publication he hoped would counteract the Sierra Club exhibit books, and he planned to release it in early 1965 just before congressional hearings on the project would begin.

Unbeknownst to Richard Bradley, Anthony Smith, and possibly even Leopold, Interior Secretary Udall charged Assistant Secretary for Water and Power Kenneth Holum with the task of studying comparisons between hydropower and alternative energy and water sources. An April report from the department's science advisor, John C. Calhoun Jr., suggested that the technology for large-scale nuclear desalinization plants had advanced to the point that it might soon be feasible to construct facilities that could produce power and fresh water at rates competitive with water importation and hydroelectric power plants.

Holum created a task force to conduct in-depth studies of desalinization that included Reclamation Commissioner Dominy and personnel from the Atomic Energy Commission. New Budget Bureau Director Kermit Gordon, whose agency had blocked the PSWP over this very issue in April, directed Holum to initiate economic studies to determine whether desalinization might constitute the most economical water source for the Pacific Southwest.[41]

In December, with the preliminary studies complete, Holum wrote Udall and told him that his task force had completed a cost comparison of desalinization and the importation of fifteen million acre-feet of water from the Columbia River—an amount that would double the

Colorado's flow—and his astonishingly optimistic report concluded that desalting sea water was the cheapest way to augment the water supply of the Colorado Basin.

Although Holum's figures reflect the faith that Interior personnel had in technological solutions, optimism that had been reinforced by pronouncements from the scientific community, they also reveal that the Bureau of Reclamation had conducted secret studies of importations from the Columbia River without consulting Senator Jackson. Holum wrote Jackson to assure him that the Interior Department was "plan[ning] no project," to soothe Jackson's fears that the Southwest might try a backdoor move to steal some of his constituents' water. Whether the report had this effect is a matter for debate, but it certainly put Jackson on notice that stronger measures than a mere amendment to the CAP bill would have to be taken if he hoped to stop studies of water augmentation from the Columbia River.[42]

Despite Holum's reassuring letter, strong evidence suggests the bureau's studies of a Pacific Northwest importation were far more than just a hypothetical alternative to desalinization. In early December Secretary Udall flew to Los Angeles for a series of secret meetings to discuss the PSWP with California politicians and water officials in order to bolster California support, which had waned following Senator Jackson's amendment to Senator Hayden's 1964 CAP bill. During a meeting with Governor Brown, California officials belittled Udall's argument that adequate water could be salvaged by phreatophyte control and lining canals with concrete but expressed enthusiasm for a regional plan that provided for the importation of water from outside the Colorado Basin.[43]

Udall also met with representatives of the MWD, as well as Otis Chandler, publisher of the *Los Angeles Times*. Joe Jensen of the MWD argued optimistically that "only the question of accepting a substitute for the twenty-five-year guarantee of 4.4 million acre-feet separates Arizona and California." Knowing that sufficient basin augmentation would render the 4.4 million guarantee relatively meaningless, Udall brought Commissioner Dominy along to reveal a plan that the Bureau of Reclamation had been studying secretly since mid-November—the importation of ten to fifteen million acre-feet of water from the Columbia River, a proposal that would "cost billions of dollars" in Udall's estimation.

California congressman Chet Holifield insisted that California's interest must be protected by the authorization of "the entire project," and that California politicians would only support it if the Pacific Northwest diversion was backed by a feasibility grade study, certified by the interior secretary. Udall reemphasized that this Columbia River water would be made available "at the present price of Colorado River water," the difference to be subsidized by the "first power revenues" generated by Bridge and Marble Canyon Dams. In response to questions about Senator Jackson's probable opposition, Udall replied that he hoped to entice the Washington senator by offering him a "stepped-up reclamation program" to make up for the scheduled closure of several important federal installations in his home state.[44] Udall left California convinced that he was close to working out a compromise to gain California's support—and it appeared that he had, provided he could persuade Senator Jackson to go along.

During 1964 the advocates and opponents of dams in Grand Canyon created and implemented the strategies that they would pursue for the length of the campaign. The preservationists abandoned legal challenges except, perhaps, for rhetorical purposes, and began to focus upon disproving the figures that the bureau was using to justify the project. They also appealed to the public, distributed literature, showed films, and hired experts to suggest alternative means of power generation reliant upon either existing coal deposits or technological solutions that appeared to be imminent. By December 1964, with membership in most conservation organizations growing and public awareness of environmental issues increasing rapidly as a result of the recent passage of the Wilderness Act and the publication of Rachel Carson's *Silent Spring* in 1962, leading preservationists believed that they stood an excellent chance of generating a massive public outcry against the Grand Canyon dams.

People who wanted the dams built could also point to some gains. Although the CAP bill appeared stymied by the Bureau of the Budget and had not received President Johnson's blessing in this election year, Hayden and Udall had joined forces and the senator was now convinced that the best chance for the CAP lay in a scheme that incorporated some elements of Udall's regional solution. This development was sure to please Aspinall who, as chair of the House Interior Committee, had the power to move a bill quickly through that chamber once his committee approved it. Technological answers to many of the Southwest's water problems also appeared to be within reach and Interior Department agencies were working frantically to attain them.

Finally, and perhaps most important of all, California and Arizona appeared to be on the brink of the improbable agreement that Udall had envisioned, raising the possibility that the California roadblock that had stood in the way of the CAP in the House of Representatives for almost two decades might be overcome. With House approval now within reach, and the pro-reclamation LBJ having just won the presidency in his own right by a landslide, the passage of a CAP bill seemed closer than ever at the end of 1964.

Only one obstacle to the Grand Canyon dams remained. Udall's hard-won agreement depended entirely upon the importation of additional water into the Colorado River Basin. The most available source of that water, at least in the short term, was the Columbia River. Now all eyes turned toward the enormous water surplus of the Pacific Northwest and the Senate gatekeeper who had sworn to defend it. Even though Henry Jackson had already objected to the idea of diverting water from the Columbia River, Udall believed he could be convinced to come on board if given new federal incentives that promised economic benefits for the citizens of Washington state. With Jackson out of the way, no congressional opposition would be strong enough to prevent both houses from passing the massive regional plan. With the Columbia River discharging 140 million acre-feet of fresh water every year into the Pacific Ocean, Udall truly believed he could persuade Jackson to give one-tenth of that wasted water to his thirsty neighbors to the south.

6

"A Little Closer to God"

The United States of America was a nation in turmoil by the mid-1960s. Social anxieties, long repressed as a result of Cold War ideology, McCarthy era paranoia, and America's systemic racism, emerged at the forefront of American political and social thought. African Americans attained several milestones in their struggle to realize the full rights of citizenship conferred by the constitutional amendments passed during Reconstruction—rights that had been eroded through the efforts of white supremacists, a complacent populace and its representatives, and a Supreme Court more concerned about preserving the status quo than with upholding constitutional principles inalienable to all individuals.

In the aftermath of the 1954 Supreme Court decision in *Brown v. Board of Education* and inspired by the nonviolent example of Martin Luther King Jr., African Americans reclaimed these rights of citizenship. In August 1963, hundreds of thousands of Americans of all races descended upon the capitol itself, where, on the steps of the Lincoln Memorial, King called upon all Americans to put their hatreds aside and accept one another as human beings untarnished by the artificial barriers of skin color and archaic prejudices. President Kennedy called for a nation where the rights and privileges of citizenship would accrue to people of all colors, and after his death Lyndon Johnson continued JFK's program and pushed for the passage of landmark civil rights legislation in Congress. The issue of civil rights burned brightly in January 1965 and served as a catalyst for other social impulses that would also transform America during the rest of the decade.

The concern over civil rights fueled protests over civil liberties such as freedom of speech and expression. Mario Savio, a student radical who participated in the "Freedom Summer" of 1964, and other young people who marched in local civil rights demonstrations, protested against the University of California's restrictions upon the free speech rights of students in autumn of 1964. The tension smoldered for two months until it finally ignited into a firestorm of mass protest that resulted in a student takeover of the campus administration offices.

The Berkeley police arrested hundreds of students, including Terry Sumner, a close friend of the David Brower family. Partially because of the crackdown on the Berkeley campus, in January 1965 student groups around the country began protesting a wide range of issues related to freedom of speech and expression. Students also began to demonstrate against America's increasing involvement in Vietnam. The student anti-war movement would dominate the rest of the decade and create the gravest divisions within American society since the Civil War.[1]

Citizens against American military involvement in Vietnam would soon have civil liberties concerns of their own, as the government began cracking down on their protests. The antiwar movement would fuel public concerns about First Amendment rights for the rest of the decade and culminate in two landmark Supreme Court holdings. In 1969 the Supreme Court ruled in *Brandenburg v. Ohio* that individuals had First Amendment rights to engage in speech and expression, which, though perhaps repugnant to the majority of Americans, were permissible so long as the speech or conduct did not have a likely chance of inciting lawless behavior. The court also addressed First Amendment rights in *New York Times Co. v. United States* and upheld the right of the *New York Times* to publish excerpts from the Pentagon Papers in 1971.[2]

The Rise of Modern Environmentalism

The modern environmental movement burst into the public consciousness along with these social and cultural transformations. By 1965, important publications such as Stewart Udall's *The Quiet Crisis*, Udall's own public involvement in outdoor activities, the passage of the Wilderness Bill in 1964, and Lady Bird Johnson's Beautification campaign had amplified public awareness of environmental issues. No event generated as much public awareness—or as much controversy—as Rachel Carson's 1962 book *Silent Spring*, in which the soft-spoken marine biologist warned of the hazards of pesticide and herbicide usage, consequences that, because of humanity's position at the top of the food chain, were inescapable.

Carson's book, as well as the unprecedented efforts by the chemical industry, scientific community, and their political allies, to counter her arguments and disparage her individually showed millions of people that environmental issues could affect them personally, and that their government often chose corporate profit over public health. As a result, large numbers of people who didn't care whether dams were built in western canyons became vociferous environmental advocates when contaminated food, water, and air endangered their own health and the health of their loved ones.[3]

Thus as 1965 began, the American public was grappling with issues that it had only recently begun to confront, issues in political, social, legal, and environmental philosophy that would change, perhaps irreversibly, how many people viewed their government, big business, and the costs of America's affluence. Politicians as well as the public looked to science and technology as offering solutions for many of these concerns, and by 1965 people who both favored and opposed dams in Grand Canyon had presented scientific solutions to the American people. The fight to save Grand Canyon reached its climax during this turbulent period.

This latest struggle to keep dams out of Grand Canyon played out in the court of public opinion and within the byzantine process of the American political system. These two arenas, while at times closely related, were also mutually exclusive; a massive public outcry would not necessarily result in changes in policy. A formal process to ensure transparency and review of the environmental consequences of government and corporate projects did not exist . . . at least not yet. The transformative issues of the mid-1960s, the enormous public protests they generated, and the lack of transparency within the political system would all play decisive roles in deciding the outcome of the Grand Canyon dam fight and the lasting impressions it would leave on American society.

Udall conceived of the Pacific Southwest Water Plan (PSWP) as a technological solution to political and environmental constraints. In 1963 Udall introduced it as a radical attempt to break the political deadlock in the House of Representatives, which, he believed, had thwarted Arizona's efforts to construct the Central Arizona Project (CAP) since the late 1940s. Now, a year and a half after the US Supreme Court had adjudicated the water rights of the lower basin, Udall appeared to be on the brink of success.

Despite the battering he had taken in the Arizona press and accusations of favoring California leveled by Arizona Senator Carl Hayden, Arizona Governor Paul Fannin, and other Grand Canyon State water officials, Udall returned to Washington from his trip to Los Angeles in late December 1964 with something that no one else had ever accomplished: a commitment from California's water leaders to support the CAP. Ebullient about the chances of obtaining congressional passage of the regional proposal, and perhaps about his own place in history, Udall, along with Reclamation Commissioner Floyd Dominy, started building public support for the project by telling the American people that the water crisis of the Southwest was on the brink of being solved.

Udall and Dominy began to publicly state that the acquisition of Columbia River water would guarantee that future projects would not create shortages in the lower Colorado River Basin. Udall's staff pleaded with him to stop talking so cavalierly about the Columbia diversion, fearing that it would anger Washington Senator Henry Jackson, who might view these efforts as an attempt to generate so much public support as to present him with a fait accompli. Udall unwisely dismissed these warnings, to his later regret, for when the Senate Interior Committee chairman returned from his holiday break in January 1965, he was very, very annoyed.[4]

Despite Jackson's ire, now that the possibility of water importation from the Pacific Northwest was being openly discussed, the Arizona-California negotiations began to bear fruit when Congress reconvened. On January 6, 1965, Senators Hayden of Arizona and Kuchel of California introduced new CAP bills in the Senate, and a few days later California Representative Craig Hosmer, an outspoken opponent of the CAP since his election to Congress in the early 1950s, introduced a bill identical to Kuchel's in the House.

An amazed Rich Johnson of the Central Arizona Project Association wrote: "The unbelievable had happened. There were California bills before the Congress which proposed authorization of the Central Arizona Project after more than 20 years of uncompromising opposition in the Congress and the Court." Differences remained between the Hayden and Kuchel proposals, most notably Kuchel's insistence that California's 4.4 million acre-feet of water be given priority over Arizona's CAP allocation in perpetuity—the California guarantee. Perhaps fearing Jackson's reaction, neither bill mentioned the Pacific Northwest as a possible source for water importation.[5]

The Hayden and Kuchel bills included aspects of Udall's PSWP, and both bills were regional in concept. Hayden and Kuchel continued to negotiate and on February 1, 1965, Hayden agreed to accept California's priority in perpetuity with one condition—that the bill must first pass in the House of Representatives, a ploy that would force California's congressional delegation to support the CAP, something it had never done before. Kuchel agreed and incorporated the compromise into his bill, which he amended on February 8, 1965. That same day, thirty-five of California's representatives introduced identical bills calling for the construction of a "Lower Colorado River Basin Project (LCRBP)" in the House, clearing the way for the arduous process of congressional debate.[6] Wayne Aspinall's insistence upon cooperation had paid handsome dividends to the water and power interests, and it finally appeared that significant progress could be made. Although it was no longer Udall's plan, the secretary's insistence upon a regional scheme had morphed into a project that gained California's support, an improbable achievement that virtually nobody but Udall thought would ever happen.

Moves, Countermoves, and Bean Counters

While these political maneuvers were occurring, the Interior Department moved to counter the Sierra Club's exhibit format book series with a pictorial effort of its own. In early 1965 it released a slick thirty-four-page publication, photographed and written mostly by Dominy, titled *Lake Powell: Jewel of the Colorado*. Dominy and his associates captured vivid images of the reservoir in its picturesque setting of fiery red and orange sandstone cliffs. These pictures offered compelling evidence—for those willing to be swayed by arguments such as these—that the commissioner and other supporters of new recreation opportunities were right, it *was* possible to improve upon nature, and Lake Powell was a wonderful example. Dominy attempted to mimic the Sierra Club exhibit books by composing brief captions to go with his photos, and these bits of poetry have entered the lore of American environmentalism as some of the most reviled verse ever written:

> To the sea my waters wasted
> While the lands cried out for moisture
> Now man controls me
> Stores me, regulates my flow. . . .

To have a deep blue lake
Where no lake was before
Seems to bring man
A little closer to God.

Dominy's magazine was mostly a celebration of Lake Powell (and himself), but the commissioner turned his thoughts from Glen to Grand Canyon in the last two pages of the magazine. Clearly stating the purpose of Bridge and Marble Canyon Dams, he wrote: "These dams are cash registers. They will ring up sales of electric power produced by Colorado River water." Dominy also advocated the superiority of hydroelectric energy over other potential alternative sources because of its usefulness as peaking power and argued that the dams would have only a miniscule effect upon Grand Canyon National Park and Monument.[7]

Although repugnant to environmentalists, this publication was an effective response to the Sierra Club exhibit books at a time when the Interior Department was starting to receive letters from concerned citizens opposed to the dams. *Lake Powell: Jewel of the Colorado* showed the reservoir for what it was: a paradise for people who loved outdoor recreation, set in the incomparable scenery of Glen Canyon. Millions of Americans, enjoying the prosperity of the early 1960s, engaged in boating, water skiing, and fishing during their spare time, and visitor totals at Lake Powell had increased exponentially since bureau personnel closed the gates of Glen Canyon Dam in the winter of 1963. The magazine promised more of the same recreational opportunities in Grand Canyon.[8] The Interior Department mailed copies of *Lake Powell: Jewel of the Colorado* to all members of Congress and to prominent national newspapers. The Central Arizona Project Association also distributed it in Arizona.

This and other publications, speeches, and congressional testimony helped Dominy and other advocates of the CAP build a narrative in which preservationists, who sought to keep dams out of Grand Canyon were viewed as selfish, elitist people who wanted to lock up the West's most scenic places for themselves. These arguments of elitism would be increasingly trumpeted as the year wore on, bolstered by official park service figures showing that only a few hundred people had ever seen the reach of lower Grand Canyon that Bridge Canyon Reservoir would make accessible. These, the bureau argued, were either wealthy people with the money to pay for expensive rafting trips or a tiny minority of physical specimens blessed with the stamina to hike miles of big country to see the scenic grandeur in this remote area.

In contrast, Glen Canyon Dam had created a recreational paradise enjoyed by millions and a water highway that ordinary Americans could travel to view the wonders of the canyon country of the Colorado Plateau, including Rainbow Bridge. The CAP dams would open up previously inaccessible portions of Grand Canyon to millions more. Those who wanted the dams constructed would aim charges of elitism at preservationists for the remainder of the controversy, forcing environmentalists such as Brower and Richard Bradley to scramble to find effective counterarguments that would also appeal to a mass audience.

Leaders of the Sierra Club and other environmental groups embarked on nationwide speaking tours, booking engagements with local conservation organizations, and chapters of women's clubs and garden clubs. Opponents of the dams also circulated traveling exhibits of canyon photos and distributed *Time and the River Flowing*, which received a glowing review in the *New York Times*. Now that the CAP included the high Bridge Canyon Dam, the preservationists' campaign had frequently begun to receive favorable press coverage in the *Times*, largely through the efforts of its editorial page editor and Sierra Club board member John Oakes.

By the spring of 1965 a handful of nationally circulated magazines also began printing stories about the controversy written from a pro-environmentalist viewpoint. Richard Bradley convinced the editors of *Life* magazine to print one of his anti-dam editorials, and *Fortune* magazine also carried a brief essay about the controversy. The leaders of seven major conservation organizations, including the Wilderness Society, Sierra Club, and Audubon Society, were so pleased by the "fair and factual" nature of the *Fortune* article that they ordered more than ninety thousand reprints and sent them to their members and other interested parties. However, as promising as these developments were, the *Life* and *Fortune* articles were only a page or two in length, not long enough, preservationists believed, to make a case against the dams that would resonate with the public.[9]

With the exceptions of the short *Life* and *Fortune* pieces, and occasional articles in the *New York Times*, the conservationists believed they had not caught the attention of the national media they believed necessary to get the public behind their anti-dam campaign. Richard Bradley, who wrote the article published in *Living Wilderness* earlier in the year, was alarmed that very few people seemed to know that the latest Colorado River dams were going to be built in Grand Canyon. He believed that the leaders of the same pro-dam organizations that wined and dined important congressmen and their wives at Arizona's poshest hotels and trendy restaurants the previous year were intentionally misleading the public by omitting any references to Grand Canyon in their public relations efforts.

Bradley's suspicions appear to have been well founded. Indeed, the Central Arizona Project Association sponsored a symposium at Arizona State University in the summer of 1964 called "Project Rescue" and afterwards distributed a short publication devoted entirely to the CAP. It did not mention Grand Canyon once, even though it included a large map of the affected area. Likewise, none of the bills before the House in the spring of 1965 included the words "Grand Canyon." To Richard Bradley and other opponents of the dams these and other omissions were evidence of "political skullduggery," and they believed they could only counter it with enough national publicity so that the American people would understand what was at stake. To that end, Richard and David Bradley began corresponding with the editors of *Atlantic Monthly*, a magazine with millions of mostly white, well-educated, middle- and upper-class subscribers, about publishing a full-length article about the irreplaceable scenic grandeur this latest bureau scheme would destroy. If successful, this would be the preservationists' first entrée into a constituency many times larger than that which typically made up the membership of conservationist organizations.[10]

In the winter of 1965, the Sierra Club printed another one of Brower's exhortations in the February issue of the *Sierra Club Bulletin*. The article outlined the strategy of the Grand Canyon Task Force, reemphasized the technical and aesthetic arguments against the dams, and concluded with a plea for members to join the campaign to protect Grand Canyon. One person who responded was Alan Carlin, an economist with the RAND Corporation, a southern California think tank, with a PhD in economics from MIT. Carlin informed Brower that he specialized in irrigation project analysis and knew of studies that RAND engineers conducted in 1958 showing that the cost-benefit analysis formula the bureau had used to gain congressional approval of its projects for decades was invalid.

Brower needed this type of expertise to combat the bureau specialists who would testify before the House and Senate Interior Committees, and he asked Carlin for his help. Carlin became the first of three experts holding degrees from MIT on whom the anti-dam advocates would rely to rebut the technical arguments advanced by those in support of the projects. The other two were Laurence Moss, a nuclear engineer, and Jeff Ingram, a mathematician. Together with Carlin, they made up what Brower would later call his "MIT trio."[11]

While environmentalists scrambled to mount their anti-dam campaign, the interior secretary engaged in an ongoing struggle with the Bureau of the Budget. In November 1964 Budget Bureau Director Elmer Staats met with Udall's assistant secretary for water and power, Ken Holum, to discuss Budget's continuing uneasiness about the Pacific Southwest Water Plan, including the high Bridge Canyon Dam. Staats urged the Interior Department to alter its proposal to "protect national park values," but Interior personnel refused. In late spring the Budget Bureau issued its formal report on the Lower Colorado River Basin Project bill now being advanced by representatives from Arizona and California, recommending the deferral of Bridge Canyon Dam for later consideration by a national water commission.

Hayden was reportedly "jubilant" over the recommendation, for even though it removed the greatest source of power production from the proposal, the Budget Bureau had cleared the way for congressional consideration of the rest of the project. Despite opposition from some Arizona water leaders, the "old fox" Hayden, as he was sometimes called in the Phoenix newspapers, had obtained Senate passage of a bill in 1964 placing a moratorium upon construction at the Marble Canyon site, holding it in reserve just in case problems arose with Bridge Canyon Dam. Now the Budget Bureau's action made the venerable Arizona senator look like a prophet, and Arizona newspapers chastised those who had opposed him, especially officials of the Arizona Power Authority. The release of the report also implied, perhaps erroneously, that President Johnson had at least approved of Marble Canyon Dam in principle, support that would be indispensable in the event of congressional passage of the bill. However, the Budget Bureau report also demonstrated that the president wanted to avoid any controversy over Bridge Canyon Dam.[12]

Having gained the backing of the Bureau of the Budget, Arizona's congressional team had reason to be cautiously optimistic in June 1965 about the chances of obtaining passage of the CAP in some form. The interior secretary, who had accepted the Budget Bureau's report, shared this optimism and urged Chairman Aspinall to convene hearings at the earliest possible date. Representative John Rhodes of Arizona reluctantly assented to the deferral of the Bridge Canyon Dam but argued that it should remain in the bill for "strategic reasons," presumably to keep California's support and as a negotiating tool to use against preservationist arguments.

Even Floyd Dominy resigned himself privately to the idea that the Bridge Canyon Dam might have to be reduced in height because of the conservationists' opposition to it. The measure before Congress had been hammered together as a result of trying negotiations between Arizona and California, so Rhodes viewed the deletion of Bridge Canyon Dam as a threat to the entire project. Without Bridge Canyon Dam—the major source of revenue for the basin account—the incentive used to gain California's crucial support would be removed. Consequently, the congressional delegations for both Arizona and California pressed Interior Committee Chairman Aspinall for hearings on the bill as it was originally submitted—with a high Bridge Canyon Dam, defying the Budget Bureau's recommendation. This resulted in a split between the Arizona-California congressmen who wanted the project built with both dams, and Interior Secretary Udall who, though he still favored the high Bridge Canyon Dam personally, assented to the Budget Bureau's deferral recommendation as the official position of the administration.[13]

The Taming of the Bureau and the Genesis of NEPA

The specter of Senator Jackson, the most powerful person in Congress immovably opposed to the high Bridge Canyon Dam, loomed over the preparations for these House Interior Committee hearings. Furious that the Interior Department had begun studying a diversion of Columbia River water without speaking to him about it first, and that Udall and Dominy had brazenly stated publicly that importing water from that river would solve the Southwest's water crisis, Jackson began to think of ways to ensure that they wouldn't take a single drop of water from the Pacific Northwest. Jackson's influence, thought formidable enough to bring reclamation projects to a screeching halt in the Senate, did not extend very far into the lower chamber. The senator feared that Hayden's insistence upon holding hearings in the House first was a shrewd political move calculated to create so much inertia behind the project that it would be politically impossible to stop it.

By its very nature, the congressional approval process in the first half of the twentieth century lacked the transparency that is built into it today. As a result, the bureau had opportunistically developed an uncanny ability to gain approval of its projects with little if any input from people who might oppose them. Udall and Dominy had not felt obligated to inform Jackson of their plans because they were merely following the bureau's time-honored formula. But whether they felt obligated or not, the testy Washington senator was the wrong person to leave out of this process. Now they would pay dearly for trying to steal Columbia River water behind Jackson's back.

Jackson's strategy was designed to preempt the manner in which the bureau had gained congressional approval of water projects for more than half a century. A typical Bureau of Reclamation project went through a three-step process before construction could begin. The first step was for the bureau to make a "reconnaissance" study, a preliminary assessment of whether the proposal should be considered further. The second step was called a "feasibility" study, where bureau experts conducted field assessments and calculated the project's costs versus its benefits.

These feasibility reports were then used as the basis to draft legislation. The final step, where a bill was finally introduced to Congress, was called an "authorization." The timing of these steps is critical; the reconnaissance phase took two years, and feasibility took five more. Seven years or more might pass between the initiation of a reconnaissance study and the beginning of congressional debate over whether to approve a project. But this process, most of which occurred without the knowledge of Congress, only needed the consent of the interior secretary to set it in motion. Once underway, the bureau's well-oiled engineering and publicity apparatus would generate mountains of favorable data and entice local people to get on board with promises of economic and recreational benefits to come. By the time Congress finally had its chance to weigh in, a project often had so much support that it would be folly to try to stop it, especially if one hailed from the West. Jackson realized that the only way to derail the bureau was to figure out a way to keep it from setting this process in motion in the first place.

Jackson surmised that Arizona and California were attempting to surreptitiously gain the backing of the Interior Department for water-importation studies. With action on the CAP legislation now imminent in the House, the suspicious Washington senator made an adroit parliamentary maneuver in June 1965. Now it would be clear to everyone that Udall's strategy to entice Jackson with additional reclamation projects had failed.

Jackson attached a two-sentence amendment to a minor reclamation bill that had already passed the House but was still before the Senate. This proviso required that the bureau obtain *congressional approval* of all future feasibility studies of water projects before they could begin. Dominy understood the ramifications of what Jackson was trying to do and enlisted the aid of the National Reclamation Association and Interior Department officials in an unsuccessful attempt to stop it. Despite this pressure, President Johnson signed the altered bill into law, leaving Dominy fuming and uncharacteristically speechless.[14]

Jackson had tamed the bureau, and yet few people outside of Dominy's inner circle at the time noticed his maneuver and fewer still understood its implications. Before the enactment of Jackson's provision, the bureau only needed to gain the routine approval of the interior secretary to initiate feasibility studies of any water diversion. Now supporters of the CAP would have to obtain the assent of the entire Congress to even begin a study. With two lines of text and the stroke of a pen, Jackson upended the bureau's long-established tradition of circumventing Congress to obtain the higher-level reports it had used for five decades to gain approval of its projects. Now anything beyond the initial planning would be subjected to congressional debate and public scrutiny.

After blocking the bureau's plan to take water from the Columbia River, Jackson continued to ponder the necessity of drafting a policy that required systemic analysis, public input, a discussion of feasible alternatives, and comprehensive environmental studies of all government construction. He eventually tasked his legal advisors with the mission of drafting a bill to that effect, and on January 1, 1970, President Nixon would sign that revolutionary legislation into law. Jackson's two-sentence rider, born out of frustrations that ended fifty years of bureau manipulation of the system, was the point of origin for the National Environmental Policy Act (NEPA).[15]

Jackson's maneuver also created yet another unsolvable dilemma for Udall. California's support—the primary reason Udall had conceived of a regional plan—was entirely predicated on the bill containing feasibility studies of a Columbia River diversion. So long as Jackson opposed that diversion, no bill would see the light of day; Jackson would simply bottle it up in the Senate Interior Committee, and it would never come to the floor for a vote.

But representatives from the seven Colorado River Basin states plunged doggedly ahead, despite the Jackson roadblock awaiting them in the Senate. House Interior Committee Chairman Aspinall was known as a stickler for refusing to call hearings on legislation that he knew would meet significant opposition in the upper chamber. He understood that Jackson's opposition would probably doom the bill. Yet enamored by 140 million acre-feet of "wasted" Columbia River water, he broke with his own long-standing legislative protocol and scheduled the hearings anyway.

Aspinall's unrelenting pursuit of a Columbia River diversion can be explained because he feared the completion of the CAP would create a water deficit in the upper Colorado River Basin. That the river was over-allocated was wellknown by 1965. Aspinall and other representatives from the upper basin states realized that if the CAP were built, it would bring the lower basin's total use close to its allotted 7.5 million-acre feet as stipulated by the 1922 Colorado River Compact. Since the compact supposedly divided the annual flow equally between the basins, if the lower basin used its entire amount first, it would create shortfalls upstream as a matter of mathematical certainty. Consequently, Aspinall, who hailed from the upper basin state of Colorado, believed the importation of water into the lower Colorado River Basin from an outside source was the only way to ensure that the upper basin, including his home state, would receive its full amount.[16]

1965: Drama in the House

In early August, Chairman Aspinall acquired a sudden case of cold feet and delayed the initiation of hearings in the House Interior Committee. Aspinall hired an engineering firm to analyze the effect that the CAP would have upon the water supply of the upper basin and, to his dismay, these experts confirmed his suspicions that the CAP would create water deficits upstream. Representatives John Rhodes and Morris Udall pointed to Bureau of Reclamation studies that concluded just the opposite—that water available for upper basin usage would increase as lower basin reservoirs filled—but the chairman, concerned with his constituents' future water supply, balked.

FIGURE 6.1. Floyd Dominy's photo of Marble Canyon, with the proposed Marble Canyon Dam and Reservoir superimposed. Floyd E. Dominy Collection, Box 8A, American Heritage Center, University of Wyoming.

Water strategist Northcutt Ely, long viewed with suspicion by Arizona water leaders because of his lengthy role in delaying the CAP, suggested a compromise meeting in August 1965. Representatives of the seven Colorado Basin states met and, at Ely's urging, agreed to seek a water-importation feasibility study as a part of any lower basin project, hoping they could bring so much political pressure to bear upon Jackson that he would be forced to go along. After the seven states reached this accord, Aspinall finally agreed to schedule hearings before the House Subcommittee on Irrigation and Reclamation the last week of August—the first formal House hearings on the CAP since 1951.[17]

Supporters of the dams proposed for Grand Canyon came to these hearings armed with studies of how the project would allow the states of the lower basin to continue the economic growth they had enjoyed since the end of World War II. Dominy prepared numerous charts and graphs demonstrating how the project would sustain the agricultural economy of Arizona, and he emphasized that the project would not bring any new land into cultivation. Dominy argued further that the proposal would create great opportunities for recreation and new habitat for fish and wildlife.

Then, as all present gasped in astonishment, Dominy revealed that he had personally photographed the entire length of Grand Canyon from Lee's Ferry to Lake Mead from a helicopter. The commissioner produced two sets of prints, the originals and, opposite them, duplicates onto which he had airbrushed the proposed dams and reservoirs to demonstrate that they would have no detrimental impact upon the canyon. Now, Dominy believed, every member of the committee could see just how little the effect of raising the water level a few hundred feet in a canyon a mile deep would actually have.

As if these photographs were not convincing enough, the commissioner had ordered his personnel to build a scale model of the entire Grand Canyon twenty-five feet long and thirteen feet wide that included removable plastic inlays of the proposed dams and reservoirs. Dominy "plugged the hall" just outside the hearing room with this model so that congressmen and witnesses alike could see that the dams would be located outside of the national park and monument and that the impact of the dams and reservoirs upon the canyon would be extremely small.[18]

Now that the prospect of the Columbia River diversion was out in the open, it quickly became one of the most hotly debated topics before the subcommittee. Jackson's congressional ally, Washington Representative Thomas Foley, grilled Interior Secretary Udall about the Columbia River diversion and he became so exasperated with the secretary's evasiveness that he asked Udall the same question three times hoping to get a straight answer. Udall ducked the inquiries as best he could and though he finally admitted to seeking a feasibility study, he said that it was only so that other augmentation options could be compared with a Columbia diversion in terms of cost.

Foley then asked the secretary whether the CAP was feasible without the importation of water and Udall answered that it was, to the surprise of Commissioner Dominy, who had just testified that without water augmentation, the CAP by itself would merely delay the inevitable destruction of Arizona's agricultural economy. Leaping into the fray, Representatives Craig Hosmer of California and Morris Udall of Arizona headed off this damaging line of questioning by taking the proceedings to a higher moral plane. For a single state such as Washington to hoard its plentiful water resources was not only selfish, they contended, it also contradicted President Johnson's directive to Congress to assist him in building a "Great Society" for the entire nation.[19]

The preservationists showed up in force. Twenty-five witnesses representing environmental organizations, including the Sierra Club, Wilderness Society, Izaak Walton League, National Parks Association, and Audubon Society, testified before the subcommittee. However, a surprise awaited them when they arrived in Washington. Chairman Aspinall had scheduled two days of opposition testimony commencing on Monday, August 30, but when the morning session began, Aspinall manipulated the schedule and called former Arizona senator Barry Goldwater to testify instead. Goldwater's strong argument in favor of the dams stole much of the press coverage, and many of the reporters hurriedly left the room after Goldwater finished. Some annoyed conservationists reflected that this appeared to be a prearranged attempt on the part of the pro-dam forces to steal their publicity.[20] Indeed, it appears to have been exactly that.

When the preservationists finally took the stand, most of them stressed that they understood Arizona's need for water and that their objections lay not with the concept of the CAP, just with the method proposed to generate power for it. Why, argued Charles Callison of the Audubon Society, was it necessary to desecrate Grand Canyon with hydroelectric dams and power plants when thermal plants, using the plentiful fossil fuel available in the Four Corners region, could generate the power at an even lower cost? Why, protested Anthony Wayne Smith of the National Parks Association, scar one of the world's great natural wonders with dams and reservoirs when the Interior Department's own Office of Science and Technology predicted that atomic power would soon sell for less than hydropower. Smith also invoked the president's rhetoric against the committee members who had advanced it, arguing that a "truly Great Society," would preserve the entire stretch of the Grand Canyon from Glen Canyon Dam to Lake Mead.[21]

Although Brower made impassioned arguments, many conservationists and CAP supporters agreed that Smith of the NPA was the most formidable anti-dam witness as he presented the Raushenbush proposal as an alternative and rebutted unrelenting objections from Representative Hosmer. Preservationists also introduced an economic analysis of the project conducted by Alan Carlin of the RAND Corporation, in which he demolished the Bureau of Reclamation's economic justification for Marble Canyon Dam by using projections of the future cost of nuclear energy as an alternative power source.[22]

Many other conservationists testified, including Madelyn Leopold, the seventeen-year-old daughter of USGS hydrologist Luna Leopold and granddaughter of naturalist Aldo Leopold. A moment of levity occurred when Morris Udall was questioning Bruce Knight of the Wasatch Mountain Club. Frustrated after hearing Knight repeat the now-familiar refrain that nuclear energy would soon replace hydroelectric power, Udall broke the first rule of trial practice by asking a question to which he did not know the answer. Hoping to embarrass Knight by revealing his lack of expertise, the congressman asked him several leading questions before setting him up for the coup de grâce. What credentials, Udall wondered aloud, did the witness have that would qualify him to speak on the promise of nuclear power? Knight replied, "I am a nuclear physicist." "That," a furiously backpedaling Udall exclaimed, "is all I have."[23]

However, Morris Udall was far more effective when he attacked the Sierra Club's book *Time and the River Flowing*, which, Brower had testified, represented a photographic record of what the dams actually threatened. Udall gave a detailed analysis of the book and accused the Sierra Club of misrepresenting the effect that Bridge and Marble Canyon Dams would have upon Grand Canyon. Critiquing the book photograph by photograph, Udall concluded that of the seventy-nine pictures of Grand Canyon presented, only twelve showed scenes that would be inundated by the proposed reservoirs, while another ten were of scenes that "would be altered to some degree." Furthermore, six of *these* pictures were of areas that would be affected by Marble Canyon Dam, which, Udall argued, was "completely outside Grand Canyon," meaning, of course, Grand Canyon

National Park. Forty-five of the photos were of rock formations, flora, and fauna far removed from the areas that would be flooded. Morris Udall, like Dominy before him, showed the committee overlays of the twelve photos of areas that would be affected, in order to demonstrate just how minimal the intrusion into the canyon would be.[24]

Brower pointed out that the book intended to present the canyon as a complete "geological entity" that could not be divided into separate parts. To deface one part with a dam and reservoir, he contended, would injure the canyon in its entirety. Echoing Newton Drury's arguments from the 1940s, he explained that the river, though altered by Glen Canyon Dam to some degree, still flowed and constituted the single most important element of Grand Canyon. To replace the free-flowing river with slack-water reservoirs would effectively ruin the major interpretive aspect that people came to see, a living river still in the process of creating the greatest geological spectacle in the world.[25]

Several of the committee members, along with Commissioner Dominy, accused the preservationists, and the Sierra Club in particular, of elitism. Calling the club's position "the height of exclusion," Hosmer said angrily that he could not understand why Congress should heed the wishes of a few people who did not "have sense to stay out of the river" and keep out the "vast majority of the American people," including his own family, who would enjoy a boating experience in Grand Canyon. Morris Udall agreed, lamenting that only nine hundred people had braved the rapids of the Colorado in all of recorded history. Udall asked the rhetorical question, "How many cabdrivers, carpenters, and bricklayers, and ordinary God-fearing taxpaying citizens are members of the Sierra Club?"[26] Pounding on the theme of elitism again and again, pro-dam members of the subcommittee contended the Bridge and Marble Canyon Dams would create new recreational opportunities for all Americans as opposed to a wealthy, hardy few.

CAP advocates also arranged for George Rocha, chief and chairman of the Hualapai Nation, to testify in favor of the dams along with Hualapai counsel Royal Marks. The Hualapai had negotiated a lucrative contract with the state of Arizona in 1960 when the APA was exploring the possibility of building Bridge Canyon Dam as a state project. Rocha argued that although his people favored the construction of the dam because of the economic benefits that would accrue to them, the present CAP proposals contained no provision for compensating the Hualapai for the 20,132 acres of reservation land the project would require. Rocha testified that the federal government should at least offer what the APA agreed to pay in 1960.

Additionally, he revealed that the Hualapai would demand money up front to avoid problems like those encountered by the Sioux and Seneca Nations when Congress refused to award them compensation after approving dams that flooded parts of their reservations. Rocha and Marks each testified that the Hualapai Nation would seek a license from the Federal Power Commission to build the dam in the event that Congress upheld the Budget Bureau's deferral of that project, and they insisted that the dam be renamed "Hualapai Dam" no matter who constructed it. If the Hualapai Nation developed the site, Marks argued, it proposed to build a low dam in accordance with existing FPC guidelines that forbade dams that would cause intrusions into parks and monuments.[27]

Takeaways

The hearings before the House Subcommittee on Irrigation and Reclamation ended on September 1, 1965. Both sides defended their positions well, and they each spent the next few weeks assessing the strengths and weaknesses of their own arguments as well as those of their opponents. Rhodes and Morris Udall, though clearly impressed by the expert testimony the environmentalists presented, had rebutted these witnesses effectively. They seemed more troubled by signs that the agreement between the seven states of the Colorado River Basin might be unraveling. While Arizona and California maintained a tenuous truce after the hearings ended, representatives from the upper basin states began voicing their concerns about the unlikely prospects of gaining the approval of their counterparts from the Pacific Northwest for the study of importation from the Columbia River. Aspinall, however, was satisfied because now all the respective positions of the basin states and the preservationists were out in the open. Aspinall announced that he intended to push for passage of the project in the spring of 1966, provided that the seven-state agreement held for a few more months.[28]

CAP supporters developed two arguments during the 1965 House subcommittee hearings they would use to great effect during future confrontations with the environmentalists opposed to the Grand Canyon dams. First, they portrayed the preservationists as selfish people who wanted to keep the lower reaches of Grand Canyon all to themselves, an argument with the potential for considerable mass appeal. Second, the preservationists' attempt to influence the legislative process—and its potential tax consequences—had been raised. Representative Hosmer queried Callison of the Audubon Society about his association's lobbying activities and asked him specifically whether the society had attempted to generate a national letter-writing campaign in violation of the 1946 Lobbying Act. Callison denied the charge.

Morris Udall also questioned Brower about the purpose of *Time and the River Flowing* and claimed that it was intended to influence legislation. Brower replied that the book was intended to be used as an educational tool, and that it was the constitutional right of the Sierra Club to petition Congress. Thus, by early September 1965 conservationists were now aware that political supporters of the CAP were questioning their opposition tactics in light of the provisions of the Lobbying Act of 1946, looking for possible violations of the IRS code.[29]

The hearings also revealed a potentially ruinous oversight on the part of CAP advocates, for they had completely ignored the American Indian people who might be affected by the project. Chief Rocha testified that the federal government had not included the Hualapai Nation in their plans even though the construction of Bridge Canyon Dam would involve taking more than twenty thousand acres of his people's land. In 1965 public sensitivity to issues of race relations was particularly high as a result of the civil rights movement; to have the chief of the Hualapai tribe testify during a public hearing that Congress and the Interior Department had virtually ignored the rights of the Native Americans the project was most likely to affect was a potentially devastating development.

A related issue that concerned CAP advocates was that Hualapai attorney Marks had also outlined a compromise position that might appeal to the many conservationists who had not accepted the Sierra Club's stand against all development within the canyon. If the federal project failed to pass and the Hualapai Nation built a low dam on its own, Grand Canyon National Park and Monument would be completely out of danger.[30]

Blindsided by this unexpected development, Morris Udall, Rhodes, and other CAP advocates immediately tried to minimize the damage. Udall was angry at Marks, who, Udall believed, had "bragged" to the committee that the Hualapai could construct the dam on their own. But the crafty Udall also saw in the Hualapai testimony a potential weapon that might save the high Bridge Canyon Dam and the political alliance between Arizona and California that depended upon it. Udall believed the Native American position could be used to gain a public windfall for the CAP at the very least, and it might even be possible to paint the Sierra Club and possibly even Jackson as racist at the height of the civil rights movement.[31]

Those opposed to the Grand Canyon dams had also learned some lessons from the hearings in autumn of 1965. First and perhaps most frustrating, the letter-writing campaigns begun by several of the conservation organizations had already succeeded in generating a great deal of mail to Congress and the Interior Department. But the jury was still out with respect to its impact, and the preliminary signs were troubling. It looked as though the Interior Committee members thought the letter writers were the victims of a misinformation campaign conducted by the environmentalists. These politicians believed an informed public would agree that the preservation of more than one hundred miles of free-flowing river in Grand Canyon National Park and Monument, combined with the two reservoirs and their recreation potential, was a reasonable compromise. The Interior Committee kept track of the volume of mail but only considered it as an "imponderable."[32]

Some environmentalists were openly frustrated that the policy-making process seemed to promote development at the expense of wilderness. Richard Lamm of the Colorado Open Space Coordinating Council (COSCC), a Sierra Club member and future governor, met with the Colorado congressional delegation, including Aspinall, and came away convinced that the issue was much more complex and the process far more difficult to influence than he and other preservationists initially realized. Although the preservation of the canyon and upholding the integrity of the National Park System were of paramount importance to conservationists, Lamm observed that these considerations were only a secondary concern to politicians, a "flea on the elephant," to members of the Interior Committee.[33]

Instead, most of the political players from the western states were concerned with the "Gordian Knot" of political intrigue that surrounded the legislation. Arizona, they argued was now in a strong bargaining position because of its influence in the House and Senate, and western politicians who opposed the CAP risked having the formidable Hayden use his influence to block their own reclamation projects. Most alarming to

Lamm, however, was that politicians considered reclamation to be such a time-honored political formula for power development that it appeared as though the bureau's cost-benefit justification of its projects was virtually unassailable because it created the illusion that hydroelectric projects were not a direct federal subsidy.[34]

The environmentalists' experts had demonstrated that thermal steam plants could generate power cheaper than hydroelectric dams, but western politicians believed that federally owned steam plants would be viewed as "creeping socialism," even though many hydroelectric power projects that had spurred development and economic growth were also federally funded. Lamm succinctly outlined the situation conservationists hoping to preserve Grand Canyon faced: "Despite the fact that there are more economic, more practical solutions, they are not enough at this point to overcome the tendency to allow these matters to flow in the accepted orthodox political channels."[35]

Lamm also observed that many of the major political players in this drama were willing to dismiss the environmentalists' major argument—that the construction of dams in Grand Canyon would create a precedent that would endanger the rest of the National Park System—in favor of political pragmatism, and he communicated these concerns to Brower and other preservationist leaders.[36]

Preservationists also confronted accusations by Morris Udall, Dominy, and others that they were deliberately trying to mislead the American people into believing that the dams would flood out a substantial portion of Grand Canyon National Park and create a lake that people could see from the popular tourist overlooks on the South Rim. In his analysis of *Time and the River Flowing*, Morris Udall charged that the club intended for the reader to infer that all of the scenes displayed in the book would be inundated, a charge that Brower vehemently denied.[37]

But in fending off these charges of misrepresentation, preservationists failed to see that the dam supporters themselves were guilty of misleading the Interior Committee as well as the public. During the hearings, Mo Udall and Dominy referred to the Albright-Mead correspondence of 1933 and used it to assert that the park service had agreed to a high Bridge Canyon Dam years before.[38] Albright's communications with Mead clearly show that he only agreed to a low dam that would back water through the monument.

However, the misuse of the Albright correspondence did not escape the notice of Park Service Director George Hartzog, who had voiced his concern about Dominy's misuse of this exchange of letters since 1964. Hartzog asked his subordinates to confirm Dominy's misrepresentation of the park service position during the 1965 hearings, but no evidence exists to suggest that he took action to stop it. Hartzog also refused to allow park service personnel to speak out against Bridge Canyon Dam, despite Interior Secretary Udall's acceptance of the Budget Bureau's recommendation that it be deferred. Although Conrad Wirth voiced his opposition to the Dinosaur dams when he was park service director, without apparent consequences, Hartzog took disciplinary action against a park service employee who was caught handing out literature opposing Bridge Canyon Dam in October 1965.[39] Hartzog's actions further alienated him from conservation organizations whose leaders felt that service employees should be free to express their opposition should they feel so inclined.

Looking Ahead

Slowly, as a result of the efforts of many concerned individuals and environmental groups, the preservationists' campaign began to pick up steam after the 1965 hearings. Although leaders from the major organizations carried on the most publicized aspects of the effort, such as testifying before Congress and producing literature for distribution, ordinary members of these societies also began to take action at the grassroots level. Concerned citizens and influential environmentalists had been writing letters to Congress since Stewart Udall first proposed the Pacific Southwest Water Plan in August 1963. After the spring hearings ended, the volume of letters began to increase noticeably during the summer of 1965.[40]

Many of these letters came from professionals such as businesspeople, college professors, doctors, and lawyers. Many of them wrote the Sierra Club and asked what they could do to help, and/or explained what they had already done. For example, Frank Griffin, an insurance consultant from Chicago, wrote Brower offering to help pay for the distribution of *Time and the River Flowing* to all members of Congress. He also informed Brower that he and his wife sent letters to all one hundred senators, and he asked for reprints of articles from the *Sierra Club Bulletin* to distribute to friends and neighbors.[41] Many such letters can be found in the Sierra Club files.

An examination of this correspondence reveals that although the rank and file of the Sierra Club and other environmental societies responded to Brower's pleas for support, the letter-writing campaign had not created much of a response from people who were not members of these organizations. Few letters arrived without their author claiming an affiliation with an environmental group. Although some conservationists looked to the Sierra Club to provide leadership, others believed that the creation of a national "save the Grand Canyon" organization would be a better way to coordinate the effort. When asked about this possibility, Brower responded that he believed all the conservation organizations needed to do was to continue their present efforts and communicate with each other more closely.[42]

By now Brower was immersed in speaking engagements and only rarely appeared at Sierra Club headquarters. The club hired two full-time staff members to keep up with his schedule and answer his mail. Brower believed that the Sierra Club's decisions to form its own "Grand Canyon Task Force" and risk its tax-deductible status to generate public awareness were enough and that another organization was not necessary.[43] If it was possible to stop the Grand Canyon dams, it would be an angry tide of public protest, rather than a bureaucracy created by environmentalists, that would do it.

Indeed, some people interested in participating in the fight to save Grand Canyon began to create organizations of their own. One good example of this type of grassroots activity was the COSCC, a group begun by Eugene and Ruth Weiner of Denver. Starting with a nucleus of fifty people in March 1965, including Lamm and professors Richard and William Bradley, this organization was created solely to oppose the Grand Canyon dams. By September 1965 the group had increased to about two hundred members, distributed eight thousand "fact sheets," dispensed countless bumper stickers and buttons, and contacted 350 conservation organizations. By December the group had scheduled public debates between CAP supporters and prominent preservationists and booked the Sierra Club's Glen Canyon movie for screenings all over the state of Colorado.[44]

In addition to his activities with the COSCC, Richard Bradley continued his own efforts to combat the Grand Canyon dams. He kept trying to convince the editors of Atlantic Monthly to publish an article from the preservationist perspective during the last half of 1965, and he attempted to enlist distinguished environmental author Wallace Stegner in the fight. But Stegner begged off, citing his demanding teaching and research responsibilities at Stanford University.[45]

Devereux Butcher, former executive secretary of the National Parks Association and a longtime conservationist, persuaded John Vosburgh, the editor of *Audubon* magazine, to ask Bradley whether he would be willing to write an article for a forthcoming issue. Vosburgh made clear to Bradley that he was free to write a no-holds-barred excoriation of the proposed Grand Canyon dams. "We are interested in a hard-hitting piece exposing the bold and thoughtless plan which would ruin much of the Grand Canyon if the Marble Gorge and Bridge Canyon Dams should be constructed," Vosburgh wrote. "Much of the public is unaware of this scheme of the Bureau of Reclamation."[46] Although *Audubon* was not a magazine with the national circulation for which Bradley had hoped, he drafted an article that Vosburgh scheduled for publication in the early spring of 1966. More importantly, this signaled that the Audubon Society, one of the oldest and most respected conservation organizations in the United States, had embraced the new style of activist environmentalism that was rapidly emerging in the mid-1960s.

Grand Canyon dam supporters also intensified their publicity efforts after the 1965 hearings, and in September representatives from the Central Arizona Project Association, the Metropolitan Water District of Southern California, and several large lobbying groups, including the American Public Power Association, met in Washington, DC, to discuss strategy. They quickly reached a consensus that the next few months would prove decisive in the struggle for the Lower Colorado River Basin Project and formed a committee based in Washington, DC, to lead the effort. These officials agreed that the primary purpose of creating this centralized strategy was to combat the "preservationists' opposition" to the Grand Canyon dams. CAP supporters drew up a comprehensive plan of attack, and delegates were tasked with contacting the national media, influential industrial lobbyists, and key members of Congress. Literature counteracting the preservationists' arguments was also proposed, and a special emphasis was to be placed upon developing "favorable relationships" with the states of the Pacific Northwest.[47]

Morris Udall was optimistic following the hearings and looked forward to their resumption in 1966. Udall believed that negotiations with Jackson and Foley would eventually bear fruit because, in his opinion, these politicians had been "shamed" into admitting that they wanted to hang on to their surplus water even while the Southwest was running out of it. Meanwhile, Dominy and Stewart Udall stumped the American

West, trying to gin up additional public support. The bureau also produced a film titled *Power for the Nation,* narrated by actor Frederic March and accompanied by music from the US Air Force Band, that emphasized the economic and recreational benefits of hydroelectric dams. Anthony Wayne Smith criticized the bureau and the Interior Department for using public funds to generate this propaganda, and he wrote the board of trustees of the National Parks Association and asked them to create a strategy to combat it.[48]

By the winter of 1965, conservation leaders such as Smith, Bradley, and Brower realized that the pro-dam advertising must be countered in the mass media to generate the public outrage they believed would get Congress's attention. Using the national media constituted the third incarnation of the evolving strategy they had pursued since the latest fight to save Grand Canyon began in 1963. When Stewart Udall first introduced the Pacific Southwest Water Plan, environmentalists attempted to create a legal argument against the dams based upon the reclamation provision in the Park Establishment Act of 1919 and the Federal Power Acts of 1920, 1921, and 1935. However, the dubious nature of these arguments soon became apparent, and preservationists had largely abandoned them by 1965. The second tactic the environmentalists adopted was to attack the proposals with a two-pronged approach that included technologically viable alternatives and strong rhetorical arguments emphasizing that congressional approval of dams that would create invasions of Grand Canyon National Park and Monument would set a harmful precedent, allowing development in the rest of the National Park System.

Although the technological argument was relatively new, the invocation of precedent originated with Park Service Director Drury when he used it to defend Grand Canyon National Park against the high Bridge Canyon Dam and the destructive Marble Canyon–Kanab Creek Project during the CAP debates of the 1940s. Congress did not approve of these proposals; however, conservation organizations adopted Drury's strategy and used it, along with expert testimony to call the bureau's data into question to defend Dinosaur National Monument during the Echo Park Controversy.

When the conservationists defeated the Dinosaur dams, some viewed it as a reversal of the Hetch Hetchy verdict and argued that Congress had established a new principle: that the lands held by the National Park Service could no longer be violated for development. However, they were bitterly disappointed only a few years later when the rising waters of Lake Powell threatened Rainbow Bridge National Monument, and Congress refused to construct the protective measures environmentalists thought were needed to protect it. Despite the angry rhetoric, many congressmen were not convinced that the intrusion of a small sliver of water into Rainbow Bridge National Monument constituted a precedent that would endanger the National Park System. Senator Frank Moss of Utah argued that a lake beneath the bridge would "add greatly to its scenic lure," while Aspinall and Commissioner Dominy favored the intrusion because they believed it would enable millions to see the arch rather than just a privileged few.[49]

Environmentalists fighting to preserve Grand Canyon in 1965 had no choice but to rely upon the precedent argument once the weakness of their initial legal arguments had been exposed because, although diminished by the Rainbow Bridge fiasco, it still was their strongest weapon. However, many of the same arguments used to defeat the environmentalists' position during the Rainbow Bridge dispute reappeared during the House Interior Committee hearings of 1965. Congressmen contended that a lake would improve the scenery of the canyon, open it up to public access, and that the environmentalists who were fighting against it were selfish—the antithesis of President Johnson's Great Society. Even more troubling were the allegations of racism that could be leveled toward environmentalists if they objected to the Hualapai Nation's proposal to build the Bridge Canyon Dam. Obviously the already-weakened precedent argument would not be nearly powerful enough to defeat the rhetorical onslaught to which the preservationists would certainly be subjected when the hearings resumed in 1966.

Leading preservationists realized in the winter of 1965 that they needed a new strategy that would transcend arguments based upon legal interpretations and precedent to gain widespread public appeal. In Grand Canyon environmentalists had the world's greatest symbol of natural grandeur to defend, but despite numerous articles in conservation magazines, traveling photo exhibits, grassroots protests, and the stunning book *Time and the River Flowing*, they had not figured out how to trigger a national wave of protest against the impending threat to Grand Canyon . . . at least not yet.

Richard Bradley, who had been pressing his efforts to gain publicity in the national media for more than a year, could claim only mixed results by winter of 1965. While he had not been able to convince the editors of *Atlantic Monthly* to publish his article, they put him in touch with *Life* magazine, which agreed to print a short anti-dam editorial. *Harper's* also printed a short satirical piece, criticizing Stewart Udall for endorsing "piddling enterprises" such as Glen Canyon, Marble Canyon, and Bridge Canyon Dams, and called instead for a dam "one mile high" across the entire canyon. However, when Bradley tried to publish a more conventional article in *Harper's*, longtime essayist Bernard DeVoto's former employer turned him down. And though the *New York Times* carried regular articles about the controversy, *Time* magazine featured an article on conservation in late September 1965, just after the House hearings, that didn't mention the threats to Grand Canyon at all. Some preservationists suspected that the bureau had managed to apply pressure behind the scenes to influence the editors of *Time* to avoid publicizing the dams.[50]

Although Brower was unable to determine whether these allegations were true, soon conservationists would see just how far the bureau and other proponents of the CAP would go to prevent them from arguing their case in the national media. Barring the occurrence of something dramatic, it appeared as though Morris Udall, Rhodes, Hayden, Stewart Udall, and other supporters of the Lower Colorado River Basin Project had finally forged enough alliances and cut the political deals necessary to break the bill free in the House during the next session of Congress. Environmentalists such as Brower and Bradley believed that if they could not draw the attention of the national media to the threats looming over Grand Canyon in 1966, the opportunity to save America's most spectacular scenic wonder from massive hydroelectric projects would, like Glen Canyon before it, soon be irretrievably lost.

7

"Permanent Massive Things"

At the outset of the new year, environmentalists and supporters of the Grand Canyon dams were still honing strategies to win the day in Congress and to convince the American people to support them. Which side would prevail—those who wanted to continue developing the West's water resources to support skyrocketing population growth and develop new recreational opportunities, or advocates of preservation who fought to preserve the free-flowing Colorado River in a stretch of Grand Canyon few people would ever see? Would the outcome reflect progress as it had been defined since the founding of the nation, or would it reflect progress of a different sort—a recognition that intangible aesthetic values were sometimes worth more than dollars and cents?[1]

Was there still a place in such a wealthy country for John Muir–style preservation, or could this affluence only be sustained by continuing to sacrifice America's natural grandeur? Could technology save the day and allow America to have both? In the firmament of the mid-1960s, with the nation more divided than at any time since the Civil War, how the fight to save Grand Canyon would be affected by the civil rights movement, concerns about free speech, protests against American intervention in Vietnam, and the rising tide of the new environmentalism, was impossible to predict.

As American society grappled with these and other issues, the political process continued to grind forward. Morris Udall, John Rhodes, Carl Hayden, Stewart Udall, Barry Goldwater, and others who were attempting to gain passage of the Central Arizona Project waited impatiently for Wayne Aspinall to reconvene the House hearings that had ended the previous year. All hoped that the seven states of the Colorado River Basin would honor the compromises, so painstakingly negotiated during the previous two years, long enough for the bill to reach the floor of the House for a vote.

Although hundreds of people were working on obtaining passage of the Central Arizona Project bill, by January 1966 Morris Udall emerged as the quarterback of the effort in the House. Mo Udall, the "one-eyed Mormon" as he laughingly referred to himself, took office in May 1961 upon winning a special election for his brother's vacant congressional seat, after Stewart's appointment as interior secretary. Twice reelected, he now held Arizona's only seat on the vital House Committee on Interior and Insular Affairs. Generally a supporter of conservation, in the case of CAP, Morris Udall found himself caught in the same conundrum as his brother. He found himself opposing conservationists with whom he was usually allied, all the while fighting a personal struggle to reconcile his obligations to his Arizona constituency and his desire to develop Arizona's water resources with his own environmentalist sympathies. Possessed of a self-deprecating wit, by 1966 Morris Udall also was known among his colleagues as a politician of keen intellect with a tireless work ethic, a man who was not above playing hardball politics when the situation called for it.[2]

Jackson and the Hualapai: Removing the Roadblocks

Potential opposition from the Pacific Northwest still threatened the Central Arizona Project bill, especially in the Senate. However, Morris Udall believed that, through tactful negotiations and Carl Hayden's influence, Senator Jackson could be persuaded to approve of at least a feasibility-grade study of the importation of water from the Columbia River.[3] The promise of water augmentation was all that held the fragile seven-state coalition together. Although Udall was optimistic, he was also aware that if he failed, the upper basin states as well as California would withdraw their support. Udall knew he could do little about the position held by politicians from the Pacific Northwest at the beginning of the year; the real negotiations, he believed, would occur while the bill was under consideration, probably during the joint House/Senate conference committee meetings after passage, which he anticipated would occur in the summer of 1966.

But before these deals could be cut, the bill had to somehow make it through both the House and Senate. Udall realized that if the conservationists grew strong enough to prevent the passage of a high

Bridge Canyon Dam the regional proposal would be doomed, because California's representatives and Aspinall all believed that without the high dam the development fund would take a great deal longer to accrue enough revenue to build water-importation works—too long in their view, given the imminence of the Southwest's water crisis.

Thus by 1966 the high Bridge Canyon Dam had become the focal point of the entire debate because the project's supporters believed it alone promised an immediate cash windfall large enough to fund the Columbia diversion. The Budget Bureau's approval of Marble Canyon Dam—and recommendation that Bridge Canyon Dam be deferred—posed an additional barrier to passage. Marble Canyon Dam alone could not fund the water importation that California and Aspinall desired. Defeat the high dam, and it might doom the entire scheme. Win its approval, and the project would be virtually impossible to stop.

Supporters of the CAP now moved to strengthen their position against the environmentalists, and they launched a preemptive strike to prevent the alliance of conservationists and the Hualapai Nation over the construction of a low dam at Bridge Canyon. During the autumn 1965 hearings, Royal Marks, the attorney for the Hualapai Nation, had testified that the Hualapai would build Bridge Canyon Dam itself if it could gain the approval of the Federal Power Commission. Since the FPC did not have the authority to approve a dam that would flood national monument or park lands, the Hualapai project would, by law, have to be a dam lower than any currently under consideration.[4] Arizona water advocates viewed this testimony as a threat, and it became a matter of utmost priority to get the Hualapai behind the high dam for its "public relations value" and because it would remove a potential obstacle to passage. Fearing that the removal of threats to the park and monument would appease some of the conservation organizations, Arizona Representatives Morris Udall, Rhodes, and George Senner wrote a joint letter to the Hualapai Nation and asked what it would take to gain their support.[5]

Getting the Hualapai on board would take some deft political maneuvering. The Hualapai Nation began voicing its concerns about a federally constructed Bridge Canyon Project almost as soon as the Arizona delegation introduced CAP legislation in June 1963. Marks, whose law firm had represented the nation since 1948, wrote John Rhodes and expressed his concern that the legislation contained no provision for compensating the Hualapai, given that only three years previously the Hualapai had been promised a generous payment by the state of Arizona for use of the damsite. Rhodes pled ignorance and said that he had taken Senator Hayden's word that the legislation introduced in 1963 was "identical" with that submitted in 1950, which did in fact guarantee compensation. Marks's co-counsel, Arthur Lazarus, made similar inquiries of Interior Secretary Udall in October 1963, but despite these queries both the interior secretary and the Arizona congressional delegation failed to take any action until after the House hearings in autumn of 1965.[6]

By then, the "Indian problem," as some Arizonans had begun to call it, could no longer be ignored in the face of the explosive civil rights issues involved.[7] The surprise threat from the Hualapai threw the Arizona delegation into a panic, and Mo Udall asked the Bureau of Reclamation to assess the impact that the Hualapai contract of 1960 would have upon the development fund Bridge Canyon Dam was designed to create. The bureau's analysis revealed the stunning and inescapable fact that the annual payments the agreement called for would reduce the development fund by more than $65 million by 2025 and almost $93 million by 2047.

Attorneys for the Hualapai Nation confirmed that they expected, at the minimum, for the Interior Department to compensate it at the rate the Arizona Power Authority (APA) agreed to in 1960 when the authority was seeking to build a low dam. These demands would probably increase because the Interior plan called for a high dam. The Hualapai also expected to be able to buy power at the lowest market rate, control the revenue generated by tourists using the south shore of the reservoir, have the bureau construct a road to the reservoir for recreational purposes, and for the name of the dam to be changed from Bridge Canyon to "Hualapai."[8]

As if potential conflicts with the Hualapai Nation were not enough, the Arizona delegation also knew that the Navajo Nation was interested in a substantial portion of revenue from Marble Canyon Dam. However, because the Navajo failed to convince the FPC during the APA proceedings that it had a legitimate claim to the dam site in the early 1960s, Arizona politicians concluded that they did not constitute a serious threat and focused their efforts on getting the Hualapai on board.[9] Although perhaps a defensible decision from legal and economic perspectives, ignoring the Navajo Nation, one of the largest American

Indian groups in the United States, was an inexcusable blunder. The same Arizona politicians who had so painstakingly crafted the intricate compromises necessary to create the seven-state alliance had unwittingly handed the conservationists a potent weapon they could use against the project. And use it they would.

Morris Udall and Rhodes met with Marks in early January 1966 to try to get the Hualapai to budge on some of their demands. But Marks was adamant, essentially telling the Arizona representatives to take it or leave it. A dismayed Morris Udall wrote his brother shortly after this encounter, and Stewart Udall issued an immediate directive to his staff to get moving on a solution. Mo Udall now faced a difficult choice. Giving in to the Hualapai position would result in a great depletion of the development fund and anger the states hoping for water importation at the earliest possible date. Because the amount of money that would accrue to the fund depended upon the height of Bridge Canyon Dam, this reduction in revenue practically guaranteed that a high dam had to be built for the project to be economically feasible. His support of a high dam was sure to incur the wrath of the conservationists. However, Udall believed he had little choice because to ignore the Hualapai demands at a time when civil rights issues were front page news would create a public relations disaster that could imperil the entire project.[10] It appeared yet another deal had to be made.

Virtually everyone working toward the passage of the Central Arizona Project recognized the importance of avoiding a conflict with the Hualapai Nation. Spurred on by Secretary Udall to find a solution, Interior Department staff came to him with their recommendations. Assistant Secretary for Public Land Management Harry Anderson argued that the department should agree to the Hualapai demands as a matter of "public policy" and "equity." He also contended that the Hualapai stood in danger of being "exploited nationally" by the conservationists if supporters of the CAP failed to gain their support.

Les Alexander of the Arizona Interstate Stream Commission put the situation more bluntly in a conversation with Rhodes: The price of giving in to these demands must be the Hualapais' enthusiastic and unyielding support of the project. If this could be achieved, it presented the opportunity to turn the Hualapai desire to have Bridge Canyon/ Hualapai Dam built "to our advantage against the so-called conservationists." Alexander urged a professional advertising agency should be hired to mount "a professional type rebuttal," against the conservationists, arguing that "the plight of the poor Hualapais" would be a great way to generate pressure to build Bridge Canyon Dam.[11] Alexander, Rhodes, and other Arizona water advocates believed it was possible to portray the preservationists as racist, themselves as civil rights advocates, and gain a tremendous public windfall as a result.

A Toehold in the National Media

Meanwhile, environmentalists kept trying to find a way to carry the fight to the American people. By late January 1966 two schools of thought had emerged among conservationists: one led by Richard Lamm, who believed in a centralized, coordinated anti-dam campaign; the other, championed by David Brower and Richard Bradley, who thought that a grassroots effort stood the best chance of success. The latter group believed if they could gain access to the national media and make the public aware of the threats looming over America's most spectacular natural wonder, that massive numbers of people would rise up in wrathful protest.

With hearings but a few short months away, preservationists had acquired some important allies, including the *New York Times*. The newspaper had opposed only Bridge Canyon Dam in previous editorials, but now it took a stand against Marble Canyon Dam as well, even though it was upstream of the park and monument. The editors of the *Times* published an editorial in January criticizing the potential destruction of Grand Canyon, and they questioned why hydroelectric dams were necessary at all given recent advances in thermal and atomic energy.[12] Encouraged, but knowing time was growing short, Brower and Bradley continued their efforts to gain more media coverage.

In January the defenders of Grand Canyon received their first break when the Audubon Society came through on its promise to publish Richard Bradley's hard-hitting article solicited the previous fall. Richard and his brother David had not succeeded in having the widely circulated *Atlantic Monthly* publish their essay because, as Richard put it later, the editors "couldn't believe that Stewart Udall would support such a dumb project."

The piece appeared in the January–February issue, an event that was to have far-reaching consequences for the remainder of the campaign. The article, titled "Ruin for the Grand Canyon," stressed many of the arguments environmentalists had been advancing since 1963: Alternative energy sources were available; the Kanab Creek tunnel still loomed as a potential threat; the dams would desecrate Grand Canyon; and other familiar themes. Although written forcefully, the article only reached the relatively small membership of the Audubon Society, a total of about 48,500 people, not an audience of the size that Bradley and Brower sought.[13]

Alone, Bradley's article was no more significant than other essays published in environmental and scientific magazines that had circulated among a dedicated but limited number of readers interested in environmental issues. However, during the last week of January 1966 Bradley received an unsolicited letter from Marjorie Nicholson, a reprint editor at *Reader's Digest*, asking if she could run the *Audubon* article in an upcoming issue. This was what the preservationists had been waiting for; *Reader's Digest* had an estimated readership of thirty-five million in the US and twenty million more in foreign countries, twice that of *Life* or the *Saturday Evening Post*. An employee of the *Digest*, who was also a Sierra Club member, told Brower the magazine received seventy-eight thousand unsolicited manuscripts every six months and that an estimated one out of every four Americans read it. Gaining access to one of the most widely circulated publications in the world was a coup of stupendous proportions for the preservationists, one they hoped would ignite the public outrage necessary to swing the momentum of the anti-dam crusade in their favor.[14]

This potential threat to the CAP was not lost on Floyd Dominy, and the commissioner did everything in his power to stop the publication of Bradley's article. When *Reader's Digest* called Dominy to confirm some of Bradley's assertions, the commissioner responded with a four-page point-by-point rebuttal of "known errors or misstatements," criticizing Bradley for comparing the proposed Grand Canyon dams with Hetch Hetchy; "raising the ghost of the Kanab Creek diversion," which had been abandoned for "several decades"; and arguing that steam plants could produce peaking power. Dominy contended that the park service had long approved the high Bridge Canyon Dam and included a copy of Park Service Director Albright's 1933 letter as evidence to support this latter point.

Although it appears that both Bradley and Dominy made some erroneous assertions, the editors of the *Digest* gave Bradley a chance to rebut the commissioner's claims. After sending his response, an incredulous Bradley informed Brower that Dominy's letter was full of "bluff and bluster and misstatements" and speculated that perhaps it could be used to get him fired from the bureau. After receiving Bradley's reply, and checking some of the facts on its own, *Reader's Digest* accepted Bradley's article as written and decided to publish it in April 1966. Bradley was cautiously optimistic. However, he feared that Interior Secretary Udall possessed the influence to "kill the article" by leaning on the *Digest's* editorial staff, and he told Brower that he wouldn't believe he had succeeded until he had "seen [the article] in print."[15]

The Colorado Open Space Coordinating Council (COSCC) also continued its efforts in spring of 1966 and scheduled a television debate between Dominy and Daniel Luten, Sierra Club treasurer and a geography professor at UC Berkeley. Also seeking national media exposure, the council, along with the Rocky Mountain chapter of the Sierra Club and the Colorado Mountain Club, raised enough funding to place a full-page ad in the *Denver Post* in March. The advertisement featured a breathtaking photo of the Colorado River from Toroweap Point, the tallest sheer face in Grand Canyon, and it urged readers to write their congressional representatives, President Johnson, and, perhaps most importantly, TV and radio stations, magazines, and newspapers. "Tell them it is your Grand Canyon," the article urged, "and you want it left as it is," invoking the language of Teddy Roosevelt. Encouraged by the local response, the COSCC began to raise money so it could run advertisements in national newspapers such as the *New York Times* and the *Christian Science Monitor*.[16]

But those in favor of the Grand Canyon dams also won a substantial victory in March 1966. The two-million-member National Wildlife Federation had not taken an official position on the Lower Colorado Basin Project, despite pressure from Anthony Smith, Brower, and other prominent conservationists. During the second week of March, the New Mexico Wildlife and Conservation Association offered a resolution at the NWF annual convention, calling for the national leadership to oppose the two dams proposed for the Colorado River because of the evaporation they would cause and their effect upon Grand Canyon National Park.

However, Phil Clemons and Bill Winter of the Arizona Game Protective Association offered a counter-resolution, calling for a "balance between conservation and full development of the water and power resources" of the Colorado River. Winter and Clemons persuaded the executive committee of the NWF to table the New Mexico resolution.[17] As a result, the largest conservation organization in the world remained on the sidelines as the fight to save Grand Canyon moved toward its climax.

Meanwhile, preparations for the publication of Richard Bradley's article continued. *Reader's Digest* mailed out offprints of the essay in March, including one to new Arizona Governor Sam Goddard, who suggested that the magazine send some of its staff to Grand Canyon so that they could see what the uproar was all about. The editors agreed and asked David Brower to organize a symposium on March 30–31 at the iconic El Tovar Hotel on the south rim of the canyon to allow the preservationists to present their arguments to the national press. *Reader's Digest* hired New York's J. Walter Thompson Company, one of the largest and most respected public relations firms in the world, to lay the groundwork and send invitations to members of the press. The firm chartered an airplane and invited eighty members of the national media, who would soon descend upon the south rim of Grand Canyon expecting to learn more about the controversy from the environmentalists' point of view.

The Battle of El Tovar

Although *Reader's Digest* intended the symposium to be a celebration of the publication of Bradley's article and an opportunity for preservationists to present their side of the controversy, the staff at J. Walter Thompson misunderstood, and they asked Governor Goddard to send them a list of pro-dam people he thought should attend. Unbeknownst to environmentalists, who were simply planning to make their case against the dams, Morris Udall, Northcutt Ely, Barry Goldwater, and other high-powered dam supporters made plans to crash the meeting. Additionally, Dominy, though unable to attend himself, arranged for the bureau to send several people along with its huge scale model of the canyon with the plastic inlays for the dams and reservoirs. All these arrangements were made without the consent or knowledge of the preservationists, and as a result, things soon spun wildly out of control.[18]

On the evening of March 29, Brower and MIT mathematician Jeff Ingram arrived to assess the situation and make preliminary seating arrangements. Brower fired the preservationists' opening salvo, sending a telegram to Stewart Udall in which he accused him of "muzzling the National Park Service" by not allowing park service personnel to voice objections to the dams. Brower claimed that he had received a copy of an Interior Department memo, "leaked" to the Sierra Club by a park service employee, outlining the official position of the agency and requesting that all recipients destroy it after reading it.[19]

The next day the conference degenerated into a free-for-all. Before the beginning of the day's scheduled activities, Ingram and Brower left the hotel to take a short walk along the rim of Grand Canyon. While they were gone, bureau personnel arrived and commandeered the El Tovar dining room where the meeting was scheduled to take place. They set up Dominy's scale model of Grand Canyon that had been used to great effect during the fall 1965 House hearings. A furious, red-faced Brower demanded that they remove it. When they refused, he threatened to throw the model out himself—along with the people who had set it up—while Ingram, according to Ely, threatened to "punch one of the bureau people in the eye."[20]

Bureau personnel and representatives of the Thompson Company immediately placed a series of frantic phone calls to the upper echelons of the Interior Department. They eventually reached Interior Secretary Udall, who apparently ordered that the model was to be left where it was. Dominy said later that order was restored and only the timely arrival of the Grand Canyon National Park Police averted an outright brawl. A tenuous truce was hammered out, and the bureau's model stayed.[21] The near donnybrook of March 30, 1966, has entered the lore of the Bureau of Reclamation as "The Battle of El Tovar"; however, the real battle, the war of words, would begin later on that afternoon.[22]

Although *Reader's Digest* and Hilda Burns of the J. Walter Thompson Company had assured Brower that the preservationists would be allowed to use the conference to present their anti-dam message exclusively, actual events soon rendered these previous arrangements moot. Morris Udall insisted that as a US congressman he should have the chance to talk to the reporters who were planning to attend. On March 30 Udall managed get aboard the press's charter plane in New York and he used the long transcontinental flight to lobby for the dams. When the plane landed, Udall discovered that although he, Ely, and other dam supporters would be welcome to mingle with the guests at a cocktail party that night, they would not be allowed to participate in the evening's panel discussion.

When more pro-dam advocates and a contingent of the Arizona press arrived, including the CBS affiliate from Phoenix, Udall threatened to call his own press conference unless he and other CAP supporters were allowed to speak. Brower claimed later that Burns backed down in the face of this pressure. As a result, Udall and Ely were given the chance to

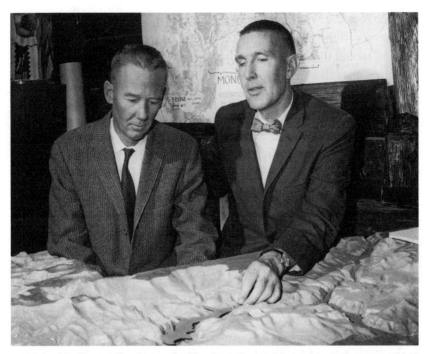

FIGURE 7.1. Left to right: physicist Richard Bradley and Representative Morris Udall with Floyd Dominy's scale model of Grand Canyon. Morris K. Udall Papers, box 478, folder 9, courtesy of University of Arizona Libraries, Special Collections.

present their pro-dam arguments that night, and the morning session was reconfigured to accommodate them and Barry Goldwater, who was anticipated to attend. Brower relinquished his position as moderator to Stephen Spurr from the University of Michigan, a "neutral" observer, because as a "partisan" Brower believed he could not be unbiased toward the supporters of the dams.[23]

According to author and Sierra Club member George Steck who attended, Mo Udall verbally attacked Brower so savagely that "David . . . cried right there on the podium." Harold Bradley, former Sierra Club president, father of Richard and David, and a veteran of the Echo Park fight, recalled that "[Morris] Udall made an ass of himself" by being so aggressive. The verbal skirmishes continued throughout the evening. Catcalls and boos from the largely anti-dam audience rained down upon Udall and Ely when they tried to speak. When Udall claimed that neither dam would create a reservoir visible from any point to which one could drive, environmentalists in the audience shouted "Toroweap," forcing

Udall to recant. Ely tried to show the press just how extremist a position the preservationists had taken. When he asked the audience how many of them would like to see Glen Canyon Dam torn out, he was met with thunderous applause.[24] The first day ended with the conservationists in disarray, feeling they had been "steamrollered" by the strong-armed tactics of Udall, Ely, the bureau, and the rest of the pro-dam contingent.[25]

The next day Goldwater arrived in time for the morning session. Goldwater told the audience in a regretful tone that while he wished the dams didn't have to be built, he also had a duty to speak for the millions of people in the Phoenix area who would someday need the water and power the dams would provide for future growth and prosperity. Ultimately, he admitted he was not enthusiastic about Marble Canyon Dam but believed strongly that Bridge Canyon Dam should be constructed. Goldwater also emphasized that the dam would bring tremendous economic benefits to the Hualapai Nation, reiterating the argument that other Arizona lobbyists had made early in the spring.

Goldwater's comment about the Hualapai piqued the interest of Stephen Jett, a twenty-seven-year-old assistant professor of geography at the University of California, Davis, who had no formal affiliation with any conservation organization. Jett, who wrote his dissertation and a soon-to-be-published book about Navajo country's scenic resources and tourism potential, posed as a member of the press and asked Goldwater whether the CAP would benefit the Navajo Nation. Goldwater replied that to the best of his knowledge, the Navajo possessed no legal rights in the Marble Canyon damsite, and so they had "not been consulted." Given that the Hualapai stood to benefit handsomely from Bridge Canyon Dam, Goldwater's response struck Jett as being "unjust" because the east abutment of Marble Canyon Dam and the eastern half of the reservoir would need to be on Navajo land. Goldwater's talk turned the morning session to the advantage of the dam supporters. Environmentalists complained later that Goldwater dominated the panel because his status as a former senator and recent presidential candidate overawed the moderator. Indeed, a glance at the transcript reveals that Goldwater spoke for almost seventy-five percent of airtime during the morning session.[26]

The preservationists in the audience refrained from their disruptive tactics of the previous evening, and the anti-dam panel participants gave a good account of themselves in the time remaining. After Richard

Bradley spoke, the supporters of the dams could not counter his arguments about alternative energy sources on either technical or economic grounds. Morris Udall could only respond that reclamation policy prevented the bureau from undertaking studies of alternatives such as thermal power plants.[27] The Sierra Club members present even managed to show their poignant film *Glen Canyon* during breaks in the presentation. However, when the session ended and members of the press waited their turn to fly over the canyon in Martin Litton's plane, most of the environmentalists were disappointed because they felt that the pro-dam faction had upstaged them. "Barry Goldwater is pretty hard to beat on his home ground," a dejected Brower wrote afterward.[28]

From all outward appearances, it looked like the CAP interlopers had successfully derailed the conference. After struggling to gain access to the national media for the better part of a year, some environmentalists believed that these efforts had all been for naught because the hard-won opportunity to present their case to a nationwide audience had been crushed by the hubris and prestige of political heavyweights such as Mo Udall and Goldwater. But pro-dam advocates who thought they had distracted the media, and preservationists who believed the symposium a disaster, failed to consider the dramatic effect that the last conference event—the flights over the canyon with Litton—would have.

After landing on the north rim, far from Udall and Goldwater, and in the presence of the canyon proper—rather than the bureau's puny model of it—the reporters were treated to a fiery jeremiad from Litton. Standing at the edge of the dramatic Toroweap overlook, a nearly sheer drop of 3,500 vertical feet, he showed them explicitly just how damaging the dams would be. There was no better place in all the canyon to make this argument. Toroweap overlooks the world-famous Lava Falls, one of the most intense stretches of navigable whitewater in North America with a drop of almost forty feet. With this spectacular setting as a backdrop, Litton thundered that it was imperative to stop the bureau from desecrating any portion of the canyon, not just what was protected by Grand Canyon National Park. Litton's overflights and impassioned oratory brought the reporters face-to-face with the appalling reality that Lava Falls and other mighty Grand Canyon rapids would be silenced forever if Bridge Canyon/Hualapai Dam were built.

Litton salvaged the conference for the preservationists. Several members of the press who had supported the project, such as columnist

Bert Hanna of the *Denver Post* and Jean Ensign, general manager of radio station WVIP in suburban New York, wrote later that they now understood the conservationists' side of the story.[29] Richard Bradley, Brower, Ingram, and others returned home believing that their opportunity to take their crusade to the national press had been hijacked. The fight to save Grand Canyon now became front-page news across the country, and several other leading magazines began to consider publishing articles about it.

Yet at least one prominent dam supporter knew his effort to derail the conference had failed. Although he made his best case for the CAP, Morris Udall immediately understood how difficult it was to combat the passion of the preservationists with Grand Canyon as a backdrop. Twenty years after the *Reader's Digest* symposium, Udall wrote:

> The weakness of the arguments in favor of the dams was borne home to me the day I had to debate David Brower—as clever, tough, and tenacious an opponent as you could want—in front of a gaggle of national press at the worst possible venue: the *rim of the Grand Canyon*. This was a tough assignment—comparable to debating the merits of chastity in Hugh Hefner's hot tub in front of an audience of centerfold models and me being on the side of abstinence [emphasis Udall's].[30]

The *Reader's Digest* conference and the publication of Richard Bradley's article had a tremendous impact on the battle over the Grand Canyon dam. Large numbers of people who had not been aware of the threat to Grand Canyon were now finding out about it through the national media. CAP advocates Rich Johnson and Dominy believed that the preservationists had gained the upper hand by the spring of 1966, and they also knew there was nothing they could do to match it. These claims appear at first to be ridiculous. After all, the Central Arizona Project Association had an enormous amount of money, ranking twenty-second in terms of money spent on lobbying out of the thousands of registered Washington, DC, lobbying groups. And Dominy was commissioner of an immensely powerful and well-funded government agency. But the facts bear out these arguments.

Despite his energetic and sometimes bellicose opposition, Dominy had published exactly one magazine-quality brochure, *Lake Powell: Jewel of the Colorado*, and distributed only sixty thousand copies of it.

Bureau and CAPA personnel tried to match the preservationists speech for speech and handed out tens of thousands of flyers, but the bureau was prevented by law from mounting an outright counteroffensive. The Central Arizona Project Association was not restricted by such regulations. At John Rhodes's suggestion, it hired a public relations agency to launch a media counteroffensive. The firm it consulted, Hill and Knowlton, said that a publicity blitz powerful enough to counteract the *Reader's Digest* article and symposium would cost at least $250,000, a figure far beyond what the association could afford.[31]

Reaping the Fruits of Success

Even if such a campaign were launched, it was too late to counteract the preservationists' publicity in time for the upcoming spring 1966 hearings. Thus the responsibility to counter the preservationists fell back upon Rich Johnson and other members of the CAPA, who began to prepare their own in-house lobbying strategy. The Central Arizona Project Association, with help from the *Arizona Republic*, kicked off a letter-writing campaign of its own and urged Arizonans to write *Reader's Digest* voicing their displeasure about Bradley's article and the Grand Canyon conference. Soon the magazine's editors received hundreds of angry letters from dam supporters. Dominy and other bureau personnel also continued their indefatigable efforts, handing out literature and giving speeches across the West, including a presentation at the Los Angeles "Sportshow," an outdoor recreation and boating convention that drew more than five hundred thousand people in one weekend.[32] But the damage had already been done. By early April 1966, the preservationists had broken through to the mass media and used this coverage to publicize their fight against the dams to the American public.

Just more than a month after the conference at Grand Canyon, articles sympathetic to the preservationists' anti-dam position appeared in the May issues of *Life* magazine, *Newsweek*, and *Outdoor Life*. Almost immediately, an avalanche of mail flooded Congress, Interior Secretary Udall's office, and the White House. Other publications began to print satirical pieces about the proposed dams, and they lampooned Dominy in particular. In an exceptionally biting essay, *Biophilist*, a bimonthly newsletter published by a small group of preservationists in Denver, printed lyrics to a tune it titled "America the Bureautiful," the first verse and chorus of which reads:

Bureautiful for specious tries
To obfuscate the plain
And concretize falliciousness
For departmental gain!
America! America!
Bow down to Dominy
Poo-Bah who dreams to dam all streams
From sea to shining sea.

Burns of the J. Walter Thompson Company wrote Brower in early May, confirming what many conservationists were now beginning to suspect, that the conference had not been the debacle they had feared. "We're just delighted with the way this thing is turning," Burns wrote. "It's a completely different story now that the national people are making themselves heard."[33] As a result of the conference and the media attention it attracted, the aroused public that Richard Bradley and Litton had sought, the only force that environmental leaders believed could stop the Grand Canyon dams, was at last making its presence felt.

On March 31, 1966, as the conference was occurring at Grand Canyon, Representatives John Saylor of Pennsylvania and John Dingell of Michigan introduced legislation calling for an expansion of Grand Canyon National Park. This bill, drafted by members of the Sierra Club, sought to include the entire 277-mile length of Grand Canyon within the new park boundaries and to remove and vacate all reservations previously made by the Federal Power Commission and the Bureau of Reclamation. The bill also proposed to add parts of the Hualapai Reservation and Kaibab National Forest to the park. As a result, the legislation drew opposition from wildlife organizations such as the Arizona Game Protective Association because it sought to include most of the north Kaibab Plateau, a world-renown trophy mule deer-hunting destination, within the expanded park.[34] Destined for defeat, the bill represented the first attempt to enlarge Grand Canyon National Park to include all 277 miles of Grand Canyon. It also demonstrated that on the eve of the resumption of the CAP hearings, deep divisions still separated various conservation groups.

Although the environmentalists had gained the upper hand in the national media, evidenced by the growing tide of public sentiment, the people who wanted the dams built still held the advantage in Congress.

FIGURE 7.2. The grass roots campaign: Sierra Club Executive Director David Brower and supporters at Grand Canyon in March 1966. Arthur Schatz, The LIFE Picture Collection, Getty Images.

Morris Udall, Aspinall, and other project supporters feverishly began to prepare for the resumption of hearings before the House Subcommittee on Irrigation and Reclamation. Arizona representatives also pressed Roy Elson, aide to Senator Hayden, to convince him to initiate action in the upper chamber, but Elson responded that Hayden would only move on the bill after the entire House passed it.[35]

May 1966: The Hearings Resume

By the end of April, a new threat to the passage of the Lower Colorado Basin Project bill had arisen. The state of New Mexico now demanded fifty thousand acre-feet of water from the lower basin in exchange for its continued support of the project. Udall and Rhodes were bewildered by this latest threat, while Rich Johnson termed it "blackmail." But they could not ignore this demand because New Mexico senator Clinton Anderson chaired the Senate Subcommittee on Irrigation and Reclamation. Not even Hayden possessed enough power to overcome the objections of both Anderson and Jackson, so Udall and Rhodes confronted this latest problem while an exasperated Aspinall bowed to mounting pressure and scheduled the hearings to commence on May

9, 1966. Seventy-three witnesses were slated to testify and, despite Morris Udall's attempts to exclude all anti-dam testimony, Aspinall included fourteen dam opponents. Among these were Brower's MIT trio: mathematician Ingram; Alan Carlin, the economist from the RAND Corporation; and Laurence Moss, a nuclear engineer, who intended to offer powerful new arguments designed to undermine the bureau's technical justifications for the project.[36]

Thomas Kimball, executive director of the National Wildlife Federation, was also scheduled to appear as a witness. Despite the neutral position the NWF took in March, Kimball intended to testify against the dams and advocate the substitution of alternative power sources for the Central Arizona Project. In early May it appeared as though the NWF and its two million members were about to weigh in against the Grand Canyon dams. But Winter of the Arizona Game Protective Association learned of Kimball's pending testimony, called him, and convinced him to cancel his appearance before the committee. Understating his victory, Winter wrote Rhodes and said that the members of the AGPA believed that for Kimball to testify against the dams would have been "highly detrimental to the CAP."

Winter also believed that when the time came, he could convince Kimball to oppose the proposed expansion of Grand Canyon National Park because of its inclusion of the north Kaibab deer herd. Winter understood that because the NWF included numerous big game hunting associations, Kimball would ultimately step back from publicly taking controversial positions that would divide his own organization. He told Rhodes that the AGPA would continue its efforts to keep the NWF from adopting an official position against the dams.[37] Consequently, as the crucial hearings began, preservationists seeking to keep dams out of Grand Canyon were still without the support of the largest conservation organization in the world.

Although Aspinall planned for the hearings to last only three or four days, this soon proved unrealistic because of the sheer number of witnesses. The supporters of the dams testified first. Once again Dominy's mastery of the art of persuasion was on full display as he offered exhaustive testimony to justify the projects on technical grounds. While being questioned by Morris Udall, Dominy, in a surprising turn, stated that the project was "theoretically possible" without Bridge/Hualapai and Marble Canyon Dams, if irrigation water costs to Arizona farmers were subsidized by the sale of power revenues from other sources—something that went against "long-standing reclamation policy."[38]

Hayden, now in his late eighties, did not testify, but his statement supporting a regional concept with the CAP as its centerpiece was read into the record. Arizona's congressmen Udall, Rhodes, and Senner then presented a joint statement in support of the bill, and Stewart Udall also prepared a statement. An unexpected development occurred when Representative George Mahon of Texas appeared and demanded fifteen million acre-feet of Columbia River water for the Texas Panhandle! This ridiculous suggestion only hardened the resolve of Senator Jackson, Representative Thomas Foley, and other politicians from the Pacific Northwest. Soon Foley subjected Mahon and other Texas representatives to a blistering cross-examination.[39]

The most dramatic exchanges while pro-dam witnesses were on the stand took place between Assistant Secretary for Water and Power Kenneth Holum and Aspinall. The chairman asked why the Interior Department had agreed with the Budget Bureau's recommendation that Bridge Canyon Dam be deferred until it and the proposed Columbia diversion had been studied by a national water commission. Such a commission, Aspinall feared, would constitute another bureaucratic hurdle to overcome and would result in additional delays.

Foley, alarmed by the intentions of the Pacific Southwest and the demands by Mahon, subjected Holum to a withering interrogation, forcing Holum to admit that the Interior Department had not determined that water importation from the Columbia River was the best approach to water augmentation. "Is there any reason why this Committee [sic] should direct a feasibility study . . . for importation rather than desalinization or weather modification or some other means of augmenting water?" Foley asked. "No sir," Holum replied.[40]

Preservationists from all over the country came to Washington, DC, to support the testimony in opposition to the dams. In contrast to the well-financed efforts of the Central Arizona Project Association and other pro-dam organizations from the Colorado Basin states, the conservationists' war room was in effect a microcosm of their nationwide grassroots effort. Despite successfully gaining access to the national media, their Grand Canyon campaign was still underfunded. For the hearings the preservationists established a temporary headquarters in a room at the Dupont Plaza Hotel and relied upon volunteers to type up testimony and make exhibits. Brower remembered that people "pounded away on a couple of old typewriters" and slept on the floor in the wee hours of the night. In response to Brower's invitation, Morris Udall stopped by while the hearings were taking place to see the nerve center of the opposition effort. "He came in and saw this bunch of devoted people working hard to beat his dams," Brower recalled. "I think he was impressed by that."[41]

The dam opponents' testimony began on May 13. From the moment they took the stand, it became apparent that not all members of the committee were happy with Aspinall's decision to allow them to testify. Craig Hosmer of California began verbally attacking Brower even before his testimony began, establishing a pattern of rude behavior that would continue for the duration of the conservationists' appearances.

Each time a witness attempted to speak, Hosmer objected on the grounds that the testimony was repetitious—though he never objected to hours of repetitive testimony from Dominy and other pro-dam witnesses. Aspinall, or the acting chair, would be forced to overrule the objection. This happened time and time again, sometimes touching off testy exchanges between Hosmer and Representative Saylor of Pennsylvania who opposed the dams. Although Aspinall wanted the project desperately, to his credit he conducted the hearings with fairness, granting the same courtesies to the preservationists as to advocates of the projects. So did Morris Udall. However, Aspinall could only control the procedural aspects of the hearings; he had little control over how the committee members treated witnesses once they were on the stand, something Hosmer used to his advantage to make vituperative, mostly baseless attacks.

Ingram, the first of the Sierra Club's technical experts, took the stand. He endured spurious and nonsensical objections from Hosmer, including an accusation that the environmentalists wanted to create another Pike's Peak(!). Ingram used the bureau's own figures to demonstrate how the construction of Bridge/Hualapai and Marble Canyon Dams would actually reduce the amount of revenue available in the development fund for construction until 2021, fifty-five years in the future. Since the dams were not needed to generate power for the Central Arizona Project specifically, but were only to generate power to sell at a profit to undetermined markets, Ingram reasoned the Arizona portion of the project could be powered by other means and the power purchased at off peak times at a low cost.[42]

The bureau had argued that revenue in excess of maintenance and operating costs from Hoover, Parker, and Davis Dams would begin accruing in the development fund in 1987 once they were paid off. This capital was designed to finance water augmentation into the Colorado River Basin. However, Ingram demonstrated that the tremendous cost of $1.2 billion needed to construct the two dams and their appurtenant structures would delay this accrual of funds until 2004. Even if the revenue stream were projected out over seventy-five years, the profit generated by the Grand Canyon dams plus the revenue from other hydroelectric plants would still only amount to a measly return of 1.33 percent.[43]

If the CAP were built without dams, Ingram showed that the development fund would begin accruing money in 1995, nine years earlier than if the cost of the dams were included. If the dams were built, the funds in the development fund would only surpass those generated by a damless CAP in 2021. Additionally, without the dams there would be more water because there would be no reservoirs and thus no evaporation loss, which the bureau estimated at one hundred thousand acre-feet per year.[44]

Ingram pointed to studies that indicated silt from the Paria River would render Marble Canyon Dam useless in a relatively short period of time, although this data was rather incomplete. Hosmer objected, stating that "the mathematician seems not to be aware of where the water comes from that is going to Marble Canyon Dam. It is already desilted by Lake Powell." In this exchange, Hosmer demonstrated his own ignorance of geography, for the Paria River is *downstream* from Glen Canyon Dam and does not deposit any silt into Lake Powell.[45]

Ingram also attacked the scaled-down Interior Department proposal that only included Marble Canyon Dam. Ingram demonstrated that without the "subsidy" from Hoover, Parker, and Davis Dams, Marble Canyon Dam would not be able to pay for itself. If true, this would violate the bureau's own long-established policy stipulating that projects must break even and have a cost/benefit ratio of at least 1:1. Saylor confirmed, from separate documentation, that Ingram's figures matched those compiled by the bureau "to the penny" and little if any rebuttal was offered by the rest of the committee.[46]

RAND Corporation economist Carlin testified next, and his new analysis of the proposal was even more devastating than his testimony in fall of 1965. Carlin submitted his report, cowritten with William Hoehn, also of the RAND Corporation. The report used figures supplied by the bureau, the Atomic Energy Commission, and Dominy in his 1965 testimony to demonstrate that nuclear power plants combined with pumped storage plants could generate more and cheaper power than both Grand Canyon dams at little loss to the development fund. The Carlin/Hoehn report also showed that a nuclear power plant would contribute more money to the development fund than Marble Canyon Dam alone, effectively undermining the Interior Department's position as well.[47]

In a stunning display of classlessness in violation of House protocol, Hosmer launched a scorching attack upon Carlin, who struggled with a speech impediment that made it difficult for him to testify. Hosmer cut him off repeatedly with rude and irrelevant remarks clearly intended to distract him from responding to questions from the committee. Saylor was so embarrassed by Hosmer's tactics that he intervened, and his apology to Carlin for the "abuse you have taken" made it into the record. Saylor's action restored a semblance of civility to the hearings and allowed Carlin to address some unresolved issues, as well as testify to his expertise in evaluating the economics of hydroelectric projects, something he had not yet had an opportunity to do.[48]

Nuclear engineer Laurence Moss took the stand next. Although his arguments paralleled those of Carlin to some degree, he contended that Carlin's figures actually gave the bureau the benefit of the doubt and made the Grand Canyon dams look better in terms of costs versus benefits than they actually were. Aspinall took the opportunity to voice his concerns that despite the optimism surrounding the potential for nuclear power, it appeared as though its future was still uncertain. Moss replied that private utilities ordered more than 5,700 megawatts of nuclear-generating capacity in 1965 and during the first fifteen weeks of 1966 ordered between 8,815 and 12,315 more, a definite sign that nuclear energy was now increasingly perceived as a viable alternative to hydroelectric power. Moss then confirmed Ingram's arguments independently that the development fund would accrue revenue much more quickly if neither dam were built.[49]

The Impact of Civil Rights

George Rocha, chief of the Hualapai Nation, also testified earlier that week. In late April Aspinall told Mo Udall that he believed it would be a good strategic move to "have an Indian, preferably the Chief of the Hualapai tribe," testify in favor of the bill. Aspinall explained that this would be a good opportunity to charge the Sierra Club and others "who opposed Bridge Canyon Dam . . . [as] being anti-Indian." He also suggested that the Hualapai do some lobbying of their own and emphasized that the dam would lift them out of poverty and ensure the economic success of their reservation. Rocha's testimony gave the CAP backers everything they hoped for. He told the committee that the dam was the Hualapai Nation's only hope for economic salvation and stressed that without it his people would continue to languish in poverty while the rest of the nation prospered.[50]

Preservationists anticipated this move and they attempted to enlist the aid of Cornell University anthropology professor Henry Dobyns, a leading authority on the Hualapai who had done extensive archeological assessments and excavations in lower Grand Canyon. However, this move backfired. Instead, Dobyns replied that he would not oppose the dams but that he in fact would be "very happy to testify . . . in favor" of Bridge Canyon Dam. He believed it offered economic opportunity for the Hualapai Nation and would help them to become integrated into the

FIGURE 7.3. Left to right: Representative John Rhodes, Hualapai Chief George Rocha, and Representative Morris Udall in front of an artist's depiction of the proposed Hualapai Dam ca. 1966. Morris K. Udall Papers, box 735, folder 20, courtesy of University of Arizona Libraries, Special Collections.

"United States' body politic." Blasting the preservationists' campaign, Dobyns wrote Sierra Club member Eugene Weiner and accused the environmentalists of racial discrimination and of attempting to hold the Hualapai tribe in "economic, social, and political subordination."[51]

Many supporters of the dams now believed Dobyns and the Hualapai were the perfect counter to the preservationists' anti-dam offensive. The Phoenix newspapers soon published Dobyns's remarks, and Morris Udall gleefully referenced Dobyns's letter to Weiner during a speech on the floor of the House of Representatives titled "The Conservation Plot That Failed." Udall inserted the letter into the *Congressional Record*. Dobyns testified before the House Committee on May 13, and he admonished Brower and his "fellow liberals" for not seeing "the wisdom of the conservation of Indians as well as rocks and ducks." Indeed, the promise of American Indian support had gained so much traction that during the questioning Utah Representative Laurence J. Burton stated that he might bring the Echo Park Dam before Congress for reconsideration and call it "Chief Washiki" or "Hualapai Dam." "It might pass then," he reflected.[52]

But the preservationists offered a devastating counterargument. Dr. Stephen Jett, who had questioned Goldwater about the potential benefits for the Navajo Nation at the *Reader's Digest* Grand Canyon conference, also appeared. Jett worked with Brower and other preservationist leaders before and during the hearings, and the Sierra Club paid his way so he could participate. However, Jett had not joined the club and testified as a private individual because he believed that the "interests of the tribe should be represented" and feared that his testimony would be discounted by the pro-dam contingent on the committee if he were seen as an instrument of a conservation organization.

Jett's testimony lacked the official blessing of the Navajo Tribal Council. The Navajo Nation had only just learned of the hearings—from Jett, not the government—and had not had enough time to prepare a response. Jett assured the committee that he had the approval of the tribal chairman, who was very concerned about the proposed inundation of forty-six miles of spectacular scenery in Marble Canyon on the western edge of the Navajo Reservation. He also inserted a detailed statement into the record highlighting the federal government's failure to consult with the Navajo on the proposed legislation.

Jett argued that national projections indicated that the demand for "scenic tourism" would increase greatly over that for water-based recreation during the next four decades. In anticipation of that, he said the Navajo could develop profitable tourist overlooks along the "Navajo Rim" of the gorge. If the CAP were built using nuclear power or coal-fired plants as power and revenue sources, it would also create opportunities for the poverty-stricken Navajo and Hopi peoples because the two reservations contained vast undeveloped deposits of coal, petroleum, natural gas, and uranium. Jett managed to change the order of witnesses so he could testify after Dobyns and have the last word on American Indian issues. He also entered a statement demonstrating how the Hualapai could also benefit from scenic tourism if tribal parks were developed in lower Grand Canyon.[53]

Although supporters and opponents of the Grand Canyon dams attempted to gain the approval of American Indians in the region, the preservationists only had this opportunity because the CAP lobby failed to fully anticipate the potential impact Native American testimony would have in a larger social context. Between 1957 and 1962, Arizona water leaders seeking a state-constructed Marble Canyon Dam antagonized the seventy-five thousand members of the Navajo Nation by refusing to acknowledge that they might have a valid claim to the economic benefits that would accrue from the dam and reservoir that would be partially located on their land. The Navajo had not forgotten this . . . and they had also not forgotten that these same politicians offered compensation to the Hualapai Nation for the Bridge Canyon project farther downstream.

Even with the opportunity to right this injustice, which occurred at the height of the civil rights movement, Stewart Udall's proposed Pacific Southwest Water Plan and subsequent lower basin project bills refused to consider the Navajo claims. Yet, beginning in 1965, these same federal proposals included compensation for the Hualapai Nation that had a total population of just more than nine hundred people. The CAP lobby missed a tremendous opportunity in the spring of 1966 to secure the backing of all Native Americans in the region. CAP lobbyists gained the support of several other Arizona Native American nations, including the White Mountain Apache, San Carlos Apache, and Akimel O'odham (formerly known as Pima) Nations, and could argue truthfully that most Arizona Native American *groups* approved of the project. But the preservationists could counter with a truthful argument of their own—that most Arizona American Indian *people* opposed it. The inhabitants of the

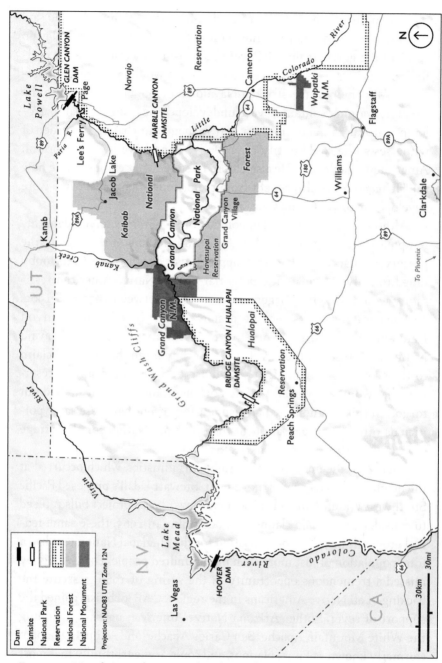

FIGURE 7.4. Map showing the proposed Bridge Canyon/Hualapai Dam and Marble Canyon Dam as they appeared in the Pacific Southwest Water Plan and Lower Colorado River Basin Project between 1964–1967 and their proximity to the Hualapai, Havasupai, and Navajo reservations. Map by Nathaniel Douglass, ndcartography.com.

Navajo Nation far outnumbered the combined population of the rest of Arizona's Native American groups.

Aspinall concluded the hearings and announced that he would remand the proposal to the House Subcommittee on Public Works to work out compromises in closed sessions and then pass the bill to the full House Interior Committee. Both Marble and Bridge/Hualapai Dams remained in the bill despite the Bureau of the Budget's recommended deferral of the latter. Although the Department of the Interior adopted the Budget Bureau's position, Secretary Udall believed privately that if Congress passed the bill with both dams in it, Hayden's influence would prove decisive and the senator would be able to persuade President Johnson to sign it.[54]

These were heady times for people fighting to obtain water for central Arizona. Not since 1951 had a proposal including the CAP come before the full House Interior Committee. Morris Udall and Rhodes canvassed the committee members from both sides of the aisle to see where they stood. Rhodes and Udall also conducted preliminary head counts of the House Rules Committee—the last stop before a debate on the floor of the House of Representatives.

The results were encouraging. Despite the preservationists' offensive and the increasing volume of mail, the anti-dam publicity appeared to be having little or no effect upon Congress. At the conclusion of the subcommittee hearings in late May, Rhodes and Udall reported to members of the Arizona contingent that they believed they had the votes to gain passage of the bill in the Rules Committee and in the House as a whole, although Rhodes stated that the bill's chances would be greatly improved if they could convince President Johnson to back it.[55]

Opponents and advocates of the Grand Canyon dams now steeled themselves for the floor debate that both sides believed was coming. With Aspinall behind the bill, and the Arizona-California alliance still intact, the bill stood a good chance of gaining a favorable report from the full Interior Committee, a milestone in Arizona's struggle to obtain the CAP.

Despite the preservationists' media blitz, the dam advocates appeared to had retained their hold on the Congress, and the only imminent danger to passage lurked in the form of the opposition from the Pacific Northwest. Morris Udall still believed that he could convince Foley and Jackson of Washington to agree to a solution that would benefit everyone involved. The numerous compromises they had made to gain political support swelled the bill to a cumbersome size, but these deals forged a formidable political juggernaut that representatives opposed to the dams would find difficult if not impossible to stop once the legislation made it to the House floor.

Supporters of the dams worked around the clock to sway Congress and public opinion. Morris Udall and Rhodes organized a series of luncheons the first week of June 1966. They invited all members of Congress to "have a steak on Arizona" and hear presentations by Goldwater and themselves that demonstrated why the dams needed to be part of the Lower Colorado River Basin Project. They of course added that, contrary to the Sierra Club's "misrepresentations," the dams would not harm Grand Canyon National Park at all. The bureau's scale model of Grand Canyon was again pressed into service. A detailed memorandum refuting the Carlin and Moss analyses that extolled the cost savings of nuclear power was distributed at each meeting.

The response was very favorable, and the action savvy. By using their incumbency and celebrity status to their advantage, the personal touch of Rhodes, Udall, and Goldwater had a much greater effect upon members of Congress than letters from faceless constituents using language copied from the *Sierra Club Bulletin* or other conservation publications. Morris Udall's informal vote projections and his correspondence from colleagues suggested that the preservationists' media campaign had a great effect upon public opinion but had not translated into meaningful congressional opposition.[56]

Arizona water lobbyists also planned a massive letter-writing campaign to try to counteract the effect of the national publicity by the preservationists; however, their audience was not as widespread. Seeking to make up for their lack of mass appeal, the CAP task force selected its targets with care, aiming to sway individuals of great influence or to associate the CAP with issues that would resonate with the American public. In early June the task force met and agreed to target corporate America through its registered Washington, DC, lobbyists. An examination of the lobbying plan reveals a veritable "who's who" of American business, with letters sent to dozens of lobbyists including fifty major oil companies, General Electric, Goodyear, the Southern Pacific Railroad, and US Steel.[57]

Morris Udall, Aspinall, and other CAP supporters also increased their efforts to paint environmentalists as racist, with a devious public relations campaign. Arizona's CAP task force decided to send an avalanche of letters from the Hualapai chief and other Arizona and Colorado Native

American groups to Congress, President Johnson, the National Council of Churches, Secretary Udall, and twelve thousand "Indian friends," emphasizing that Hualapai Dam would enable the Hualapai people to cast off their bonds of poverty. An additional letter, ostensibly written by Chief George Rocha to Brower, was released to the press in a move designed to taint the Sierra Club executive director personally. However, Rocha was not entrusted with the actual writing of these letters; that task was delegated to Central Arizona Project Association President Rich Johnson. All Chief Rocha was asked to contribute was his signature and some Hualapai Tribal Council letterhead.[58]

Johnson, the high-powered Phoenix attorney and lobbyist, ghost-wrote the following excerpt taken from a letter signed by Rocha, as a plea for support from selected "Indian friends":

> My people have lived in isolation and poverty for so long that we have almost forgotten how to hope for a better way. The progress and prosperity of the nation have not touched our lives. Our world is the canyon country of the Colorado River in Arizona. There are no jobs for us. We have no businesses to run and no resources to sell, but now there is a new hope for us. I will tell you about it because we need your help to make the dreams of our people come true. . . . [Hualapai Dam] will make jobs and businesses for us and we will not be a poor and forgotten people any longer.

Johnson also wrote similar letters that were signed by the chiefs of the San Carlos Apache, Akimel O'odham, and the White Mountain Apache Nations, while Felix Sparks from the Upper Colorado River Commission wrote similar letters for the chiefs of the Southern Ute and Ute Mountain Nations.[59] This approach, though paternalistic and obnoxious, demonstrates that the CAP contingent understood the larger social context in which the fight over the dams was taking place.

The dam supporters were already portraying the environmentalists as elitists who wanted to keep lower Grand Canyon all to themselves. Now they sought to add the charge of racism as well by demonstrating that the Sierra Club and other conservationists were actively working to deny the Hualapai people the right to profit from their own resource. The vast majority of the people who belonged to environmental organizations in the mid-1960s were white and at least of middle-class means. To charge these groups with pursuing a racist agenda at the height of the 1960s civil rights struggle had the potential to devastate the environmentalists' hard-won gains in the court of public opinion.

Bottom Up and Top Down

Opponents of the Grand Canyon dams, unaware that they were about to be accused of racism and believing that the critical phase of the anti-dam struggle lay just ahead, also continued to take their "save Grand Canyon" message to the American public.[60] Richard Bradley—who, after the publication of his *Reader's Digest* article, received a steady stream of correspondence from people asking how they could help—continued his correspondence with the editors of *Atlantic Magazine* to try to convince them to carry the story. However, to his frustration, the magazine refused to commit.[61]

Meanwhile, at the grassroots level, two intrepid ninth graders, Jeff Mandell and Kenneth Light, from East Meadow, New York, started an anti-dam club they called "the Grand Canyoneers" and recruited seventy-five compatriots. These youngsters wrote letters to all the members of the House and Senate and they even received a token donation from US Supreme Court Justice William O. Douglas.[62]

The members of the Colorado Open Space Coordinating Council's Grand Canyon Task Force also continued scheduling anti-dam events. By June it had purchased four Glen Canyon films from the Sierra Club and shown them an estimated two hundred times. The COSCC also consulted with *Science* magazine about a proposed article, started branches in Baltimore and Detroit, and organized a three-day, anti-dam "marathon" at the University of Colorado, where members showed movies and handed out literature. However, after successfully running ads in local newspapers, the COSCC leadership realized that they could not place an ad in the *New York Times* as they had originally planned because they simply could not afford the $10,000 to $15,000 it would cost.[63]

The Sierra Club was also in dire need of cash—its financial woes would drive Brower from the club less than three years later—as a result of publishing books such as *Time and the River Flowing* and its simultaneous campaigns to preserve the North Cascades, create a national park for Coastal Redwoods, and protect Grand Canyon from dams.[64] Although its technical experts had offered devastating arguments against the Grand Canyon dams during the just-concluded congressional hearings, it appeared as though most committee members had ignored this testimony.

Less than two weeks later, members of various House procedural committees were hammering out compromises in accordance with existing reclamation policy. Arizona politicians were taking straw polls to see how the votes would line up, and the preliminary indications were very favorable. The critical debate in the House Interior Committee, where the entire battle might be won or lost, was imminent, and preservationists needed to find a way to sustain the momentum of their stunning success in gaining coverage in *Reader's Digest* and *Life* magazines. Despite the expense, Brower decided to run ads in national newspapers, a tactic he had already used in December 1965 to raise public awareness of the Sierra Club's crusade to establish a Redwood National Park.[65]

Brower turned to the San Francisco advertising firm of Freeman, Mander & Gossage to plan this strategy. But, Brower's conferences with Howard Gossage and Jerry Mander revealed sharp differences in philosophy over what approach they believed stood the best chance of generating a public reaction. Brower, the self-described amateur, wanted a simple clear message, one that would reiterate the arguments he and other conservationists had been making for a couple of years to a national audience. However, Gossage and Mander believed that an ad should be more than just a recitation of facts and arguments; it needed to be "an event," something people would react to and keep talking about long after they had read it. Otherwise, Gossage argued, "there's no point." But Brower was reluctant because he thought the idea reflected too much "Madison Avenue" influence and differed sharply from the Sierra Club's style of advocacy.

Ultimately, neither side could convince the other and so Brower and his professional admen remained divided over tactics. "I was a bit chicken," Brower admitted to me later. He called his ally John Oakes, the *New York Times* editorial page editor, and asked him if the paper could run one ad in the earliest editions and switch to the other ad for later editions on the same date. The paper had never done that before, but Brower and Oakes thought it might be a good way to compare the public response to both approaches—amateur and professional—would generate.

Despite these disagreements, with legislation calling for the construction of dams in Grand Canyon on the threshold of approval in the House Interior Committee, there was one issue that Brower, Mander, and Gossage all agreed was of utmost importance. The release of the ads had to be timed flawlessly to have its maximum effect upon public opinion.[66] As events were soon to prove, the timing of the Sierra Club's *New York Times* advertisements was absolutely perfect.

8

Be Careful What You Wish For . . .

In *The Quiet Crisis,* Stewart Udall praised visionaries such as John Muir, who had argued for wilderness preservation and battled to protect Yosemite National Park with relentless perseverance and powerful rhetoric. Despite deep divisions within the Sierra Club and the seemingly unstoppable momentum of early twentieth-century Progressive Conservation, Muir fought gamely, using fiery language as his most effective weapon. Although he ultimately lost the fight to save Hetch Hetchy, this struggle was one of the most important factors that led Congress to create the National Park Service in 1916. Turning to the mid-twentieth century, Udall wrote that wilderness, parks, rivers, and wildlife must have advocates—"modern Muirs," he called them—who were willing to fight "with blood and bone" to save the natural world. Now as the latest incarnation of Udall's regional water project entered the most crucial phase of the political process, the secretary was about to get his wish in the form of David Brower who, as it would turn out, was willing to risk everything, even the financial ruin of Muir's beloved Sierra Club itself, to save the earth and to stop dams from being built in Grand Canyon.[1]

Ever since the beginning of this most recent and greatest fight to save Grand Canyon, the advocates of Bridge and Marble Canyon Dams argued that they would create vast new water recreational opportunities and open the lower canyon to millions of people. Floyd Dominy, Craig Hosmer, Morris Udall, and Wayne Aspinall accused the environmentalists of wanting to keep the lower canyon for the handful of people who were either wealthy enough to take float trips down the river or who had the physical stamina to explore this remote region on foot. Citing Lake Powell as an example of how reservoirs could improve upon nature, those who wanted the Grand Canyon dams built portrayed preservationists as a selfish minority, out of step with President Johnson's Great Society.

These accusations of elitism stung preservationists, who were trying desperately to distance themselves from these very ideas that they had supported only a short time before. Brower had voted in favor of dams in Grand Canyon in 1949, and Sierra Club leaders such as Bestor Robinson and other longtime members still argued that recreational reservoirs were an appropriate use of national park lands. The National Park Service had accommodated reservoir construction until the tenure of Newton Drury. Even Drury, though steadfast in his defense of Grand Canyon National Park, wavered over whether reservoirs and national monuments were irreconcilable, in all probability because he believed that monuments could not be defended, at least until the opening salvos of the Dinosaur campaign. Robinson's arguments in favor of recreation began appearing in bureau and Interior Department publications during the 1960s, to the great regret of leading preservationists.[2]

Public awareness of environmental issues increased tremendously in the twenty years after the conclusion of World War II; by the mid-1960s, in addition to the pressing social conflicts that divided the country, a revolution of sorts was occurring within the environmental movement itself. People were not only becoming increasingly concerned over threats to national parks, monuments, and wildlife, they were also worried about the dangers of pesticides, air and water pollution, chemical wastes, and other environmental hazards that threatened their quality of life. This increasing public awareness is reflected in the steady rise in the numbers of people who joined conservation organizations of various types during this time period. By the end of the decade, a National Wildlife Federation poll would show that fewer people were concerned about the preservation of open spaces, parks, and individual examples of natural curiosities than about contaminated air, water, food, and other threats to their health and well-being.[3]

Environmentalism had now become personal, and in 1966 leaders of the movement sought to determine the direction in which it was headed. Even more radical environmental thinkers cast off the ideologies that promoted the protection of mere physical features such as mountains and canyons, i.e., Muir-style preservation, altogether. The increasing public response to health issues and a more ecologically defined environmentalism now threatened to make preservation an anachronism as well.

As events would soon prove, it wasn't dead yet. Preservationists defending Grand Canyon began to make inroads with the American people, not with complex ecological arguments, but through a simple, direct, emotional approach that demolished the bureau's accusations of elitism. They were serendipitously aided by the social and political context of the 1960s—and by young people, and many who were not so young, who were questioning the status quo of virtually everything.

Grand Canyon belonged to everyone, environmentalists argued, it had become a sacred icon of American wilderness and, indeed, of America itself. It was those who sought to deface it with needless dams who were selfish, not the people trying to save it. In fact, those who wanted the dams were not merely selfish, they—the faceless government agencies staffed with robotic bureaucrats, the unresponsive political process, the ESTABLISHMENT!—were not just selfish, they were the enemy! Grand Canyon was the whole canyon, not just the one-hundred-mile section contained within the artificial political boundaries of the National Park System. Brower knew that the vast majority of people who visited Grand Canyon only experienced it from the park's overlooks on the south rim; the river, when visible, appeared to them as a gossamer blue-green thread far below. Drawing upon Drury's arguments from two decades before, Brower's primary objective was to convince the public that the river and canyon were one. Compromise, the strategy that had led to the loss of Glen Canyon and other spectacular places, was no longer an acceptable option.[4]

"Activating the Public"

The Sierra Club ran full-page advertisements in the *New York Times* and other national newspapers starting on June 9, 1966, an event that changed the fight to save Grand Canyon, and perhaps the entire environmental movement, forever. The professional copy Jerry Mander composed was confrontational, eye-catching, and, intentional or not, echoed John Muir's scorching rhetoric from a half century before.

In 1912 Muir wrote, "These temple destroyers, devotees of ravaging commercialism, seem to have a perfect contempt for Nature, and, instead of lifting their eyes to the God of the mountains, lift them to the Almighty Dollar." Mander's 1966 ad screamed in large headline-sized type, "Now Only You Can Save Grand Canyon From Being Flooded . . . For Profit!"

(If they can turn Grand Canyon into a "cash register"
is any national park safe? You know the answer.)

Now Only You Can Save Grand Canyon
From Being Flooded...For Profit

Yes, that's right, *Grand Canyon!*
The facts are these:

1. Bill H.R. 4671 is now before Rep. Wayne Aspinall's (Colo.) House Committee on Interior and Insular Affairs. This bill provides for two dams—Bridge Canyon and Marble Gorge—which would stop the Colorado River and flood water back into the canyon.

2. Should the bill pass, two standing lakes will fill what is presently 130 miles of canyon gorge. As for the wild, running Colorado River, the canyon's sculptor for 25,000,000 years, it will become dead water.

3. In some places the canyon will be submerged five hundred feet deep. "The most revealing single page of the earth's history," as Joseph Wood Krutch has described the fantastic canyon walls, will be drowned.

The new artificial shoreline will fluctuate on hydroelectric demand. Some days there will only be acres of mud where the flowing river and living canyon now are.

4. Why are these dams being built, then? For commercial power. They are dams of the sort which their sponsor, the Bureau of Reclamation of the Department of the Interior, calls "cash registers."

In other words, these dams aren't even to store water for people and farms, but to provide *auxiliary* power for industry. Arizona power politics in your Grand Canyon.

Moreover, Arizona doesn't need the dams to carry out its water development. Actually, it would have more water without the dams.

5. For, the most remarkable fact is that, as Congressional hearings have confirmed, seepage and evaporation at these remote damsites would annually *lose* enough water to supply both Phoenix and Tucson.

As for the remainder, far more efficient power sources are available right now, and at lower net cost. For the truth is, that the Grand Canyon dams will cost far more than they can earn.

6. Recognizing the threat to Grand Canyon, the Bureau of the Budget (which speaks for the President on such matters) has already suggested a moratorium on one of the dams and proposed a commission consider alternatives.

This suggestion has been steadily resisted by Mr. Aspinall's House Committee, which continues to proceed with H. R. 4671. It has been actively fought by the Bureau of Reclamation.

7. At the same time, interestingly, other Bureaus within Secretary Udall's domain (notably National Parks, Fish and Wildlife, Indian Affairs, Mines, Outdoor Recreation, Geological Survey) have been discouraged from presenting their findings, obtained at public expense. Only the Reclamation Bureau has been heard.

8. Meanwhile, in a matter of days the bill will be on the floor of Congress and—let us make the shocking fact completely clear—it will probably pass.

The only thing that can stop it is your prompt action.

The Grand Canyon: How man plans to improve it. (*Newsweek, May 30, 1966.*)

9. What to do? Letters and wires are effective, and so are the forms at right once you have signed them and mailed them. (You will notice that there is also one in the box below to the Sierra Club; that's us.)

10. Remember, with all the complexities of Washington politics and Arizona politics, and the ins and outs of committees and procedures, there is only one simple, incredible issue here: This time it's the Grand Canyon about to flood. *The Grand Canyon.*

WHAT THE SIERRA CLUB IS FOR

The Sierra Club, founded in 1892 by John Muir, is nonprofit, supported by people who sense what Thoreau sensed when he wrote, "in wildness is the preservation of the world." The club's program is nationwide, includes wilderness trips, books, and films—and a major effort to protect the remnant of wilderness in the Americas.

There are now twenty chapters, branch offices in New York, Washington, Albuquerque, Seattle, and Los Angeles, and a main office in San Francisco.

This advertisement has been made possible by individual contributions, particularly from our Atlantic, Rocky Mountain, Rio Grande, Southern California and Grand Canyon chapter members, and by buyers of Sierra Club books everywhere, especially the twelve in the highly praised Exhibit Format Series, which includes books on Grand Canyon, Glen Canyon, the Redwoods, the Northern Cascades, Mount Everest, and the Sierra.

```
David Brower, Executive Director,
Sierra Club
Mills Tower, San Francisco, California
☐ Please send me more of the details of the battle to save
  Grand Canyon.
☐ I know how much this sort of constructive protest costs.
  Here is my donation of $_____to help you continue
  your work.
☐ Please send me a copy of "Time and the River Flowing,"
  the famous four-color book by Philip Hyde and François
  Leydet which tells the whole story of Grand Canyon and
  the battle to save it. I am enclosing $25.00
☐ I would like to be a member of the Sierra Club. Enclosed
  is $14.00 for entrance fee and first year's dues.

Name_____
Address_____
City_____

Note: All contributions and membership dues are deductible.
```

PLEASE CLIP THESE AND MAIL THEM

No. 1
THE PRESIDENT
THE WHITE HOUSE
WASHINGTON 25, D.C.

THANK YOU FOR YOUR STAND, THROUGH THE BUREAU OF THE BUDGET, PROTECTING GRAND CANYON. WOULD YOU PLEASE ASK CONGRESS TO DEFER BOTH GRAND CANYON DAMS PENDING INVESTIGATION OF THE ALTERNATE POWER SOURCES. THANK YOU AGAIN.

Name_____
Address_____
City_____State____Zip____

No. 2
SECRETARY OF THE INTERIOR STEWART UDALL
WASHINGTON 25, D.C.

ALL YOUR SPLENDID CONSERVATION WORK OF THE PAST WILL BE BLIGHTED IF YOU ALLOW THE LIVING GRAND CANYON TO DIE AT THE HANDS OF YOUR BUREAU OF RECLAMATION. WOULD YOU PLEASE ALLOW THE FINDINGS OF YOUR OTHER BUREAUS TO BE REPORTED FULLY TO CONGRESS BEFORE THE VOTE ON H. R. 4671? THANK YOU.

Name_____
Address_____
City_____State____Zip____

No. 3
REPRESENTATIVE WAYNE ASPINALL
HOUSE OF REPRESENTATIVES
WASHINGTON 25, D.C.

I URGE YOU TO HALT PROCEEDINGS ON H. R. 4671, NOW IN YOUR COMMITTEE, AND TO SEEK EXPERT TESTIMONY FROM THE MANY INTERIOR DEPARTMENT AGENCIES THAT HAVE NOT YET APPEARED BEFORE YOU. THANK YOU.

Name_____
Address_____
City_____State____Zip____

No. 4 (To your Congressman)
REPRESENTATIVE
HOUSE OF REPRESENTATIVES
WASHINGTON 25, D.C.

PLEASE JOIN IN THE FIGHT TO SAVE GRAND CANYON BY URGING DELETION OF BOTH DAMS PROPOSED IN H. R. 4671. THANK YOU.

Name_____
Address_____
City_____State____Zip____

No. 5 (To one of your U. S. Senators)
SENATOR
UNITED STATES SENATE
WASHINGTON 25, D.C.

PLEASE JOIN IN THE FIGHT TO SAVE GRAND CANYON BY URGING DELETION OF BOTH DAMS PROPOSED IN H. R. 4671. THANK YOU.

Name_____
Address_____
City_____State____Zip____

No. 6 (To your state's other Senator)
SENATOR
UNITED STATES SENATE
WASHINGTON 25, D.C.

PLEASE JOIN IN THE FIGHT TO SAVE GRAND CANYON BY URGING DELETION OF BOTH DAMS PROPOSED IN H. R. 4671. THANK YOU.

Name_____
Address_____
City_____State____Zip____

FIGURE 7.5. The first of the brilliant Grand Canyon "Battle Ads" created by the San Francisco advertising firm of Freeman, Mander & Gossage and commissioned by the Sierra Club, this full-page advertisement ran in the *New York Times* and other national newspapers on June 9, 1966. This ad triggered the Internal Revenue Service's revocation of the Sierra Club's tax-deductible status and generated a tsunami of public sympathy for the club and its fight to save Grand Canyon from dams. Image courtesy of Jerry Mander.

Both Muir and Mander described in stark terms the crassness of destroying areas of irreplaceable natural splendor for mere economic gain. Mander's ad also included a summary of the arguments and accused Stewart Udall of silencing agencies within the Interior Department such as the National Park Service, whose personnel opposed the dams. The ad encouraged readers to make contributions to the Sierra Club, write letters, or clip and send the attached coupons that had the names and addresses of key government officials already printed on them. Emphasizing that the canyon belonged to all Americans, the ad closed with this admonition: "Remember, with all the complexities of Washington and Arizona politics and the ins and outs of committees and procedures, there is only one simple, incredible issue here: This time it's the Grand Canyon they want to flood. *The Grand Canyon* [emphasis in the original]."[5]

Outraged dam supporters claimed the ads distorted the truth. They accused the Sierra Club of trying to dupe the American people into believing that the dams would flood the entire canyon from rim to rim. Aspinall angrily scolded Brower and said the ads were "nasty, indecent," and "ignorant," while Barry Goldwater denounced them as a "Big Lie." Aspinall never forgave Brower and refused to pose for pictures with him when they crossed paths later.[6]

Morris Udall delivered a blistering speech on the floor of the House in which he excoriated the Sierra Club's tactics the same day the advertisements appeared. Udall raged that the advertisements were "dishonest," "inflammatory," and the most "distorted and flagrant hatchet job" he had ever seen. He argued that the ads were misleading because they included a photo of lower Grand Canyon upon which the bureau had superimposed the Bridge Canyon Dam and reservoir. However, this part of the canyon lay far outside the boundaries of the national park; hence, he felt that the Sierra Club's contention that Hualapai Dam would inundate part of Grand Canyon was simply untrue because he believed the language implied that what would really be flooded was Grand Canyon National Park.[7] But Mander had described the Sierra Club's position in rhetoric designed to evoke an emotional response. The magnificent canyon and the river that carved it transcended paltry human attempts to cut them into pieces by drawing arbitrary lines on a map. All of the river and canyon should be protected, whether they lay within the park or not.

Were the Sierra Club advertisements misleading as Morris Udall charged, or merely the product of professional advertising? Brower himself wrote Udall shortly before the ads were published and emphasized that while, in his view, a lake five hundred feet deep would "flood" the Colorado River, for anyone to accuse him of trying to deceive the public into believing that the dams would create reservoirs that would inundate the canyon from rim to rim was simply "preposterous."[8]

Mander designed his ad to generate mass appeal through an eye-catching headline. A person who only read the headline could have easily concluded that Grand Canyon would be flooded from rim to rim. However, the small print of the ad clearly stated that the canyon would be flooded to a maximum depth of five hundred feet. Even Brower's more understated ad, though it did not specify the actual depth of the reservoirs, included the photo of the Bridge Canyon site, which also had recently been published in a *Newsweek* article, upon which the bureau had superimposed Hualapai Dam and Reservoir. The picture clearly demonstrated that at its deepest point the reservoir would only flood the inner gorge of the canyon and would not even inundate that completely.

Thirty years after these ads were printed, Brower and Floyd Dominy were still fighting about them. In the mid-1990s Dominy angrily recalled that the misleading public perception Brower intentionally created was believed by so many people that visitors to popular tourist overlooks in Grand Canyon National Park would ask park rangers where the lake was going to be. Brower argued that he never said that the canyon would be "flooded out" but only "flooded," a fine semantic distinction perhaps, but, depending on one's perspective, a serious one. The inclusion of the bureau's own pictures, Brower contended, undermined any accusation that the Sierra Club advertisements were deceptive. Nonetheless, Dominy railed, "It was an absolute lie, and Brower knew it. So that sanctimonious bastard deliberately lied!"[9]

Perhaps it is possible to draw a distinction between the language Brower used and the impression the ads actually created. The ads were written and structured strategically to tap into the symbolic importance Grand Canyon had attained in the minds of most Americans by the mid-1960s. By emphasizing the term "Grand Canyon" as opposed to "national park" or "Colorado River," the ads were designed to evoke "disbelief and outrage" that anyone would dare to harm it. Susan Senecah, in her fascinating analysis of the Sierra Club's "advocacy advertising," describes this interplay between ad and reader: "Using hyperbole and sensationalism, the lines are drawn between the two dichotomous choices available to the reader: dams or no dams, evil or good. The issue demands a moral decision . . . [The language empowered people] to act in an individual capacity to achieve collective results."[10]

Brower could honestly claim he never said that the Grand Canyon dams would flood the canyon from rim to rim or be located within Grand Canyon National Park, yet he could also write and support advertising that intentionally created the inference in people's minds that they would do exactly that. Americans who read and reacted to these ads did so because Grand Canyon, *their* Grand Canyon, was threatened by self-serving politicians and "bungling government agencies" intent upon destroying it for short-term economic gain.[11] In their minds, the location of the boundaries, and where the dams would be built, simply didn't matter.

In the same speech where he accused the Sierra Club of lying, Morris Udall made at least two false assertions on the floor of the House himself: that former Park Service Director Albright approved of a high Bridge/Hualapai Dam and that both dams were to be utilized as run of the river projects that would not create surges of water downstream. Albright's approval of a low dam, and only a low dam, has already been well-documented and Floyd Dominy had testified in the recent subcommittee hearings that one of the reasons the dams were absolutely indispensable was because of their ability to generate peaking power. Preservationists loathed peaking power plants because the reservoir fluctuations they caused created an unsightly dead zone because of silt and mineral deposition. One only had to look at the before and after photos of Hetch Hetchy the Sierra Club was circulating to see these effects.

In addition, Morris Udall, Rhodes, and other dam advocates kept insisting that the Bridge/Hualapai and Marble Canyon dam sites and reservoirs were not in Grand Canyon—meaning Grand Canyon National Park—a strategy clearly designed to keep the public from learning that vast stretches of the canyon lay unprotected *outside* of the park. The semantic gymnastics of these CAP supporters was every bit as misleading as what the Sierra Club's ads implied, that the dams would flood out Grand Canyon National Park.[12]

Police-State Tactics

Scarcely had the smoke cleared from Morris Udall's verbal salvo against the Sierra Club's Grand Canyon "Battle Ads," then an event that has become part of the mythology of the environmental movement occurred. On June

10, 1966, less than twenty-four hours after the publication of the Sierra Club's advertisements, the Internal Revenue Service notified the club leadership that the organization was now under investigation for violating IRS regulations governing lobbying. Specifically, the IRS charged that the club's ads were designed to have a "substantial" influence on the pending legislation, a direct violation of IRS statutes and the Supreme Court's 1954 *Harriss* decision. The IRS stated that it could no longer guarantee the tax deductibility of contributions made to the club while it investigated the club's lobbying activities. Sierra Club President Edgar Wayburn remembered later that "a small faceless man in a dark blue suit" hand-delivered the IRS notice to the Sierra Club office in San Francisco, while Brower insisted at the time that it was delivered by a "federal marshal . . . for dramatic effect."[13]

Although it has never been determined with any degree of certainty who initiated the IRS action, many prominent conservationists blamed Morris Udall for sparking the investigation. The popular account as related by many preservationists is that on June 9, 1966, while Mo Udall was having either lunch or drinks at the Congressional Hotel bar in Washington, DC, with IRS Commissioner Sheldon Cohen, he showed Cohen the Sierra Club ad in the *Washington Post* and shouted, "How the hell can the Sierra Club get away with this?" Brower and Wayburn insisted that Udall later admitted to them personally that he had not only called for the IRS action, but also recognized it as a colossal blunder on his part because of the public reaction that followed.[14]

Cohen stated later that the IRS started the investigation on its own; a treasury undersecretary indicated that someone must have heard part of Udall's conversation with Cohen and concluded, erroneously, that Udall was asking Cohen to investigate. Dominy also credited Mo Udall, "based on some pretty good surmising," for "being smart enough" to think of it and, holding true to his mercurial personality, is on record both as saying he wished he had thought of it himself and believing that it was the biggest mistake the dam supporters made. Stewart Udall steadfastly defended his brother and stated that anyone who accused Mo of initiating the IRS action was guilty of taking a "cheap shot." In a letter to Ansel Adams, the secretary even said he had been told that the investigation had originated with a US Treasury Department official who was also a member of the Sierra Club![15]

For his part, Morris Udall vehemently denied the charges that he asked Cohen to revoke the Sierra Club's tax-deductible status. Roy

Elson, aide to Senator Hayden, rejected the notion that Hayden had anything to do with the IRS action, although he admitted in an interview that he suggested it to Hayden but that "the Senator would have no part of it."[16] California Representative Craig Hosmer, perhaps the most antagonistic opponent conservationists faced, asked preservationist witnesses point-blank about the expenditures their organizations incurred in trying to defeat the Grand Canyon dams during the September 1965 congressional hearings with Morris Udall in the room. It is a matter of historical fact that the issue of the club's lobbying activities and their potential for violating the Federal Lobbying Act was openly discussed during these hearings.[17]

Sierra Club Director William Siri believed that Mo Udall brought the ad to the attention of an IRS official without actually suggesting that the IRS investigate the club's tax status. This version of events is supported by the evidence: Mo Udall wrote Cohen on June 10, 1966, the day after the ads were placed, inquiring as to whether contributions to the Sierra Club elicited by the newspaper ads were tax deductible; however, he did not ask for an investigation into the Sierra Club's activities.[18] Perhaps Cohen, prompted by Udall's letter, or perhaps after their alleged conversation at the Congressional Hotel, initiated the investigation himself. It is also possible that the suggestion was made over the telephone by Udall or someone else and that no record of it exists.

To state definitively, as some preservationists have done, based upon hearsay evidence that Morris Udall initiated the investigation and intended to use the IRS revocation as a weapon to damage the Sierra Club, is not conclusively supported by the records. But regardless of who was ultimately responsible, and despite Commissioner Cohen's claims that the IRS was merely trying to "administer the tax laws as they have been enacted by Congress," it is indisputable that the Internal Revenue Service reacted to the Sierra Club advertisements with unprecedented speed.[19]

Considering that the IRS rendered its permanent decision later that year and applied its decree retroactively to include all contributions made after June 9, the club's assertions that it had been singled out ring true. It also appears, given that the IRS revoked the club's tax-*deductible* status as opposed to its tax-*exempt* status—two entirely different tax issues that many people have conflated—the IRS was trying to undercut the Sierra Club at its very foundation because the small tax-deductible gifts and dues of its individual members were the lifeblood of the club. Possibly the most enduring mystery of the IRS revocation is not who ordered it, but rather why it took so long for someone to do so, given the widely held hostility for the preservationists' position and the club in particular.

When the mass media began broadcasting the news of the IRS action, tens of thousands of people immediately reacted and fired off angry letters to Congress. Estimates of the volume of mail vary, and the tabulations are scant, but California Senator Thomas Kuchel later recalled that it was "one of the largest letter-writing campaigns I have ever seen." Stewart Udall's staff counted more than twenty thousand letters mailed just to the interior secretary, while the archived papers of Hayden, Rhodes, Mo Udall, Barry Goldwater, Stewart Udall, and other important political players contain tens of thousands more.

How many letters came in to Washington as a result of the ads and IRS action is open to debate; Morris Udall described the mail as a "deluge," while some historians have put the figure at "millions." Marc Reisner, in *Cadillac Desert*, cited an interview with a bureau official who claimed that dump trucks were used to haul it to congressional offices.[20] It's difficult to obtain an exact figure, but clearly a tsunami of letters inundated the offices of federal officials in the wake of the IRS revocation of the Sierra Club's tax-deductible status.

A representative sample of the letters in the archived papers of the Interior Department, Sierra Club, Wilderness Society, Mo and Stewart Udall, Hayden, John Saylor, and Rhodes demonstrate that a shift in public focus occurred after the IRS revocation. Before the IRS action, the letter writers generally claimed affiliation with one or more conservation organizations and wrote only that the Grand Canyon dams should be stopped. After the IRS action of June 10, 1966, people expressed outrage that the club's rights of free speech, petition, and due process had been violated, in addition to concerns about the dams. Others wrote the Sierra Club, stating that they wanted to become members as an act of protest because they believed the IRS action threatened fundamental rights that constituted the bedrock of the republic itself.[21]

Editorials appeared in newspapers across the nation criticizing both the proposed damming of Grand Canyon and federal interference with basic constitutional rights. Terms such as "police-state" and "tyranny" frequently appeared in correspondence and newspaper editorials, while the *New York Times* accused Secretary Udall of prohibiting free speech within his own department by "silencing" agencies that could be presumed to oppose the dams while at the same time allowing the Bureau of Reclamation to "lobby the public shamelessly and tirelessly with the public's own money."[22]

Whether Stewart Udall muzzled the National Park Service is a matter of debate. Udall responded to Brower's March 1966 accusations by stating that once the Interior Department adopted a position as a matter of policy, it would inhibit his agency's ability to function if it were torn by dissension. However, Park Service Director George Hartzog censured a park service employee for distributing literature against Bridge Canyon Dam in October 1965, six months *after* Udall adopted the Budget Bureau's recommendation that Bridge Canyon Dam be deferred. The interior secretary failed to communicate this policy shift to park service personnel for more than a year, and it was only after Brower's March 30 telegram from Grand Canyon that Udall informed park superintendents that their subordinates could oppose Bridge Canyon Dam.[23]

Even after Udall's message was distributed in June 1966, Yosemite National Park Superintendent John Davis, with Director Hartzog's subsequent approval, prevented a concessionaire from showing the Sierra Club's Glen Canyon film because it opposed the bureau's proposed dams for Grand Canyon, an incident that evoked accusations of censorship from Sierra Club officials. Merrill Beal, Grand Canyon National Park naturalist during the controversy, contended that he was "instructed" to not oppose the programs of the Bureau of Reclamation, which favored Bridge Canyon Dam. It appears park service personnel received orders to refrain from opposing Bridge Canyon Dam from the upper echelons of either the National Park Service or the Interior Department even after Secretary Udall accepted the Budget Bureau's deferral of Bridge Canyon Dam in April 1965.[24]

Although the Sierra Club leadership had decided to challenge the Federal Lobbying Act on First Amendment grounds, when the IRS finally acted they did not realize the great potential for public sympathy it created . . . at least at first. Evidently the club's leadership was not Machiavellian enough to try to antagonize the IRS into taking away its tax-deductible status in anticipation of a public windfall. Brower commented upon the serendipitous nature of the enormous public reaction, later telling me that "I was just lucky it worked out that way." However, in the wake of the June 9 advertisements and the IRS response, club leaders immediately recognized that larger social forces were at work and released two more ads during the congressional debate of the summer of 1966, each of which gave prominent space to the club's IRS travails.[25]

Ironically, it was the dam supporters who first understood that the controversy was playing out in a much larger social context. Although unable to capitalize on public concerns about federal interference with individual rights, they tapped into public unrest about civil rights and portrayed dam opponents as being racially prejudiced against American Indians. Rich Johnson's letters, "written" by Hualapai Chief Rocha and other Native Americans, began arriving in the offices of congressmen, newspaper editors, and other intended recipients at the beginning of July. Arizona Representative George Senner read one aloud on the floor of the House and inserted it into the *Congressional Record*. Western newspapers began running articles arguing that the Hualapai Dam would confer great benefits upon the Hualapai Nation, some reprinting the passages "written" by Chief Rocha.[26]

In addition, Morris Udall, John Rhodes, Floyd Dominy, and other project advocates launched a media blitz of their own and scheduled TV and radio appearances nationwide. Udall argued his case so convincingly that the editors of the *Washington Post* wrote in August that, contrary to the Sierra Club's assertions, "it is plain nonsense to speak of these proposed minor changes ruining the Grand Canyon." When Carolyn Pierce, president of the General Federation of Women's Clubs, wrote an opposition letter to Saylor, which the Pennsylvania representative entered into the *Congressional Record*, Arizona's Rhodes produced a letter and resolution favoring the dams from the president of the Arizona Women's Club. The *Arizona Republic* and *Arizona Daily Star* encouraged their subscribers to write Congress, and the *Republic* claimed later that more than seven thousand of its subscribers sent coupons to Congress. An ephemeral pro-CAP citizen's group, the Southwest Progress Committee, sponsored the production of a movie, *Grand Canyon, The Ever-Changing Giant*, and scheduled it for television broadcasts across the United States.[27]

One Sierra Club member from Tucson alleged that the editor of the *Arizona Daily Star* made threatening phone calls to local library officials and to the sisters of a Catholic hospital who hosted a Sierra Club film and anti-dam presentation at their facilities. Pro-dam newspapers also reminded their readers that the Sierra Club, including David Brower, had once supported the Grand Canyon dams.[28] This counteroffensive began to yield results, and less than one month after the Sierra Club advertisements of June 9, a steady stream of pro-dam letters began trickling into congressional mailboxes.

By mid-August Rhodes could write to a CAP supporter that many of his congressional colleagues were receiving as much mail in favor as opposed. The *Arizona Republic* began to print letters from disgruntled Sierra Club members who disapproved of Brower's tactics and felt that he and his allies had hijacked their organization. The volume of pro-dam mail never came close to the deluge sent by the opposition, but it was enough to remind members of Congress that there were two sides to the issue. Several of them told Morris Udall that they resented the Sierra Club's tactics and had received many letters from people who favored the dams.[29]

Virtually ignored by most people who contend that the Sierra Club advertisements and the IRS revocation constituted the turning point at which the defeat of the dams became inevitable, is that key House committees kept pushing the bill forward in the summer of 1966. The political alliance among the basin states, forged by almost two years of tense negotiations and exasperating behind-the-scenes intrigue, somehow remained intact. Despite heated debates over the deals upon which representatives had already agreed, and numerous anti-dam speeches delivered on the House floor by Saylor and Michigan Representative John Dingell, the House Subcommittee on Public Works released its final bill on June 10. One day after the Sierra Club's ads ran, the bill included: (1) both dams; (2) a payment of $16,398,000 to the Hualapai Nation; and (3) a feasibility-grade study of water importation to be initiated by a national water commission.[30]

The Lower Colorado River Basin Project now moved back to the House Subcommittee on Irrigation and Reclamation, chaired by Walter Rogers from Texas. Once there, representatives from the seven basin states blocked another attempt by Saylor to remove both dams and Foley's amendment to delete the feasibility study. On June 28, when the debate concluded, the subcommittee voted 13–5 in favor of the existing bill, the dissents coming from Saylor and four representatives from the Pacific Northwest. Now with the subcommittee hurdles cleared, the bill moved to the full House Committee on Interior and Insular Affairs, the first time that the Central Arizona Project in any form had come before the Interior Committee since the CAP defeats of 1950 and 1951. Senator Hayden looked forward to the coming floor debate and announced that despite Jackson's opposition to water importation from the Northwest, the Senate Interior

Committee chairman had promised him that he would move on the bill immediately after the lower house passed it.[31]

Cape Disappointment

On the southernmost tip of the Washington coast, a stone outcropping called Cape Disappointment rises like a sentinel above the mouth of the mighty Columbia River. Despite well-known hazards plotted on maritime maps and the incandescent beam of a lighthouse built in 1856, the rocks, riptides, and sandbars where the river joins the Pacific Ocean have claimed more than two thousand vessels and seven hundred lives since 1792. It is for good reason that sailors call this area "the Graveyard of the Pacific."[32] Southwestern politicians enamored of importing water from the Columbia River would encounter their own Cape Disappointment in the unyielding form of Senator Jackson, who had sworn to protect the Columbia from anyone who tried to steal water from it. As chair of the Senate Committee on Interior and Insular Affairs, it was well within his power to destroy their best-laid plans, and despite tactics that ranged from public shaming to the promise of governmental largess, Jackson refused to give up even one drop of water. And so it was on the rhetorical shoals of Jackson's steadfast opposition that this latest version of the CAP—the last containing dams to reach the House Interior Committee—would run aground forever.

On July 13, 1966, the Lower Colorado River Basin Project came before the full House Interior Committee, and once again the representatives from the Pacific Northwest tried to amend the bill to remove the feasibility study. Saylor pushed his amendment to delete both dams and, as in the subcommittee, these attempts were defeated easily. However, after a week of tumultuous debate, Aspinall dropped a bombshell that threatened to unravel the fragile seven-state alliance for good.

Aspinall realized that Jackson would never allow a bill containing a feasibility study to leave the Senate Interior Committee even if it passed in the House. He argued that the feasibility language should be downgraded to a reconnaissance study and recommended the creation of a national water commission with jurisdiction over any proposal to import water into the Colorado Basin.

California's representatives were furious that Aspinall had buckled under Jackson's opposition and threatened to walk out of the proceedings. Although it was a practical move by a pragmatic politician, Aspinall's amendment threatened to tear the seven-state agreement apart. Morris

Udall, caught in an agonizing dilemma, voted in favor of the amendment although he lamented the probable loss of California's support. On July 21, the House Interior Committee voted 20–9 to downgrade the importation analysis from a feasibility to a reconnaissance study.[33]

Frantic water officials from the seven basin states, faced with the prospect that years of painstaking negotiations would come to naught, met to try to work out a compromise solution; however, it looked like their differences were now irreconcilable. One side would have to give, and the prospects for that seemed unlikely, especially now that Aspinall himself had told some of his House colleagues that he "had a deal in the Senate" based upon his new proposal. California's support appeared irretrievably lost.

But the wily Mo Udall, with the future of the alliance and the Central Arizona Project hanging by a thread, framed a creative solution that demonstrated his skills as a parliamentary tactician and his astute political instincts. Udall's strategy involved some freewheeling semantics that would give Aspinall more flexibility to fight for the bill on the floor of the House and the use of a rare parliamentary tactic—a "motion to recommit" the bill briefly back to the subcommittee for a quick revision.

Instead of language calling for a feasibility study outright, Udall suggested that the bill be revised to include a reconnaissance study initially, with the promise that a feasibility study would follow immediately if the proposed national water commission determined that water importation was feasible. With Aspinall's blessing, Udall secretly brokered this agreement with California unbeknownst to Saylor and Foley, who believed that Arizona and California were at odds once again.[34]

On July 28, 1966, the House Interior Committee met to vote on the Lower Colorado River Basin Project bill. Saylor and Foley were confident that the legislation would go down to defeat because of Aspinall's controversial amendment of the week before. Before the final vote, Californian Craig Hosmer implemented Udall's strategy and moved to recommit the bill back to the reclamation subcommittee for alteration. The motion passed 20–10 despite vehement objections from Foley and Saylor. Aspinall immediately sent the bill to the subcommittee, which added and approved Udall's reconnaissance/feasibility language and sent it back to the Interior Committee chair after a couple of hours of discussion.

Aspinall then brought the altered bill back before the full Interior Committee, which was still obligated to vote on July 28. After a bitterly contested session, during which an outraged Saylor accused the "selfish interests" from California and Arizona and Aspinall of "nefarious legislative shenanigans," the House Interior Committee voted 22–10 to send the bill to the floor.[35] Despite strong objections in the committee and another full-page Sierra Club ad that had appeared in the *New York Times* on July 25, now only the House Rules Committee, which was responsible for making sure the bill conformed to House procedural protocols, stood in the way of a floor debate that would probably result in the passage of the Central Arizona Project with two Grand Canyon dams.[36]

Morris Udall had canvassed the members of the Rules Committee in early May to see whether the committee would object to releasing the bill to the floor in the event of a favorable Interior Committee report, and the fifteen members overwhelmingly supported the bill. Now with the long-awaited floor debate seemingly imminent, Udall and Rhodes asked their House colleagues again to determine whether the bill stood a good chance of passage. On August 22, Udall's count revealed that 156 of his colleagues supported the bill outright, with another seventy leaning in favor of it. Calculating a "reasonably optimistic" assessment of the probable and undecided votes, Mo Udall believed that about 260 representatives would vote in favor of the bill—and he only needed 218 to pass it. Udall, Rhodes, and the rest of the Arizona task force now swung into action to try to influence the probable and undecided votes by calling influential constituents within their districts. Udall even "nailed down" a colleague's vote with the gift of a framed picture of Grand Canyon he paid for himself.[37]

Environmentalists also continued their efforts, although many of them were now resigned to the inevitability that the bill would come before the House. Richard Bradley ventured into hostile territory toward the end of July and delivered an address to the Los Angeles Town Hall to rebut a speech Dominy had made several weeks earlier. By the end of August, the Colorado Open Space Coordinating Council had produced and circulated two anti-dam television documentaries in response to a film produced by CAP advocates, while the July–August *Sierra Club Bulletin* featured a cover photo of the upper reaches of Lake Powell with driftwood and other floating debris covering the reservoir's surface, captioned "A Portent of Things to Come in Grand Canyon?" People also continued lobbying at the grassroots level. Many wrote the Sierra Club and asked for reprints of articles to distribute to friends and neighbors, including Helen Skelton of Fremont, Indiana, who also took $150 of her own money and placed full-page ads in two local newspapers.[38]

Preservationists also managed to effectively negate the accusations of racism made by the reclamation lobby. This smear campaign had grown more intense as the summer progressed. Brower asked Stephen Jett, who had testified against the dams during the May hearings, to speak to the Navajo Tribal Council and, in particular, Navajo Tribal attorney Norman Littell, whom, coincidentally, Stewart Udall had been trying to fire since 1963. In July Jett had his pilot fly Littell and himself over the Marble Canyon damsite prior to a scheduled council meeting. Jett, like Martin Litton the previous March, allowed the canyon to work its magic. By the time they landed the attorney was convinced that the dams were a bad idea and, according to Jett, the situation also provided Littell a serendipitous opportunity to "give his adversary Stew Udall, a poke in the eye."[39]

Jett also convinced him that the creation or expansion of large tribal parks along the rim of Marble Canyon could bring great economic benefits to the Navajo Nation. By the time the council met in early August, Jett and Littell had drafted a resolution opposing the dams. They had also observed that if a coal-fired plant were built as an alternative source of CAP power, the Navajo could supply the fuel for it from the vast coal deposits located on their reservation.[40]

Despite ongoing conflict between the "traditionist" and "progressive" factions within the Navajo Tribal Council, on August 3 it repudiated its 1961 resolution in favor of Marble Canyon Dam and overwhelmingly approved a measure condemning both Grand Canyon dams and the "tactics of the Udalls." The council also approved the final version of a contract Littell had been negotiating with Peabody Coal Company to develop the reservation's coal resources to supply several of the region's existing and planned power plants. In a powerful statement against the dams, Navajo Tribal councilman Howard Gorman testified in Navajo (and simultaneously translated into English), "Sheep can reproduce. So can humans. But the land is not like these. Once it is destroyed, it is gone forever." Councilwoman Annie Wauneka, a Presidential Medal of Freedom recipient, helped write a press release that condemned the dams. The national media picked up the story, effectively destroying the pro-dam lobby's attempt to paint the environmentalists as racist.[41]

Although twice-defeated in committee, Saylor continued his offensive against the project. He announced that he intended to offer an amended bill during the floor debate that would eliminate California's annual 4.4 million acre-foot guarantee, both Grand Canyon dams, Aspinall's Colorado projects, and the water-importation studies. Saylor argued that his proposal would "save one billion dollars—and Grand Canyon too," and that it offered Congress a relatively noncontroversial alternative to the CAP with the House midterm elections just more than three months away.[42]

With the bill one step away from a floor debate, the Sierra Club struck again on August 23. With exquisite timing, it began publishing full-page advertisements in the *Wall Street Journal, San Francisco Chronicle*, and several other prominent newspapers and magazines that, unlike the *New York Times*, could run last-minute ads with very little notice.[43] This advertisement, perhaps the most famous of them all, once again hearkened to Muir's defense of Hetch Hetchy.

In 1912 Muir wrote, "Dam Hetch-Hetchy! As well dam for water-tanks the people's cathedrals and churches, for no holier temple has ever been consecrated by the heart of man."[44]

Fifty-four years later, in response to arguments that the Grand Canyon reservoirs would make the canyon's scenic wonders more accessible, Brower, Mander, and Gossage penned this headline: "Should We Also Flood the Sistine Chapel So Tourists Can Get Nearer the Ceiling?"[45] Yet despite these headlines and a deluge of anti-dam mail, the isolated committee process ground forward, virtually unaffected by what was happening in the court of public opinion.

California's "Third Senator"

When the Rules Committee had not released the bill to the floor by mid-August, Morris Udall began to suspect that the California representatives on the committee were obstructing the proceedings. Udall and John Rhodes met with California's water strategists to determine whether that was the case. Northcutt Ely, who wielded so much power behind the scenes that Dominy occasionally referred to him as "California's third senator," still masterminded California's water strategy.

On August 22, 1966, Ely told them he had spoken with some California congressmen who believed that Saylor had the votes to pass his substitute bill during the upcoming floor debate. Even worse, Ely claimed Aspinall approved of the delay because he believed that if Saylor succeeded, Jackson would ram a similar bill through the Senate, and thus both California and Colorado would lose the project's features that were

SHOULD WE ALSO FLOOD THE SISTINE CHAPEL SO TOURISTS CAN GET NEARER THE CEILING?

EARTH began four billion years ago and Man two million. The Age of Technology, on the other hand, is hardly a hundred years old, and on our time chart we have been generous to give it even the little line we have.

It seems to us hasty, therefore, during this blip of time, for Man to think of directing his fascinating new tools toward altering irrevocably the forces which made him. Nonetheless, in these few brief years among four billion, wilderness has all but disappeared. And now these:

1) There is a bill in Congress to "improve" Grand Canyon. Two dams will back up artificial lakes into 148 miles of canyon gorge. This will benefit tourists in power boats, it is argued, who will enjoy viewing the canyon wall more closely. (See headline.) Submerged underneath the tourists will be part of the most revealing single page of earth's history. The lakes will be as deep as 600 feet (deeper for example, than all but a handful of New York buildings are high) but in a century, silting will have replaced the water with that much mud, wall to wall.

There is no part of the wild Colorado River, the Grand Canyon's sculptor, that will not be maimed.

Tourist recreation, as a reason for the dams, is in fact an afterthought. The Bureau of Reclamation, which backs them, prefers to call the dams "cash registers." They are expected to make money by sale of commercial power.

They will not provide anyone with water.

2) In Northern California, four lumber companies are about to complete logging the private virgin redwood forests, an operation which to give you an idea of its size, has taken fifty years.

Soon, where nature's tallest living things have stood silently since the age of the dinosaurs, the extent of the cutting will make creation of a redwood national park absurd.

The companies have said tourists want only enough roadside trees for the snapping of photos. They offer to spare trees for this purpose, and not much more. The result will remind you of the places on your face you missed while you were shaving.

3) And up the Hudson, there are plans for a power complex —a plant, transmission lines, and a reservoir on top of Storm King Mountain—destroying one of the last wild and high and beautiful spots near New York City.

4) A proposal to flood a region in Alaska as large as Lake Erie would eliminate at once the breeding grounds of more wildlife than conservationists have preserved in history.

5) In San Francisco, real estate developers are day by day filling a bay that made the city famous, putting tract houses over the fill; and now there's a new idea—still more fill, enough for an air cargo terminal as big as Manhattan.

There exists today a mentality which can conceive such destruction, giving commerce as ample reason. For 74 years, the 40,000 member Sierra Club has opposed that mentality. But now, when even Grand Canyon can be threatened, we are at a critical moment in time.

This generation will decide if something untrammelled and free remains, as testimony we had love for those who follow.

We have been taking ads, therefore, asking people to write their Congressmen and Senators; Secretary of the Interior Stewart Udall; The President; and to send us funds to continue the battle. Thousands *have* written, but meanwhile, the Grand Canyon legislation has advanced out of committee and is near a House vote. More letters are needed and more money, to help fight a mentality that may decide Man no longer needs nature.*

```
David Brower, Executive Director
Sierra Club
Mills Tower, San Francisco

☐ Please send me more details on how I may help.
☐ Here is a donation of $_____ to continue your effort
   to keep the public informed.
☐ Send me "Time and the River Flowing," famous four color
   book which tells the complete story of Grand Canyon,
   and why T. Roosevelt said, "leave it as it is." ($25.00)
☐ Send me "The Last Redwoods" which tells the complete
   story of the opportunity as well as the destruction in the
   redwoods. ($17.50)
☐ I would like to be a member of the Sierra Club. Enclosed is
   $14.00 for entrance and first year's dues.

Name_____
Address_____
City_____State_____Zip_____
```

*The previous ads, urging that readers exercise a constitutional right of petition, to save Grand Canyon, produced an unprecedented reaction by the Internal Revenue Service threatening our tax deductible status. IRS says the ads may be a "substantial" effort to "influence legislation." Undefined, these terms leave organizations like ours at the mercy of administrative whim. (The question has not been raised with any organizations that favor Grand Canyon dams.) So we cannot now promise that contributions you send us are deductible—pending results of what may be a long legal battle.

The Sierra Club, founded in 1892 by John Muir, is nonprofit, supported by people who, like Thoreau, believe "In wildness is the preservation of the world." The club's program is nationwide, includes wilderness trips, books and films—as well as such efforts as this to protect the remnant of wilderness in the Americas. There are now twenty chapters, branch offices in New York (Biltmore Hotel), Washington (Dupont Circle Building), Los Angeles (Auditorium Building), Albuquerque, Seattle, and main office in San Francisco.

(timeline markings on chart: AGE OF TECHNOLOGY; FIRST MAN 2 MILLION YRS. AGO; FIRST ELEPHANTS 60 MILLION YRS. AGO; FIRST REDWOODS 130 MILLION YRS. AGO; FIRST MAMMALS 180 MILLION YRS. AGO; FIRST DINOSAURS 180 MILLION YRS. AGO; FIRST TREES 280 MILLION YRS. AGO; FIRST REPTILES 275 MILLION YRS. AGO; FIRST FISHES 400 MILLION YRS. AGO; GRAND CANYON 550 MILLION YRS. AGO; FIRST CORALS 575 MILLION YRS. AGO; FIRST SPONGES 650 MILLION YRS. AGO; BIRTH OF THE EARTH 4 BILLION YRS. AGO)

FIGURE 7.6. The Sistine Chapel Ad was first published in the *Wall Street Journal* on August 23, 1966 and it appeared in five other newspapers over a period of several weeks. Although it had little impact upon the political debates that were occurring behind closed doors, it has become the most famous of the Sierra Club's Grand Canyon "Battle Ads" because of its rhetorical elegance. Image courtesy of Jerry Mander.

most important to them. To prevent this from happening, Ely told Udall and Rhodes that he had instructed the California members of the committee to hold the bill so that Saylor would not have the opportunity to alter it during the floor debate.

Stunned, Udall and Rhodes, citing a poll Udall completed that very day, contended that they already had a firm commitment of three-quarters of the votes needed to pass the legislation in its present form along with enough "probables" so that the bill should pass with ease. However, Ely was adamant, so long as the possibility existed that Saylor's amended bill might gain approval, he had instructed the two California representatives on the Rules Committee to hold the bill indefinitely to keep it from the floor.

The Arizona representatives argued that even if Saylor succeeded, they had enough political support to reinsert whatever Saylor managed to delete, and so there was little chance that the House would pass a stripped-down version of the bill. For the next two weeks, Morris Udall frantically worked to overcome the roadblock, even conducting a new poll on August 26, the day after the appearance of the Sierra Club's "Sistine Chapel" ad, that indicated support for the bill had *grown*.[46]

Rhodes briefly considered attaching the CAP bill as a rider to an appropriations bill to circumvent the Rules Committee altogether, but decided that there was not enough time left in the current session to begin such a move. Even though Rhodes and Udall cited convincing evidence indicating that the House would pass the legislation with a solid majority, Ely continued to instruct the Rules Committee members from California to delay it indefinitely. The bill eventually died, its last gasp coming in mid-September 1966 when Rhodes and Udall gave up after determining that the support they had in August had evaporated because of the upcoming November election.[47]

Did Ely and Aspinall have legitimate reasons to fear Saylor's threats to amend the bill to delete the Colorado/California provisions as well as the Grand Canyon dams in August 1966? If so, it would appear as though the preservationists' campaign had bridged the public and political aspects of the Grand Canyon debate, and that environmental groups such as the Sierra Club could claim that they saved the canyon by stopping the dams. Environmental historians who argue that the preservationists were the primary cause of the bill's defeat base their arguments upon this presumption.

However, Ely never cited any hard evidence to support his claim that Saylor possessed the political strength to alter the bill. When pressed by Arizona's representatives, Ely could not produce any concrete data and stated that his actions were based upon a "consensus" of senior California congressmen. Furthermore, when Rhodes and Udall asked Ely which congressmen he spoke with, he refused to reveal their identities. It appears as though Ely either was unwilling or unable to demonstrate that his manipulation of the Rules Committee was based upon any hard evidence that would indicate Saylor possessed the strength to follow through on his threat.[48]

Meanwhile, Morris Udall and Rhodes had been canvassing their House colleagues since May. Virtually all of these polls suggested that the bill stood a good chance of passage and had gained support throughout the summer of 1966 despite the Sierra Club's ad campaign and the public outcry against the dams. Les Alexander of Udall's staff reflected that it was common practice for the speaker of the House to recommend that a bill be introduced to the floor when its sponsors could guarantee 150 solid votes in favor of it.[49] On August 26, Udall and Rhodes took a new poll that indicated they could count on 170 sure votes and sixty-seven "probables," along with seventy-six members who were undecided or believed themselves uninformed who could go either way. Even Udall's conservative assessment of how, in his opinion, each "probable" and "undecided/uninformed" member would vote yielded a worst-case total of 228, ten more than the 218 they needed to pass it.[50] Based upon this evidence, it appears that Rhodes and Udall had good reason to believe that the House would pass the CAP and the Grand Canyon dams by a comfortable margin.

Although Ely claimed that Aspinall shared his views, Aspinall gave Rhodes and Udall his word on September 10 that if the bill should emerge from the Rules Committee, he would fight for it on the floor.[51] Clearly Ely was the driving force behind the Rules Committee debacle and, though he claimed Aspinall supported him, he could not substantiate his arguments with solid evidence. In the face of strong indications that Rhodes and Udall had enough votes to obtain passage of the legislation as originally written, it appears Ely used the Saylor threat as an excuse to hold up the Lower Colorado River Basin Project bill to further another agenda.

Ely's actions can only be understood within the overall historical context of the acrimonious Arizona-California water dispute. For almost a half century, Arizona and California had battled over the lower basin allocation of the Colorado River in the courts and Congress. The two states came to the brink of exchanging gunfire when Arizona Governor

Benjamin Moeur called out the National Guard in 1934 to prevent California from building a diversion dam on the lower reach of the river.

Since the 1940s Ely had been deftly manipulating the strings of California's water strategy like a puppetmaster, and in the wake of Arizona's 1963 Supreme Court victory he was quoted widely as saying that California could negate the court's decision through legislative intrigue. Ely believed that in accordance with the doctrine of prior appropriation, California's 4.4 million acre-foot allotment should be guaranteed over any water Arizona claimed for the CAP.

It is difficult to separate the issues from the mutual suspicions that built up during forty-five years of subterfuge, but the record provides ample evidence about whether Ely was bargaining in good faith. When Rhodes and Udall met with Ely in late August to try to convince him that they had the votes to pass the project over Saylor's threatened amendments, Ely indicated that he would be satisfied if the guarantee was preserved. He also stated that his fears were based upon what might happen if a bill were allowed to "go to the Senate with the 'guarantee' eliminated."[52]

Believing that they could take Ely at his word, Rhodes and Udall then spoke to Saylor about preserving the "California guarantee." They received Saylor's counteroffer in September. Incredibly, Saylor, the most vocal dam opponent in Congress, wrote Arizona's representatives and told them he would support a bill that included both the California guarantee *and a low dam at the Bridge Canyon site*—one that would back water through the length of the national monument.[53] Here then would come the test of whether Ely was negotiating in good faith, for Saylor had given his word to Udall and Rhodes that he would now support the retention of the California guarantee during the floor debate.

Saylor's counterproposal is revealing both of his own perception of strength as well as of Ely's true intentions. For Saylor to propose a compromise bill that included a reservoir that would stretch the entire length of Grand Canyon National Monument is indicative that he believed he stood little chance of amending the bill on the floor. It was a desperate move by a shrewd politician who thought Rhodes and Udall had the votes to pass a two-dam bill.

However, in the context of Ely's Rules Committee antics, Saylor's support of one Grand Canyon dam, despite months of intense Sierra Club rhetoric, is of secondary importance. Had Ely been bargaining with Rhodes and Udall in good faith, Saylor's inclusion of the 4.4 million acre-foot provision should have removed Ely's doubts, for California's priority was now guaranteed by the very politician whom, Ely claimed, had sworn to delete it. Yet when the two Arizonans presented the Saylor compromise to Ely, the latter balked, even though several of California's own representatives indicated that they would support it.[54]

When Ely refused to grant his assent to Saylor's compromise, the bill's fate was sealed because it was too late for further negotiations in the eighty-ninth Congress as all members of the House were hitting the campaign trail. It is clear from this exchange that Ely used the Saylor threat as a pretext to mask his true intentions—to manipulate the political process to delay the implementation of the Supreme Court decision of 1963 so that California could continue using eight hundred thousand acre-feet of Arizona's water every year.

Arizona water advocates began assessing the blame for this catastrophic defeat even before the bill was officially pronounced dead in mid-September. Amazingly, Rhodes and Udall were reluctant to publicly blame California, probably because they still hoped for its political support, and they even released a report that emphasized the positive accomplishments of 1966 that could be built upon in the next Congress. A bitter Aspinall blamed the defeat first and foremost upon President Johnson for failing to back the proposal.[55]

A Texas Hill Country Enigma

It is difficult to determine where President Johnson stood on the issue of dams in Grand Canyon through the end of 1967. LBJ had a long history of supporting reclamation projects, voting in favor of the CAP both times it came before the Senate in 1950 and 1951, and he maintained a close friendship with Hayden throughout his presidency. Because the Bureau of the Budget is an executive agency, its recommendations that Bridge Canyon Dam be deferred became the official position of the administration, though not necessarily of the president, as early as 1965. However, LBJ shrewdly avoided taking a public position on the dams himself until the issue was no longer in doubt.

Stewart Udall believed Johnson would have backed the project had Senator Hayden asked for his support. However, Udall also warned Arizona's congressional representatives on June 30, 1966, that the passage of a bill including both dams would place LBJ in a quandary, because the Budget Bureau recommended that Bridge Canyon Dam be deferred.[56] In any event, President Johnson never had to make a decision because that bill died in committee.

Despite Johnson's history of support for reclamation, many preservationists viewed him as being sympathetic to environmental issues, a perception created by Johnson's 1964 address to Congress on the importance of preserving natural beauty and his support of the Wilderness Act. However, most Americans seeking to voice their concerns to the administration about Grand Canyon wrote the First Lady. Lady Bird Johnson had become one of the administration's chief spokespersons on environmental issues as a result of her beautification campaign. Ordinary citizens concerned with the possible damming of Grand Canyon wrote her in ever-increasing numbers during 1966 as the political battle reached its crescendo.[57]

Sharon Francis, who collaborated with Wallace Stegner in helping Stewart Udall write *The Quiet Crisis,* worked for Lady Bird Johnson on beautification issues, and she also helped the First Lady with the mail she received from people concerned about Grand Canyon. Francis's involvement alarmed pro-dam officials within the Interior Department. "Sharon Francis is about as 100 percent a preservationist as they come, and I deeply regret her influence in Mrs. Johnson's office," Udall's chief of staff wrote in July. [58] The First Lady commented to Francis that the letters against the dams, which totaled about fifty a week, were the "highest caliber" letters she had seen on "any subject." Johnson insisted on answering many of them herself, rather than turning them over to the Interior Department for a standard form-letter reply. She believed that people would think she didn't care if she sent a perfunctory response.[59]

Lady Bird Johnson thought she should take a position because to "preach natural beauty and ignore what was happening to the greatest beauty of them all—Grand Canyon—would be hypocritical." But because the president had not committed either way, the First Lady never opposed the dams unequivocally. The closest she came was when she told Secretary Udall that she would like to see studies and public discussions of alternatives to them.[60] Francis also suggested to Udall that the Bureau of the Budget should authorize the study of other options. Although the amount of influence Lady Bird Johnson was able to exert is a matter for conjecture, Francis indicated in a 1997 interview that she believed LBJ "deferred" to the First Lady on environmental issues.[61]

Perhaps one way to gauge the degree of influence the First Lady had with the president and the public is evidenced by the efforts of bureau personnel. At the height of the fight to save Grand Canyon, they man-aged to schedule her to dedicate Glen Canyon Dam, a public relations victory of the highest magnitude. The effect upon public perception is difficult to determine. But clearly the bureau hoped that the widely dis-tributed photos and news accounts of Johnson's speech—a speech Francis believed was written by someone within the bureau—delivered while standing atop Glen Canyon Dam would create the impression that she favored dams and approved of the construction of them downstream in Grand Canyon. At the time, Brower realized that the First Lady's speech could potentially influence the public to support the Grand Canyon dams and he feared the negative impact it might have.[62]

One thing can be stated with certainty, however. Lyndon Johnson would have been forced to make a very difficult decision had Congress passed the Lower Colorado River Basin Project in 1966. Whether the president signed or vetoed the bill, he would most certainly have come under fire, either from influential pro-dam politicians who could threaten his legislative agenda in Congress, or fiscal conservatives, the First Lady, and an angry public on the other.

"The Power Centers"

Given the high level of House support indicated by Mo Udall's canvass-ing during the summer of 1966, why did the legislation fail? In their postmortems of the 1966 congressional session, Udall, Rhodes, Aspinall, and other advocates of the Grand Canyon dams tried to determine why they could not pass the bill they had brought to the brink of success. Although each of them acknowledged the preservationists' anti-dam of-fensive as being important, they also indicated that it was only one of many factors that contributed to the defeat of the Lower Colorado River Basin Project. The primary reason the bill failed was that it had become so encumbered with compromises that it bogged down when these po-litical deals began to unravel.[63]

Water augmentation, the incentive Stewart Udall used in 1963 to "finagle" California's support, came with an unforeseen cost—intracta-ble opposition from Jackson, the Washington senator who chaired the Senate. The Pacific Northwest's refusal to compromise on water impor-tation from the Columbia River put Rhodes and Morris Udall in an un-tenable position because California's support hinged upon a successful resolution of this problem.[64]

Complicating matters further, Aspinall had also become a staunch supporter of water importation because he thought building the CAP as a single project would take water from the upper basin. He believed only through basin augmentation could the upper basin's allotment from the 1922 Compact, including that of his home state of Colorado, be preserved. And like Jackson in the Senate, Aspinall had the power to stop any water project bill in its tracks. Thus the issue of interbasin water transfers brought three indispensable sources of potential support—California, Aspinall, and Jackson—into irreconcilable conflict for which there was no politically acceptable solution.

Stewart Udall's grand strategy of 1963 now lay in ruins, undone by the very compromises that had held so much promise only a short time before. In early fall of 1966, the secretary realized that in advocating a regional solution contingent upon water importation, he unwittingly sowed the seeds of the bill's failure even though he had accomplished his initial goal of gaining California's backing. Although essentially sidelined while his brother championed the recently defeated two-dam proposal in the House, he realized that Jackson's adamant opposition to water importation placed him in a dilemma worse than the situation he had faced in 1963. He now had the added burden of dealing with the fallout from Arizona's recent legislative failure.

Udall understood that as a federal official he had much greater latitude than his brother or other Arizona water advocates. His position as interior secretary was reasonably insulated from Arizona politics, and it shielded him somewhat from the cacophony of criticism emanating from angry Arizona state water officials and newspaper editors. Udall believed it was his responsibility to once again assume the leadership of the CAP effort in the wake of the bill's failure in the House. But he also realized that it would be very difficult to undo the deals that had been cut the previous two years without incurring a great deal of political fallout. Udall believed he must try to find a solution, even if it took a change in reclamation policy. In early September he told his Interior Department staff to study alternatives to hydroelectric dams in Grand Canyon. He also quietly consulted with a few trusted confidants including USGS hydrologist Luna Leopold, who told him that if he were to abandon the Grand Canyon dams he would "be famous for the rest of time."[65]

Rhodes and Morris Udall also started planning a new strategy to maximize the possibility of passing a federal CAP bill in the upcoming

Ninetieth Congress that would meet in winter of 1967. They now felt a skeletal approach, similar to the bills Carl Hayden had advocated since the 1963 Supreme Court decision, would have a much better chance of making it through Congress than a regional proposal.

Morris Udall offered a candid assessment of why the 1966 bill failed. In a September 22 memo titled "The Power Centers," Udall evaluated potential supporters of a 1967 CAP bill, labeling them as either "indispensable" or "important." It is revealing to note Udall's list of five "indispensable" power centers consisted of Senators Hayden, Jackson, and Clinton Anderson of New Mexico, along with Aspinall and President Johnson. "Important" supporters included Saylor, the preservationists, and southern California.[66] By late 1966 Mo Udall believed that the support of Jackson was more important than that of California, and he focused upon attaining it. However, if this new strategy was to succeed, he also had to somehow convince Aspinall to approve a less grandiose proposal than the bill he had unsuccessfully backed in 1966. And although in Udall's estimation the support of the conservationists was desirable, he did not view their opposition as decisive.

Representative Senner of Arizona predicted that a slimmed-down federal project would pass in the Ninetieth Congress, although he thought one dam might have to be eliminated. Dominy also recommended the elimination of Marble Canyon Dam and the enlargement of Grand Canyon National Park to include Marble Canyon, an ironic position for the commissioner to take considering he had denied that Marble Canyon was a part of Grand Canyon for so long. Nevertheless, Dominy had first broached the idea of compromise in April 1966 because he realized the difficulty of getting both dams through Congress.[67]

Prominent environmental historians credit Stewart Udall with playing a major role in formulating the environmental ideology of the Kennedy and Johnson administrations during the formative period of the modern environmental movement.[68] Udall is revered by many environmentalists today as a strong advocate of preservation. However, as interior secretary he was often torn between his emerging preservationist consciousness and his deep belief in Gifford Pinchot's tradition of Progressive Conservation.

In the case of Grand Canyon, Udall's struggle became even more acute because he also was trying to reconcile his environmentalist leanings with his desire to obtain the Central Arizona Project for his native state. Many people have argued that the preservationists' anti-dam campaign and the public outcry it generated forced him to decide between the development of water resources and the preservation and eventual protection of the entire Grand Canyon. They contend that Udall bowed to this pressure and that as a result he experienced a shift in his own environmental consciousness and rejected the Grand Canyon dams he had formerly endorsed.[69]

From the environmentalists' perspective this is a feel-good story. However, it fails to take into account that Udall was a political realist to the core. He consistently demonstrated this characteristic throughout his congressional career and tenure as interior secretary. In 1963 Udall thought he had pieced together a practical political solution and believed that he could support dams in Grand Canyon and still advocate in favor of preservation elsewhere. In the autumn of 1966 Udall's regional plan had failed and Hayden's health was so bad that he was planning to retire after the 1968 election. Stewart Udall assessed the situation and concluded: (1) his own tenure as interior secretary would end in early 1969; and (2) Richard Nixon, a Californian, was the favorite to to take on a steadily weakening Johnson. Udall knew Arizona's disproportionately powerful political influence would end in a little over two years and there would be no chance of obtaining congressional approval of the CAP after the election of 1968.

"I did not reverse myself!" Stewart Udall told me emphatically. Rather, Udall determined that "the smart thing to do politically [was] to take the dams out" and sponsor a less controversial bill while Arizona still had the influence to get it through Congress. In the end, Udall dropped the Grand Canyon dams, not because he had been pressured into it by the environmentalists, but because he understood that his window of political opportunity was closing fast.[70]

The Art of the Possible

Udall chose his alternative power source based upon practical reasons as well. Although he remained optimistic about the potential for nuclear power through the end of his tenure as interior secretary, he also realized that the approval and construction of nuclear power plants was time-prohibitive. It often took more than ten years from conception to completion. Ultimately he believed that nuclear-powered desalinization plants would solve the problem of water augmentation. But by mid-autumn of 1966 he also understood that thermal power was the most realistic way to obtain power for the Central Arizona Project because coal plants would not take as long to build and they relied upon existing technology.[71]

In October Udall went public and stated that the administration was considering legislation that would offer alternatives to the Grand Canyon dams. By early December, after the studies of alternatives were finished, Udall decided to persuade President Johnson to back a CAP proposal without dams at the Bridge and Marble Canyon damsites.[72]

Given that they had zero chance of Senate passage and no support from the interior secretary, by January of 1967 the Grand Canyon dams were dead—and yet they wouldn't lie down. Despite these insurmountable political obstacles, when Congress reconvened Rhodes, Morris Udall, and Representative Sam Steiger, who defeated Senner in the November election, presented a new CAP bill that eliminated Marble Canyon Dam but kept the high dam at Bridge Canyon. Aspinall introduced another bill reminiscent of the measure the Sierra Club's Bestor Robinson had written in 1949. Instead of eliminating the Bridge/Hualapai Dam, Aspinall proposed to: (1) shift the park's western park boundary to just upstream of the new Hualapai reservoir; and (2) extend the eastern park boundary a like distance to include some of Marble Canyon and eliminate Marble Canyon Dam.

Intended as compromises, both of these bills were eighteen years too late. When these futile proposals came before the House Reclamation Subcommittee in 1967, Brower emphatically testified that the Sierra Club was unwilling to approve of a dam of any height in Grand Canyon. An exasperated Morris Udall listed a number of concessions he was willing to make, including: (1) the deletion of Marble Canyon Dam; (2) the expansion of Grand Canyon National Park; and (3) the construction of a Bridge Canyon Dam so low that it would only create a reservoir in the monument and not invade the park at all. Facing Brower he said, "What will the Sierra Club accept? If we have a low, low, low, Bridge Canyon Dam maybe 100 feet high, is that too much? Is there any point where you compromise here?" Brower replied, "You aren't giving us anything that God didn't put there in the first place."[73]

Even then, Aspinall wouldn't relent and suggested that the national monument be abolished, in his mind eliminating much of the controversy.[74] Instead, Aspinall's idea provided more fodder for the Sierra Club, which unleashed yet another full-page newspaper ad on March 13, 1967, with the headline, "(Better Hold Up On The Flowers and Cheery Wires, Just A Bit Longer), Grand Canyon National Monument Is Hereby Abolished."[75]

Additionally, the Sierra Club emphasized that it was still battling the IRS, fanning the flames of public outrage generated by the agency's revocation of its tax-deductible status in June 1966.[76] Interior Secretary Udall and Jett, who had recently written the text for yet another stunning Sierra Club exhibit format book, titled *Navajo Wildlands: 'As Long as the Rivers Shall Run,'* also testified. They cited the benefits that would accrue to the Navajo Nation from the development of its coal reserves and tourism to the three tribal parks along the rim that the Navajo had recently created. Jett was confronted about the damage that strip-mining would do to portions of the Navajo Reservation. He stated that he didn't favor strip-mining, but when compared with Grand Canyon, the areas that would be mined were far the lesser in terms of size and scenic value, that the surface could be reclaimed, and that the emissions from coal-fired plants could be controlled at relatively low cost.[77]

Rupert Parker, the new Hualapai tribal chairman, urged the committee to include Hualapai Dam in the bill. Reiterating some of the rhetoric from Rocha's testimony of the previous year, Parker stated that the Hualapai and most Arizona American Indian nations favored the dam and that they resented the Sierra Club's desire to reserve the canyon for "a select few." Finally, he accused the Sierra Club of misinforming the American people by stating that the Havasupai people opposed the Hualapai Dam, and he inserted a resolution from the Havasupai Tribal Council that confirmed support for it.[78]

Committee members also sat through the presentation of some fantastic schemes at these hearings. The ghost of Fred Colter and his Arizona Highline Canal appeared in the form of a tunnel ninety-two miles in length proposed by mining engineer F. C. Ramsing. This gravity-fed tunnel, Ramsing argued, would require little power to operate, generate power, and divert water from Lake Powell to the Verde River north of Phoenix.

Another witness, Floyd Goss, an engineer with the Los Angeles Department of Water and Power, argued that if Bridge Canyon Dam were constructed as a pumped storage project, it would have an annual generating capacity of 5.1 million megawatts, four times greater than that of Hoover Dam. Hosmer trumpeted this project's virtues as a way to undercut the preservationists' economic arguments against the dam. However, the downside to the Goss proposal, which quickly sank from view, was that

FIGURE 8.1. The committee that saved Grand Canyon: the 1967–1968 Senate
Committee on Interior and Insular Affairs. Chairman Henry Jackson is in front of
the door. Senator Carl Hayden is fourth from the left. University of Washington
Libraries, Special Collections, UW21832.

it required an additional dam downstream. Even Dominy opposed Goss's
plan because operating Bridge Canyon Dam this way would release tremendous surges of water down the river, making the lower canyon, in
Dominy's words, "a very dangerous place."[79] After five days of testimony,
these hearings adjourned without setting a date for the presentation of
this latest CAP measure to the full Interior Committee.

As these doomed proceedings moved forward in the House,
Stewart Udall presented the Interior Department's new CAP proposal
at a press conference on February 1, 1967. This plan eliminated both
dams in Grand Canyon and included an expansion of Grand Canyon
National Park to include Marble Canyon. The secretary suggested
that Congress decide how to use the Bridge Canyon site and reserved
any study of water importation to a national water commission per
Jackson's proposal the previous year. Aspinall immediately attacked
the new scheme and flatly declared that Congress would never pass
it. Arizona's "go it alone" faction was also disappointed because the
plan included the Marble Canyon site within Udall's proposed expansion of the national park, and they accused him of "double crossing" his native state.

But Stewart Udall's plan also won acceptance, especially in the Senate.
Henry Jackson said he was delighted with Udall's proposal and endorsed
it completely. The most important development though, was the reaction
of Carl Hayden, who indicated that he might approve of the measure if it
would "get the project moving." This represented a landmark change on

Hayden's part, for he had been the most vocal advocate of building hydroelectric dams in Grand Canyon for almost fifty years.[80]

On February 16, 1967, Arizona Senators Carl Hayden and Fannin of Arizona cosponsored CAP legislation that did not include hydroelectric dams in Grand Canyon. Instead, the measure called for the construction of a coal-fired steam plant to generate the power required to pump water through the proposed aqueduct. Jackson of Washington submitted a similar proposal. These bills were immediately criticized by California Senator Thomas Kuchel who had already introduced legislation calling for a regional plan and the construction of Hualapai Dam. After Hayden begrudgingly assented to the inclusion of the California guarantee, Jackson guided the damless bill through his committee with ease, and on June 29 it voted 11–3 to report it to the floor after rejecting, by a similar margin, efforts by a trio of senators to amend it to include dams and water importation.[81]

Jackson's virtually omnipotent power over reclamation projects would be further showcased during the Senate floor debate. When Kutchel and Colorado Senator Gordon Allott attempted to add dams to Jackson's bill, the Senate rejected their amendment by the crushing roll-call vote of 70–12. It was now obvious that Jackson's original bill had so much support that it could be approved by a simple voice vote. On August 7, 1967, at the conclusion of the floor debate, a loud chorus of "ayes" echoed through the Senate chamber in affirmation of Jackson's bill, the third time that the Senate had passed CAP legislation but the first without dams in Grand Canyon. Vigilant to the last, Jackson insisted that the bill contain a provision prohibiting the study of water importation for ten years. So complete was Jackson's victory that Mo Udall later recalled that to "even dream about" water importation from the Columbia River would be a violation of the law.[82]

Although Interior Secretary Udall introduced legislation recommending against the construction of additional dams on the Colorado River, he still remained undecided about whether a dam should be built at the Bridge Canyon site. He had reluctantly directed his department to study alternatives because he knew it was politically impossible to gain the approval of a CAP with dams in it, and during the February 1 press conference he expressed his belief that if Congress ever authorized a dam there, that it should be a high one.

But in June 1967 the secretary took his family and some National Park Service personnel on a guided Colorado River trip to examine the disputed damsites first hand. Casting off from Lee's Ferry, the river crossing established by his great-grandfather in 1872, Udall felt a sense of awe as he drifted through the Colorado gorge as well as occasional terror while riding the rapids. Udall wrote an article about the experience and published it in *Venture* magazine several months later revealing that his river trip had forced him to rethink his position. Udall chastised himself for making an "armchair judgement" when framing the Pacific Southwest Water Plan in 1963 and called for the enlargement of Grand Canyon National Park to include both damsites if power could be provided by other means. "The burden of proof, I believe, rests on the dambuilders," Udall wrote. "If they cannot make out a compelling case the park should be enlarged and given permanent protection."[83]

Others had yet to experience this ideological transformation, and on August 2, 1967, Aspinall decreed there would be no further action on the CAP because he planned to adjourn the House Interior Committee for the remainder of the year. The committee approved, and the chairman flew home to Colorado. Angered by Aspinall's intractability, frustrated with California's continued opposition, and believing that they had substantial support from their House colleagues, Rhodes and Morris Udall decided to circumvent Aspinall's opposition by bypassing the Interior Committee altogether. Knowing that the Senate was currently debating a public works appropriations bill that the House had already passed, Rhodes and Udall spoke with Hayden about the possibility of attaching the CAP to the Senate version of the appropriations bill, a rarely used procedure that required enormous power and prestige in the Senate as well as a suspension of the rules.[84]

But Hayden had finally run out of patience with Aspinall as well, and though not a hardball politician by nature, he agreed to pressure Aspinall in two ways. First, as chair of the Senate Appropriations Committee, he blocked authorization of the Fryingpan–Arkansas Mountain Diversion Project slated for Aspinall's home state of Colorado. In addition, per Rhodes's and Udall's suggestion, he threatened to attach the Central Arizona Project to the public works appropriations bill as a rider, and convinced the Senate to suspend its rules so he could do it.[85] As a result, Aspinall scrambled back to Washington and promised Hayden that he would bring the CAP bill to a House vote in early 1968.[86]

When Congress reconvened, President Johnson finally endorsed the CAP publicly and called upon Congress to pass it with all possible speed.

True to his word, Aspinall reopened the CAP hearings and on March 26, 1968, the Interior Committee approved the bill. Aspinall, the last influential dam proponent, had finally capitulated—the bill omitted all hydroelectric dams from the project. Elated by their good fortune, Arizona's congressional delegation shepherded the CAP bill through the rules committee and onto the House floor for a vote. On May 15, 1968, the House of Representatives overwhelmingly passed legislation authorizing the construction of the CAP by the federal government, its electricity to be provided by an immense coal-fired power plant located in Page, Arizona. The bill contained Aspinall's five upper basin projects and the California 4.4 million acre-foot guarantee in perpetuity, concessions Arizona's representatives made to gain the political support of these two factions. After the joint conference committee ironed out some minor

FIGURE 8.2. President Lyndon Baines Johnson signs the "damless" Lower Colorado River Basin Project bill into law on September 30, 1968. Left to right: Representative John Rhodes, Senator Carl Hayden, Representative Sam Steiger, Interior Secretary Stewart Udall, Representative John Saylor, Arizona Governor Paul Fannin, Lady Bird Johnson, and President Johnson. Morris K. Udall Papers, box 735, folder 56, courtesy of University of Arizona Libraries, Special Collections.

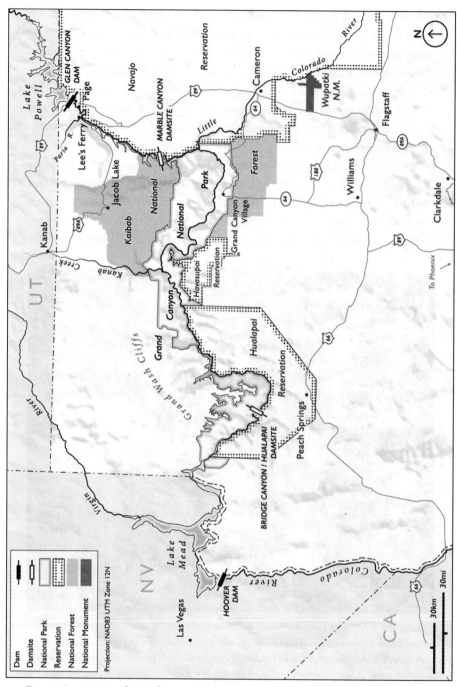

FIGURE 8.3. A map of Grand Canyon National Park after the 1975 park expansion. Map by Nathaniel Douglass, ndcartography.com.

differences that were approved by both houses, the final version of the CAP bill, one that did not include hydroelectric dams on the main stem of the Colorado River in Grand Canyon, was ready for LBJ's signature.

All eyes were on the ex-sheriff of Maricopa County as ninety-year-old Senator Carl Hayden walked into the East Room of the White House on September 30, 1968. Numerous dignitaries, including the Udall brothers, the rest of Arizona's delegation, and David Brower waited anxiously for this historic moment. Lyndon and Lady Bird Johnson strode into the room, LBJ sat down, made a few brief remarks, and signed the Colorado River Basin Project Act into law. The president, smiling broadly, turned to his old friend Carl Hayden, handed him his pen, and shook his hand. Hayden thanked past and present members of the Arizona congressional delegation and declared: "Today is the high-water mark in my career as a US senator."[87] With that, the dean of the US Senate, weeping, walked out of the room and into retirement, having finally attained his dream of a Central Arizona Project.

Shortly before leaving office, Johnson, at the urging of Stewart Udall, created Marble Canyon National Monument and brought the damsite there under the jurisdiction of the National Park Service. Six years later, Congress passed Goldwater's bill to enlarge Grand Canyon National Park to include all 277 miles of the canyon—including both the Marble and Bridge Canyon damsites—from Lee's Ferry to the Grand Wash Cliffs. The 1975 Grand Canyon National Park Enlargement Act amended the reclamation provision from the original 1919 establishment act so that the interior secretary can only authorize reclamation projects in the western portion of the enlarged park that was once part of the Lake Mead National Recreation Area. It preserved the 1968 Colorado River Basin Project Act's reclamation provisions as well. Although the enlargement act gave Marble Canyon a great deal of protection, it specifically reserved the possibility that a dam could someday be built at the Bridge Canyon Damsite in lower Grand Canyon.[88] In 1975, with the bureau tamed, Jackson's National Environmental Policy Act in place, and the environmental movement now part of America's political and social mainstream, it appeared, at least outwardly, that the threat to build dams in Grand Canyon had finally been defeated. And in a kind twist of fate, former National Park Service Director Newton Drury, who stood steadfastly against the Grand Canyon dams during the 1940s without any help from environmental organizations, lived to see his last line of defense—the national park boundary—extended to protect all of the canyon and the free-flowing Colorado River within it.[89]

And yet the dam builders still clung to the hope that the wheel of history would someday turn in their favor. While it is true that CAP was passed without dams in 1968, the law did not preclude that possibility in the future as this language from Title III section 303 of the Colorado River Basin Project indicates: "Provided: That nothing in *this* section or in *this* Act contained shall be construed to authorize the study or construction of any dams on the main stream of the Colorado River between Hoover Dam and Glen Canyon Dam." [emphasis mine] Thus, Congress left open the possibility that it or perhaps some other entity could reconsider the issue of dams at a later date. As a result, through the 1980s the APA and Hualapai Nation tried unsuccessfully to gain authorization to build Hualapai Dam.[90]

The Grand Canyon National Park Enlargement Act of 1975 also called for the park service to designate areas within Grand Canyon to be added to the national wilderness system. The service finished these studies in 1980 and updated them in 1993 and 2010. Each version recommended removing the reclamation provision from the enlargement act, but the Interior Department has never forwarded these findings to Congress. The studies also required public hearings and during the resulting testimony the APA, Hualapai Nation, and the bureau registered strong objections because they still harbored the hope that a dam or dams still might be built. Because the NPS wilderness designation has yet to be adopted, this added degree of protection has not been given to Grand Canyon. Environmental law experts contend that it is unlikely this will ever occur because of competing agendas within government agencies that oversee the public lands. Thus although no serious discussion about building the Grand Canyon dams has occurred for half a century, with the population of the West exploding, water levels in Lakes Mead and Powell dropping precipitously, the need for power climbing, and concerns over carbon emissions mounting, it is far, *far*, too early to pronounce them dead.[91]

9

Alternative Realities

Ira Gabrielson, the "grand old man of conservation," is supposed to have once said, "If you can't save Grand Canyon, what the hell can you save?"[1] In 1968 Grand Canyon had been saved, or at least as saved as anything can be that is subject to the whims of Congress. The story of how this happened is incredibly complicated. There are many reasons people wanted the dams built, and a like number why others did not. I have researched and pondered these questions for more than a quarter century, and I am still finding out new answers, and more importantly, asking new questions. As a historian I have pursued the questions of why—why the struggle happened, why the plans of the dam builders were foiled, and why any of this still matters today.

The Making of a Narrative

Environmental historians were the first to tackle the question of where the epic battle to save Grand Canyon from dams should fit within the historical literature of modern environmentalism. That it was one of the most hotly contested environmental controversies in American history in terms of public reaction was obvious, but whom should receive credit for defeating the dams? The point of origin for this historiography is a Sierra Club exhibit format book published in 1970 titled *Grand Canyon of the Living Colorado*. Printed less than two years after President Johnson signed the Central Arizona Project authorization into law, it contained stunning color photographs of the canyon and essays about various aspects of the Grand Canyon struggle, including a reprint of Stewart Udall's February 1968 *Venture* article, an article by David

Brower about the Grand Canyon "Battle Ads," and an essay summarizing the political aspects of the fight to save Grand Canyon, that emphasized the pivotal role the Sierra Club played in defeating the dams written by the book's editor, Sierra Club member Roderick Nash.[2]

Even while Nash worked on this Sierra Club publication, he was also starting his career as an environmental historian and assistant professor of history at the University of California, Santa Barbara. In 1967 Nash published *Wilderness and the American Mind,* an iconic book in the fields of US intellectual and environmental history. Nash gained national acclaim for his account of how the concept of wilderness has evolved in the American psyche over the past four hundred years. He published a second edition of *Wilderness* in 1973, which added a section about the Grand Canyon dams, and in 1983 a third edition in which he expanded this discussion.

Taken almost *verbatim* from his 1970 essay in *Grand Canyon of the Living Colorado,* Nash's 1983 analysis was replicated in fourth (2001) and fifth (2014) editions of the book. Nash states categorically that environmentalists achieved the impossible in stopping the Grand Canyon dams. After contending that the environmental movement had gained enough influence by the 1950s and 1960s to "influence the political process," he elaborated further about Grand Canyon:

> The result in terms of Grand Canyon was unprecedented. Dams that originally had the full backing of the administration, the personal enthusiasm of the secretary of the interior, and nearly unanimous support from senators and representatives of the seven Colorado Basin states, as well as the determined boosting of water and power user's lobbies—dams, in other words, that seemed virtually certain of authorization—were stopped.[3]

According to Nash, environmentalists, and the Sierra Club in particular, were the decisive factor in the defeat of the dams because they were able to: (1) influence Congress directly; and (2) mobilize the public into pressuring Congress into accepting alternative sources of power. Although numerous environmental societies took part in the anti-dam campaign, most notably the National Parks Association, the Sierra Club is the only environmental organization Nash mentions by name in his discussion about the Grand Canyon dams. Nash also argues that Stewart Udall's trip down the river in June 1967 led to the secretary's change of mind, which was also pivotal in stopping the dams. Because of his formidable reputation as scholar and status as one of the generation of university professors who founded the field of environmental history, Nash's analysis of the fight to save Grand Canyon has scarcely been challenged by environmental historians and others who have written about the epic struggle. Most have accepted his account at face value and have cited his interpretation in their own work for almost fifty years.[4]

Journalists and environmental writers have also written that the Sierra Club, virtually single-handedly, stopped the Grand Canyon dams and this version of events has been widely published and republished over the past five decades. Two highly readable books, John McPhee's *Encounters with the Archdruid*, published in 1971 after its syndication in the *New Yorker*, and Marc Reisner's *Cadillac Desert* (first edition, 1986; second, 1993), also argue that the Sierra Club defeated the Grand Canyon dams. Both appealed to enormous popular audiences. A host of essays and articles in environmental magazines and elsewhere have also repeated—and perpetuated—the mantra that the Sierra Club saved Grand Canyon.

Environmentalists and Grand Canyon enthusiasts have also succeeded in spreading the word through articles, documentaries, websites, and even blogs. Recent examples include Carl Pope's 2011 article, "We Can Only Mar It," and Ken Brower's 2015 tribute to Martin Litton titled, "Appreciations: Lessons from the Man Who Stopped Grand Canyon Dams."

Of the documentaries, three stand out in particular: Reisner's *Cadillac Desert: An American Nile* (1997), which features short interviews with important environmentalists such as Brower and Litton and dam supporters such as Dominy and Barry Goldwater; a film about the life of Martin Litton titled *The Good Fight: The Martin Litton Story* (2010), featuring lengthy interviews with Litton; and the massive 2012 documentary titled *A Fierce Green Fire: The Battle for a Living Planet*.

Although numerous blogs and websites about Grand Canyon discuss the dam battle, easily the most comprehensive and informative website and blog is Jeff Ingram's *Celebrating the Grand Canyon*, which he has been building since at least 2009. Ingram, whose testimony at various committee hearings demolished the bureau's cost-benefit analyses and development fund projections, has created a website that is truly monumental. Given his close association with these events, his numerous entries are unabashedly (and understandably) biased in favor of promoting the argument that the Sierra Club's role in the fight to save Grand Canyon was decisive. Finally, on the occasion of its 125th anniversary in 2017, the Sierra Club itself, now three million members strong, posted a brief history to its website that stated "arguably [its] most renowned preservation victory was leading the fight to prevent Grand Canyon from being dammed."[5]

Thus in the five decades since Congress authorized the dam-free CAP, filmmakers, authors of popular accounts, websites, conservation magazines, bloggers, and environmental historians have overwhelmingly accorded preservationists, and the Sierra Club in particular, an almost omnipotent ability to influence policymaking in the mid-1960s. Many of these people argue that the fight to save Grand Canyon was the most climactic confrontation between advocates of utilitarian water development and preservationists that has ever occurred. Some leading environmental historians state that it was during the defense of Grand Canyon that the environmental movement "came of age."[6]

When assessing these historical events, it is important to remember that the fight to save Grand Canyon from dams occurred before the passage of the National Environmental Policy Act, which became law on January 1, 1970. Before NEPA, detailed studies of the environmental consequences of such projects—the environmental impact statements that are so commonplace today—were nonexistent. Although environmentalists and other interested parties were frequently invited to testify at congressional committee hearings, they did not have the right to do so. Whether they appeared was entirely at the whim of committee chairs such as Wayne Aspinall and, as Fred Packard of the National Parks Association found out during the CAP debates of the early 1950s, they would not always be included.

Other than testimony—when they had the chance to give it—there was little else environmentalists could do to influence the process from within. The only other option they had was to generate enough public outrage that the politicians making these decisions would feel the pressure from without. The vast majority of the accounts cited here are based upon the assumption that the Sierra Club's ability to mobilize public opinion breached the barrier that separated public activism from the committee system, which, in turn, created the opportunity for the preservationists to shape policy. Arguably this was how environmentalists defeated the dams planned for Dinosaur National Monument during the

1950s. Across the spectrum of historical and popular interpretation, the Sierra Club has emerged as the savior of Grand Canyon because people believe it had the clout to bring about political change as it had during the Dinosaur struggle. But is that actually the case?

Two Arenas, Two Outcomes: The Case for Complexity

The fight to save Grand Canyon revolved around several pivot points that affected the outcome of the struggle in the minds of the public and within the political process. People who have written about these events recognize that the debate over Grand Canyon took place in both of these arenas. Clearly the preservationists' campaign and the IRS revocation had a great effect upon public opinion, as judged by the volume of mail and the tremendous grassroots efforts ordinary people made to save the canyon.

However, to assume that a victory in the court of public opinion automatically resulted in a change of federal policy fails to consider decades of complex political and legal intrigue that framed Colorado River water issues—and the Arizona-California struggle in particular—for most of the twentieth century. It also does not consider the isolated and intricate nature of the policymaking process at that time, particularly the workings of the committee system and the power held by each committee chair. According to Stewart Udall, chairmen such as Aspinall in the House, and Hayden and Jackson in the Senate, wielded power that was virtually absolute during the 1960s; Udall even called Aspinall "a one-man committee" when I interviewed him in 1997. Committee chairs opposed to legislation could be circumvented rarely. Only through the sheer weight of numbers did California overcome Interior Committee Chairman and Arizona Representative John Murdock during the early 1950s. Only through seniority, power, and respect, did Hayden gain the two-thirds majority necessary to suspend the rules of parliamentary procedure and bypass the committee system altogether.[7]

The complexity of the political battle to obtain the Central Arizona Project is staggering. Beginning with the first decades of the twentieth century, Arizona was embroiled in a bitter political battle to obtain the right to use water from the Colorado River. The nature of this fight was largely determined by the constraints imposed by the Colorado River Compact of 1922. From that point forward, Arizona and California would be pitted against each other over the allocation of lower basin water. While California successfully used its political power to obtain projects to tap the Colorado River, it also wielded this power to prevent Arizona from doing the same, a pattern that continued until the passage of the Central Arizona Project in 1968.

Even when Arizona gained a disproportionate amount of political influence during the 1940s and 1950s, with Hayden's seniority in the Senate, Ernest McFarland's election as Senate majority leader, and Murdock becoming chair of the House Interior Committee, it was not enough to overcome California's opposition in 1950 and 1951. California's large congressional bloc proved strong enough in the House to negate Murdock's chairmanship, obtain passage of a CAP moratorium in 1951, and delay Arizona's ambitions until the US Supreme Court settled the issue of lower basin water rights. As a result, Arizona representatives Stewart Udall, Morris Udall, and Rhodes, having experienced California's raw political power firsthand, came to view California's support as indispensable to obtaining the CAP.

When Special Master Simon Rifkind released his recommendations to the Supreme Court in 1960, which upheld Arizona's water claims, it shifted the political landscape. In addition to California, Arizona politicians now had to deal with opposition from representatives of the upper basin states, particularly Colorado. Aspinall understood that there wasn't enough water in the river and feared that the construction of another large water project in the lower basin would permanently reduce the upper basin's allotment.

Although Arizona's political influence arguably increased after Stewart Udall's appointment as secretary of the interior, it appeared the political obstacles to obtaining the CAP were also greater than ever. California and Colorado, the two most populous states in the Colorado Basin, were now allied against it. Carl Hayden believed that his influence in the Senate would be enough to gain passage of the CAP in both houses. After corresponding with Aspinall in 1963, however, Stewart Udall believed that the only way to get his and California's support was a regional water development that included water augmentation.

The political situation changed again in the wake of the 1963 Supreme Court decision in *Arizona v. California*. Assured that Arizona now held legal title to enough water to justify pursuing the CAP, Stewart Udall stepped up his efforts to create regional water harmony, and he gained the support of both California and Aspinall with the promise of water augmentation from outside the Colorado River Basin. However, this tactic created a division between himself and Hayden, who sought a bare-bones project. This rift in the Arizona effort never completely healed during the entire period Congress debated the regional scheme. Udall's decision to pursue a regional water plan was perhaps the most critical political decision made during the fight to save Grand Canyon. In all likelihood, the regional plan, though promising initially, is ultimately what doomed any project that included dams in Grand Canyon.

When Udall decided that the additional water for the Colorado River Basin would come from the Columbia River, it solidified the Arizona-California-Aspinall alliance in the House. However, it also raised the unanticipated ire of Senator Jackson. As chair of the Senate Interior Committee, Jackson wielded as much power as Aspinall did in the lower chamber. The Columbia diversion also redefined the purpose and symbolic meaning of the high Bridge Canyon Dam, which, per Hayden's original 1950–1951 CAP proposals, was intended to generate hydroelectric power for a bare-bones project within Arizona's borders.

Udall's Pacific Southwest Water Plan *repurposed* Bridge Canyon Dam and turned it into a "cash register" to bankroll the funding and generate the hydroelectric power necessary for the importation of water from the Pacific Northwest. Since the much smaller Marble Canyon Dam could not have generated enough power to do this alone, the high Bridge Canyon Dam became the most important, and most objectionable, element of Udall's massive regional project. Jackson understood that if Bridge Canyon Dam could be defeated, the Columbia River would be safe. And as chair of the Senate Interior Committee, Jackson had the power to kill it all by himself.[8]

Once Udall gained California's backing with the prospect of additional water, the high Bridge Canyon Dam became nonnegotiable because it was the revenue source for the augmentation. Udall made the painful decision to build the high dam even though he knew environmentalists would oppose it because of its infringement upon Grand Canyon National Park. However, with California on board, Udall believed that the political momentum behind the regional proposal would be impossible to stop, especially since the conservation organizations dramatically curtailed their lobbying in the aftermath of the Supreme Court's 1954 *Harriss* decision.

The Sierra Club's decision to risk its tax-deductible status was also a turning point, because it freed the club to mount a far more intensive opposition campaign than Udall anticipated. By the early summer of 1966 the national media was devoting considerable attention to the club's anti-dam efforts. This coverage became even more widespread after the publication of the club's full-page newspaper ads and the IRS revocation of the club's tax-deductible status they triggered. Within the congressional process, environmentalists presented expert testimony that, if read objectively, demolished the bureau's financial justification for the projects and promoted viable alternatives to provide power without damming Grand Canyon. It is reasonable to conclude as many have done, that these events caused the bill to fail in the fall of 1966.

And yet, in the summer of 1966, despite this expert testimony and the massive public outcry the opposition campaign generated, the bill moved forward and came within a whisker of reaching the House floor. The political alliance between Arizona, California, and Wayne Aspinall unraveled not because of the environmentalists' campaign but because no one could find a way to overcome the opposition of Henry Jackson, who refused to compromise on the issue of water importation from the Columbia River.

As the bill's supporters frantically attempted to figure out how to appease Jackson, California water strategist Northcutt Ely seized his chance to deal the bill a deathblow by holding it in the House Rules Committee. Ely's primary objective for almost twenty years had been to delay the CAP and preserve California's annual use of almost one million acre-feet of Arizona's water. Not even the Supreme Court decision of 1963 could dissuade him from pursuing that objective, and he accomplished it in the fall of 1966. These political developments occurred within the isolated committee system, far removed from the preservationists' crusade and the national outcry it generated. The bill would have died in 1966, and for the very same reasons, had there not been any environmentalists to oppose it.

In the wake of this defeat, Stewart Udall, knowing Arizona's powerful political position would evaporate with Hayden's retirement and his own impending departure from the Interior Department in January 1969, tried to find a CAP alternative that would be palatable to Congress while Arizona still possessed the political influence to obtain it. By the winter of 1966, Udall had conceived of the proposal that eventually passed—a bare-bones project without dams in Grand Canyon—believing it would remove the Jackson roadblock in the Senate. Udall's assessment proved correct when Jackson sponsored a damless CAP bill in spring of 1967 and, with Hayden's assistance, gained overwhelming approval of it in the upper chamber.

Although there was greater opposition in the House, including from California, which refused to support it without a perpetual prioritization of its 4.4 million acre-feet of water, the Interior Committee hearings of 1967 and Mo Udall's informal polling of his colleagues revealed strong support for the damless project. Aspinall also opposed it because he was still enamored with obtaining water from the Columbia River.[9] When Aspinall refused to budge, Hayden used his power and prestige to suspend the Senate rules and force him into holding the hearings in 1968 that finally resulted in a House floor debate and passage. California's guarantee and Aspinall's five upper basin projects were added late in 1968, but it is clear that the House would have passed the CAP over the objections of both in 1967 had Hayden used his power earlier to force Aspinall's hand.

A Wrong Turn?

The way the events played out suggests that Interior Secretary Udall's single-minded pursuit of a regional water plan may have had the unintended consequence of dooming the Bridge and Marble Canyon Dams from the start. When he took office in 1961, Udall believed California's support was still indispensable. The congressional climate had changed because President Eisenhower's policy of "no new starts" was no longer in effect. Reclamation budgets dramatically increased after JFK became president, and western politicians soon found it possible to move their projects through Congress once again.[10] Because none of these projects could have been passed without Hayden's blessing, Arizona's senior senator amassed an enormous reserve of goodwill that, if tapped, could have—and eventually was—used to turn the tide in the House.

California's opposition proved immovable in the climate of fiscal conservatism of the 1950s, but Arizona's House support increased during the Kennedy/Johnson administrations because of these changed budget conditions and an increasing belief on the part of House members that Arizona deserved the CAP in the wake of the 1963 Supreme Court decision. It appears as though Udall misjudged the power of California's House influence in the 1960s. If he had not been so fixated upon gaining its support at all costs, Arizona's representatives would have been free to negotiate over the high Bridge Canyon Dam and offer a compromise that would not have threatened the national park. Perhaps the best evidence of this possibility is that even Pennsylvania's John Saylor, the most vocal opponent of the high Bridge Canyon Dam in the House, wrote Mo Udall on September 7, 1966, with the regional project stalled in the Rules Committee, and stated that he would support a bare-bones Central

Arizona Project that included a low Bridge Canyon Dam that would have backed water through the national monument—this after months of intense preservationist rhetoric, the IRS action, and the publication of the Sierra Club's Grand Canyon "Battle Ads" in national newspapers.[11]

Additionally, Jackson never stated that he opposed dams in Grand Canyon *per se*, just the threat of water importation they represented. If one considers all of these factors, it appears as though Carl Hayden's political instincts of 1963 were correct; Arizona could have obtained passage of a bare-bones Central Arizona Project that did not include water augmentation from the Pacific Northwest with *at least* a low Bridge Canyon Dam and probably Marble Canyon Dam as well. A strong supporter of reclamation, Jackson, who had a warm working relationship with Carl Hayden, would not have opposed these dams because they would not have posed a threat to the Columbia River.

The sympathy Hayden had already gained by supporting reclamation projects for other states could have been mobilized to defeat California much earlier, and he could have used the threat of a rider to overcome Aspinall's opposition as easily in 1965 as he did in 1967. Ironically, by seeking to construct a regional water project, though it offered the tantalizing possibility of gaining California's and Aspinall's support, Stewart Udall actually increased the possibility that the Grand Canyon dams would be defeated in the political arena with each promise he made.

Tactics and Countertactics

The secretary's regional proposal contained the seeds of its own demise. When the bill died in committee in the fall of 1966, Udall, mindful of the time constraints under which he labored, abandoned the Grand Canyon dams and the regional approach in favor of a politically practical solution. Udall based his regional plan upon pragmatics that might have worked during the 1950s but failed in the political climate that emerged after the 1960 election and the 1963 Supreme Court decision. As the events of 1967 and 1968 demonstrate, California and Aspinall were no longer indispensable parties to the passage of the CAP.

Ultimately, the isolated nature of policymaking at the committee level, the continuing enmity between Arizona and California, and the unwieldly nature of the legislation itself led to the defeat of the Grand Canyon dams in 1966. After surveying the wreckage of his previous efforts, Stewart Udall's damless February 1967 proposal and Hayden's approval of it constituted an astute move by two practical politicians who understood that they were rapidly running out of time.

Both preservationists and advocates of the Grand Canyon dams struggled to gain public approval of their respective agendas, but the environmentalists launched the more vigorous campaign. The pro-dam lobby focused primarily upon trying to cut deals in the political arena in addition to seeking public support. CAP advocates tried initially to generate public appeal for the projects by emphasizing Arizona's need for water and the promise of more recreational opportunities. Arizona's water leaders realized that with Congress and reclamation policy on their side, they did not have to achieve complete victory. They only needed to avoid a catastrophic public relations defeat similar to when Brower demolished the bureau's justification for the Dinosaur dams using the bureau's own figures during the Echo Park controversy a decade earlier. The people in favor of the dams did not make these mistakes in the Grand Canyon fight. Hammering on the idea that the preservationists were selfish elitists, they attacked the conservationists' opposition campaign in three ways.

First, whenever a person with impressive credentials such as physicist Richard Bradley opposed the dams, bureau or congressional experts offered rebuttals to prevent the preservationists from monopolizing the technological high ground. Despite the exhaustive expert testimony of "the MIT trio" Ingram, Alan Carlin, and Laurence Moss, the preservationists never succeeded in extracting an admission from bureau personnel that the Grand Canyon dams were not economically justifiable.[12] These witnesses presented figures, thorough analyses, and reasonable alternatives during the congressional hearings, but supporters of the project countered with their own witnesses and analyses. This enabled them to negate the opinions of the environmentalists' experts at least during the Interior Committee debates of 1965–1966 when the dams were still very much alive in the political realm.

Second, dam supporters intensified their public relations effort in the wake of the publication of Richard Bradley's article "Ruin for Grand Canyon?" in the April 1966 issue of *Reader's Digest*. Although Dominy tried and failed to convince *Reader's Digest* to withdraw the article, Mo Udall and Barry Goldwater managed to co-opt much of the *Reader's Digest*–sponsored Grand Canyon symposium at the end of March 1966. In addition, Morris Udall and Rhodes granted concessions to the Hualapai Nation in exchange for its public support of the project. By eliminating the Hualapai as potential antagonists, dam advocates took advantage of American society's increasing concerns about civil rights and racial issues to try to portray the preservationists as being racist.

However, this tactic failed, largely because they ignored the Navajo Nation and left the door open for a preservationist response. Rich Johnson's letters and Henry Dobyns's testimony received national publicity in 1966, but the full effect of these racial arguments was neutralized by Stephen Jett's committee testimony on behalf of the Navajo people. It was largely because of Jett's efforts that the Navajo became dam opponents in the fall of 1966. Although the Hualapai tribal chairman testified in favor of the Hualapai Dam during the 1967 House committee hearings, less than a year later even the CAP supporters began to extol the project's benefits for the Navajo Nation. The Hualapai Nation became expendable the day the dam was dropped from consideration.

Perhaps most importantly, the pro-dam lobby played a pivotal role in driving wedges between preservationist associations such as the Sierra Club and Wilderness Society on the one hand, and wildlife-oriented organizations such as the National Wildlife Federation, the largest conservation group in the world, on the other. During the Echo Park conflict, the leadership of the National Wildlife Federation voted to oppose the dams slated for Dinosaur National Monument and any further intrusions into the National Park System.[13] Scarcely ten years later, the federation remained neutral until the issue of dams had been decided despite threats to both Grand Canyon National Park and Monument and appeals from Brower and other environmental leaders.

In the case of Grand Canyon, the National Wildlife Federation only took a position after the decisive blow had been dealt to the dams in 1966. The NWF finally voted to endorse steam plants in March 1967, but it favored the construction of a high Bridge/Hualapai dam and moving the national park boundaries east away from the reservoir if steam plants were not approved by Congress. An angry Brower even accused National Wildlife Federation Executive Director Thomas Kimball of advocating that the park be "dismembered piecemeal" in favor of economic interests.[14] Thus the pro-dam lobby neutralized the political pressure of the federation's two million members for the duration of the controversy, and as a result the preservationists' Grand Canyon effort failed to achieve the unity it attained during the fight over Dinosaur National Monument a decade earlier.

Power Imagined

Although Brower and other preservationists had not yet gained entrée to the inner workings of the political process in 1965, apart from their invited testimony at the committee hearings, they understood that the symbolic importance of Grand Canyon itself offered the opportunity to unite diverse elements within the environmental movement and to gain widespread public sympathy.

Even though pure ecological arguments were easy to refute because the Grand Canyon ecosystem had been altered by Glen Canyon Dam, the canyon itself was far from destroyed. The living river constituted the most visible reminder that the forces that carved the canyon were still at work. Many people wrote Congress, expressing that from a psychological perspective it was important to know that the Colorado River still flowed and was still creating Grand Canyon. Even in the optimistic euphoria surrounding the promise of post–World War II technological advances, Americans also understood that humanity now possessed the capacity to destroy the Earth through radiation, pollution, overpopulation, the dumping of toxic wastes, and a myriad of other potential hazards one person could not combat alone.[15] Writing a letter to protest the damming of Grand Canyon appealed to many people because it was something they could do individually to combat the faceless agencies and bureaucrats that were destroying the environment and their own geography of hope.

The club's success in bringing its fight against the Grand Canyon dams to the attention of the national media brought the threats to America's greatest scenic wonder—and the environmental organization leading the fight against them—to the attention of millions of people. If Echo Park constitutes the point in time when the Sierra Club took its place among activist environmental organizations, Grand Canyon is when other conservation groups and the American public recognized the club as the most activist environmental organization then in existence and began looking to it to spearhead this and other environmental crusades.[16]

The aura of the Sierra Club's influence was greatly strengthened by the presentations its experts made during the congressional hearings of 1965, 1966, and 1967. Although meritorious and sincere, the expert testimony did not appreciably influence the key subcommittee and committee votes in 1966 because most committee members had already made up their minds. However, the testimony of Moss, Carlin, and Ingram did influence public opinion by creating a foundation of scientific legitimacy for arguments in favor of alternative energy sources. Many letters and newspaper editorials opposed to the dams quoted their arguments, as well as those of Richard Bradley.

During the 1960s, many Americans had come to believe that science held the answers to almost every problem, large and small. And why not? Almost on a daily basis they were treated to the promises of the nuclear physicists, the amazing achievements of the space program, and a multitude of other scientific and technological advancements. The public's frequent use of the experts' arguments suggests that gaining a foundation of scientific legitimacy proved crucial for the opposition campaign's widespread appeal. These experts recommended the same alternatives the Interior Department had been studying. Udall was aware of these arguments and there is little doubt that they influenced his eventual choice of coal-fired power plants as an alternative source of electricity. By the fall of 1966, Udall was formulating a way to defuse the political opposition the dams—and the water importation from the Pacific Northwest that they were designed to pay for—had unwittingly caused.

On June 10, 1966, another pivotal event occurred when the IRS clouded the Sierra Club's tax-deductible status because of the advertisements it placed in the New York Times and other national newspapers. The IRS revocation occurred during the tumultuous social upheavals of the 1960s, and it received front-page coverage in newspapers across the country. As a result, the Sierra Club gained an enormous public windfall of sympathy from Americans concerned with governmental repression of civil liberties and those who resented federal meddling with the club's fundamental constitutional rights. Although Grand Canyon was of great symbolic importance and the Sierra Club's ad campaign generated a large response through June 9, 1966, public involvement grew tremendously after the IRS revocation the following day.

This increase in public activism is not only measured in the amount and content of the mail received by members of Congress after that date, but also in the growth statistics for the Sierra Club membership and dramatic increases in small contributions. Thousands of people joined to protest the IRS action, while tens of thousands more gleefully sent small amounts of money to aid the club in its Grand Canyon fight. People also sent accompanying letters that stated how glad they were that their gifts were *not* tax deductible. In the social context of the 1960s, large numbers of people who did not identify as environmentalists viewed the Sierra Club as a "symbol of American freedom" that refused to back down from the most powerful and hated governmental agency in the United States.[17]

The Sierra Club emerged from the fight to save Grand Canyon bloodied but unbowed, having created the public perception that its activism and willingness to risk its very existence are the reasons Grand Canyon remained free of dams, a heroic narrative it and people who admire its efforts agressively promoted. Thus the aura of political influence the club first attained as a result of Echo Park had been reinforced. The political debates that led to the unraveling of the compromises made among the basin states in August 1966 were well publicized—and Stewart Udall announced his intention to study alternatives in September 1966. But the vast majority of people, along with the historians who have written about it, have ignored the political aspects of the controversy in favor of the heroic story of the Sierra Club's "victory," a situation that was to have important ramifications for the future of the environmental movement.

The Care and Feeding of a "Noble Myth"

Despite the Sierra Club's inability to influence the political process in 1966, the decisive year when it became politically impossible to pass any regional plan that depended upon hydroelectric dams in Grand Canyon and power water augmentation from the Columbia River, that same year the club became the face of the anti-dam fight in the court of public opinion. Four major reasons explain why the idea that the Sierra Club defeated the dams has so much appeal: (1) its success in gaining access to the national media; (2) its continuing and highly publicized anti-dam efforts of 1967 and 1968, even though the dams had been defeated in 1966; (3) the final project being passed without any dams in it; and (4) the social context of the late 1960s.

Had the Colorado River Basin Project passed with even one Grand Canyon dam, it would have continued the string of preservationists' defeats that began with Rainbow Bridge and Glen Canyon. If the environmentalists had lost the Grand Canyon fight it would have been catastrophic. Nothing less than the credibility of the entire preservationist agenda was at stake. To defeat the dams—or to create the perception of doing so—would add to the aura of the political influence they had used to block the dams proposed for Dinosaur National Monument the previous decade.

The dams were defeated by political intrigues at the committee level, but the Sierra Club took credit for this result so that it could make subsequent appeals to a public that believed the club had forced the political process to work in its favor. Because of Grand Canyon's status as an American national treasure and one of the seven wonders of the natural world, for the Sierra Club to claim the mantle of having saved it—and to successfully convince other environmental organizations and the public that it had done so—conferred upon it a tremendous amount of legitimacy and prestige among environmentalists and the public alike.

The club's "saving" of Grand Canyon also occurred at the exact moment in time when public fears about health and safety had moved environmentalism beyond Muir-style preservation and created a groundswell of people willing to fight for these new environmental causes. Of all the existing environmental organizations, the Sierra Club, despite internal strife in the wake of its Grand Canyon campaign, was positioned to embrace this new environmentalism and lead it into the next decade and beyond.

However, for the public to buy the idea that the Sierra Club defeated the dams by pressuring Congress into removing them, people had to be willing to accept the club's version of these events. In June 1966, after the publication of the full-page newspaper ads and the IRS action they triggered, the Sierra Club's twin battles to save Grand Canyon and defend itself from the IRS became national news. Millions of people who had little interest in environmental causes identified with the club because of the government's repression of its First Amendment rights of speech and petition.

Although the dams became a political impossibility in fall of 1966, the Sierra Club continued to battle against both the idea of them and the IRS for another two years in the national media spotlight. Thus, by the time Congress passed the CAP without dams in 1968, the public assumed it was the Sierra Club's anti-dam crusade that had defeated them. Despite their declining faith in government, vast numbers of American citizens wanted desperately to believe that the process still worked and that their elected officials would respond to individuals and groups working at the grassroots level. After a decade of social unrest and amid rising fears of increasing governmental interference, many people viewed the passage of the CAP in 1968 without dams as not only a victory for preservationists but also as a victory for American democracy itself.

The assumption that the Sierra Club saved Grand Canyon from dams has become such an article of faith that it has scarcely been challenged in scholarly and popular accounts of these events for more than fifty years. The story has been repeated—and embellished—so often that several recent, widely distributed documentaries have broken free from the historical record itself.

For example, Academy Award–nominated filmmaker Mark Kitchell wrote and directed the "first big picture film" (and the only one to date) of the rise of modern environmentalism, a five-act epic titled *A Fierce Green Fire: The Battle for a Living Planet,* which premiered at the Sundance Film Festival in 2012. In the years since, Kitchell has released it to hundreds of theaters, churches, libraries, environmental groups, and other organizations. Almost two hours in length, the movie depicts the rise of modern environmentalism from its origins in the 1960s and it is narrated by celebrities such as Robert Redford, Ashley Judd, and Meryl Streep. The film has recently been available to stream on Netflix and YouTube, and PBS began posting short excerpts from it as part of its *American Masters* podcasts on Earth Day starting on April 22, 2014.[18]

Act One is titled "Conservation," and a substantial portion of it focuses on the Sierra Club and Brower's role in the fight to save Grand Canyon from dams. The short segment of Act One PBS posted to its website is titled "When the Sierra Club Saved the Grand Canyon."[19] "Conservation" is narrated by Redford, whose sincere intellectual baritone lends gravitas to documentary narration perhaps only rivaled by that of Morgan Freeman. Featuring archival photos and film, and interviews with Martin Litton, Jerry Mander, Doug Scott (a former Sierra Club conservation director), and Tom Turner (the author of David Brower's authorized biography), it is perhaps the most widely distributed version of the Sierra Club's heroic narrative to date. The interviews are passionate, compelling, and they, along with Kitchell's script, contain significant historical inaccuracies.

The film begins with a brief overview of the genesis of the environmental movement at the turn of the twentieth century. The ideas of conservation and preservation are presented along with their most important advocates, Gifford Pinchot and John Muir. The Sierra Club's unsuccessful battle to save Hetch Hetchy, its victorious Dinosaur campaign, and the loss of Glen Canyon, follow in quick succession. Brower is introduced, and the audience learns about the heartbreaking destruction of Glen Canyon from Brower himself. However, with more dams planned for the Colorado River, Brower would soon, as Redford intones, have a chance at "redemption."[20]

Voiceovers by Redford and Litton and a film clip of bureau personnel assaying a damsite introduce the audience to the threats looming over Grand Canyon. This scene is soon followed by another of two daring high-scalers traversing a vertical face while suspended by ropes above the raging Colorado River. Although these clips are very dramatic, they are taken from a 1961 Bureau of Reclamation documentary about the construction of Glen Canyon Dam. The map is clearly of Glen Canyon above Lee's Ferry, and the high-scalers are on a sheer wall at the Glen Canyon Damsite, fifty miles upstream of any damsite the bureau contemplated developing in Grand Canyon during the 1960s. Although this montage appears to be a seemingly innocuous bit of artistic license, it sets the stage for what follows.[21]

Redford, in a grave tone, then explains that the Bureau of Reclamation released plans in 1965 "to build two power dams, and a tunnel to connect them through the heart of the Grand Canyon" that "would have killed the river," statements affirmed with great passion by Litton. While it is true that the bureau studied this possibility in the 1940s and 1950s, and Los Angeles's bid to build it as a state project had been rejected by the FPC in 1961, the Marble Canyon–Kanab Creek project had long been abandoned by the bureau when Stewart Udall began framing his regional plan in 1963. Udall briefly toyed with the idea but by the time he released the final version of the PSWP in 1964, he had discarded it for good. At no time during the 1960s was the Kanab Creek tunnel a part of any final plan endorsed by the Interior Department or the bureau. Nor was it ever part of any bill that appeared before Congress. In 1966 even Bureau of Reclamation Commissioner Dominy referred to it as a "ghost."[22]

Immediately following this assertion, Scott states that "the dams in the Grand Canyon [were] going to be a fight to the death." The Sierra Club would not accept a dam of any height because "[they weren't] going to allow dams to be built in a national park." This misstatement is an outright articulation of what the Sierra Club hoped the public would infer from the newspaper ads it published in 1966 and 1967—that the dams were going to be built in Grand Canyon National Park. But at no time during the epic dam debate of the 1960s did any proposal dreamed up by Stewart Udall or contemplated by Congress include a dam that would be built within either Grand Canyon National Park or Monument as they existed at that time. And although Scott's statement is an obvious reference to Brower's dramatic 1967 testimony before the House Reclamation Subcommittee in which he refused to accept even a "low,

low, low, Bridge Canyon Dam," that committee never took a vote on the project in 1967 because the dams were already a lost cause.[23]

Next, in an extraordinary departure from the historical record, Jerry Mander, whose firm helped Brower write the brilliant full-page advertisements that appeared in the *New York Times* and other prominent newspapers, reveals the following: "The dams had already been passed in Congress, the deal was done. Udall was celebrating the great victory of these dams that were going to go in . . . everybody on that side of the story was confident that they had won the struggle."[24]

Where to begin? Not only was the deal *not* done, at no time in either house of Congress did *any* committee report a bill to the floor that included *even a single dam* in Grand Canyon. As previously noted, when Senator Gordon Allott of Colorado tried to bypass the Senate Interior Committee by amending Jackson's 1967 CAP bill to include a Hualapai Dam during the floor debate, the Senate crushed the amendment 70–12, a ringing affirmation of the virtually omnipotent power Jackson wielded over reclamation projects in the upper chamber. And although the House Interior Committee did vote to forward the CAP with dams in it to the floor in July 1966, that bill died in the Rules Committee a few weeks later. The only times even one house of Congress has ever passed bills that included even a single dam in Grand Canyon were in 1950 and 1951 when the Senate passed Hayden's doomed Bridge Canyon Dam bills that California blocked in the House Interior Committee. Contrary to Mander's assertions, *at no time* during the 1960s did *any* bill containing a Grand Canyon dam pass in *either* house of Congress.

Furthermore, Stewart Udall was not celebrating, because he had nothing to celebrate. Everybody who favored the dams knew that, because the bloated 1965–1966 regional bill was figuratively duct-taped together, it could come apart at any time, and it eventually did. Even had this ill-fated legislation somehow made it through the House, Jackson was lurking in the Senate. The 1967 Senate vote demonstrates that Jackson held all the cards in the upper chamber and that he had the power to kill the dams whether they came before his committee or the Senate as a whole. These are not matters of differing historical interpretation or conjecture; they are matters of historical fact that are clearly spelled out in the record.

After a summary of the impact of the Sierra Club's full-page ads, the IRS response, and more stunning archival film footage, Redford gives his summation in a stately narration:

The public rallied to the idea of saving the Grand Canyon. Opposition to the dams grew fast and furious. Pressure grew so strong that it turned the tide. Congress and Secretary Udall were forced to abandon the dams. Finally, Congress prohibited dams anywhere in the Grand Canyon and expanded the national park. It was a complete victory for Brower and the Sierra Club.

And there it is, the myth encapsulated, framed in breathtaking visual imagery with a celebrity endorsement! Judging by the magnitude of the incorrect historical assertions made in *A Fierce Green Fire* and in numerous other examples, after fifty years the heroic narrative of how the Sierra Club allegedly saved Grand Canyon is apparently no longer heroic enough.[25]

Although a certain amount of hyperbole is to be expected in a battle as fiercely contested as this one was—and indeed, as I have pointed out, both sides engaged in it frequently—there are potential consequences for falsifying the historical record that those who repeat and embellish the Sierra Club's heroic narrative have not considered. In a political milieu that has turned decisively to the right, and amid a social environment in which "alternative facts" are now a part of the American lexicon, remaining true to the historical record is more important than ever. People who create and perpetuate myths not firmly grounded in the primary sources are not just engaging in hyperbole, they are providing those who seek to exploit the natural world for short-term profit the ammunition they need to discredit the environmental movement as a whole, thereby increasing the threats to the very nature environmentalists have worked so hard to protect.

So how does one explain people's insistence upon magnifying the Sierra Club's achievements beyond their already-impressive historical reality? The field of philosophy may hold some clues. In the *Republic*, Plato wrote about instances where the elites of society believed it necessary to create a "Noble Lie," an intentional deception designed to unify people behind a common cause designed to bring about positive change. Had Plato written about Grand Canyon—rather than a cave—he might have distinguished between myths based upon intentional deception and those created and perpetuated by people so close to events that they cannot describe them with a reasonable degree of objectivity.[26]

Such is the case of the Sierra Club's heroic narrative. This "noble myth" as I shall call it—as opposed to Plato's "Noble Lie"—is not based upon an intentional deception; rather it is framed by unconscious overstatements of what actually occurred, made by people too close to the events to write about them from a detached perspective. In the case of the Sierra Club, historian Nash wrote his original essay as text for a Sierra Club publication. I do not fault him for finding it difficult to write about the fight to save Grand Canyon dispassionately, because he was intimately involved in it. However, Nash's account has been accepted, repeated, and embellished without critical analysis for so long that it has become exaggerated to the point of becoming factually absurd.

Noble myths, though unintentionally false, are designed to exhort the faithful to even greater heroic efforts to fight against perceived threats, in this case threats to the environment. Myths, once established and repeated, are difficult to disprove even when they conflict with documentary evidence, because people become emotionally invested in them and desperately want to accept them as truth even if they fly in the face of the verifiable record.

The Sierra Club's noble myth has become further entrenched because of three additional factors: the tenuous nature of environmental victories; the type of Sierra Club leaders that gained ascendency, at least temporarily, during the controversy; and the belief that their cause was not only just, but that it was morally righteous. Environmental victories, even those that seem permanent, are always subject to the whims of Congress and administrations. Recent reductions to Bears' Ears and Grand Staircase–Escalante National Monuments are stark reminders of the temporary nature of permanence with respect to wilderness protection. Because of the lingering uncertainty that hangs over supposedly protected places, augmented by continuing and unrelenting efforts to exploit the resources within them, environmentalists can never let down their guard.

In the 1960s this degree of vigilance required new leaders with a degree of dedication—fanaticism to some—who absolutely refused to compromise. By 1963 the old generation of Sierra Club leaders such as Bestor Robinson, who favored Marble Canyon Dam because it would have created a splendid tailwater trout fishery, had given way to people such as Brower, Litton, and Ingram. These new leaders believed that compromise only led to the destruction of nature. Nor could they disengage from their activism when assessing it. To recognize that their campaign constituted only one factor in the deletion of the dams would compromise the perception that Grand Canyon today is dam-free because of the Sierra Club's efforts.

Brower's evangelical language from the 1960s mirrors that used by Muir to defend Hetch Hetchy fifty years previously. In both struggles the rhetoric clearly framed the choice as being between "man's" worldly avarice and protecting places that still bore the imprint of the creator's hand. These parallels are not accidental. By adding a layer of righteousness to their cause, the Sierra Club's leaders claimed the moral high ground, which they used as a base to attack the dams with impressive technological and poignant emotional arguments.

Positive Outcomes in Navajo Country

Scholars have also focused upon the Sierra Club's "triumph" at the expense of discussing other important ramifications and ironies of the final resolution to the struggle over the Grand Canyon dams. For example, the controversy raises new questions about how Native Americans and environmental organizations are perceived by the American public and portrayed in the historical record. Many environmentalists, critical of how American society has abused the landscape of North America, argue that American Indians have an ecological consciousness that white society should emulate to remedy the environmental depredations that American industrial capitalism has wrought upon the landscape for the past 150 years. Historians have also engaged in this debate, with scholars ranging from Calvin Martin to Shepard Krech polarized on the issue of Native Americans as environmentalists.[27]

Ironically, at almost the same time that a weeping "Iron Eyes Cody," an actor of Sicilian ancestry named Espera Oscar de Corti who pretended he was Cherokee, appeared in an iconic anti-pollution television commerical and admonished the American public to respect rather than destroy nature, both the Hualapai and Navajo Nations were seeking to construct hydroelectric dams in Grand Canyon, perhaps the most sublime example of natural splendor in all the world.[28] While the CAP debate is only one act in a much larger drama, it illuminates the difficulties that can arise when scholars attempt to lump all American Indians into one ecologically conscious camp. This fallacy is illuminated even further when one considers that significant conflicts within individual American Indian nations—as was the case between the "traditionalist" and the "progressive" factions of the Navajo—are common. By perpetuating these inaccurate stereotypes, historians have failed to recognize the agency American Indians have exercised in determining the use of their resources, even though in wielding it Native Americans may undermine popular portrayals of themselves as proto-environmentalists.

The efforts to gain American Indian support and manipulate public opinion are also illustrative of the Machiavellian tactics Central Arizona Project supporters and environmentalists used during the fight to save Grand Canyon. The CAP supporters promised enormous economic benefits to the Hualapai Nation for much of the debate. Yet they revealed their true colors as political pragmatists when faced with Hayden's and Stewart Udall's impending departures in January 1969. They abandoned the Hualapai after it became politically expedient to delete the dams and sided with the Sierra Club in publicizing the benefits that would accrue to the Navajo people. Their lofty pronouncements about aiding the Hualapai notwithstanding, the Department of the Interior and Arizona state and federal officials instead left the Hualapai Nation with heightened expectations that never came to pass once the dams had been removed from the final CAP legislation.

Environmentalists enlisted the Navajo people in their opposition to the Grand Canyon dams and argued that scenic tourism to Marble Canyon could become an important source of revenue for them. However, in the five decades since the dam controversy ended, the Navajo Nation has not developed the rim of Marble Canyon within its reservation to facilitate sightseeing. Despite continuing poverty and the promise of economic benefits, the Navajo Nation has (thankfully) recently rejected an attempt made by a Scottsdale, Arizona–based corporation to build a monstrous hotel/casino complex near the sacred confluence of the Colorado and Little Colorado Rivers.

Regrettably, the Sierra Club, by courting the Navajo people and obtaining their opposition to the dams and support for power supplied by coal-fired plants, became a party to massive strip-mining in Navajo country. Draglines have desecrated parts of Black Mesa, which is an element of one of the most sacred land features in Navajo cosmology, and the air pollution from the Four Corners and Navajo power plants frequently obscures the view across Grand Canyon, the very place the club fought so hard to preserve.[29]

The Navajo Nation contracted to develop its coal reserves—and the Four Corners Power Plant was already coming on line—before the conclusion of the fight against the dams. But the Navajo Generating Plant near Page, Arizona, was built to provide power for the CAP. The timing of these events created the erroneous impression that the Sierra Club agreed to the sacrifice of a pristine landscape to keep the dams from being built. Although the Navajo power plant, and the strip-mining needed to fuel it, increased the mining and pollution in Navajo country, dams would not have eliminated them.

However, in 2019, the year of the Grand Canyon National Park Centennial, the tide may have turned. As of this writing, several units of the Four Corners Power Plant have been decommissioned, while a lawsuit settlement forced the utility companies that own the remaining units to significantly reduce harmful emissions. This legal action was based upon the Clean Air Act of 1970 as amended in 1990 for "major sources" of air pollution as applied to coal-fired power plants.[30] Additionally, the Navajo plant is scheduled to be decommissioned by the end of 2019, a fitting date for the demise of the worst polluting power plant in the western United States.[31]

If Navajo closes, the skies over Grand Canyon should be much clearer. Cheaper natural gas and renewable energy sources have made the plant obsolete—the outcome for which the Sierra Club wished when it suggested fossil fuel power generation as an alternative source of electricity for the CAP between 1965 and 1968. Although my previous work has been critical of the Sierra Club for "choosing political pragmatism over human concerns," the recent development of cleaner alternatives may further demonstrate the wisdom of choosing coal over hydroelectric power as a short-term expedient.[32]

Grand Canyon, NEPA, and the Rise of the Sierra Club

Environmental advocates, shut out from the political and legal process for most of the twentieth century, received their first break in 1965 when the US Second Circuit Court of Appeals handed down its ruling in *Scenic Hudson Preservation Conference v. Federal Power Commission*—better known as the Storm King decision—which granted conservation groups standing to sue to preserve scenic values.[33] This court decision only initially applied to proposals under consideration by the Federal Power Commission. Because it did not affect Bureau of Reclamation projects, preservationists fighting against the Grand Canyon dams were still without legal recourse. However, Storm King is the point where environmentalists gained another avenue into policymaking in addition to the opportunity to testify during committee hearings when invited.[34] Within five years the forces unleashed by the activism of the 1960s and the rising tide of the nascent environmental movement would result in sweeping changes in environmental law and policy more quickly than anyone could have ever imagined.

The same year as the Storm King decision, Senator Jackson's demand for transparency upended the bureau's approval process. His refusal to bargain away Columbia River water had so frightened Aspinall and Ely that they stalled the Lower Colorado River Basin Project to death in August 1966, effectively killing the Grand Canyon dams. But Jackson was not about to rest on his laurels and allow CAP supporters to salvage anything from their failure. After the defeat of the dams and the Columbia River diversion in 1966, Jackson left nothing to chance and continued his offensive against the taking of water from the Columbia River until the final CAP bill was passed in 1968.

Even while the CAP endgame played out in the political arena, some members of Congress began to consider the passage of sweeping legislation designed to create a national environmental policy in response to growing concerns about public health, pesticide use, and threats to the National Park System. Although environmental regulations have long been a part of American law, dating to the first water quality statute of 1789, no comprehensive federal policy had existed. Congress recognized that some degree of transparency should be part of the authorization process for federal projects as early as 1946 when President Truman signed an amendment to the Fish and Wildlife Coordination Act of 1934, requiring biological surveys of the impact federal and state dam proposals would have on fish and wildlife.[35]

Although important steps, none of these early environmental statutes were comprehensive in scope. As growing numbers of people became concerned about post–World War II environmental issues such as dams proposed for Dinosaur National Monument and the health consequences of nuclear testing during the 1950s, a few politicians began to foresee the need for sweeping environmental legislation. However, it wasn't until the 1960s, after environmentalism became a public concern, that a political climate conducive to the drafting of comprehensive federal environmental regulations materialized.[36]

As the modern environmental movement emerged after the appointment of Stewart Udall as interior secretary and the publication of Rachael Carson's *Silent Spring* in the early 1960s, congressional attempts to craft broad environmental policies were slowed by jurisdictional rivalries between various Senate committees. By the mid-1960s Edmund Muskie of Maine, chair of the Senate Subcommittee on Water and Air Pollution of the Senate Committee on Public Works, had sponsored the

Water Quality Act of 1965, and his subcommittee had taken the lead with respect to antipollution legislation.[37]

At that time, Senator Jackson and the Senate Interior Committee exercised little jurisdiction over environmental issues. However, Jackson's annoyance with Floyd Dominy's single-minded pursuit of massive water projects, including the Grand Canyon dams and the Columbia River diversion at the expense of environmental and other "public values," eventually led him to consider expanding the role of his committee. After Jackson obtained Senate approval of his June 1965 amendment that forced the Bureau of Reclamation to obtain congressional approval before beginning feasibility studies of water projects, he began to strategize with his staff about how to increase the jurisdiction of the Interior Committee to include environmental issues.

In 1966, Jackson hired a brilliant young attorney, Bill Van Ness, to be special counsel to the Interior Committee, and by 1967 Van Ness had been given the task of drafting a bill that included a statement of national environmental policy. Jackson insisted that the law contain an "action-forcing" provision that required federal agencies to: (1) cooperate with each other when studying a potential project; (2) consider all feasible alternatives; and (3) render environmental impact statements (EIS) that outlined the environmental consequences of their proposals.[38] Ironically, Van Ness and his co-counsel Daniel Dreyfus used the feasibility study model developed by the Army Corps of Engineers and Bureau of Reclamation, as the foundation for the National Environmental Policy Act (NEPA).[39] Spurred by threats to the Everglades National Park in 1968, and after some legislative maneuvering in both houses of Congress, Jackson introduced Senate Bill 1075 to the Senate on April 16, 1969, and when President Nixon signed it on January 1, 1970, NEPA became the law.

The origins of key components of NEPA can be traced directly to Jackson's opposition to the high Bridge Canyon Dam and the Columbia River water diversion for which it was designed to provide power and revenue. While blocking the Southwest's attempts to commandeer water from the Columbia, Jackson derailed tactics that the Bureau of Reclamation had used for more than half a century to gain approval of its projects. According to Van Ness, Jackson's legislative maneuver in June 1965 constitutes the point of origin for NEPA's Environmental Impact Statement requirement.[40]

The EIS is the primary legal mechanism by which NEPA is enforced and public input is guaranteed. Federal agencies can no longer manipulate Congress into approving projects without regard for their potential environmental consequences. Because Jackson insisted upon transparency during the debate over the Lower Colorado River Basin Project and the Grand Canyon dams in 1965, the protection of public values, the assessment of a project's environmental consequences, and opportunities for public input are all key elements of environmental policymaking today.

Final Thoughts

Although in 1970 the public gained unprecedented opportunities to participate in environmental policymaking, access to the political system did not guarantee that organizations or individuals could effect change. Hence, the American people's perception of the Sierra Club's ability to influence policy became very important after the passage of NEPA because the club's leadership was able to translate this illusion of strength, which was at its peak in the wake of the club's having just "saved" Grand Canyon, into real political power once NEPA went into effect and gave environmentalists legal avenues through which they could shape the process.

FIGURE 9.1. Senator Henry Jackson and Bill Van Ness, special counsel to the Senate Committee on Interior and Insular Affairs and primary author of the National Environmental Policy Act. University of Washington Libraries, Special Collections, UW277953z.

The fight to save Grand Canyon is the event that allowed the Sierra Club to reap the benefits of the leadership position it gained among environmental organizations because of its directors' 1960 decision to let Brower pursue public environmental activism despite the risk it posed to the club's tax-deductible status. By seeking to influence legislation in the face of the IRS threat, the Sierra Club not only gained a tremendous amount of public visibility, it also placed itself in a position to capitalize upon fortuitous circumstances should they occur.

Although it may be serendipitous from the Sierra Club's perspective that the controversy over the proposed Grand Canyon dams took place in such a turbulent social and political climate, it was certainly not a chance occurrence that the Sierra Club was in position to take advantage of it. Alone among the environmental organizations at the time, the Sierra Club and its leadership were willing to risk everything to save Grand Canyon, even if it meant the club's financial destitution and involved stretching the truth. As the eminently quotable Litton once put it, "If the end is a noble one, let the chips fall where they may. We certainly aren't sorry we kept the dams out of the Grand Canyon and if we lied to do it, fine!"[41]

Although the preservationists' anti-dam campaign did not play a decisive role in saving Grand Canyon, the public *thought* that it had. The Sierra Club capitalized on its reputation of having just "saved" America's greatest scenic wonder by converting these perceptions into actual political influence once environmentalists gained access to the policymaking process in 1970. And as a result, the Sierra Club's environmental advocacy and post-NEPA influence are certainly important reasons why the public has overwhelmingly opposed attempts to compromise the National Park System for almost fifty years and why the club is one of the most important environmental organizations in the world today.

Aldo Leopold once wrote, "We speak glibly of conservation education, but what do we mean by it? If we mean indoctrination, then let us be reminded that it is just as easy to indoctrinate with fallacies as with facts."[42] The Sierra Club's noble myth has outlived its usefulness. In this centennial year of Grand Canyon National Park, let us heed Leopold's words. Let us acknowledge the complexity of these events and rescind the opportunity that oversimplification of, and deviation from, the documented historical record has given to those who seek to exploit our national parks, monuments, and other sacred spaces.

Notes

Preface

1. David Ross Brower, interview by author, July 27, 1997.
2. Daniel P. Beard, *Deadbeat Dams: Why We Should Abolish the U.S. Bureau of Reclamation and Tear Out Glen Canyon Dam* (Boulder, CO: Johnson Books, 2015).
3. Ryder W. Miller, "Review, *Still the Wild River Runs: Congress, the Sierra Club, and the Fight to Save Grand Canyon, 1963–1968*," *Electronic Green Journal* 1, issue 18 (2003), https://escholarship.org/search/?q=Miller,%20Ryder%20W, accessed July 20, 2018; Jeff Ingram, "Celebrating the Grand Canyon" (2009–present), http://gcfutures.blogspot.com/, accessed July 8, 2018.
4. Kenneth Brower, "Appreciation: Lessons from the Man Who Stopped Grand Canyon Dams," https://news.nationalgeographic.com/news/2014/12/141202-grand-canyon-dams-colorado-river-martin-litton-conservation/, accessed July 20, 2018.

Introduction

1. Theodore Roosevelt, "Speech at the Grand Canyon," May 6, 1903, quoted in *The Coconino Sun* (Flagstaff, AZ), May 9, 1903.
2. Roderick Nash, *Wilderness and the American Mind*, 5th ed. (New Haven: Yale University Press, 2014), 227–37; Marc Reisner, *Cadillac Desert: The American West and Its Disappearing Water*, 2nd ed. (New York: Penguin Books, 1993), 272–90; Mark Kitchell, "Act 1: Conservation," in *A Fierce Green Fire: The Battle for a Living Planet*, January 23, 2012, documentary, https://www.youtube.com/watch?v=u_fW_7WzSXk, accessed May 18, 2018.
3. "Cadillac Desert 2 American Nile video merge," YouTube, March 8, 2015, published by Stanley Rubin, https://www.youtube.com/watch?v=vKIxKE-Duac&t=1490s, accessed June 25, 2018.
4. US Bureau of Reclamation, "*Pacific Southwest Water Plan Report*" (January 1964), 10, 13, https://www.usbr.gov/lc/region/programs/crbstudy/PSWPRptJan64.pdf, accessed July 15, 2018.

Chapter 1

1. Roosevelt, "Speech at Grand Canyon, May 6, 1903," printed in *Coconino Sun*, May 9, 1903. The title for this chapter is taken from the speech.
2. Joseph C. Ives, *Report Upon the Colorado River of the West* (Washington, DC: Government Printing Office, 1861), 110; John Wesley Powell, *Canyons of*

the Colorado (New York: Cosimo Publications, 2008; reprinted from 1895), 328; Robert Brewster Stanton, *Field Notes of a Survey for the Proposed Denver, Colorado Cañon and Pacific Railroad from Green River, Utah, down the Green and Colorado Rivers to the Gulf of California; Incl. Expense Accounts, etc.*, vol. 3, May 10, 1889–April 30, 1890 (transcript), 108, 40, https://digitalcollections.nypl.org/items/510d47e2-c81b-a3d9-e040-e00a18064a99/book?parent=12b78680-c5bf-012f-c9a2-58d385a7bc34#page/21/mode/2up. accessed July 20, 2018.

3. John Wesley Powell, *Report on the Lands of the Arid Region of the United States* (Cambridge: Harvard University Press, 1962; 1878), ix–xi, xvi, xxiii, 44, 48, 54.

4. Donald Worster, *A River Running West: The Life of John Wesley Powell* (New York: Oxford University Press, 2001), 467–532; Donald Pisani, *To Reclaim a Divided West: Water, Law, and Public Policy 1848–1902* (Albuquerque: University of New Mexico Press, 1992), 143–65.

5. Donald Worster, *Rivers of Empire* (New York: Pantheon Books, 1985), 194–97; Reisner, 122–24. For an entertaining account of the fiasco, see Diane E. Boyer and Robert H. Webb, *Damming Grand Canyon: The 1923 USGS Colorado River Expedition* (Logan: Utah State University Press, 2007), 24–28, http://digitalcommons.usu.edu/usupress_pubs/161.

6. Norris Hundley, Jr., *Water and the West: The Colorado River Compact and the Politics of Water in the American West* (Berkeley: University of California Press, 1975), 9–10.

7. Norris Hundley, Jr., *The Great Thirst: Californians and Water, 1770s–1990s* (Berkeley: University of California Press, 1992), 203–4.

8. William E. Warne, *The Bureau of Reclamation* (New York: Praeger Publishers Inc., 1973), 13–14; Michael C. Robinson, *Water for the West: The Bureau of Reclamation, 1902–1977* (Chicago: The Public Works Historical Society, 1979), 19–21, 28; https://www.usbr.gov/lc/phoenix/AZ100/1910/men_built_the_dam.html, accessed May 17, 2018.

9. Robinson, 38–44; Richard Berkman and Kip Viscusi, *Damming the West: Ralph Nader's Study Group Report on the Bureau of Reclamation* (New York: Grossman Publishers, 1973).

10. Hundley, *Great Thirst*, 203–9.

11. Robert Brewster Stanton, *Down the Colorado*, ed. Dwight L. Smith (Norman: University of Oklahoma Press, 1965), 272.

12. *Salt Lake City Tribune*, November 28, 1893; *Coconino Sun*, March 22, 1902.

13. *Coconino Sun*, April 13, 1901, August 30, 1902; *Phoenix Republican*, June 21, 1902; J. Donald Hughes, *In the House of Stone and Light: A Human History of The Grand Canyon* (Grand Canyon History Association, 1978), 65; A. B. West to Morris Udall, November 17, 1966, folder 23, box 483, Morris Udall Papers, Special Collections, University of Arizona (hereafter MKU).

14. *Kingman (AZ) Miner*, February 22, 1902; *Coconino Sun*, June 21, 1902.

15. Portions of this section were originally published in *Forest History Today* 18, no. 1 (Spring 2012): 3–11. Used with permission.

16. Douglas Strong, "Ralph H. Cameron and the Grand Canyon" (Parts 1 and 2), *Arizona and the West* 20, nos. 1 and 2 (Winter, Spring 1978): 41–64, 155–72.

17. Robert Shankland, *Steve Mather of the National Parks* (New York: Alfred Knopf, 1970), 225–42; Bert Cameron, interview transcribed by William E. Austin, June 21, 1939, in *Grand Canyon Items*, vol. 2, Grand Canyon National Park Research Library (hereafter GCRL); Strong, 56; *Coconino Sun*, May 24, 1912.

18. Donald Worster, *A Passion for Nature: The Life of John Muir* (New York: Oxford University Press, 2008), 396–400, 418–53; Robert Righter, *The Battle over Hetch Hetchy: America's Most Controversial Dam and the Birth of Modern Environmentalism* (New York: Oxford University Press, 2006); Michael Cohen, *The History of the Sierra Club, 1892–1970* (San Francisco: Sierra Club Books, 1988), 22–31; Holoway R. Jones, *John Muir and the Sierra Club: The Battle for Yosemite* (San Francisco: Sierra Club, 1965), 6–8; Gifford Pinchot, *The Fight for Conservation* (Garden City, NY: Harcourt, Brace, 1910), 42–50; Nash, 161–80; Stephen Fox, *The American Conservation Movement: John Muir and His Legacy* (Madison: University of Wisconsin Press, 1981), 139–46.

19. The three parks were Yosemite, Sequoia, and General Grant, a small reserve created to protect the Sierra redwood named after the Civil War hero and eighteenth president.

20. Worster, *Passion for Nature*, 426–33.

21. Ibid., 437, 451–453; Alfred Runte, *National Parks: The American Experience*, 2nd ed. (Lincoln: University of Nebraska Press, 1989), 77–82; Cohen, 22–31.

22. "The Hetch Hetchy Restoration Task Force," http://vault.sierraclub.org/ca/hetchhetchy/hetch_hetchy_task_force.html; John Muir, "The Hetch Hetchy Valley," *Sierra Club Bulletin*, vol. VI. no. 4 (1908), https://vault.sierraclub.org/ca/hetchhetchy/hetch_hetchy_muir_scb_1908.html.

23. Runte, 100–5; Muir, "Hetch Hetchy."

24. R. H. Cameron, "Informal Application for Water Development in Grand Canyon National Monument," November 18, 1914, 31, fiche GCRA-04363, Grand Canyon National Park Museum Collection (hereafter GCMC); Jerome Kerwin, *Federal Water-Power Legislation* (New York: Columbia University Press, 1926).

25. Cameron, 1; Lyle A. Whitsit, "Report on the Hydroelectric Project in Cataract Canyon," 2–3, GRCA-04363, GCMC; Boyer and Webb, 46.

26. Samuel Hays, *Conservation and the Gospel of Efficiency: The Progressive Conservation Movement, 1890–1920* (Cambridge: Harvard University Press, 1959), 168, 173; Ronald A. Foresta, *America's National Parks and Their Keepers* (Washington, DC: Resources for the Future, 1984), 17–20.

27. Harold K. Steen, *The U.S. Forest Service: A Centennial History* (Seattle: University of Washington Press, 2004), 114–22.

28. Nash, 181; Fox, 146–7; Steen, 114–22; Char Miller ed., *American Forests: Nature, Culture, and Politics* (Lawrence: University Press of Kansas Press, 1997), 91–93; Michael Frome, *The Forest Service* (New York: Praeger Publishing, 1971), 14–16.

29. Henry Graves to Secretary of the Interior, January 22, 1915, GRCA-04363, GCMC.

30. W. I. Johnson to Henry Graves, September 13, 1915; Henry Graves to Secretary of the Interior, January 22, 1915; A. F. Potter to Henry Graves, September 26, 1914, all in GRCA-04363, GCMC.

31. H. B. Greely to Stanley D. McGraw, March 18, 1915; O. C. Merrill to Barklay, Parsons, and Klapp, engineers, February 21, 1917, both in GRCA-04363, GCMC.

32. Whitsit, 3.

33. Cameron et al. v. United States, 252 U.S. 450 (1920).

34. Hughes, 85.

35. Grand Canyon National Park Establishment Act, 16 U.S.C. § 221 (1919); Steven Carothers and Bryan T. Brown, *The Colorado River Through Grand Canyon* (Tucson: University of Arizona Press, 1991), 6; "Grand Canyon National Park," *Congressional Record*, House, H1769–1774 (January 20, 1919).

36. Establishment Act, sec. 227; "Grand Canyon National Park," *Congressional Record*, House, January 20, 1919.

37. US Department of the Interior, *The Colorado River: A Natural Menace Becomes a National Resource* (Washington, DC: Government Printing Office, 1946), 168; Bureau of Reclamation, *Memorandum Report on Reconnaissance Studies Marble Canyon Kanab Creek Power Development* (Boulder City, Nevada: 1961), 3, GCRL.

38. E. C. La Rue, *Water-Supply Paper 395: Colorado River and Its Utilization* (Washington, DC: Government Printing Office, 1916), 179–80; Cameron, 9, GRCA-04363, GCMC.

39. Joe Gelt, "Sharing Colorado River Water: History, Public Policy and the Colorado River Compact," 1997, https://wrrc.arizona.edu/publications/arroyo-newsletter/sharing-colorado-river-water-history-public-policy-and-colorado-river, accessed May 21, 2018.

40. Norris Hundley, *Dividing the Waters* (Berkeley: University of California Press, 1966), 48–51; Department of the Interior, *The Colorado River*, 59–66; Gelt.

41. *Colorado River Compact of 1922*, https://www.usbr.gov/lc/region/pao/pdfiles/crcompct.pdf, accessed July 3, 2018; "Lee's Ferry History," https://www.nps.gov/glca/learn/historyculture/leesferryhistory.htm, accessed July 3, 2018. Lee Ferry, the compact point a mile downstream of the Paria River, is a different location than the historical river crossing named "Lee's Ferry" upstream of the Paria River where Stewart and Morris Udall's great-grandfather, John D. Lee, began transporting Mormon settlers south across the Colorado River in 1872.

42. National Academy of Sciences, *Water and Choice in the Colorado Basin: An Example of Alternatives in Water Management* (Washington, DC: Printing and Publishing Office, National Academy of Sciences, 1968), 21.

43. *San Francisco Chronicle*, June 3, 1921; June 6, 1921.

44. Fred Colter, *The Highline Book* (Phoenix, AZ: Fred Colter, 1934), 13–14; Porter Preston to Project Manager, July 25,1923, in RG-115, BOR, Series: CAP Reports, Federal Records Center, Denver (hereafter FRCD).

45. E. C. La Rue, *Water-Supply Paper 556: Water and Flood Control of Colorado River Below Green River, Utah* (Washington, DC: Government Printing Office, 1925), 134–164; *New York Daily Tribune*, December 12, 1923; *Washington Post*, November 11, 1923; Diary of Emery Kolb, 1923, Emery Kolb Papers, Special Collections, Cline Library, Northern Arizona University (hereafter EK); Boyer and Webb, frontpiece, 263. River miles are calculated both up- and downstream from Lee's Ferry, which is mile zero.

46. Colter, 37–38, 44–47; *Arizona Republic*, January 14, 1952; Byron Pearson, "The Marble Canyon–Kanab Creek Project: Grand Canyon, the Bureau of Reclamation, and the Limits of Utilitarianism," *Locus* 8, no. 1 (Fall 1995): 65–80.

47. Colter, 13; Hundley, *Dividing the Waters*, 48–51; A. P. Davis to F. S. Dellenbaugh, August 8, 1922, Box 4, Folder 1, Dellenbaugh Papers, Special Collections, University of Arizona (hereafter FD).

48. Reisner, 125; Phillip Fradkin, *A River No More: The Colorado River and the West*, (Tucson: University of Arizona Press, 1981), 272.

49. Joseph E. Stevens, *Hoover Dam* (Norman: University of Oklahoma Press, 1988), 46, 53; Russell Martin, *A Story That Stands Like a Dam* (New York: Henry Holt and Company, 1989), 3.

50. UCLA Library Digital Collections, http://digital2.library.ucla.edu/Search.do?selectedProjects=all&viewType=1&keyWord=colorado+river, accessed December 18, 2018.

51. Nadine Arroyo Rodriguez, "Arizona Navy Deployed in 1934," Mojave Desert Archives, November 22, 2013, http://mojavedesertarchives.blogspot.com/2013/11/arizona-navy-deployed-in-1934.html, accessed May 23, 2018; Reisner, 258–59.

52. *Arizona Daily Star*, September 30, 1945; January 21, 1947; June 20, 1947; Stevens, 230, 258; Fradkin, 189–90; Reisner, 258–59 and *Arizona Republic*, March 11, 2014.

53. George Hartzog to Stewart Udall, January 27, 1964; R. F. Walter to Dr. Elwood Mead, Commissioner of Reclamation, June 7, 1932, GRCA-04848, GCMC; Kerwin, 380.

54. Mead to Albright, June 14, 1932; Albright to Roger Toll, August 3, 1932; Albright to Mead, January 11, 1933, all in GRCA-04848, GCMC.

55. John Ise, *Our National Park Policy: A Critical History* (Manchester, NH: Ayer Company Publications, 1979), 354.

56. M. R. Tillotson to Director, National Park Service, June 27, 1938, GRCA-04848 (GCMC).

57. Harold Ickes to Chairman, Federal Power Commission, May 27,1939, GRCA-04848 (GCMC); Foresta, 45–47.

58. J. Humlum, *Water Development and Planning in the Southwestern United States* (Copenhagen, Denmark: Carlsberg Foundation, 1969).

59. Rich Johnson, *The Central Arizona Project, 1918–1968* (Tucson: University of Arizona Press, 1977).

Chapter 2

1. Portions of this chapter were originally published in *Pacific Historical Review* 68 (August 1999): 397–424. Used with permission.

2. "Timeline," *The Life and Legacy of Rachel Carson*, http://www.rachelcarson.org/TimelineList.aspx, accessed November 28, 2018.

3. Foresta, 48–49.

4. Ibid., 51; Susan Rhoades Neel, "Irreconcilable Differences: Reclamation, Preservation, and the Origins of the Echo Park Dam Controversy" (PhD diss., University of California, Los Angeles, 1990), 276, 280, 337, 364; Richard West Sellars, *Preserving Nature in the National Parks: A History* (New Haven: Yale University Press, 1997), 155–203.

5. Harvey, 34; Albright to Mead, January 11, 1933, GRCA-04848, GCMC.

6. Newton Drury completed his bachelor's degree in English at UC Berkeley in 1912. He also took a concurrent program of study in the law but graduated three hours short of completing it. Thus, Drury, although he was awarded an honorary Doctor of Laws LLD from UC Berkeley for his work in conservation later in life, never attained the professional law degrees of LLB, or JD required to practice law. Although he was a brilliant legal analyst and tactician, ironically, he was not an attorney. Newton B. Drury, "Parks and Redwoods, 1919–1971," interview by Susan Schrepfer (Bancroft Library, Regional Oral History Office, 1972) 56.

7. La Rue, *Water-Supply Paper 556*, 74; Boyer and Webb, 266–67.

8. Drury to Bryant, October 9, 1942; Frederick Law Olmsted, "Preliminary Survey," 5–6, folder "GCNP," both in box 8, Newton Drury Records, Record Group 79, Records of the National Park Service, National Archives, College Park, MD (hereafter NDR); Edwin D. McKee, "Report on Portions of Grand Canyon That May Be Affected by Proposed Bridge Canyon Dam, Arizona," 1942, fiche L-7423, "Dams on the Colorado River 1948–1954," GCRL.

9. Drury to Merriam, October 30, 1942, fiche L-7423, "Dams on the Colorado River 1948–1954," GCRL. See also Drury to Superintendent, Grand Canyon National Park, October 9, 1942, folder "GCNP," box 8, NDR.

10. R. James Oppedahl, "Conflicts Between Resource Development and Preservation at Glacier National Park" (master's thesis, University of Montana, 1976), 87–88, 91, https://scholarworks.umt.edu/cgi/viewcontent.cgi?article=9671&context=etd, accessed May 27, 2018; see also C. W. Buchholtz, "The Historical Dichotomy of Use and Preservation in Glacier National Park" (master's thesis, University of Montana, 1969), 74, https://scholarworks.umt.edu/cgi/viewcontent.cgi?article=3566&context=etd, accessed May 28, 2018.

11. US Department of the Interior, Bureau of Reclamation, *Preliminary Report on Colorado River–Phoenix Diversion Project, Arizona* (March 1944), 3–4, 10; Pearson, "Marble Canyon–Kanab Creek," 65–80.

12. Reisner, 259–260; Richard White, *It's Your Misfortune and None of My Own* (Norman: University of Oklahoma Press, 1991), 514, 542.

13. US Department of the Interior, Bureau of Reclamation, *The Colorado River: A Natural Menace Becomes a National Resource; A Comprehensive Report on the Development of the Water Resources of the Colorado River Basin for Irrigation, Power Production, and other Beneficial Uses in Arizona, California, Colorado, Nevada, New Mexico, Utah, and Wyoming* (Washington, DC: Government Printing Office, March 1946), 168–84.

14. Ibid.; John S. McLaughlin to the Director of the National Park Service, October 24, 1961, fiche L-7423; Bureau of Reclamation, "Marble Canyon–Kanab Creek," GCRL.

15. US Department of the Interior, *The Colorado River*, 168; Olmsted, "Preliminary Survey," folder "GCNP," box 8, NDR.

16. *Los Angeles Times*, July 30, 1945; and Scoyen to Director, August 6, 1945, GRCA-04848, GCMC.

17. Oppedahl, 94.

18. John U. Terrell, *The Western Web: A Chronological Narrative of the Case against the State of Arizona and the Bureau of Reclamation in the Long Fight to Defeat the Proposed Multi-billion Dollar Central Arizona Project* (Los Angeles: The Colorado River Association of California, 1952), 8–12; *Arizona Republic*, May 1, 1948; Carl Hayden to Howard J. Smith, Executive Secretary, Central Arizona Project Association, May 13, 1948, folder 1, box 019, Carl T. Hayden Papers, Special Collections, Hayden Library, Arizona State University, Tempe, AZ (hereafter CTH); and Tolleson to Drury, September 12, 1947, folder "GCNP," box 8, NDR.

19. Terrell, 89; Johnson, 29–37.

20. Bill Van Ness, interview with author by phone, August 14, 2012.

21. Drury to Krug, March 22, 1948, fiche L-7423, "Bridge Canyon Dam 1948–1954," GCRL.

22. Newton Drury to Secretary of the Interior, March 22, 1948, fiche L-7423, "Bridge Canyon Dam 1948–1954," GCRL.

23. Johnson, 47.

24. "Minutes," Sierra Club Board of Directors, September 5, 1948, folder 19, carton 3, Sierra Club Records, Bancroft Library, University of California, Berkeley (hereafter SCR).

25. Cohen, 301; Drury to Conrad Wirth, June 9, 1948, folder "GCNP," box 8, NDR; Drury to Leonard, June 16, 1948, fiche L-7423, "Bridge Canyon Dam 1948–1954," GCRL.

26. Michael W. Straus to J. A. Krug, May 22, 1946; Drury to Leonard, June 16, 1948, both in fiche L-7423, "Bridge Canyon Dam, 1948–1954," GCRL.

27. Oppedahl, 116.

28. Larry M. Dillsaver and William C. Tweed, *The Challenge of the Big Trees* (Three Rivers, CA: Sequoia Natural History Association, 1990), chapter 7, https://www.nps.gov/parkhistory/online_books/dilsaver-tweed/chap8c.htm, accessed May 28, 2018.

29. Drury to Leonard, August 18, 1948; Charlotte Mauk to Drury, September 16, 1948, both in folder "GCNP," box 8, NDR.

30. Drury to Secretary of the Interior, February 25, 1949, folder "GCNP," box 8, NDR.

31. Johnson, 57–69.

32. Robinson to Senator Joseph C. O'Mahoney, March 28, 1949, folder "GCNP," box 8, NDR.

33. Drury to Robinson, April 12, 1949; Drury to Director of Information, May 10, 1949; Olmsted to Drury, May 10, 1949, all in folder "GCNP," box 8, NDR.

34. George F. Baggley to Director of Region Three of the Department of the Interior, July 18, 1949, fiche L-7423, "Dams in Colorado River 1948–1954," GCRL.

35. Drury, "Parks and Redwoods," 523, partly quoted in Harvey, 93.

36. From the documentary evidence, the person who read the memo to Straus is impossible to determine.

37. US Bureau of Reclamation, "Notice of Intention of Investigation," May 12, 1949; William Warne to Michael Straus, June 14, 1949; William Warne to Michael Straus, July 30, 1949; William Warne to J. A. Krug, August 10, 1949; all in fiche L-7423, "Dams on the Colorado River, 1948–1954," GCRL. The bureau built two construction camps on the rim of Marble Canyon's inner gorge that were supplied by cableways, one (pictured) at an alternative "Redwall" site at river mile 32.7 just downstream of Vasey's Paradise, and another at the Marble Canyon Damsite at river mile 39.2.

38. Fred Packard, "Grand Canyon Monument in Danger," *National Parks* magazine, July–September 1949, 3–8; Fred Packard, "Grand Canyon National Park and Dinosaur Monument in Danger," *National Parks* magazine, October–December 1949, 11–12; Fox, 203–4; Butcher to Robinson, June 6, 1949, folder "Colorado River 1947–1959," box 6:102, WSP/CCDPL.

39. J. A. Krug to Richard Leonard, October 21, 1949, "Log of Features to be Covered by a High Dam at Bridge Canyon," fiche L-7423, "Bridge Canyon Dam, 1948–1954," GCRL.

40. "Director of the National Park Service to the Director of Information," May 10, 1949, folder "GCNP," box 8, NDR; "Minutes," Sierra Club Board of Directors, September 4, 1949, folder 20, carton 3, SCR.

41. "Minutes," "Special Meeting of the Board of Directors," November 12, 1949, folder 20, carton 3, SCR.

42. Newton B. Drury to Richard Leonard, February 15, 1950, fiche L-7423, "Dams on the Colorado River 1948–1954," GCRL; Robinson, "Thoughts," 24.

43. Foresta, 48.

44. Smith to Hayden, February 20, 1950, folder 12, box 19, CTH; Drury to McFarland, February 7, 1950; Director to Assistant Director Wirth, February 15, 1950, both in folder "GCNP," box 8, NDR; Fred Packard to Senator Matthew M. Neely, February 9, 1950, folder "Colorado River 1947–1959," box 6:102, WSP/CCDPL; US Congress, Senate, Committee on Interior and Insular Affairs, *Colorado River Storage Project: Hearings before the Subcommittee on Irrigation and Reclamation of the Committee on Interior and Insular Affairs,* 84th Cong., 1st sess. (February 28–March 5, 1955), 692; Johnson, 70–71.

45. Packard to Senator Matthew N. Neeley, February 9, 1950; James to Richard

Leonard, February 16, 1950, both in folder "Colorado River 1947–1959," box 6:102, WSP/CCDPL; *Arizona Republic*, April 4, 1950.

46. Harvey, 74–77; Reisner, 140–41.

47. Packard to President, Phoenix Chamber of Commerce, July 31, 1950, folder "Colorado River 1947–1959," box 6:102, WSP/CCDPL.

48. "Minutes," "Special Meeting of the Sierra Club Board of Directors," November 12, 1949, folder 19, carton 3, SCR; and Johnson, 71.

49. Leonard to Zahniser, August 1, 1950; William Voigt to Leonard, August 9, 1950, folder "Colorado River 1947–1959," box 6:102, WSP/CCDPL; "Minutes," Sierra Club Board of Directors, September 3, 1950, folder 20, carton 3, SCR.

50. Robert Stebbins to Harold C. Bryant, August 3, 1950; Lemuel A. Garrison to Robert Stebbins, August 17, 1950; M. R. Tillotson to Superintendent, Grand Canyon National Park, August 24, 1950; Lemuel A. Garrison to Robert C. Stebbins, August 29, 1950, all in fiche L-7423, "Dams on the Colorado River 1948–1954," GCRL.

51. Harvey, 95–105.

52. Arthur Demaray was Drury's immediate successor, but he only served as park service director for seven months.

53. *A Bill Authorizing the Construction, Operation and Maintenance of a Dam and Incidental Works in the Main Stream of the Colorado River at Bridge Canyon, Together with Certain Appurtenant Dams and Canals, and for Other Purposes*, S.75, 82nd Cong., 1st sess. (1951), fiche L-7423, "Dams on the Colorado River, 1948–1954," GCRL.

54. US Congress, House, Committee on Interior and Insular Affairs, *Central Arizona Project: Hearing before the Committee on Interior and Insular Affairs*, 82nd Cong., 1st sess. (March 18, 1951).

55. Morris Udall to David F. Brinegar, October 1968, folder 6, box 482, MKU.

56. US Congress, House, Committee on Interior and Insular Affairs, *Central Arizona Project: Hearing before the Committee on Interior and Insular Affairs*, 82nd Cong., 1st sess. (March 18, 1951), 2.

57. Ibid.

58. Bestor Robinson, "Thoughts on Conservation and the Sierra Club," interview by Susan R. Schrepfer (Sierra Club History Committee, 1974), 24–26, Regional Oral History Office, Bancroft Library, University of California Berkeley (hereafter ROHOBL).

59. *The Daily News* (Chicago), June 11, 1951; Voigt to the Editor, July 12, 1951, folder, "Colorado River 1947–1959," box 6:102, WSP/CCDPL.

Chapter 3

1. Elmo Richardson, "Federal Park Policy in Utah: The Escalante National Monument Controversy of 1935–1940," *Utah Historical Quarterly* 33 (Spring 1965): 110–33.

2. *Reisner, Cadillac Desert: An American Nile*, https://www.youtube.com/watch?v=vKIxKE-Duac&t=2804s, accessed June 1, 2018.

3. See Nash, Harvey, Fox, and Reisner.

4. Harvey, 80–91.

5. Ibid., 186–87, 201–2.

6. US Congress, Senate, Subcommittee on Irrigation and Reclamation of the Committee on Interior and Insular Affairs, *Colorado River Storage Project: Hearing before the Subcommittee on Irrigation and Reclamation*, 84th Cong., 1st sess. (February 28–March 5, 1955), 692.

7. Ibid., 693–94.

8. US Congress, House, Subcommittee on Irrigation and Reclamation of the Committee on Interior and Insular Affairs, *Colorado River Storage Project: Hearings before the Subcommittee on Irrigation and Reclamation*, 84th Cong., 1st sess. (March 17–19, 1955), 733, 797.

9. Ibid., 1132–33.

10. Stewart Udall to Killian and Brinegar, April 5, 1955, folder 3, box 12, Stewart L. Udall Papers, Special Collections, University of Arizona, Tucson, AZ (hereafter SLU); Udall to O. M. Lassen, May 9, 1956, folder 4, box 12, SLU.

11. *Arizona Republic*, June 2, 1955; *Arizona Daily Star*, June 2, 1955; *Arizona Daily Star*, June 10, 1955.

12. Director, National Park Service to Commissioner, Bureau of Reclamation, August 4, 1949, fiche L-7423, "Dams on the Colorado River 1938–1954," GCRL.

13. United States v. Harriss, 74 S.C. 808, 814 (S.C. 1954).

14. Fox, 279.

15. *Harriss*, 74 S.C. 808, 814.

16. Ibid., 808, 813, 815.

17. Martha Hubbard Davis v. Commissioner of Internal Revenue, 22 T.C. No. 131., 1051 (T.C. 1954); John Skinner, Esq., to Leonard, December 1, 1954, folder 15, carton 86, Richard Leonard Papers, Sierra Club Members Papers, Bancroft Library, University of California Berkeley (hereafter RLP/SCMP); and David Brower, "'Environmental Activist, Publicist and Prophet," interview by Susan Schrepfer (Sierra Club History Committee, 1974–1978), 136, ROHOBL.

18. Richard Leonard, "Mountaineer, Lawyer, Environmentalist," interview by Susan Schrepfer (Sierra Club History Committee, 1975) 144, ROHOBL.

19. "Minutes," Sierra Club, Special Meeting of the Board of Directors, November 21, 1954, folder 25, carton 3, SCR.

20. Leonard to Zahniser, January 3, 1958, folder 5, carton 86, RLP/SCMP.

21. "Los Angeles Department of Water and Power Bulletin" (1954), folder 1, box 321, CTH; *Arizona Republic*, December 12, 1957; *Arizona Republic*, November 21, 1958.

22. *Arizona Republic*, April 6, 1956; *Phoenix Gazette*, May 14, 1956; *Williams (AZ) News*, April 5, 1956.

23. Wirth to Assistant Secretary Lewis, April 29, 1954, fiche L-7423, "Bridge Canyon Dam, 1954–1966," GCRL.

24. McLaughlin to Regional Director, Region Three, November 21, 1957; Hugh

Miller, Region Three Director to Director, November 27, 1957; Director, National Park Service to Project Review Coordinator, Office of Assistant Secretary, Water and Power Development, n.d.; Fred Aandahl to Kuykendall, January 17, 1958, all in fiche L-7423, "Bridge Canyon Dam 1954–1966," GCRL; Howard Stricklin, "Through the Eyes of Howard Stricklin," interview by Julie Russell, August 26, 1981, Grand Canyon Oral History Project, GCMC, 41.

25. "Minutes," Sierra Club Board of Directors Meeting, January 19–20, 1957, folder 25, carton 3, SCR; "Sierra Club Opposes Bridge Canyon Dam," July 30, 1957, folder "Colorado River 1947–1959," box 6:102, WSP/CCDPL.

26. Harza Engineering Company, "Preliminary Planning Report: Colorado River Development within the State of Arizona: Colorado River Projects" (Chicago, December 15, 1958), GCRL; and *Arizona Daily Sun* (Flagstaff), June 28, 1958.

27. Harza, "Preliminary."

28. Ibid.; Philip Fradkin, *Fallout: An American Nuclear Tragedy* (Tucson: The University of Arizona Press, 1989), 146–47; "Application for License: Arizona Power Authority," Before the US Federal Power Commission, July 1958, GCRL; see also *Arizona Republic*, January 19, 1959. The height of Harza's proposed dams above the riverbeds: Bridge, 359 feet; Prospect, 276 feet; Marble, 290 feet; Coconino, 276 feet.

29. Portions of this section were originally published in *Western Historical Quarterly* 32 (Autumn 2000): 297–318. Used with permission.

30. The Anglocentric term "Indian Problem" has been used throughout American history and it appears in correspondence related to the CAP. I use it with sarcasm here. George F. Baggley to the Director of Region Three of the Department of the Interior, July 18, 1949, fiche L-7423, "Dams in Colorado River 1948–1954," GCRL.

31. White, 579–80.

32. Federal Water Power Act, Statutes at Large, 41, sec. 10 (a), 1074 (1920); Federal Power Act, Statutes at Large, 49, sec. 201–202, 803 (1935).

33. W. S. Gookin to Morris Udall, March 22, 1965; and "Hualapai Contract," executed August 30, 1960, both in folder 4, box 8, CTH.

34. Arizona Enabling Act, Statutes at Large, 36, sec. 28, 575 (1910); and Navajo Indian Reservation Extension Act, Statutes at Large, 48, sec. 1, 960 (1934); "Decision Upon Application For License Under Section 4(e) of the Federal Power Act: Arizona Power Authority, Project No. 2248," US Federal Power Commission, issued September 10, 1962, 3, folder 1, box 321, CTH.

35. George A. Hillery Jr. and Frank J. Essene, "Navajo Population: An Analysis of the 1960 Census," *Southwestern Journal of Anthropology* 19, no. 3 (Autumn 1963): 300, https://www.jstor.org/stable/3629209?read-now=1&loggedin=true&seq=4#page_scan_tab_contents, accessed June 3, 2018.

36. Robert Dallek, *Lone Star Rising: Lyndon Johnson and His Times, 1908–1960* (New York: Oxford University Press, 1991), 564–75; on Udall's role see Floyd Dominy, interview by author, November 1, 1996.

37. John F. Kennedy, "Special Message on Natural Resources," February 23, 1961,

folder 4, box 90, SLU; Stewart Udall, interview by Charles Coate, Santa Fe, NM, April 23, 1997.

38. Dominy interview, November 1, 1996; and Stewart Udall, interview by W. W. Moss, January 12, 1970, transcript John F. Kennedy Library, Boston MA.; Udall interview by Charles Coate, April 23, 1997.

39. Stegner's catchphrase "geography of hope" is quoted in Cohen, 261; Sharon Francis, phone interview by author, August 14, 1997; and Ansel Adams to Stewart Udall, December 15, 1960, folder 1, box 190, SLU.

40. Stewart Udall, *The Quiet Crisis* (New York: Avon Books, 1963), 186–87.

41. Ibid., 179; and Udall interview, March 13, 1997.

42. "Minutes," Sierra Club Board of Directors, December 5–6, 1959, folder 25, carton 3, SCR; Brower interview, July 27, 1997.

43. Brower, "Environmental Activist"; David Brower, "Transcript of Remarks before Sierra Club Executive Committee in Spring 1960 leading to the organization of the Sierra Club Foundation," February 24, 1961, folder 4, box 55, DBP/SCMP; Edgar Wayburn, "Sierra Club Statesman, Leader of the Parks and Wilderness Movement: Gaining Protection for Alaska, the Redwoods, and Golden Gate Parklands," interview by Ann Lage and Susan Schrepfer (Sierra Club History Committee, 1976–1981), 290–91, ROHOBL; Leonard, "Mountaineer," 144; Cohen, 163–66, 277.

44. "Application," Arizona Power Authority, July 1958 (GCRL); and *Arizona Republic*, May 3, 1961.

45. *Arizona Daily Star*, May 3, 1961; *Arizona Republic*, May 3, 1961; Roy Elson, interview by Pam Stevenson, https://www.cap-az.com/about-us/oral-history-transcripts?view=download&fileId, accessed July 3, 2018.

46. Wayne Akin, Chairman, Arizona Interstate Stream Commission and C. A. Calhoun, Chairman, Arizona Power Authority to Governor Paul Fannin, February 1, 1961, folder 1, box 166, SLU; Governor Paul Fannin to Interior Secretary Stewart Udall, October 23, 1961, folder 3, box 166, SLU.

47. US Bureau of Reclamation, "Marble Canyon Kanab Creek" (October 1961), 2, fiche L-7423, "Marble Canyon–Kanab Creek Project," 1961–1962, GCRL.

48. Director, National Park Service to Secretary of the Interior, May 31, 1961, fiche L-7423, "Marble Canyon–Kanab Creek Project, 1961–1962," GCRL.

49. Udall, interview, March 13, 1997; Special Assistant to the Director, June 30, 1961, folder "Assistant Secretary Carr's Staff Minutes," box 5, Conrad Wirth Records, Record Group 79, Records of the National Park Service, National Archives, College Park, MD (hereafter CWR); Johnson, 130; *Arizona Republic*, December 29, 1963.

50. Smith to Udall, August 23, 1961; Udall to Smith, October 11, 1961, both in folder 10, box 168, Record Group 48, Department of the Interior, National Archives, College Park, MD (hereafter IDR); *Washington Post*, March 27, 1977.

51. Director, National Park Service to Secretary of the Interior, October 24, 1961, folder 10, box 168, IDR; Doty to Wirth, October 27, 1961; Smith Brookhart to

Wirth, November 14, 1961, both in folder "Region 3 Correspondence: 1961," box 19, CWR.

52. Udall to Charles Reed, Wayne Akin, and Rich Johnson (memo unsent but shared with Morris Udall), folder 3, box 166, SLU.

53. Dominy interview, November 1, 1996; "Trouble at the Bridge," *National Parks* magazine, April 1960, 19.

54. Dominy interview, November 1, 1996; Kim Engel-Pearson, *Writing Arizona, 1912–2012: A Cultural and Environmental Chronicle* (Norman: University of Oklahoma Press, 2017), 135.

55. "Testimony of Conrad Wirth," December 6, 1961, fiche L-7423, "Marble Canyon–Kanab Creek Project, 1961–1962," GCRL; and *Phoenix Gazette*, November 8, 1961.

56. *Arizona Republic*, April 27, 1962; "Brief for Intervenor, National Parks Association," April 9, 1962; "Decision," US Federal Power Commission, issued September 10, 1962, 31, 37, 39. The FPC (abolished in 1977) proceedings were conducted under the auspices of administrative law. The hearing examiners were somewhat akin to judges in the civil court system.

57. Anthony Wayne Smith, "The Attack on Grand Canyon," *National Parks* magazine (January 1962), 2.

58. Brower to Kuchel, September 22, 1960, folder 13, carton 21, DBP/SCMP.

59. *Arizona Republic*, May 3, 1961; *Arizona Daily Star*, May 3, 1961; "Resolution of the Navajo Tribal Council: Urging Construction of Marble Canyon Dam as a Bureau of Reclamation Project," May 22, 1961; Paul Jones to Morris Udall, October 19, 1961, all in file 7, box 477, MKU.

60. Morris Udall to Wayne Aspinall, October 16, 1961, folder 7, box 477, MKU.

61. Johnson, 130–31; Dominy, interview, November 1, 1996; and Brit Storey, phone interview by author, October 17, 1996.

62. Dominy interview, November 1, 1996.

63. Udall interview, March 13, 1997.

64. Dominy interview, November 1, 1996; Udall interview, March 13, 1997.

65. "Petition of Stewart L. Udall, Secretary of the Interior, for Intervention," October 1, 1962; "Answer and Objection of Arizona Power Authority to Petition for Intervention, Motion for Leave Out of Time, Motion for Re-Opening the Record for Presentation of Evidence of Stewart L. Udall, Secretary of the Interior," October 10, 1962; "Order Granting Limited Intervention Out of Time," November 2, 1962, all in fiche L-7423, "Marble Canyon–Kanab Creek Project 1961–1962," GCRL.

66. *Arizona Republic*, January 1, 1963.

67. Udall interview, March 13, 1997.

Chapter 4

1. Udall interview, March 13, 1997; Stewart Udall, *The Myths of August: A Personal Exploration of Our Tragic Cold War Affair with the Atom* (New York: Pantheon Books, 1994), 250–71.

2. Floyd Dominy to the Secretary of the Interior, November 9, 1962, folder 4, box 162, SLU; *New York Times*, September 9, 1961.

3. Udall, *The Quiet Crisis*, 191.

4. Udall Interview, March 13, 1997.

5. Aspinall to Udall, November 27, 1962, folder 7, box 166, SLU; Udall interview, March 13, 1997.

6. Udall to Aspinall, January 18, 1963, folder 7, box 166, SLU.

7. John C. Miles, *Guardians of the Parks: A History of the National Parks and Conservation Association* (Washington, DC: Taylor and Francis, 1995), 215.

8. Ibid., 214–15.

9. The phrase "think big" had come to symbolize the Interior Department's conservation program under President Kennedy and was widely used in national publications by 1962.

10. David Brower, *For Earth's Sake: The Life and Times of David Brower* (Salt Lake City, UT: Peregrine Books, 1990), 347; Martin, 208; Brower interview, July 27, 1997.

11. "Wild By Law," *American Experience*, 35 min., Corporation for Public Broadcasting, 1991, videocassette.

12. Reisner, 285.

13. *New York Times*, January 22, 1963; *Oregonian* (Portland, OR), September 12, 1962; Brower interview, July 27, 1997.

14. *New York Times*, January 22, 1963; *Oregonian* (Portland, OR), September 12, 1962.

15. Udall Interview, March 13, 1997.

16. Ibid.; "Statement of the President," October 26, 1964, folder 4, box 162, SLU; Stewart Udall, interview by W.W. Moss, January 12, 1970, 480.

17. *New York Times*, January 22, 1963; *Oregonian* (Portland, OR), September 12, 1962.

18. *New York Times*, August 27, 1963.

19. Commissioner of Reclamation to Secretary of the Interior, February 14, 1962, folder 4, box 166, SLU.

20. Eliot Porter, *The Place No One Knew: Glen Canyon on the Colorado* (San Francisco: Sierra Club Books, 1963), 7; Engel-Pearson, 130; Brower interview, July 27, 1997.

21. David Brower, quoted in Porter, 5.

22. "Minutes," Sierra Club Board of Directors, May 4, 1963, folder 2, carton 4, SCR; and Martin Litton, "Sierra Club Director and Uncompromising Preservationist, 1950s–1970s," interview by Ann Lage (Sierra Club Oral History Series, 1980–1981), 73, ROHOBL; Brower, "Environmental Activist," 143.

23. Johnson, 120–21.

24. Arizona v. California, 83 S. Ct. 1468; Johnson, 140.

25. Ted Riggins, "An Ode—From California," folder 9, box 174, SLU.

26. "Memorandum," Orren Beaty to Stewart Udall, June 5, 1963; "Memorandum," Hayden to Arizona Congressional Delegation, May 10, 1963, both in folder 8, box 166, SLU.

27. "Memorandum," Hayden to Arizona Congressional Delegation, May 10, 1963, folder 8, box 166, SLU.

28. Secretary of the Interior, "Report to the President," June 11, 1963, folder 7, box 107, SLU; Udall to Hayden, June 12, 1963, folder 8, box 166, SLU; Udall to Hayden, July 22, 1963, folder 10, box 166, SLU.

29. Keith Brown, Arizona Republican Party Chairman, "Press Release," June 21, 1962, SLU.

30. *New York Times*, June 12, 1963.

31. Brower to Udall, June 22, 1963; Brower to Udall, June 24, 1963, both in folder 4, box 321, CTH.

32. *Arizona Republic*, August 22, 1963.

33. *New York Times*, August 22, 27, 1963.

34. *New York Times*, January 22, 1963.

35. *New York Times*, August 27, 1963; *Arizona Republic*, August 27, 1963.

36. Assistant Regional Director, Resource Planning to Acting Superintendent, Grand Canyon National Park, July 5, 1963; Wirth to the Secretary of the Interior, August 13, 1963 both in fiche L-7243, "Bridge Canyon Dam, 1954–1966," GCRL.

37. US Department of the Interior, Bureau of Reclamation, "Marble–Kanab Creek Power Development," October 1961, GCRL.

38. US Department of the Interior, "National Park Service Appendix to Pacific Southwest Water Plan," August, 1963, box 172, SLU.

39. Beaty, "Memo," February 6, 1963.

40. Excerpts from Carver's remarkable speech are quoted in Michael Frome, *Regreening the National Parks* (Tucson: University of Arizona Press, 1992), 65–67.

41. Superintendent, Grand Canyon National Park to Regional Director, Region Three, November 21, 1957; Regional Director, Region Three to Director, November 27, 1957; both in fiche L-7423, "Bridge Canyon Dam, 1954–1966," GCRL.

42. Anthony Wayne Smith, "The Mighty Colorado," *National Parks* magazine, October 1963, 2; and Weldon Heald, "Colorado River of the West," *National Parks* magazine, October 1963, 4–9.

43. Clyde Thomas, "The Last Days of Grand Canyon Too?," *Sierra Club Bulletin*, October 1963, 2–4.

44. Hayden to Udall, February 7, 1964, folder 6, box 167, SLU; Johnson, 146.

45. *Los Angeles Times*, November 13, 1963; Hayden to Udall, December 5, 1963, folder 3, box 167, SLU.

46. Johnson, 147.

47. Stewart Udall to LBJ re: PSWP, n.d., folder 3, box 174, SLU.

Chapter 5

1. Stewart Udall, "Enroute Back to Washington," handwritten notes taken aboard the cabinet plane, November 22, 1963, folder 3, box 109, SLU.

2. Ibid.; Robert Caro, *The Years of Lyndon Johnson, The Path to Power* (New York: Alfred Knopf, 1982), 458–68; Dallek, 175, 179–81; Udall interview, March 13, 1997; McFarland to the President, August 1, 1966, folder 2, box 476, MKU.

3. Caro, 77–78, 125, 552.

4. Udall to Moyers and attached "Memo to the President," November 27, 1963, folder 9, box 197, SLU.

5. *Arizona Daily Star*, December 12, 30, 1963; Udall to Hayden, December 19, 1963, folder 2, box 167, SLU.

6. Remarks by Commissioner Floyd E. Dominy, Bureau of Reclamation, Tucson, AZ, December 11, 1963, https://server16127.contentdm.oclc.org/cdm4/document.php?CISOROOT=/udallcoloradoAZU&CISOPTR=4382 , accessed July 22, 2018; Dominy interview, November 1, 1996.

7. Beaty to Udall, December 16, 1963, folder 2, box 167, SLU.

8. *Arizona Republic*, December 27, 29, 1963; *New York Times*, February 15, 1964; Udall interview, March 13, 1997.

9. McLaughlin to Director, December 13, 1963; McLaughlin to Director, February 4, 1964, both in fiche L-7423, "Bridge Canyon Dam, 1954–1966," GCRL.

10. Director Hartzog to the Secretary of the Interior, January 27, 1964, fiche L-7423, "Bridge Canyon Dam, 1954–1966," GCRL.

11. Carl Hayden to George B. Hartzog, February 17, 1964; Superintendent McLaughlin to his staff, February 26, 1964; John A. Carver Jr. to Carl Hayden, March 6, 1964; Regional Director National Park Service to Southwest Region Superintendents, March 16, 1964; all in fiche L-7423, "Bridge Canyon Dam, 1954–1966," GCRL; *Arizona Daily Sun*, February 20, 1964; *Arizona Republic*, February 20, 1964.

12. Brower, "Environmental Activist," 61; George Hartzog, interview by author, November 2, 1996.

13. Hartzog interview, November 2, 1996.

14. Ibid.

15. US Department of the Interior, National Park Service, *Appendix to Pacific Southwest Water Plan*, August 1963, box 172, SLU. The title to this chapter is taken from this document.

16. *Grand Canyon National Park Establishment Act, Statutes at Large* 40, sec 1, 1178; and Jasperson to Brower, April 28, 1964, folder 13, box 21, DBP/SCMP.

17. Jasperson to Brower, April 28, 1964, folder 13, box 21, DBP/SCMP.

18. *Arizona Republic*, December 29, 1963.

19. Regional Director to Southwest Region Superintendents, March 26, 1964, fiche L-7423, "Bridge Canyon Dam, 1954–1966," GCRL.

20. O. N. Arrington, Chief AZGF Special Services Division, to Governor Fannin, March 20, 1964, folder 6, box 167, SLU.

21. Morley Fox, "A Report on Conservation Groups," 1965, folder 9, box 478, MKU.

22. Transcript of Udall/Hayden exchange at the CAP hearings before the Senate Committee on Interior and Insular Affairs, prepared by Floyd Dominy, file 7, box 167, SLU; Udall to Senator Henry Jackson, April 9, 1964, folder 8, box 167, SLU.

23. Stewart Udall, "Before the Subcommittee on Irrigation and Reclamation, Committee on Interior and Insular Affairs," US Senate, April 9, 1964, folder 1, box 2, CAP/88, John Jacob Rhodes Papers, Department of Archives and Manuscripts, Arizona State University, Tempe, AZ (hereafter JJR).

24. Mead to Albright, June 14, 1932; Albright to Roger Toll, August 3, 1932; Albright to Mead, January 11, 1933, GRCA-04848, GCMC.

25. E. B. Debler, "Speech," June 27, 1938, GRCA-04848, GCMC; United States Department of the Interior, Bureau of Reclamation, "Colorado River–Phoenix Diversion," 3–4, 10.

26. Staats to Udall, January 20, 1964, folder 5, box 167, SLU; Joseph Califano, Department of the Army to Kermit Gordon, April 1, 1964; Staats to Udall, April 25, 1964, both in folder 8, box 167, SLU; Staats to Udall, March 11, 1964, folder 3, box 1, CAP/88, JJR.

27. Udall to LBJ, February 14, 1964, folder 1, box 476, MKU; and *Arizona Republic*, April 16, 1964; Stewart Udall, "Reports to the President," January 2, February 2, March 3, March 24, April 7, 1964, all in folders 7–9, box 115, SLU; and Carl Hayden to the President, May 5, 1964, folder 1, box 168, SLU; Udall interview, March 13, 1997.

28. Central Arizona Project Association, *Newsletter*, Phoenix, AZ, August 1964, folder 2, box 1, JJR; *Phoenix Gazette*, July 28, 1964; Johnson, 143–44.

29. Central Arizona Project Association, *Newsletter*; "1964, Action on Public Lands, Water and Reclamation," https://library.cqpress.com/cqalmanac/document.php?id=cqal64-1303213, accessed July 22, 2018.

30. *Arizona Republic*, June 20, 1964.

31. David Brower, "The New Threat to Grand Canyon: Action Needed," *Sierra Club Bulletin*, January 1964, 18. The heading quote is taken from this article. Stephen Raushenbush, "A Bridge Canyon Dam Is Not Necessary," *National Parks* magazine, April 1964, 4–9.

32. Anthony Wayne Smith, "The Editorial Page," *National Parks* magazine, April 1964, 2.

33. Brower, "New Threat," 18; David Brower, "Gigantic Southwest Water Plan Offers More Reservoirs than Water," *Sierra Club Bulletin*, September 1964, 12–13; Luna Leopold "Confidential" to Bradley and Brower, November 10, 1964, folder 12, box 21, DBP/SCMP.

34. *Arizona Republic*, February 28, 1964; and Francois Leydet, *Time and the River Flowing: Grand Canyon* (San Francisco: Sierra Club, 1964); David Brower, "Our Special Grand Canyon campaign needs . . .," 1964, folder "Grand Canyon General," box 209, SCMP; *New York Times*, November 9, 10, 1964.

35. Harvey, 162–66; and David Brower tape, untitled, 1977, GCMC.

36. Richard Bradley, "The Controversial Colorado," September 24, 1964, folder "The Controversial Colorado," box 1 "Grand Canyon Dams," Richard Bradley Papers, Conservation Collection, Western History/Genealogy Department, Denver Public Library, Denver, CO (hereafter RBP).

37. Leopold "Confidential" to Bradley and Brower; Bradley to Saylor, November 15, 1964, both in folder 12, box 21, DBP/SCMP.

38. *Denver Post*, September 25, 1964; Dominy to Bradley, October 26, 1964, folder 12, box 21, DBP/SCMP; *Denver Post*, October 19, 1964; Richard Bradley, "Attack on Grand Canyon," *The Living Wilderness*, Winter 1964–1965, 3–6; Richard C. Bradley, "Grand Canyon of the Controversial Colorado," *Sierra Club Bulletin*, December 1964, 73–78.

39. Rhodes to Governor Fannin, Mo Udall, and others regarding the November field hearings, September 3, 1964, folder 2, box 477, MKU; Larry Mehren to Morris Udall, September 1, 1964, folder 2, box 2, JJR.

40. Roy Webb, *If We Had A Boat* (Salt Lake City: University of Utah Press, 1986), 131; US Department of the Interior, Bureau of Reclamation, *Bridge and Marble Canyon Dams and Their Relationship to Grand Canyon National Park and Monument* (Washington, DC: Government Printing Office, 1964).

41. Science Advisor to the Secretary, April 10, 1964, folder 4, box 162, SLU; Commissioner of Reclamation to the Secretary, October 29, 1964, folder 1, box 168, SLU.

42. Assistant Secretary, Water and Power Development to Secretary of the Interior, December 30, 1964; Holum to Jackson, December 11, 1964, both in folder 2, box 168, SLU.

43. Orren Beaty to Udall, December 31, 1964, folder 2, box 168, SLU.

44. Joe Jensen, "Confidential Report to MWD Directors," December 1964, folder 2, box 168, SLU.

Chapter 6

1. US Department of the Interior, *Lake Powell: Jewel of the Colorado* (Washington, DC: Government Printing Office, 1965); William O'Neil, *Coming Apart* (New York: Times Book Company, 1971), 278–87; Barbara Brower to author, December 19, 1997.

2. Brandenburg v. Ohio, 89 S. Ct. 1827; and New York Times Co. v. United States, 91 S. Ct. 2140.

3. O'Neil; Stewart Burns, *Social Movements of the 1960s* (Boston: Twayne Publishers, 1990).

4. *Los Angeles Times*, December 15, 1964; Orren Beaty, "Memorandum to the Secretary," December 31, 1964, folder 2, box 108, SLU.

5. Johnson, 149–50.

6. Ibid., 152.

7. US Department of the Interior, *Lake Powell*.

8. Ibid., inside front cover; Assistant Director, Resource Planning to Departmental Task Force—Lower Colorado River, box 321, folder 4, CTH; US Department of the Interior, "National Park Service Appendix to Pacific Southwest Water Plan," August, 1963," box 172, SLU.

9. Michael Nadel, editor of *The Living Wilderness*, to Mrs. Alfred Hudson, May 21, 1965, folder "Colorado River, 1960–1965," box 106, WSP/CCDPL; *New*

York Times, December 20, 1964; Russell Butcher to Brooks Alexander, April 28, 1965, folder 32, box 11, DBP/SCMP; "Grand Canyon 'Cash Registers,'" *Life Magazine*, May 7, 1965; Bradley to Brower, January 8, 1965, folder 29, box 19, DBP/SCMP; Bradley to Wallace Stegner, 1965, folder "Atlantic," box 1 "Grand Canyon Dams," RBP/CCDPL.

10. Bradley to Charles Morton, Editor, *The Atlantic Monthly*, March 10, 1965; Bradley to Wallace Stegner, fall 1965; Stegner to Bradley, November 25, 1965, all in folder "Atlantic," box 1 "Grand Canyon Dams," RBP/CCDPL; and "Proceedings: Project Rescue, A Seminar on the Central Arizona Project," co-sponsored by Arizona State University and the Central Arizona Project Association, July 6, 8, 10, 1964, folder 5, box 3, JJR.

11. David Brower, "The Chips Are Down for Grand Canyon," *Sierra Club Bulletin*, February 1965; Carlin to Brower, March 8, 1965, folder 9, box 21, DBP/SCMP; Brower interview, July 27, 1997.

12. *Phoenix Gazette*, April 30, 1965; *Phoenix Gazette*, May 10, 1965; *Arizona Republic*, May 11, 1965; Assistant Secretary—Water and Power to Secretary of the Interior, November 3, 1964, folder 2, box 168, SLU; Staats to Stewart Udall, March 18, 1965, folder 4, box 164, SLU.

13. Stewart Udall to Aspinall, May 17, 1965; Udall to Budget Director, April 15, 1965, both in folder 5, box 168, SLU; Johnson, 155.

14. *Oregonian* (Portland, OR),, July 18, 1965; Reisner, 279.

15. Van Ness interview, August 14, 2012.

16. Johnson, 161–63.

17. Ibid.

18. US Congress, House, Subcommittee on Irrigation and Reclamation of the Committee on Interior and Insular Affairs, *Lower Colorado Basin Project: Hearings before the Subcommittee on Irrigation and Reclamation of the Committee on Interior and Insular Affairs*, 89th Cong., 1st sess., 109, 166–88, 736; Dominy interview, November 1, 1996. According to Dominy, two of these scale models were actually built.

19. *Hearings*, 201–10.

20. Ibid., iv–vi; Richard Lamm, "Report to the Colorado Open Space Coordinating Council on Testifying before the House Interior and Insular Affairs Subcommittee on Irrigation and Reclamation," September 1, 1965, folder 21, box 20, DBP/SCMP; Bradley to Charles Morton, April 3, 1966, folder "Atlantic," box 1 "Grand Canyon Dams," RBP/CCDPL.

21. *Hearings*, 716–19, 751–52.

22. Johnson, 161–63.

23. *Hearings*, 872; Lamm, "Report," 1–3.

24. *Hearings*, 800–808; and "'Time and the River Flowing,' An Analysis by Representative Morris K. Udall of Francois Leydet's book on the Grand Canyon of the Colorado," box 321, folder 5, CTH.

25. *Hearings*, 809–10.

26. Ibid., 644–45.

27. Ibid., 646–53.
28. Johnson, 170–74.
29. *Hearings*, 757–58, 803.
30. Ibid., 646–53.
31. Udall to Dominy, August 28, 1965, folder 5, box 477, MKU; Mo Udall to Stewart Udall, January 20, 1966, folder 6, box 166, SLU.
32. *Hearings*, 147; and Lamm, "Report."
33. Lamm, "Report," 1.
34. Ibid., 2–3
35. Ibid.
36. Ibid.
37. *Hearings*, 802–809, 812.
38. Ibid., 201, 736; David Brower, "Grand Canyon: Department of Amplification," *Sierra Club Bulletin*, December 1965, 14–15.
39. Hartzog to Larry Hadley, December 11, 1964, folder 266, box 36, George B. Hartzog Papers, Special Collections, Clemson University, Clemson, SC (hereafter GHP); Hartzog to Frank Harrison, October 6, 1965, folder 269, box 36, GHP; Director to all Regional Directors, October 18, 1965, folder 1, box 169, SLU.
40. The influx of mail is difficult to measure; however, my assessment of approximately two thousand letters contained in the collections of Carl Hayden, Stewart Udall, Morris Udall, John Rhodes, Interior Department, National Park Service, and John Saylor reveals that the number of letters increased dramatically after the August–September 1965 hearings, tapered off for the first quarter of 1966, and increased again after the May 1966 hearings, the Sierra Club's ad campaign, and the IRS revocation of June 10, 1966.
41. Griffin to Brower, August 10, 1965, folder 19, box 29, DBP/SCMP.
42. Richard Lamm to David Brower, October 28, 1965, folder 10, box 21, DBP/SCMP.
43. Ibid.; Mrs. Hasse Bunnelle to Lamm, October 29, 1965; Estella Leopold to Hasse Bunnelle, October 15, 1965; Hasse Bunnelle to Leopold, October 29, 1965, all in folder 10, box 21, DBP/SCMP.
44. "Activity Highlights 1965–1966: Future Goals," Colorado Open Space Coordinating Council, Inc., September 24, 1966, folder "Colorado Mountain Club," box 1 "Grand Canyon Dams," RBP/CCDPL.
45. Bradley to Stegner, 1965; Stegner to Bradley, November 25, 1965, both in folder "Atlantic," box 1 "Grand Canyon Dams," RBP/CCDPL.
46. Vosburgh to Bradley, August 6, 1965, folder "Audubon," box 1 "Grand Canyon Dams," RBP/CCDPL.
47. Rich Johnson, "Minutes: Meeting of Joint Public Relations Committee," September 23, 1965, folder 1, box 3, JJR.
48. "Memo on CAP hearings from MKU," August 28, 1965, folder 2, box 3, JJR; *Arizona Republic*, October 27, 1965; *Arizona Daily Star*, December 14, 1965; Smith to the National Parks Association Board of Trustees, September 28, 1965, folder 34, box 11, DBP/SCMP.

49. Mark W. T. Harvey, "Defending the Park System: The Controversy over Rainbow Bridge," *New Mexico Historical Review* 73 (January 1998): 45–60.

50. Richard Bradley to Wallace Stegner, 1965, folder "Atlantic," box 1, "Grand Canyon Dams," RBP/CCDPL; Bruce Stewart, "Think Big," *Harper's*, August 1965, 62–63; Estella Leopold to Hasse Bunnelle, October 15, 1965, folder 10, box 21, DBP/SCMP.

Chapter 7

1. The title for this chapter is a quote from Martin Litton taken from *Cadillac Desert: An American Nile*, https://www.youtube.com/watch?v=vKIxKE-Du-ac&t=1490s, accessed June 25, 2018.

2. Morris Udall, *Too Funny to Be President* (New York: Henry Holt and Company, 1988), 92. Mo Udall lost his eye as a result of a childhood accident; however, in typical good humor, he made light of it throughout his political career.

3. "Notes on March 15 Conference," folder 2, box 476, MKU.

4. *Hearings*, 646–53.

5. "Minutes of Meeting held at 10:00 o'clock, A.M., January 4, 1966 in the Arizona Room of the Hotel Adams, Phoenix, Arizona," 4–5, 7, folder 4, box 1, JJR.

6. Marks to Rhodes, June 19, 1963; Rhodes to Marks, June 26, 1963, both in folder 1, box 1, CAP/88, JRP; Lazarus to Stewart Udall, October 4, 1963, folder 2, box 1, JJR.

7. Quoted in Douglas Wall, Chairman, Arizona Interstate Stream Commission, "Confidential Memorandum," forwarded to John Rhodes by Ray Killian, Secretary, Arizona Interstate Stream Commission, March 8, 1965, folder 1, box 2, JJR.

8. Acting Commissioner of Reclamation to Morris Udall, October 12, 1965, folder 5, box 477, MKU; "Statement of Arthur Lazarus: Re Interest of Hualapai Tribe in CAP," attached to Udall to Rhodes and Senner, March 18, 1965, folder 5, box 477, MKU.

9. Byron Pearson, "We Have Almost Forgotten How to Hope": The Hualapai, the Navajo, and the Fight for the Central Arizona Project, 1944–1968," *Western Historical Quarterly* 31 (Autumn 2000): 297–316.

10. Johnson to Morris Udall, December 25, 1965; Marks to Rhodes, Udall, and Senner, January 17, 1966; Morris Udall to Stewart Udall, January 20, 1966, all in folder 5, box 477, MKU.

11. Assistant Secretary—Public Land Management to Secretary Udall, March 14, 1966, folder 6, box 169, SLU; Les Alexander, "Memo to the files," March 30, 1966, folder 1, box 169, SLU.

12. *New York Times*, August 28, 1963; *New York Times*, January 17, 1966.

13. Richard Bradley to Barbara Walton, Curator of the Western History Collection at the Denver Public Library, 1995, box 1 "Grand Canyon Dams," RBP/CCDPL; *Audubon*, January–February 1966, 34–41.

14. Nicholson to Bradley, January 27, 1966, folder "Reader's Digest Article," box 1

"Grand Canyon Dams," RBP/CCDPL; Nancy Weston to David Brower, July 28, 1959, folder 47, box 11, DBP/SCMP.

15. Acting Commissioner Bennett to Regional Director, Boulder City, NV, March 23, 1966, folder 9, box 478, MKU; Bradley to Brower, March 1, 1966; Bradley to Brower, February 11, 1966, folder 32, box 19, both in DBP/SCMP.

16. *Denver Post*, March 6, 1966; and "COSCC: Activity Highlights, 1965–1966," September 24, 1966, folder "Colorado Mountain Club," box 1 "Grand Canyon Dams," RBP/CCDPL.

17. *Arizona Republic*, March 27, 1966; and Bill Winter to John Rhodes, June 6, 1966, in folder 4, box 3, JJR.

18. Rich Johnson, "Memorandum," April 1, 1966; Commissioner of Reclamation to Regional Director, Boulder City, NV, March 23, 1966, both in folder 9, box 478, MKU; Brower to Robert Kellogg, April 28, 1966, folder 16, box 22, DBP/SCMP.

19. Brower to Udall, March 30, 1966, folder 6, box 6, DBP/SCMP; Regional Director to Southwest Region Superintendents, March 16, 1964, fiche L-7423 "Bridge Canyon Dam, 1954–1966" GCRL.

20. Johnson, *Central Arizona*, 182; and Northcutt Ely to Sterling Fisher of *Reader's Digest*, April 19, 1966, folder 1, box 5, JJR.

21. Johnson, "Memorandum;" April 1, 1966, folder 9, box 478, MKU; Brower to Kellogg, April 28, 1966, folder 16, box 22, DBP/SCMP; Dominy interview, November 1, 1996.

22. Dr. Brit Storey, phone interview by author, October 17, 1996; Dominy interview, November 1, 1996.

23. Brower to Kellogg, April 28, 1966, folder 16, box 22, DDBP/SCMP; Johnson, "Memorandum," April 1, 1966, folder 9, box 478, MKU; see also Jeff Ingram to Richard Bradley, April 8, 1966, folder "Reader's Digest article," box 1 "Grand Canyon Dams," RBP/CCDPL.

24. George Steck, interview by Michael Quinn, September 3, 1995, GCMC; Harold Bradley to Brower, April 16, 1966, folder 26, box 22, DBP/SCMP; *Reader's Digest*, "Press Information and Itinerary," March 31, 1966, fiche L-7423, "Bridge Canyon Dam 1954–1966," GCRL; "*Reader's Digest* Enlists in the Fight to Save Grand Canyon," *Sierra Club Bulletin*, May 1966, 6–7; *Arizona Republic*, March 31, 1966.

25. Bradley to Brower, April 12, 1966, folder 33, box 19, SCMP.

26. The title for this chapter is a quote from Martin Litton taken from *Cadillac Desert: An American Nile*, https://www.youtube.com/watch?v=vKIxKE-Duac&t=1490s, accessed June 25, 2018; Stephen Jett to author, February 6, 1998; Jett to author, August 11, 2018; Brower to Kellogg, April 28, 1966, folder 16, box 22, DBP/SCMP.

27. Commissioner to Regional Director, Boulder City, NV, March 23, 1966, folder 9, box 478, MKU.

28. *Arizona Republic*, April 1, 1966; Stephen Jett to author, February 6, 1998; Brower to Kellogg, April 28, 1966, folder 16, box 22, DBP/SCMP.

29. Richard Bradley to Brower, April 12, 1966, folder 33, box 19, SCMP; Ingram to

Richard Bradley, April 8, 1966, folder "Reader's Digest Article," box 1 "Grand Canyon Dams," RBP/CCDPL; "Reader's Digest Conference News," box 1, "Grand Canyon Dams," RBP/CCDPL; Clifton Merritt to Stewart Brandborg, April 20, 1966, folder "Colorado River," box 6:102, WSP/CCDPL; Larry Stevens, *The Colorado River in Grand Canyon: A Guide*, 3rd ed. (Flagstaff, AZ: Red Lake Books, 1990), 90; Colorado Open Space Coordinating Council, "Open Space Report," April 15, 1966, folder 21, box 20, DBP/SCMP; Jean T. Ensign to Brower, June 3, 1966, folder 34, box 19, DBP/SCMP.

30. Udall, *Too Funny*, 59.

31. Johnson, 183; Dominy interview, November 1, 1996; Robert Gray to John Rhodes, April 26, 1966, folder 4, box 3, JJR; *Arizona Republic*, May 26, 1966.

32. William and Elisabeth Layton to Stewart Udall, May 6, 1966, folder 33, box 19, DBP/SCMP.

33. John W. Ragsdale, "Anno Dominy MCMLXVI," *Biophilist*, March–April 1966, folder 2, box 012, CTP; Burns to Brower, May 11, 1966, folder 16, box 22, DBP/SCMP; "Knight Errant to Nature's Rescue," *Life*, May 27, 1966; and "Dam the Canyon?," *Newsweek*, May 30, 1966.

34. "The Entire Grand Canyon Must Be Protected," *Sierra Club Bulletin*, May 1966, 8–9; *Arizona Republic*, April 17, 1966.

35. Johnson, 185; *Arizona Republic*, April 3, 1966; *New York Times*, May 2, 1966; Ozell Trask, "Memo to the Files," April 29, 1966, folder 2, box 476, MKU.

36. Johnson, 172; Ray Killian, "Memorandum to the Files," April 6, 1966, folder 2, box 476, MKU.

37. Winter to Rhodes, June 6, 1966, folder 4, box 3, JJR.

38. US Congress, House, Subcommittee on Irrigation and Reclamation of the Committee on Interior and Insular Affairs, *Lower Colorado River Basin Project: Hearings before the Subcommittee on Irrigation and Reclamation of the Committee on Interior and Insular Affairs*, 89th Cong., 2d sess., 9–13, 1378, 1390.

39. *Hearings*, 1086; Johnson, 186, 1307.

40. Johnson, 188; and *Hearings*, 1362–65, 1380.

41. Brower, "Environmental Activist."

42. For Hosmer's treatment of opposition witnesses, see *Hearings* starting on 1429 and especially 1513–15, 1544 to the end of the record.

43. Ibid., 1469, 1470, 1491, 1488, 1490.

44. Ibid., 1468–71.

45. Ibid., 1491. Ingram started to rebut Hosmer but was interrupted and never had a chance to finish.

46. Ibid., 1469, 1488, 1491, 1493.

47. Ibid., 1497–1538. Pumped storage can be built in canyons of low scenic value. Water can be brought in from outside. During periods of low demand, the power generated by the upper dam can be used to pump water from the lower reservoir back upstream. During periods of high demand for power, the water is released from the upper reservoir at a faster rate, providing all the peaking advantages of hydropower.

48. Ibid., 1514–15.
49. Ibid., 1540–76.
50. Portions of this section were originally published in *Western Historical Quarterly* 32 (Autumn 2000): 297–318. Used with permission; Morris Udall to Les Alexander, April 26, 1966, folder 2, box 476, MKU; John Rhodes, "Memorandum," April 18, 1966, folder 4, box 3, CAP/89, JJR; *Hearings*, 1294.
51. Eugene Weiner to Henry Dobyns, April 2, 1966; Dobyns to Weiner, April 6, 1966, folder 4, box 3, CAP/89, JRP.
52. *Hearings*, 1484, 1577, 1579; Ray Killian to Rich Johnson, April 18, 1966; John Rhodes to Henry Dobyns, April 20, 1966, folder 4, box 3, JJR; *Arizona Republic*, May 8, 1966; US Congress, House, Speech of Morris K. Udall, "The Conservation Plot That Failed," *Congressional Record* (May 10, 1966), A2507–A2508.
53. Hearings, 1585–1587; Stephen Jett to author, December 28, 1997; Jett to author, February 6, 1998; Jett to author, August 11, 2018.
54. Udall interview, March 13, 1997.
55. Mo Udall, "Rules Headcount," May 2, 1966; Mo Udall, "Summary of 1st Headcount," May 1966, both in folder 11, box 480, MKU; Rhodes to Lewis Douglas, May 26, 1966, folder 4, box 3, JJR. Morris Udall's analysis of early May, just prior to the hearings, reveals a strong predisposition toward passage on the part of the House members. Udall's tally of the 435 members of Congress breaks down as follows: in favor—68; probable—202; undecided—159; opposed—6. A total of 218 votes were needed for passage, and Mo Udall's tally shows that 270 members were at least leaning in favor of the bill.
56. Morris Udall to "Dear Colleague," June 3, 1966; Les Alexander to Task Force, June 8, 1966, both in folder 4, box 477, MKU; Morris Udall, "June 8 Luncheon," folder 5, box 477, MKU; Udall to Les Alexander, June 7, 1966, folder 2, box 476, MKU.
57. L. M. Alexander, "Memorandum—A Lobbying Plan," June 8, 1966; L. M. Alexander, "Subject: A Lobbying Plan (Ref. June 8, 1966 Memo)," July 6, 1966, both in folder 5, box 477, MKU.
58. Ibid. That Johnson was assigned the task of writing the letters and sent them is confirmed within these two memos.
59. George Rocha to "Friend," n.d., folder 5, box 4, JJR; and L. M. Alexander, "Memorandum"; L. M. Alexander, "Subject: A Lobbying Plan." Although the Rocha letter is undated, comparable letters to Brower, LBJ, the National Council of Churches, and all congressmen were sent on June 24, 1966.
60. Henry Dobyns to Representative Richard Ottinger, August 3, 1966, folder 5, box 477, MKU.
61. Bradley to Brower, regarding list of names, June 4, 1966, folder 11, box 21, DBP/SCMP; Bradley to Brower, April 12, 1966, folder 33, box 19, DBP/SCMP; Bradley to Charles Morton, editor, April 3, May 10, August 27, 1966, folder "Atlantic," box 1 "Grand Canyon Dams," RBP/CCDPL.
62. Mandell to Brower, June 4, 1966, folder 34, box 19, DBP/SCMP.

63. Colorado Open Space Coordinating Council Inc., "Activity Highlights 1965–1966: Future Goals," September 24, 1966, folder "Colorado Mountain Club," box 1 "Grand Canyon Dams," RBP/CCDPL; Joy Coombs to Stewart Brandborg, June 23, 1966, folder "Colorado River 1966," box 106, WSP/CCDPL.

64. Robert Wyss, *The Man Who Built the Sierra Club: A Life of David Brower* (New York: Columbia University Press, 2016), 242–72.

65. Cohen, 355.

66. Brower, "Environmental Activist," 146–47; Brower's handwritten notes of May 8, 23, 1966, folder 46, "Notes 1966," box 15, DBP/SCMP; Brower interview July 27, 1997.

Chapter 8

1. Udall, *The Quiet Crisis*, 134, 186–87, 191, 202; Wyss, 242–72.

2. See chapter two. For a good example, see US Department of the Interior, *Lake Powell: Jewel of the Colorado*.

3. Runte, 190; Fox, 302.

4. Susan Louise Senecah, "The Environmental Discourse of David Brower: Using Advocacy Advertising to Save the Grand Canyon" (PhD diss., University of Minnesota, 1992), 168, 170–74, 182–84. The title for the subsequent heading is taken from Senecah.

5. *New York Times*, June 9, 1966. Sierra Club advertisements also appeared in the *Washington Post*, *San Francisco Chronicle*, and the *Los Angeles Times* on the same day.

6. Wyss, 214–15.

7. US Congress, House, Speech of Morris K. Udall, "Flooding the Grand Canyon: A Phony Issue," *Congressional Record* (June 9, 1966), 12315–17.

8. Ibid.; *New York Times*, June 9, 1966; "Dam the Canyon?," *Newsweek*, May 30, 1966, 27.

9. Senecah, 195–200; Wyss 208–9; Dominy in *Cadillac Desert: An American Nile*.

10. Senecah, 164–65.

11. Ibid.

12. US Congress, House, Speech of Morris K. Udall, "Flooding," 12315–17.

13. Edgar Wayburn, "Sierra Club Statesman, Leader of the Parks and Wilderness Movement: Gaining Protection for Alaska, the Redwoods, and Golden Gate Parklands," interviews by Ann Lage and Susan Schrepfer (Sierra Club Oral History Committee, 1976–1981), 29, ROHOBL; *Arizona Republic*, June 12, 1966.

14. Brower, "Environmental Activist," 146; and Wayburn, "Sierra Club Statesman," 293.

15. Wyss, 210; Senecah, 151; Dominy interview, November 1, 1996; Udall interview, March 13, 1997; Udall to Adams, June 21, 1966, folder 1, box 190, SLU.

16. Roy Elson, "Administrative Assistant to Senator Carl Hayden and Candidate for the United States Senate, 1955–1969," interviews by Donald Richie (April 27–August 21, 1990), 203 (Senate Historical Office, Washington, DC), John F. Kennedy Library.

17. *Hearings,* 757–58, 803.

18. William E. Siri, "Reflections on the Sierra Club, the Environment, and Mountaineering, 1950s–1970s," interview by Ann Lage (Sierra Club History Series, February 11, 1976), 56, ROHOBL; Morris Udall to Sheldon Cohen, June 10, 1966, folder 2, box 477, MKU.

19. For a recent reiteration of this argument see Tom Turner's *David Brower: The Making of the Environmental Movement* (Berkeley: University of California Press, 2015).

20. *Congressional Quarterly,* November 1, 1966, 3024; Orren Beaty to William Welsh, Assistant to the Vice President, October 16, 1966, box 124, Central Classified Files/DIR; Udall, *Too Funny,* 56; Daniel Dreyfus quoted in Reisner, 286.

21. A good example of this type of letter is John Cohan to Leo Irwin, Chief Council of the House Ways and Means Committee, August 11, 1966, folder 2, box 20, SCMP.

22. *Bakersfield Californian,* June 28, 1966; *New York Times,* June 17, 1966.

23. Hartzog to All Regional Directors, October 20, 1965, folder 4, box 190, SLU; H. N. Smith to Superintendent, June 7, 1966; Superintendent, Fort Clascop to Superintendent, Grand Canyon, September 7, 1966, both in "Colorado River Dam Proposals Collection, 1931–1968," #2670, GCNPMC.

24. Superintendent, Yosemite, to Director, June 21, 1966; George Marshall, President, to George Hartzog, June 21, 1966; George Marshall to George Hartzog, June 30, 1966; and Hartzog to Marshall, July 1, 1966, all in folder 5, box 9, GHP; Merrill Beal, interview by Julie Russell, July 20, 1981 (Grand Canyon National Park Oral History Project), GCMC. Despite the efforts to repress park service opposition, there are occasional glimpses of it. On June 7, 1966, Regional Director Dan Beard lauded the efforts of David Brower and the Sierra Club, as well as those of *New York Times* editor John Oakes. See Beard to John Osseward, June 7, 1966, fiche L-7423, "Dams on the Colorado River, 1954–1966," GCNPRL.

25. Ibid., and *New York Times,* July 25, 1966; David Brower to Frank Masland, December 28, 1966, folder 36, box 19, DBP/SCMP. The Sierra Club also ran these and other ads in other national publications during the summer of 1966, including *Harper's, Saturday Review, Ramparts, National Review,* and *Scientific American.*

26. US Congress, House, Speech of George Senner, "Letter from White Mountain Apache Tribe," *Congressional Record* (August 2, 1966), A-4075; *Oakland (CA) Tribune,* July 16, 1966; *Arizona Republic,* July 16, 1966; and *Riverside (CA) Daily Enterprise,* July 20, 1966.

27. *Washington Post,* August 14, 1966; Mrs. E. M. Bredwell to Mrs. E. P. Pierce, August 1, 1966, folder 5, box 4, JJR; *Arizona Republic,* July 27, 1966; and Robin Way to Mr. Frederick Kellerman, and attached television listing from the *New York Times,* August 17, 1966, folder 73, box 218, SCMP.

28. Rawson to Robin Way, small note attached to *Arizona Daily Citizen,* August 10,

1966; and Way to Rawson, August 17, 1966, folder 73, box 218, SCMP; *Rocky Mountain News*, August 11, 1966; Assistant Commissioner to Commissioner, Bureau of Reclamation, July 1, 1966, folder 23, box 483, MKU.

29. John Rhodes to James O'Malley, August 25, 1966, folder 5, box 4, JJR; *Arizona Republic*, June 19, 1966; MKU, "Memo to CAP," August 22, 1966, folder 11, box 480, MKU.

30. *New York Times*, June 11, 1966.

31. Water for the West, "Progress Report," July 1, 1966, folder 2, box 476, MKU; *New York Times*, July 28, 1966.

32. *Cape Disappointment State Park*, https://parks.state.wa.us/486/Cape-Disappointment, accessed June 29, 2018; "Washington's Long Beach Peninsula," https://funbeach.com/shipwrecks-graveyards-pacific/, accessed June 29, 2018.

33. J. A. Riggens, "Memorandum to the Files Re: July 20, 1966," July 21, 1966; J. A. Riggens, "Memorandum for the Files Re: July 21, 1966," both in folder 2, box 476, MKU.

34. Rich Johnson, "Memorandum," July 22, 1966; J. A. Riggins, "Memorandum to the Files," July 26, 1966, folder 2, box 476, MKU.

35. *Wall Street Journal*, July 29, 1966; J. A. Riggens, "Memorandum to the Files," July 26, 1966; Morris Udall to "Honorable ____ [in the original]," July 27, 1966, all in folder 2, box 476, MKU.

36. *New York Times*, July 25, 1966.

37. "Rules Headcount," May 2, 1966; Udall to Les Alexander and John Rhodes, August 22, 1966; Morris Udall to Les Alexander, August 23, 1966, all in folder 11, box 482, MKU.

38. Richard Bradley, "Ruin for the Grand Canyon," *Town Hall* 28, no. 28, July 12, 1966; Colorado Open Space Coordinating Council Inc., "Grand Canyon Workshop: Activity Highlights 1965–1966: Future Goals," September 24, 1966, both in folder "Colorado Mountain Club," box 1 "Grand Canyon Dams," RBP; *Sierra Club Bulletin*, July–August 1966, front cover; Helen Skelton to David Brower, August 5, 1966; Robin Way to Mrs. Helen Skelton, August 10, 1966, folder 73, box 218, SCMP.

39. Stephen Jett, "The Grand Canyon Dams Fight," 4–6, undated, unpublished manuscript. In an April 24, 2018, email to which it was attached, Dr. Jett stated that he had written it "a few weeks ago"; Jett to author, April 24, 2018; Jett to author August 11, 2018.

40. Ibid.

41. Stephen Jett to author, January 16, 2016; Stephen Jett, "Navajos Enter Fight Against Grand Canyon Dams," August 1966, 1–10, unpublished manuscript; *Gallup (NM) Independent*, August 4, 1966; Orren Beaty, "Notes to SLU," September 5, 1966; T. W. Taylor, Bureau of Indian Affairs Acting Commissioner to Secretary Udall, August 5, 1966, both in folder 1, box 127, SLU.

42. *Arizona Republic*, August 16, 1966.

43. Senecah, 157.

44. John Muir, *The Yosemite* (New York: Century, 1912), 255–57, 260–62.

45. *Wall Street Journal*, August 23, 1966. A slight variant of this phrase also appears in small type in the July 25 *New York Times* ad. Sierra Club historian Michael Cohen credits Ansel Adams for originating the phrase (Cohen, 363).

46. The heading quote is from Floyd Dominy, phone interview by author, December 1, 2005; L. M. Alexander, "Memo to the CAP Files," August 26, 1966, folder 4, box 477, MKU; L. M. Alexander, "Memo to the CAP files," August 30, 1966, folder 2, box 476, MKU.

47. Ozell Trask and Ralph Hunsaker to Task Force, August 30, 1966, folder 2, box 476, MKU; *Arizona Republic*, August 27, 1966; and *Arizona Republic*, September 1, 1966; see also "News of Conservation and the Club," *Sierra Club Bulletin*, September 1966, 2; and *Arizona Republic*, September 17, 1966.

48. L. M. Alexander to CAP Files, August 25, 1966, folder 4, box 477, MKU.

49. "Confidential Report from Les Alexander," August 19, 1966, folder 2, box 476, MKU.

50. MHR to MKU, "Memo," August 29, 1966, folder 11, box 480, MKU.

51. L. M. Alexander to CAP Task Force Members and Congressional Delegation, September 15, 1966, folder 1, box 481, MKU.

52. L. M. Alexander, "memo to CAP Files," August 26, 1966, folder 4, box 477, MKU.

53. MKU to John Rhodes, September 7, 1966, folder 2, box 476, MKU.

54. L. M. Alexander, "Memo to CAP Files," August 30, 1966, folder 2, box 476, MKU.

55. Rich Johnson, "Press Release," August 31, 1966, folder 1, box 4, CAP/89, JJR; *Arizona Republic*, September 8, 11, 15, 1966; Wayne Aspinall, "Colorado's Involvement in Westwide Water Planning," remarks made before the annual meeting of the Colorado State Grange, Cortez, CO, October 1, 1966, folder 2, box 4, CAP/89, JJR.

56. Orren Beaty, "Notes to SLU," August 5, 1966, folder 1, box 127, SLU.

57. Sharon Francis, phone interview by author, August 14, 1997.

58. Beaty, "Note to SLU," July 16, 1966, folder 1, box 127, SLU.

59. Francis interview, August 14, 1997.

60. Sharon Francis to Stewart Udall, August 18, 1966, folder 2, box 145, SLU.

61. Francis interview, August 14, 1997; Sharon Francis, interview by Dorothy Pierce McSweeney, May 20, 1969, AC 81-68, Lyndon Baines Johnson Library, Austin, Texas.

62. Francis interview, August 14, 1997; Brower interview, July 27, 1997.

63. *Arizona Republic*, September 8, 16, 1966.

64. Udall interview, March 17, 1997.

65. Assistant Secretary to Secretary, September 12, 1966, folder 4, box 168, SLU; "Weekly Report to the President from the Secretary of the Interior," August 8, 1966, folder 9, box 126, SLU; Luna Leopold, interview by Dunne Thomas and Ann Lage, "Hydrology, Geomorphology, and Environmental Policy: US Geological Survey, 1950–1972 and UC Berkeley, 1972–1987," ROHOBL, 1993, 189.

66. Morris Udall to John Rhodes, "The Power Centers," September 22, 1966, folder 2, box 476, MKU. The heading quote is taken from this memo.

67. *Arizona Republic*, September 8, 17, 21, 1966; Orren Beaty to Stewart Udall, April 6, 1966, folder 1, box 127, SLU; *Arizona Republic*, October 18, 1966.

68. See for example, Samuel Hays, *Beauty, Health, and Permanence: Environmental Politics in the United States, 1955–1985* (New York: Cambridge University Press, 1987), 52–58.

69. Cohen, 387–88; Nash, 235; Reisner, 285–90. Reisner and Nash imply that preservationist pressure caused Udall to change his mind; Udall interview, March 13, 1997.

70. Udall interview, March 13, 1997; Stewart Udall, phone interview by author, June 21, 2007; "News of Conservation and the Club," *Sierra Club Bulletin*, September 1966, 2; *New York Times*, October 9, 1966; *Arizona Republic*, October 14, 18, 1966.

71. Udall interview, March 13, 1997; Science Advisor to the Secretary, May 17, 1968, folder 3, box 139, SLU; *Arizona Republic*, June 1, 1968.

72. *New York Times*, October 9, 1966; and "Weekly Report to the President from the Secretary of the Interior," December 6, 1966, folder 7, box 126, Stewart Udall Papers; see also Assistant Secretary—Water and Power to Secretary of the Interior, January 26, 1967, folder 7, box 169, Stewart Udall Papers. Judging by his report to President Johnson of December 6, 1966, it appears as though Udall had decided to remove the dams from the project by this date.

73. US Congress, House, Subcommittee on Irrigation and Reclamation of the Committee on Interior and Insular Affairs, *Lower Colorado Basin Project: Hearings before the Subcommittee on Irrigation and Reclamation of the Committee on Interior and Insular Affairs*, 90th Cong., 1st sess., 1967, 458.

74. "News of Conservation and the Club," *Sierra Club Bulletin*, March 1967, 3.

75. Senecah, 163.

76. "News of Conservation and the Club," *Sierra Club Bulletin*, March 1967, 2–3; *New York Times*, March 13, 1967; *Arizona Republic*, March 7, 1967.

77. *Hearings*, 490–96.

78. Ibid., 552–56.

79. Ibid., 402–6; RL to MKU, March 28, 1967, folder 7, box 481, MKU; *Arizona Republic*, January 22, 1967.

80. *Arizona Republic*, February 2, 1967.

81. *Arizona Republic*, February 2, 3, 1967; *New York Times*, February 2, 1967; "Senate Passes Central Arizona Project Bill," in *CQ Almanac 1967*, 23rd ed., 10-1015-10-1021 (Washington, DC: Congressional Quarterly, 1968), http://library.cqpress.com/cqalmanac/cqal67-1313328, accessed July 15, 2018.

82. "Senate Passes"; *Arizona Republic*, February 8, 16, August 8, 1967; *New York Times*, August 4, 8, 1967; Udall, *Too Funny*, 61.

83. Stewart Udall, "Wilderness Rivers: Shooting the Wild Colorado," *Venture*, February 1968, 62–71.

84. *Arizona Republic*, October 4, 1967; O. M. Trask to Paul Fannin, August 5, 1967;

and O. M. Trask to Mo and John, August 5, 1967, both in folder 12, box 481, MKU; Morris Udall, "Memo to the Files," September 28, 1967, folder 13, box 481, MKU.

85. Although it was an unusual move, precedent existed for Hayden's action including, ironically, the approval of the Big Thompson Project in Aspinall's home state. This is how it would have worked: Having obtained a suspension of the Senate rules, Hayden would have attached the CAP rider to the appropriations bill. After Senate passage of the bill, selected members of the House and Senate would meet in conference committee to iron out the differences in the two bills, and given the CAP's overwhelming popularity in autumn of 1967 and the respect in which Hayden was held, it is highly unlikely that the conference committee would have deleted the rider. The committee would have released the bill to the floors of both houses for a final vote, thus bypassing Aspinall and the House Interior Committee completely.

86. *New York Times*, October 11, 1967; *Arizona Republic*, September 28, 29, October 11, 1967.

87. Morris Udall to Honorable ____[in original], March 11, 1968, folder 2, box 6, JJR; *Arizona Republic*, January 30, March 27, May 8, 16, August 2, September 6, 13, October 1, 1968; *New York Times*, May 17, 1968. LBJ publicly endorsed the CAP for the first time in his message on conservation delivered to Congress on March 8, 1968, referenced in the Udall letter.

88. *Colorado River Basin Project, US Code*, vol. 43, sec. 1555; *Arizona Republic*, September 4, 1969; March 5, April 8, August 1, 1974; February 25, 1985; *The Grand Canyon National Park Enlargement Act, U.S. Code*, vol. 16, sec. 228, *et seq.*; and John McComb, "Regional Rep's Report: Southwest," *Sierra Club Bulletin*, June 1972, 20–21.

89. Drury died in 1978.

90. "The Hualapai (Bridge Canyon) Project," folder 6, box 2, JJR.

91. Public Law 90-537, title III sec. 303 (a). Colorado River Basin Project 890, https://www.gpo.gov/fdsys/pkg/STATUTE-82/pdf/STATUTE-82-Pg885-3.pdf#page=1, accessed July 5, 2018; "Final Wilderness Recommendation Update: 2010 (DRAFT) Grand Canyon National Park Arizona," National Park Service, https://www.nps.gov/grca/learn/management/upload/Draft_2010_Final_Wilderness_Rec.pdf, accessed July 6, 2018; John D. Leshy, "Legal Wilderness, Its Past and Some Speculations on Its Future," *Environmental Law* 44, no. 2, 2014, http://elawreview.org/articles/volume-44/issue-44-2/legal-wilderness-past-speculations-future-2/?hilite=%22Grand%22%2C%22Canyon%22, accessed July 6, 2018.

Chapter 9

1. Brower interview, July 27, 1997. The quote is often attributed to Brower; however, he told me in 1997 that Ira Gabrielson said it first.

2. Roderick Nash, ed., *Grand Canyon of the Living Colorado* (San Francisco: Sierra Club Books, 1970).

3. Nash, 235.

4. Fifty years of historiography yield an almost countless number of interpretations based upon the assumption that the environmentalists stopped the dams. See Nash, *Wilderness,* 227–37; Nash, ed., *Grand Canyon,* 99–107; Runte, 191, which originated as a dissertation under the direction of Nash; Fradkin, 228–34; Martin, 250–74 (Fradkin cites both *Wilderness* and *Grand Canyon of the Living Colorado* as support for his argument; Martin cites *Wilderness* and Fradkin); Fox, 320, also cites *Wilderness,* along with some primary sources, but holds to Nash's conclusion; Reisner, 285–90, discusses the controversy in much greater detail than the aforementioned historiography but concludes that the dams were deleted because of the Sierra Club's campaign; Senecah's "The Environmental Discourse of David Brower" is a fascinating analysis of the rhetoric used in the "Battle Ads"; Sellars, *Preserving Nature in the National Parks,* 207; Hal Rothman, *The Greening of a Nation?* (New York: Harcourt Brace Inc., 1998), 75–79; and John Opie, *Nature's Nation: An Environmental History of the United States* (New York: Harcourt Brace, Inc., 1998), 393–94, all echo Nash's arguments, as do Helen Ingram, *Water Politics: Continuity and Change* (Albuquerque: University of New Mexico Press, 1990), 55–56, 59, and Cohen, 178, 315, 357–65. Recent interpretations that do the same include Wyss, 207–23; Sara Dant, *Losing Eden: An Environmental History of the American West* (Chichester, West Sussex, UK: John Wiley & Sons Inc., 2017), 164–65, 174; a more nuanced account is Smith, *Stewart Udall: Steward of the Land,* (2016), 252–53, but he barely discusses Henry Jackson's pivotal role.

5. Carl Pope, "We Can Only Mar It," https://www.huffingtonpost.com/carl-pope/we-can-only-mar-it_b_884215.html, accessed July 7, 2018; Kenneth Brower, "Appreciations: Lessons from the Man Who Stopped Grand Canyon Dams," https://news.nationalgeographic.com/news/2014/12/141202-grand-canyon-dams-colorado-river-martin-litton-conservation/, accessed July 7, 2018; Mark Kitchell, *A Fierce Green Fire: The Battle for a Living Planet,* "Act 1" (2012), https://www.youtube.com/watch?v=u_fW_7WzSXk, accessed May 18, 2018; *When The Sierra Club Saved Grand Canyon* (April 2, 2014), PBS, American Masters, https://www.youtube.com/watch?v=qKFPsnaPjPE, accessed May 18, 2018; Mark Fraser, James Fox, and Boris Zubov, *The Good Fight: The Martin Litton Story* (2010), https://www.videoproject.com/The-Good-Fight-The-Martin-Litton-Story.html, accessed June 28, 2018; Jeff Ingram, "Celebrating The Grand Canyon" (2009–present), http://gcfutures.blogspot.com/, accessed July, 8, 2018; https://www.sierraclub.org/anniversary, accessed May 12, 2018.

6. Reisner, 285, is the most prominent example, and the quote is taken from his narrative; John McPhee, *Encounters with the Archdruid* (New York: Farrar, Straus and Giroux, 1971).

7. Udall interview, March 13, 1997.

8. The Grand Canyon dams were frequently referred to as "cash registers" in pro-dam literature; the environmentalists co-opted this language and mocked the bureau's arguments using its own words. Although it can be argued that

the preservationists could have *possibly* influenced policy-making by the time Congress convened in January of 1967, the effect of that influence would only have been felt had a bill containing dams so low that they posed no threat to the Pacific Northwest—in other words, dams acceptable to Jackson—been introduced. No such bill ever made it past the hypothetical stage, and thus, the ability of the environmentalists to force the deletion of dams Jackson might have supported was never tested.

9. Morris Udall to William Mathews, editor, *Arizona Daily Star*, October 12, 1967, folder 14, Box 481, MKU. Mo Udall stated that Arizona now had the votes to "run over California," in this letter.

10. Dominy interview, November 1, 1996.

11. MKU to John Rhodes, September 7, 1966, folder 2, box 476, MKU. According to Udall, Saylor's proposal was handwritten and stated that he would agree to support a Bridge Canyon Dam "lowered by 90 feet."

12. The closest they came is when Dominy stated that the project would be "theoretically possible" without the Grand Canyon dams. See US Congress, House, Subcommittee on Irrigation and Reclamation of the Committee on Interior and Insular Affairs, *Lower Colorado Basin Project: Hearings before the Subcommittee on Irrigation and Reclamation of the Committee on Interior and Insular Affairs,* 89th Cong., 2d sess., May 18, 1966, 1073.

13. Harvey, *Symbol of Wilderness,* 271.

14. Thomas Kimball to all members of Congress, March 24, 1967, folder 2, box 5, JJR; Brower to Kimball, June 30, 1967, folder 37, box 19, DBP/SCMP.

15. Fox, 291–327.

16. Harvey, 291.

17. David Brower to Harry Harrow, December 29, 1966, folder 36, box 19, DBP/SCMP; "Atlantic Chapter—Sierra Club, Annual Report—1966," folder 11, box 56, SCMP; Fox, 315; Cohen, 432; *Bakersfield Californian,* June 28, 1966.

18. Interview with Mark Kitchell by John Shegarian, host of GreenIsGoodradio.com, June 19, 2014, https://www.youtube.com/watch?v=SY_ZEJcSXuQ, accessed July 14, 2018; https://www.scientificamerican.com/article/a-fierce-green-fire-new-film/, accessed July 14, 2018; http://www.pbs.org/wnet/americanmasters/a-fierce-green-fire-about-the-film/2924/, accessed July 14, 2018. This documentary is not to be confused with the film *Green Fire,: Aldo Leopold and a Land Ethic for Our Time,* which was released by the Aldo Leopold Foundation at about the same time.

19. "When the Sierra Club Saved the Grand Canyon," http://www.pbs.org/wnet/americanmasters/a-fierce-green-fire-about-the-film/2924/, accessed July 14, 2018.

20. Kitchell, *A Fierce Green Fire: The Battle for a Living Planet,* "Act I: Conservation," https://www.youtube.com/watch?v=8pUREoZWILg, accessed July 15, 2018.

21. Ibid.; US Bureau of Reclamation, *Operation Glen Canyon,* 1961; http://www.foreverwildfilm.com/doug_scott.html, accessed July 15, 2018; https://www.youtube.com/watch?v=dSghEGsBqzM, accessed August 11, 2018.

22. Ibid.; Dominy to Margaret Young, February 2, 1966, box 6, folder 6, SCMC. Ironically, both Redford's narration and Litton's recollections understate the damage the MCKC project would have caused. See chapter 2.

23. US Congress, House, Subcommittee on Irrigation and Reclamation of the Committee on Interior and Insular Affairs, *Lower Colorado Basin Project: Hearings before the Subcommittee on Irrigation and Reclamation of the Committee on Interior and Insular Affairs*, 90th Cong., 1st sess., 1967, 458.

24. Kitchell, *Fierce Green Fire*.

25. Ibid.; Another egregious example is a documentary titled *Martin's Boat* that includes a computer-generated rendering of Marble Canyon Dam that, per topographical maps of the region, depicts a dam 1200–1500 feet tall! Marble Canyon Dam would have been 310 feet high above the streambed.

26. Catalin Partenie, "Plato's Myths," *The Stanford Encyclopedia of Philosophy* (Fall 2018 edition), edited by Edward N. Zalta, URL = https://plato.stanford.edu/archives/fall2018/entries/plato-myths/, accessed July 15, 2018.

27. Calvin Martin, *Keepers of the Game: Indian-Animal Relationships and the Fur Trade* (Berkeley: University of California Press, 1978); and Shepard Krech III, *The Ecological Indian: Myth and History* (New York: W.W. Norton, 1999).

28. "Iron Eyes Cody, an Actor and Tearful Anti-Littering Icon," https://www.nytimes.com/1999/01/05/arts/iron-eyes-cody-94-an-actor-and-tearful-anti-littering-icon.html, accessed July 15, 2018.

29. Sonia Dickey, "Sacrilege in Dinétah: Native Encounters with Glen Canyon Dam" (PhD diss., University of New Mexico, 2011), 235.

30. *EPA*, "Summary of the Clean Air Act 42 U.S.C. §7401 et seq. (1970)," https://www.epa.gov/laws-regulations/summary-clean-air-act, accessed July 8, 2018.

31. Julian Boggs, Travis Madsen, and Jorden Schneider, *America's Dirtiest Power Plants: Their Oversized Contribution to Global Warming and What We Can Do About It*, Environment America Research and Policy Center, 2013, 28, https://environmentamericacenter.org/sites/environment/files/reports/Dirty%20Power%20Plants.pdf, accessed December 3, 2018.

32. James Rainey, "Biggest Coal-burning Power Plant in the West Is Most Likely Shutting Down," April 11, 2018, https://www.nbcnews.com/news/us-news/biggest-coal-burning-power-plant-west-most-likely-shutting-down-n864981, accessed July 8, 2019; Pearson, *Still The Wild River Runs*, 187.

33. Portions of this section were originally published in *Journal of the West* 50:4 (Fall 2011). Copyright ABC-CLIO, LLC ©2011. Used with permission.

34. Scenic Hudson Preservation Conference v. Federal Power Commission, 354 F.2d 608 (2d Cir. 1965); Robert Lifeset, *Power on the Hudson: Storm King Mountain and the Emergence of Modern American Environmentalism* (Pittsburgh: University of Pittsburgh Press, 2014).

35. Lynton Keith Caldwell, *The National Environmental Policy Act: An Agenda for the Future* (Bloomington: Indiana University Press, 1998), 26–30.

36. Van Ness interview, August 14, 2012.

37. Ibid.

38. Robert G. Kaufman, *Henry M. Jackson: A Life in Politics* (Seattle: University of Washington Press, 2000), 202; Caldwell, 63–64; Van Ness interview, August 14, 2012.

39. William Van Ness, interview by the Henry M. Jackson Foundation, "The National Environmental Policy Act: The Model and the Passage" (February 3, 2016), https://www.youtube.com/watch?v=ROaKgJjfefY, accessed July 15, 2018.

40. Van Ness interview, August 14, 2012.

41. Martin Litton, interview by Ann Lage, "Sierra Club Director and Uncompromising Preservationist, 1950s–1970s," ROHOBL, 1980–1981, 174.

42. Aldo Leopold, "The Ecological Conscience," in *River of the Mother of God, and Other Essays*, Susan L. Flader and J. Baird Callicott, eds. (Madison: University of Wisconsin Press, 1991), 343.

Selected Bibliography

Abbreviations

CCDPL Conservation Collection. Western History/Genealogy Department. Denver Public Library, Denver, CO.

CTH Carl Trumbull Hayden Papers. Department of Archives and Manuscripts, Arizona State University, Tempe, AZ.

CWR Conrad Wirth Records. Record Group 79. Records of the National Park Service. National Archives, College Park, MD.

DBP David Brower Papers. Bancroft Library, Berkeley, CA.

EK Emery Kolb Papers. Special Collections. Cline Library, Northern Arizona University, Flagstaff, AZ.

FD Frederick Dellenbaugh Papers. Special Collections, University of Arizona, Tucson, AZ.

FRCD Federal Records Center, Denver, CO.

GCMC Grand Canyon National Park Museum Collection, Grand Canyon Village, AZ.

GCRL Grand Canyon National Park Research Library, Grand Canyon Village, AZ.

GHP George B. Hartzog Papers. Special Collections, Clemson University, Clemson, SC.

IDR Record Group 48. Records of the Department of the Interior. National Archives, College Park, MD.

JJR John Jacob Rhodes Papers. Department of Archives and Manuscripts, Arizona State University, Tempe, AZ.

MKU Morris K. Udall Papers. Special Collections, University of Arizona, Tucson, AZ.

NDR Newton Drury Records. Record Group 79. Records of the National Park Service. National Archives, College Park, MD.

RBP Richard Bradley Papers. Special Collections, University of Utah, Salt Lake City, UT.

RLP Richard Leonard Papers. Bancroft Library, Berkeley, CA.

ROHOBL Regional Oral History Office. Bancroft Library, University of California, Berkeley.

SCMP Sierra Club Members' Papers. Bancroft Library, University of California, Berkeley.

SCR   Sierra Club Records. Bancroft Library, University of California, Berkeley.

SLU   Stewart L. Udall Papers. Special Collections, University of Arizona, Tucson, AZ.

WSP   Wilderness Society Papers. Western History Department. Denver Public Library, Denver, CO.

Primary Sources

Manuscript Collections

Barry Goldwater Papers. Department of Archives and Manuscripts, Arizona State University, Tempe, AZ.

Carl Trumbull Hayden Papers. Department of Archives and Manuscripts, Arizona State University, Tempe, AZ.

Emery Kolb Papers. Special Collections. Cline Library, Northern Arizona University, Flagstaff, AZ.

Federal Records Center, Denver, CO:

Record Group 79. Records of the National Park Service.

Record Group 115. Records of the Bureau of Reclamation.

Frederick Dellenbaugh Papers. Department of Special Collections, University of Arizona, Tucson, AZ.

George B. Hartzog Papers. Special Collections, Clemson University, Clemson, SC.

George Senner Papers. Special Collections. Cline Library, Northern Arizona University, Flagstaff, AZ.

Grand Canyon National Park Museum Collection, microfiche:

GRCA numbers: 04363; 04848; 14811; 32364; 48906; 50706; 55367; 63107; 66943; 66944. These include park superintendents' reports, correspondence files, and many items about Grand Canyon dam proposals from 1900 to 1985.

Grand Canyon National Park Research Library, microfiche:

Dams on the Colorado River 1938–1954 (L-7423, 1–5).

Bridge Canyon Dam 1948–1954 (L-7423, 1–4).

Bridge Canyon Dam 1950 (L-7423, 1).

Bridge Canyon Dam 1954–1966 (L-7423, 1–4).

Marble Canyon, Reference File (L-7423, 1).

Marble Canyon–Kanab Creek Project 1961–1962 (L-7423, 1–4).

Marble Canyon–Kanab Creek Project 1963 (L-7423, 1–5).

Letters, memos, and assorted documents, Bridge Canyon Dam Project, Marble Canyon Dam Projects n.d. (L-7423, 1).

Henry Jackson Papers. Special Collections. University of Washington Library, Seattle, WA.

John Jacob Rhodes Papers. Department of Archives and Manuscripts, Arizona State University, Tempe, AZ.

John Saylor Papers. Special Collections, Indiana University of Pennsylvania, Indiana, PA.

Lemuel Garrison Papers. Special Collections, Clemson, University, Clemson, SC.

Morris K. Udall Papers. Special Collections, University of Arizona, Tucson, AZ.

National Archives. College Park, MD. Record Group 48. Records of the Department
    of the Interior:
    Central Classified Files of the Secretary of the Interior, 1940–1966.
    Office Files of Secretary Stewart L. Udall, 1960–1966.

National Archives. College Park, MD. Record Group 79. Records of the National
    Park Service:
    Central Classified Files.
    Conrad Wirth Records.
    Newton Drury Records.

Richard C. Bradley Papers. Western History Department. Denver Public Library,
    Denver, CO.

Sierra Club Members Papers. Bancroft Library, University of California, Berkeley:
    David Brower.
    Francis Farquhar.
    John Flannery.
    Richard Leonard.
    Martin Litton.
    Charlotte Mauk.
    Tom Turner.
    Robin Way.
    Francis Wolcott.

Sierra Club Records. Bancroft Library, University of California, Berkeley:
    Board of Directors meetings 1946–1969.
    Executive Committee meetings (selected) 1946–1969.
    Financial.
    Membership Activity.
    Minutes.
    Publications.

Stewart L. Udall Papers. Special Collections, University of Arizona, Tucson, AZ.

Wilderness Society Papers. Western History Department. Denver Public Library,
    Denver, CO.

Interviews and Oral Histories

Albright, Horace. Interview by Julie Russell. Grand Canyon National Park Oral
    History Project. Grand Canyon National Park Museum, April 7, 1981.

Beal, Merrill. Interview by Julie Russell. Grand Canyon National Park Oral History
    Project. Grand Canyon National Park Museum, July 20, 1981.

Beaty, Orren. Interview with author. Vienna, VA, March 19, 1997.

Brower, David. "Brower At Dam Site." Cassette recording (n.d.). Grand Canyon
    National Park Museum Collection.

Brower, David Ross. Interview by Susan Schrepfer. "Environmental Activist,

Publicist and Prophet." Regional Oral History Office. Bancroft Library, University of California Berkeley, 1974–1978.

Brower, David Ross. Interview with author. Berkeley, CA, July 27, 1997.

Brower, David Ross. "Reflections on the Sierra Club, Friends of the Earth, and Earth Island Institute." Conducted by Ann Lage in 1999. Regional Oral History Office. Bancroft Library, University of California, Berkeley, 2012.

Brower, Kenneth. Interview by Laurel Hayden. June 21, 2012. http://sierraclub.ty-pepad.com/greenlife/2012/06/kenneth-brower-remembers-father-an-interview-with-david-browers-son.html. Accessed May 19, 2018.

Cameron, Bert. Interview by William E. Austin. Grand Canyon National Park Research Library, June 21, 1939.

Carver, John. Interview with author. Denver, CO, August 20, 1997.

Dominy, Floyd. Interview by Charles Coate by telephone. July 14, 1997.

Dominy, Floyd. Interview with author. Bellevue Farms, VA, November 1, 1996.

Dominy, Floyd. Interview with author by telephone. December 1, 2005.

Drury, Newton B. Interview by Amelia Fry and Susan Schrepfer. "Parks and Redwoods, 1919–1971." Regional Oral History Office. Bancroft Library, University of California Berkeley, 1983.

Elson, Roy. Interviews by Donald Ritchie. "Administrative Assistant to Senator Carl Hayden and Candidate for the United States Senate." John F. Kennedy Library, Boston, MA, July 6, 1990.

Elson, Roy. Interview by Pam Stevenson. https://www.cap-az.com/about-us/oral-history-transcripts?view=download&fileId. Accessed July 3, 2018.

Francis, Sharon. Interview by Dorothy Pierce McSweeny. AC 81–68. Lyndon Baines Johnson Library, Austin, TX, May 20, 1969.

Francis, Sharon. Interview with author by telephone. August 14, 1997.

Greg, Frank. Interview with author by telephone. October 15, 1996.

Hartzog, George. Interview with author. McLean, VA, November 2, 1996.

Kitchell, Mark. Interview by John Shegerian, host. GreenIsGoodradio.com. June 19, 2014. https://www.youtube.com/watch?v=SY_ZEJcSXuQ. Accessed July 15, 2018.

Leonard, Richard. Interview by Susan Schrepfer. "Mountaineer, Lawyer, Environmentalist." Regional Oral History Office. Bancroft Library, University of California Berkeley, 1975.

Leopold, Luna. Interview by Dunne Thomas and Ann Lage. "Hydrology, Geomorphology, and Environmental Policy: US Geological Survey, 1950–1972 and UC Berkeley, 1972–1987." Regional Oral History Office. Bancroft Library, University of California Berkeley, 1993.

Litton, Martin. Interview by Ann Lage. "Sierra Club Director and Uncompromising Preservationist, 1950s–1970s." Regional Oral History Office. Bancroft Library, University of California Berkeley, 1980–1981.

Robinson, Bestor. Interview by Susan R. Schrepfer. "Thoughts on Conservation and the Sierra Club." Regional Oral History Office. Bancroft Library, University of California Berkeley, 1974.

Siri, William E. Interview by Ann Lage. "Reflections on the Sierra Club, the
    Environment, and Mountaineering, 1950s–1970s." Regional Oral History Office.
    Bancroft Library, University of California Berkeley, 1976.
Steck, George. Interview by Michael Quinn. Grand Canyon National Park Oral
    History Project. Grand Canyon National Park Museum. September 3, 1995.
Storey, Brit. Interview with author by telephone, October 17, 1996.
Stricklin, Howard. Interview by Julie Russell. Grand Canyon National Park Oral
    History Project. Grand Canyon National Park Museum. August 26, 1981.
Swem, Theodore. Interview with author by telephone, October 8, 1996.
Udall, Stewart. Interview with author by telephone, October 23, 1996.
Udall, Stewart. Interview with author by telephone, June 21, 2007.
Udall, Stewart. Interview with author. Tucson, AZ, March 13, 1997.
Udall, Stewart. Interview with Charles Coate. Santa Fe, NM, April 23, 1997.
Udall, Stewart. Interview with W. W. Moss. John F. Kennedy Library, Boston, MA,
    January 12, 1970.
Van Ness, William. Interview by the Henry M. Jackson Foundation. "The Creation
    of the National Environmental Policy Act." February 2, 2016. https://www.you-
    tube.com/watch?v=ssiN7M_hedw. Accessed July 15, 2018.
Van Ness, William. Interview by the Henry M. Jackson Foundation. "The National
    Environmental Policy Act: The Model and the Passage." February 3, 2016.
    https://www.youtube.com/watch?v=ROaKgJjfefY. Accessed July 15, 2018.
Van Ness, William. Interview by the Henry M. Jackson Foundation. "NEPA's
    Legacy." February 2, 2016. https://www.youtube.com/watch?v=7QCuVcD4C64.
    Accessed July 15, 2018.
Van Ness, William. Interview with author by telephone. August 14, 2012.
Wayburn, Edgar. Interview by Ann Lage and Susan Schrepfer. "Sierra Club
    Statesman, Leader of the Parks and Wilderness Movement: Gaining Protection
    for Alaska, the Redwoods, and Golden Gate Parklands." Regional Oral History
    Office. University of California Berkeley, 1976–1981.

Newspapers

Arizona Daily Star (Tucson). September 30, 1945; January 21, June 20, 1947; June
    2, 10, 1955; May 3, 1961; April 9, December 12, 13, 1963; April 21, May 17,
    December 14, 1965.
Arizona Daily Sun (Flagstaff). June 28, 1958; February 20, 1964; March 31, May 13,
    1966.
Arizona Republic (Phoenix). May 2, 1948; April 4, May 4, 1950; January 14, 1952;
    April 3, June 2, 1955; April 6, 1956; July 7, 24, December 12, 1957; November
    21, 1958; January 19, 1959; May 3, November 22, 1961; April 27, 1962; January
    11, 24, 26, August 22, December 27, 29, 1963; February 20, 28, April 16, June 20,
    1964; May 11, October 27, 1965; March 24, 27, 31, April 1, 3, 17, May 8, 13, 29,
    June 1, 19, July 29, August 4, 16, 27, September 1, 8, 11, 15–18, 21, October 14,
    18, December 7, 10, 15, 1966; January 11, 19, 22, 24, February 2, 3, 8, 16, March
    1, 7, 14, June 24, August 1, 3, 5, 8, 18, 20, 22, 23, September 28, 29, October 4, 11,

1967; January 30, 31, March 27, May 8, 16, June 1, August 2, September 6, 13, October 1, 1968; September 4, 1969; March 4, April 8, August 1, 1974; February 25, 1985; March 11, 2014.

Bakersfield Californian. June 28, 1966.

Chicago Daily News. June 11, 1951.

Coconino Sun (Flagstaff, AZ). April 13, 1901; March 22, June 21, August 20, 30, 1902; May 24, 1912.

Denver Post. September 24, October 19, 1964; March 6, 27, November 19, 1966.

Gallup (NM) Independent. August 4, 1966.

Kingman (AZ) Miner. February 22, 1902.

Los Angeles Times. July 30, 1945; July 7, 1957; November 13, 1963; December 14, 1964.

New York Daily Tribune. December 12, 1923.

New York Times. January 22, June 12, 13, July 28, August 22, 27, 28, 1963; February 16, December 20, 1964; May 11, 1965; January 17, May 2, June 1, 9, 11, 17, July 21, 25, 28, August 17, October 9, 1966; February 2, March 13, 14, June 20, August 4, 8, October 11, 1967; May 17, 1968; January 5, 1975; January 5, 1999.

Oakland (CA) Tribune. July 16, 1966.

Oregonian (Portland, OR). September 12, 1962; July 18, 1965.

Phoenix Gazette. July 29, 1952; March 25, 1953; May 14, 1956; November 8, 22, 1961; January 26, 1963; July 28, 1964; May 10, 11, 1965.

Phoenix Republican. June 21, 1902.

Riverside (CA) Daily Enterprise. July 20, 1966.

Rocky Mountain News (Denver, CO). August 11, 1966.

Salt Lake City Tribune. November 28, 1893.

San Francisco Chronicle. June 3, 6, 1921.

Wall Street Journal. July 14, 29, 1966.

Washington Post. November 11, 1923; August 14, 1966; March 27, 1977.

Williams (AZ) News. April 5, 1956.

Secondary Sources

Articles and Chapters

"1964, Action on Public Lands, Water and Reclamation." *CQ Almanac 1964*, 20th ed. Washington, DC: Congressional Quarterly, 1965. https://library.cqpress.com/cqalmanac/document.php?id=cqal64-1303213. Accessed July 22, 2018.

Bailey, James M. "Reconsideration and Reconciliation." *New Mexico Historical Review* 80, no. 2. Spring 2005.

"Blueprint for an Area Short of Water." *US News and World Report.* September 9, 1963.

Bradley, Richard C. "Attack on Grand Canyon." *The Living Wilderness.* Washington, DC: The Wilderness Society. Winter 1964–1965.

———. "Grand Canyon of the Controversial Colorado." *Sierra Club Bulletin.* December 1964.

———. "Ruin for the Grand Canyon." *Reader's Digest.* April 1966.

———. "Ruin for the Grand Canyon." *Town Hall*. Los Angeles: Town Hall, July 12, 1966.

Brower, David. "The Chips Are Down for Grand Canyon." *Sierra Club Bulletin*. February 1965.

———. "Gigantic Southwest Water Plan Offers More Reservoirs Than Water." *Sierra Club Bulletin*. September 1964.

———. "Grand Canyon 'Battle Ads.'" In *Grand Canyon of the Living Colorado*, edited by Roderick Nash. New York: Ballantine Books, 1970. https://content.sierraclub. org/brower/grand-canyon-battle-ads. Accessed May 19, 2018.

———. "Grand Canyon: Department of Amplification." *Sierra Club Bulletin*. December 1965.

———. "The New Threat to Grand Canyon: Action Needed." *Sierra Club Bulletin*. January 1964.

Brower, Kenneth. "Appreciation: Lessons from the Man who Stopped Grand Canyon Dams." *National Geographic*. December 2, 2014. https://news.nationalgeographic. com/news/2014/12/141202-grand-canyon-dams-colorado-river-martin-litton-conservation/. Accessed July 20, 2018.

"Compromise the Grand Canyon." *Sierra Club Bulletin*. March 1967.

"Dam the Canyon?" *Newsweek*. May 30, 1966.

"Dams vs. Scenery (Again)." *Izaak Walton Magazine*. March 1965.

Dean, Robert. "'Dam Building Still Had Some Magic Then': Stewart Udall, the Central Arizona Project, and the Evolution of the Pacific Southwest Water Pan, 1963–1968." *Pacific Historical Review* vol. 66. February 1997.

Desky, Robert M. "California and the Colorado River." *California Law Review* 38, issue 4, October 1950. https://scholarship.law.berkeley.edu/cgi/viewcontent. cgi?article=3469&context=californialawreview Accessed July 18, 2018.

DeVoto, Bernard. "Shall We Let Them Ruin Our National Parks?" *Reader's Digest*. November 1950.

Drake, Brian Allen. "The Skeptical Environmentalist: Senator Barry Goldwater and the Environment Management State." *Environmental History* 15 (October 2010): 587–611.

"The Entire Grand Canyon Must Be Protected." *Sierra Club Bulletin*. May 1966.

Fedarko, Kevin. "Ain't It Just Grand?" *Outside*. June 1, 2005. https://www.outsideon-line.com/1927766/aint-it-just-grand. Accessed June 30, 2018.

"For the September Board, Glacier View Dam Again." *Sierra Club Bulletin* 34. (September 1949): 3.

Gilman, Sarah. "This Will Be the Biggest Dam Removal Project in History." *National Geographic*. April 11, 2016.

"Glacier View Dam, Glacier National Park." *Sierra Club Bulletin* 33 (May 1948): 10–11.

"Grand Canyon Cash Registers." *Life*. May 7, 1965.

"Grand Canyon, Colorado Dams Debated." *Science*. June 17, 1966.

Harvey, Mark. "The Controversy over Rainbow Bridge." *New Mexico Historical Review* 73. January 1998.

Heald, Weldon. "Colorado River of the West." *National Parks* magazine. October
    1963.

Hillery, George A., Jr., and Frank J. Essene. "Navajo Population: An Analysis
    of the 1960 Census." *Southwestern Journal of Anthropology* 19, no. 3
    (Autumn, 1963): 297–313. https://www.jstor.org/stable/3629209?read-
    now=1&loggedin=true&seq=4#page_scan_tab_contents. Accessed June 3, 2018.

"How to Save the Grand Canyon and Water the Desert Too." *US News and World
    Report*. October 24, 1966.

"Internal Revenue Service Used as a Weapon Against the Sierra Club—and Against
    Grand Canyon." *Sierra Club Bulletin*. July–August 1966.

Israelsen, Brent. "3 Decades Later, 2 Still Arguing over Glen Canyon." *Deseret News*.
    October 10, 1995. https://www.deseretnews.com/article/444096/3-DECADES-
    LATER-2-STILL-ARGUING-OVER-GLEN-CANYON.html. Accessed July 6,
    2018.

"Knight Errant to Nature's Rescue." *Life*. May 27, 1966.

Langlois, Krista. "Down with the Glen Canyon Dam." *High Country News*.
    September 4, 2017.

Leopold, Aldo. "The Ecological Conscience." In *River of the Mother of God, and
    Other Essays*, edited by Susan L. Flader and J. Baird Callicott, 338–48. Madison:
    University of Wisconsin Press, 1991.

Leopold, Madelyn. "Disillusioning Dams and the Value of Beauty." *Sierra Club
    Bulletin*. October 1965.

Leshy, John D. "Legal Wilderness, Its Past and Some Speculations on Its Future."
    Environmental Law 44, no. 2., 2014. http://elawreview.org/articles/volume-44/
    issue-44-2/legal-wilderness-past-speculations-future-2/?hilite=%22Grand%22
    %2C%22Canyon%22. Accessed July 6, 2018.

Lustgarten, Abrahm. "Unplugging the Colorado River." *New York Times*. May 20,
    2016. https://www.nytimes.com/2016/05/22/opinion/unplugging-the-colorado-
    river.html.

McComb, John. "Regional Reps Report, Southwest: Grand Canyon National Park
    Diminution Act." *Sierra Club Bulletin*. February 1975.

Miller, Ryder W. "Review, *Still the Wild River Runs: Congress, the Sierra Club, and
    the Fight to Save Grand Canyon, 1963–1968*." *Electronic Green Journal* 1, issue 18.
    2003. https://escholarship.org/search/?q=Miller,%20Ryder%20W. Accessed
    July 20, 2018.

Moss, Dewitt. "Nuclear Power and NAWAPA, What Will It Take?" *21st Century
    Science & Technology*. Spring 2011. http://21sci-tech.com/Articles_2011/
    Spring-2011/Nuclear_NAWAPA.pdf. Accessed June 27, 2018.

Muir, John. "The Hetch Hetchy Valley." *Sierra Club Bulletin*, vol. VI., no. 4. 1908.
    https://vault.sierraclub.org/ca/hetchhetchy/hetch_hetchy_muir_scb_1908.html.
    Accessed May 18, 2018.

"News of Conservation and the Club." *Sierra Club Bulletin*. February 1968.

"News of Conservation and the Club." *Sierra Club Bulletin*. March 1967.

"News of Conservation and the Club." *Sierra Club Bulletin*. September 1966.

O'Connor, J. E., J. J. Duda, and G. E. Grant. "1000 Dams Down and Counting." *Science*. May 1, 2015.

Packard, Fred. "Grand Canyon National Monument in Danger." *National Parks* magazine. July–September 1949.

———. "Grand Canyon Park and Dinosaur Monument in Danger." *National Parks Magazine*. October–December 1949.

Partenie, Catalin. "Plato's Myths." In *The Stanford Encyclopedia of Philosophy*, edited by Edward N. Zalta (Fall 2018 edition). URL = https://plato.stanford.edu/archives/fall2018/entries/plato-myths/. Accessed July 15, 2018.

Paumgarten, Nick. "A Voyage Along Trump's Wall: Canoeing the Rio Grande Reveals How Life and a Landscape Would Be Changed Along the Border." *New Yorker*. April 23, 2018.

Pearson, Byron. "How the Forest Service Saved the Grand Canyon." *Forest History Today* 18, no. 1 (Spring 2012): 3–11.

———. "Newton Drury of the National Park Service, a Reappraisal." *Pacific Historical Review* 68, no. 3. August 1999.

———. "Remembering Interior Secretary Stewart Udall." *Journal of the West* 51, no. 1 (Winter 2012): 3–9.

———. "The Marble Canyon–Kanab Creek Project." *Locus* 8, no. 1. Fall 1995.

———. "We Have Almost Forgotten How to Hope: Hualapais, Navajos, and the Fight for the Central Arizona Project, 1944–1968." *Western Historical Quarterly* 32 (Autumn, 2000): 297–318.

———. "'You Can't Study It, Contemplate It or Even Dream About It': Henry Jackson, the Columbia River Diversion, and NEPA's EIS Requirement, 1963–1969." *Journal of the West* 50, no. 4 (Fall 2011): 60–73.

Pisani, Donald J. "Floyd E. Dominy." Water History.org. http://www.waterhistory.org/histories/dominy/. Accessed May 17, 2018.

"Plato's Myths." *Stanford Encyclopedia of Philosophy*. https://plato.stanford.edu/entries/plato-myths/. Accessed May 27, 2018.

Pope, Carl. "We Can Only Mar It." *Huffington Post*. The Blog. June 27, 2011. https://www.huffingtonpost.com/carl-pope/we-can-only-mar-it_b_884215.html.

Ragsdale, John. "Anno Dominy MCMLXVI." *Biophilist*. March–April 1966.

Rainy, James. "Biggest Coal-Burning Power Plant in the West Is Most Likely Shutting Down." April 11, 2018. https://www.nbcnews.com/news/us-news/biggest-coal-burning-power-plant-west-most-likely-shutting-down-n864981. Accessed July 8, 2019.

Raushenbush, Stephen. "A Bridge Canyon Dam Is Not Necessary." *National Parks* magazine. April 1964.

"*Reader's Digest* Enlists in the Fight to Save Grand Canyon." *Sierra Club Bulletin*. May 1966.

"Reclaimed by Man." *Razz Review*. June 1975.

Reinhardt, Richard. "The Case of the Hard-Nosed Conservationists." *American West* 4 (February 1967).

Richardson, Elmo. "Federal Park Policy in Utah: The Escalante National Monument Controversy of 1935–1940." *Utah Historical Quarterly* 33. Spring 1965.

Rink, Glenn. "Life at the Marble Canyon Damsites." *Boatman's Quarterly Review*. Spring 1997. https://www.gcrg.org/bqr/10-2/mcd.html. Accessed July 8, 2018.

Satchell, Michael. "Power and the Glory." *US News and World Report*. January 21, 1991.

Schilling, Ron K. "Indians and Eagles: The Struggle Against Orme Dam." *Journal of Arizona History* 41, no. 1. Spring 2000.

"Senate Passes Central Arizona Project Bill." In *CQ Almanac 1967*, 23rd ed. Washington, DC: Congressional Quarterly, 1968. http://library.cqpress.com/cqalmanac/cqal67-1313328. Accessed July 15, 2018.

Smith, Anthony Wayne. "Attack on Grand Canyon." *National Parks* magazine. January 1962.

———. "The Editorial Page." *National Parks* magazine. April 1964.

———. "The Mighty Colorado." *National Parks* magazine. October 1963.

"Southwest Gropes for New Ways to End Water Shortage." *US News and World Report*. December 12, 1966.

Stewart, Bruce. "Think Big." *Harper's*. August 1965.

"Strong Words Betray a Weak Case." *Sierra Club Bulletin*. July–August 1966.

Thomas, Clyde. "The Last Days of Grand Canyon Too?" *Sierra Club Bulletin*. October 1963.

Thompson, Robert H. "Decision at Rainbow Bridge." *Sierra Club Bulletin*. May 1973.

"Trouble at the Bridge." *National Parks* magazine. April 1960.

Turner, Tom. "The Grand Undammed." *Sierra*. July–August 1992.

Udall, Stewart. "Wilderness Rivers: Shooting the Wild Colorado." *Venture*. February 1968.

Books

Andersen, Michael. *Polishing the Jewel: An Administrative History of Grand Canyon National Park*. Grand Canyon Association, 2000.

August, Jack L. Jr. *Vision in the Desert: Carl Hayden and Hydropolitics in the American Southwest*. Fort Worth: Texas Christian University Press, 2005.

———. *Dividing Western Waters: Mark Wilmer and Arizona v. California*. Fort Worth: Texas Christian University Press, 2007.

Beard, Daniel P. *Deadbeat Dams: Why We Should Abolish the US Bureau of Reclamation and Tear Out Glen Canyon Dam*. Boulder, CO: Johnson Books, 2015.

Berkman, Richard, and Kip Viscusi. *Damming the West: Ralph Nader's Study Group on the Bureau of Reclamation*. New York: Grossman Publishers, 1973.

Billington, David P., Donald C. Jackson, and Martin V. Melosi. *The History of Large Federal Dams: Planning, Design, and Construction in the Era of Big Dams*. Denver, CO: US Department of the Interior, Bureau of Reclamation, 2005. http://citeseerx.ist.psu.edu/viewdoc/download?doi=10.1.1.733.1294&rep=rep1&type=pd.

Boggs, Julian, Travis Madsen, and Jordan Schneider. *America's Dirtiest Power Plants: Their Oversized Contribution to Global Warming and What We Can Do About It*.

Environment America Research and Policy Center, 2013. https://environmentamericacenter.org/sites/environment/files/reports/Dirty%20Power%20Plants.pdf.

Boyer, Diane, and Robert H. Webb. *Damming Grand Canyon: The 1923 USGS Colorado River Expedition.* Logan: Utah State University Press Digital Commons, 2007.

Brower, David. *For Earth's Sake: The Life and Times of David R. Brower.* Salt Lake City: Peregrine Smith Books, 1990.

———. *Work in Progress.* Salt Lake City: Peregrine Smith Books, 1991.

Brower, Kenneth. *The Wildness Within: Remembering David Brower.* Berkeley: Heyday Books, Kindle edition, 2012.

Brugge, David E. *The Navajo-Hopi Land Dispute: An American Tragedy.* Albuquerque: University of New Mexico Press, 1994.

Burns, Stewart. *Social Movements of the 1960s.* Boston: Twayne Publisher, 1990.

Caro, Robert. *The Years of Lyndon Johnson: Volume I, The Path to Power.* New York: Alfred Knopf, 1982; Random House Vintage Books, 1990.

———. *The Years of Lyndon Johnson: Volume II, Means of Ascent.* New York: Alfred Knopf, 1990.

Carothers, Steven W., and Brian T. Brown. *The Colorado River Through Grand Canyon: Natural History and Human Change.* Tucson: University of Arizona Press, 1991.

Cohen, Michael P. *The History of the Sierra Club, 1892–1970.* San Francisco: Sierra Club Books, 1988.

Colter, Fred. *The Highline Book.* Phoenix, AZ: Fred Colter, 1934.

Dallek, Robert. *Lone Star Rising: Lyndon Johnson and His Times, 1908–1960.* New York, Oxford: Oxford University Press, 1991.

Dant, Sara. *Losing Eden: An Environmental History of the American West.* Chichester, West Sussex, UK: John Wiley & Sons Ltd., 2017.

Dilsaver, Lary M., and William C. Tweed. *The Challenge of the Big Trees.* Three Rivers, CA: Sequoia Natural History Association, 1990. https://www.nps.gov/parkhistory/online_books/dilsaver-tweed/chap8c.htm. Accessed May 28, 2018.

Einberger, Scott Raymond. *With Distance in His Eyes: The Environmental Life and Legacy of Stewart Udall.* Reno and Las Vegas: University of Nevada Press, 2018.

Engel-Pearson, Kim. *Writing Arizona, 1912–2012: A Cultural and Environmental Chronicle.* Norman: University of Oklahoma Press, 2017.

Farmer, Jarred. *Glen Canyon Dammed: Inventing Lake Powell and the Canyon Country.* Tucson: University of Arizona Press, 1999.

Fleck, John. *Water Is for Fighting Over: And Other Myths about Water in the West.* Washington, DC: Island Press, 2016.

Foresta, Ronald A. *America's National Parks and Their Keepers.* Washington, DC: Resources for the Future, 1984.

Fox, Stephen. *John Muir and His Legacy: The American Conservation Movement.* Boston: Little, Brown and Co., 1981. Reprint, Madison: University of Wisconsin Press, 1985.

Fradkin, Philip L. *Fallout: An American Nuclear Tragedy*. Tucson: University of
    Arizona Press, 1989.
————. *A River No More*. New York: Alfred Knopf, 1981.
Frome, Michael. *Regreening the National Parks*. Tucson: University of Arizona Press,
    1992.
Gitlin, Todd. *The Sixties: Years of Hope, Days of Rage*. New York: Bantam Books, 1987.
Gould, Lewis. *Lady Bird Johnson and the Environment*. Lawrence: University of
    Kansas Press, 1988.
Gunther, Gerald. *Constitutional Law*, 11th ed. Mineola, NY: The Foundation Press,
    1985.
Hartzog, George B. *Battling for the National Parks*. Mt. Kisco, NY: Moyer Bell
    Limited, 1988.
Harvey, Mark W. T. *A Symbol of Wilderness: Echo Park and the American Conservation
    Movement*. Albuquerque: University of New Mexico Press, 1994.
Hays, Samuel P. *Beauty, Health, and Permanence: Environmental Politics in the United
    States, 1955–1985*. Cambridge: Cambridge University Press, 1987.
————. *Conservation and the Gospel of Efficiency: The Progressive Conservation
    Movement, 1890–1920*. Cambridge: Harvard University Press, 1959.
Hiltzik. Michael. *Colossus: Hoover Dam and the Making of the American Century*. New
    York: Free Press, 2010.
Hoxie, Frederick, ed. *Indians in American History*. Arlington Heights, IL: Harlan
    Davidson Inc., 1988.
Hughes, J. Donald. *In the House of Stone and Light*. Grand Canyon Natural History
    Association, 1978.
Humlum, J. *Water Development and Planning in the Southwestern United States*.
    Copenhagen, Denmark: Carlsberg Foundation, 1969.
Hundley, Norris. *Dividing the Waters: A Century of Controversy Between the United
    States and Mexico*. Berkeley: University of California Press, 1966.
————. *The Great Thirst: Californians and Water, 1770s–1990s*. Berkeley and Los
    Angeles: University of California Press, 1992.
————. *Water and the West*. Berkeley: University of California Press, 1975.
Ingram, Helen. *Patterns of Politics in Water Resource Development*. Tucson: University
    of Arizona Press, 1969.
————. *Water Politics: Continuity and Change*. Albuquerque: University of New
    Mexico Press, 1990.
Ingram, Jeff. *Hijacking a River: A Political History of the Colorado River in the Grand
    Canyon*. Flagstaff, AZ: Vishnu Temple Press, 2003.
Ise, John. *Our National Park Policy: A Critical History*. Manchester, NH: Ayer
    Company Publications, 1979.
Jett, Stephen. *Navajo Wildlands: As Long as the Rivers Shall Run*. San Francisco: Sierra
    Club, 1967.
Johnson, Rich. *The Central Arizona Project: 1918–1968*. Tucson: University of Arizona
    Press, 1977.

Jones, Holoway R. *John Muir and the Sierra Club: The Battle for Yosemite*. San Francisco: Sierra Club, 1965.

Kirwin, Jerome. *Federal Water-Power Legislation*. New York: Columbia University Press, 1926.

Lago, Don. *Grand Canyon: A History of a Natural Wonder and a National Park*. Las Vegas and Reno: University of Nevada Press, 2015.

Leopold, Aldo. *A Sand County Almanac and Sketches Here and There*. New York: Oxford University Press, 1949.

Leydet, Francois. *Time and the River Flowing: Grand Canyon*. San Francisco: Sierra Club, 1964.

Lifeset, Robert. *Power on the Hudson: Storm King Mountain and the Emergence of Modern American Environmentalism*. Pittsburgh: University of Pittsburgh Press, 2014.

Mann, Dean. *The Politics of Water in Arizona*. Tucson: University of Arizona Press, 1963.

Martin, Russell. *A Story that Stands Like A Dam*. New York: Henry Holt and Co., 1989.

McMillen, Christian W. *Making Indian Law: The Hualapi Land Case and the Birth of Ethnohistory*. New Haven: Yale University Press, 2007.

McPhee, John. *Encounters with the Archdruid*. New York: Farrar, Straus, and Giroux, 1971.

Miles, John C. *Guardians of the Parks: A History of the National Parks and Conservation Association*. Washington, DC: Taylor and Francis, 1995.

Minckley, W. L. *Fishes of Arizona*. Phoenix: Sims Printing Company, 1973.

Morehouse, Barbara. *A Place Called Grand Canyon: Contested Geographies*. Tucson: University of Arizona Press, 1996.

Nash, Roderick, ed. *Grand Canyon of the Living Colorado*. New York: Ballantine Books, 1970.

———. *Wilderness and the American Mind*. New Haven: Yale University Press, 1967.

———. *Wilderness and the American Mind*, 5th ed. New Haven: Yale University Press, 2014.

Needham, Andrew. *Power Lines: Phoenix and the Making of the Modern Southwest*. Princeton, NJ: Princeton University Press, 2014.

O'Neill, William. *American High: The Years of Confidence, 1945–1960*. New York: Macmillan, 1986.

———. *Coming Apart: An Informal History of America in the 1960s*. New York: Times Books, 1971.

Opie, John. *Nature's Nation: An Environmental History of the United States*. New York: Harcourt Brace, Inc., 1998.

Palmer, Tim. *Endangered Rivers and the Conservation Movement*, 2nd ed. Landham, MD: Rowman Littlefield Publishers, 2004.

Pattie, James Ohio. *The Personal Narrative of James O. Pattie of Kentucky*. Timothy Flint and Reuben Gold Thwaites, eds. Cleveland: Arthur H. Clark, 1905.

Pearson, Byron E. *Still the Wild River Runs: Congress, the Sierra Club, and the Fight to Save Grand Canyon*. Tucson: University of Arizona Press, 2002.

Pinchot, Gifford. *The Fight for Conservation*. Garden City, NY: Harcourt Brace, 1910.

Pisani, Donald, J. *To Reclaim a Divided West: Water, Law, and Public Policy, 1848–1902*. Albuquerque: University of New Mexico Press, 1992.

Porter, Eliot. *The Place No One Knew: Glen Canyon on the Colorado*. San Francisco: Sierra Club Books, 1963.

Powell, John Wesley. *Canyons of the Colorado*. New York: Cosimo Publications, 2008. Reprinted from 1895.

———. *The Exploration of the Colorado River and Its Canyons*. New York: Dover Publications Inc., 1961.

———. *Report on the Lands of the Arid Region of the United States*, 2nd ed. Cambridge: Harvard University Press, 1962.

Reisner, Marc. *Cadillac Desert: The American West and Its Disappearing Water*. New York: Penguin Books, 1993, 1986.

Richardson, Elmo. *Dams, Parks, and Politics: Resource Development and Preservation in the Truman-Eisenhower Era*. Lexington: University Press of Kentucky, 1973.

Robinson, Donald H. *Through the Years in Glacier National Park: An Administrative History*. West Glacier, MT: Glacier Natural History Association, 1960. https://www.nps.gov/parkhistory/online_books/glac/. Accessed May 27, 2017.

Robinson, Michael C. *Water for the West: The Bureau of Reclamation, 1902–1977*. Chicago: Public Works Historical Society, 1979.

Rothman, Hal K. *The Greening of a Nation*. New York: Harcourt Brace Inc., 1998.

———. *Preserving Different Pasts: The American National Monuments*. Urbana: University of Illinois Press, 1989.

Runte, Alfred. *National Parks: The American Experience*, 2nd ed. Lincoln: University of Nebraska Press, 1989.

Schulte, Stephen C. *Wayne Aspinall and the Shaping of the American West*. Boulder: University Press of Colorado, 2002.

Sellars, Richard West. *Preserving Nature in the National Parks: A History*. New Haven: Yale University Press, 1997.

Shankland, Robert. *Steven Mather of the National Parks*. New York: Alfred Knopf, 1970.

Shepherd, Jeffrey. *We Are an Indian Nation: A History of the Hualapai People*. Tucson: University of Arizona Press, 2010.

Smith, Thomas G. *Green Republican: John Saylor and the Preservation of America's Wilderness*. Pittsburgh: University of Pittsburgh Press, 2006.

———. *Stewart Udall: Steward of the Land*. Albuquerque: University of New Mexico Press, 2017.

Smythe, William E. *The Conquest of Arid America*. Seattle: University of Washington Press, 1969. Originally published by Harper, 1899, 1905.

Stanton, Robert Brewster. *Colorado River Controversies*. New York: Dodd, Mead & Company, 1932.

———. *Down the Colorado*. Edited by Dwight L. Smith. Norman: University of Oklahoma Press, 1965.

Steen, Harold K. *The US Forest Service: A Centennial History*. Seattle: University of Washington Press, 2004.

Stegner, Wallace. *Beyond the Hundredth Meridian: John Wesley Powell and the Second Opening of the West*. New York: Houghton Mifflin Company, 1954.

Stevens, Joseph E. *Hoover Dam*. Norman: University of Oklahoma Press, 1988.

Stevens, Larry. *The Colorado River in Grand Canyon: A Guide*, 3rd ed. Flagstaff, AZ: Red Lake Books, 1990.

Sturgeon, Stephen C. *The Politics of Western Water: The Congressional Career of Wayne Aspinall*. Tucson: University of Arizona Press, 2002.

Summit, April R. *Contested Waters: An Environmental History of the Colorado River*. Boulder: University Press of Colorado, 2013.

Terrell, John U. *The Western Web: A Chronological Narrative of the Case Against the State of Arizona and the Bureau of Reclamation in the Long Fight to Defeat the Proposed Multi-Billion Dollar Central Arizona Project*, vol I & II. Los Angeles: Colorado River Association, 1949–1952.

Turner, Tom. *David Brower: The Making of the Environmental Movement*. Berkeley: University of California Press, 2015.

Udall, Morris K. *Education of a Congressman: The Newsletters of Morris K. Udall*. New York: Bobbs-Merrill Company, Inc., 1972.

———. *Too Funny to Be President*. New York: Henry Holt and Co., 1988.

Udall, Stewart L. *The Myths of August: A Personal Exploration of Our Tragic Cold War Affair with the Atom*. New York: Random House, 1994.

———. *The Quiet Crisis*. New York: Avon Books, 1963.

———. *The Quiet Crisis and the Next Generation*, 2nd ed. Salt Lake City: Peregrine Smith Books, 1988.

US Department of the Interior. *The Bureau of Reclamation: History Essays from the Centennial Symposium V. 1 and 2*. Progressive Management Publications, 2017.

Ward, Evan R. *Border Oasis: Water and the Political Ecology of the Colorado River Delta, 1940–1975*. Tucson: University of Arizona Press, 2003.

Warne, William E. *The Bureau of Reclamation*. New York: Praeger Publishers Inc., 1973.

Waters, Frank. *The Colorado*. New York: Holt, Rinehart and Winston, 1946.

Webb, Roy. *If We Had A Boat: Green River Explorers, Adventurers, and Runners*. Salt Lake City: University of Utah Press, 1986.

White, Richard. *"It's Your Misfortune and None of My Own": A New History of the American West*. Norman: University of Oklahoma Press, 1991.

Wiley, Peter, and Roger Gottlieb. *Empires in the Sun: The Rise of the New American West*. Tucson: University of Arizona Press, 1982.

Wirth, Conrad. *Parks, Politics, and the People*. Norman: University of Oklahoma Press, 1980.

Worster, Donald. *A Passion for Nature: The Life of John Muir*. New York: Oxford University Press, 2008.

———. *A River Running West: The Life of John Wesley Powell*. New York: Oxford University Press, 2001.

———. *Rivers of Empire: Water, Aridity, and the Growth of the American West*. New York: Pantheon Books, 1985.

Wyss, Robert. *The Man Who Built the Sierra Club: A Life of David Brower*. New York: Columbia University Press, 2016.

Electronic Sources

"About." *A Fierce Green Fire*. http://www.afiercegreenfire.com/about.html. Accessed May 19, 2018.

American Rivers. americanrivers.org.

"Cape Disappointment State Park." *Washington State Parks*. https://parks.state. wa.us/486/Cape-Disappointment. Accessed June 29, 2018.

"Central Arizona Project." *Killing the Colorado*. ProPublica, Inc. https://projects.pro-publica.org/killing-the-colorado/explore-the-river#central-arizona-project.

Deadbeat Dams. deadbeatdams.com.

EarthTalk. "*A Fierce Green Fire* (New Film)." *Scientific American*. https://www.scien-tificamerican.com/article/a-fierce-green-fire-new-film/. Accessed July 14, 2018.

"*A Fierce Green Fire*: About the Film." PBS. http://www.pbs.org/wnet/ americanmasters/a-fierce-green-fire-about-the-film/2924/. Accessed July 14, 2018.

Gelt, Joe. "Sharing Colorado River Water: History, Public Policy and the Colorado River Compact." Tucson: University of Arizona, Water Resource Research Center, 1997. https://wrrc.arizona.edu/publications/arroyo-newsletter/sharing-colorado-river-water-history-public-policy-and-colorado-river. Accessed May 21, 2018.

Glen Canyon Institute. glencanyon.org.

Ingram, Jeff. *Celebrating the Grand Canyon* (blog). 2009–present. http://gcfutures. blogspot.com/. Accessed July 8, 2018.

National Park Service. *Glen Canyon National Recreation Area*. "Lee's Ferry History." https://www.nps.gov/glca/learn/historyculture/leesferryhistory.htm. Accessed July 3, 2013.

"Nature, Culture and History at the Grand Canyon." Grand Canyon History. Arizona State University. http://grandcanyonhistory.clas.asu.edu/. Accessed May 16, 2018.

Sierra Club. "Celebrating 125 Years." https://www.sierraclub.org/anniversary. Accessed May 12, 2018.

———. "The Hetch Hetchy Restoration Task Force." http://vault.sierraclub.org/ca/ hetchhetchy/hetch_hetchy_task_force.html. Accessed May 18, 2018.

Surveyors of the American West, Robert Brewster Stanton's Field Notes 1889–1890. New York Public Library, 2001. http://digital.nypl.org/surveyors. Accessed July 9, 2018.

"Timeline." *The Life and Legacy of Rachel Carson*. http://www.rachelcarson.org/ TimelineList.aspx, accessed November 28, 2018.

"Tucson's Stake in Arizona's Reclamation Future." *Western Waters Digital Library*. http://westernwaters.org/record/view/84979. Accessed July 22, 2018.

USA National Wild and Scenic Rivers System. https://www.rivers.gov/. Accessed May 10, 2018.

US Bureau of Reclamation. "Colorado River Compact of 1922." https://www.usbr.gov/lc/region/pao/pdfiles/crcompct.pdf. Accessed July 3, 2018.

US Bureau of Reclamation. "The Men Who Built the Dam." https://www.usbr.gov/lc/phoenix/AZ100/1910/men_built_the_dam.html. Accessed May 17, 2018.

"Washington's Long Beach Peninsula." https://funbeach.com/shipwrecks-graveyards-pacific/. Accessed June 29, 2018.

Films/Videos

American Rivers. *Leave It as It Is: The Colorado River in the Grand Canyon.* American Rivers.org. April 6, 2015. https://www.youtube.com/watch?v=P_KD0SBQ4YU.

American Rivers. *Oppose the Grand Canyon Escalade!* August 20, 2016. American Rivers.org. https://www.youtube.com/watch?v=ULS96Lv2kXA.

Canyon Light. *A River Ran Through It, Draining Lake Powell.* July 29, 2016. https://www.youtube.com/watch?v=5eCytLfHaPw. Accessed June 28, 2018.

Fraser, Mark, James Fox, and Boris Zubov. *The Good Fight: The Martin Litton Story.* 2010. https://www.videoproject.com/The-Good-Fight-The-Martin-Litton-Story.html. Accessed June 28, 2018.

Hott, Lawrence and Diane Garey. *Wild by Law: The Rise of Environmentalism and the Creation of the Wilderness Act.* 1991.

Kitchell, Mark and Celia Kitchell. "Act 1: Conservation." *A Fierce Green Fire: The Battle for a Living Planet.* 2012. https://www.youtube.com/watch?v=u_fW_7W-zSXk. Accessed May 18, 2018.

McBride, Pete. *Colorado River: I Am Red.* April 16, 2013. American Rivers.org. https://www.youtube.com/watch?v=mqYcC7jEe44.

Reisner, Marc. *Cadillac Desert: An American Nile.* Chicago, IL: Home Vision Select, 1997. https://www.youtube.com/watch?v=vKIxKE-Duac. Accessed July 8, 2018.

"Sierra Club Is Celebrating 125 Years." NationalSierraClub. May 26, 2017. https://www.youtube.com/watch?v=hwa82wGFuks>. Accessed May 12, 2018.

Scott, Doug. *Forever Wild Film.* http://www.foreverwildfilm.com/doug_scott.html. Accessed July 15, 2018.

US Bureau of Reclamation. *Operation Glen Canyon.* 1961, https://www.youtube.com/watch?v=dSghEGsBqzM. Accessed August 11, 2018.

When the Sierra Club Saved Grand Canyon. American Masters, PBS. April 2, 2014. https://www.youtube.com/watch?v=qKFPsnaPjPE. Accessed May 12, 2018.

Where Grand Canyon Rivers Converge, Economic and Preservation Needs Collide. PBS News Hour. June 3, 2015. https://www.youtube.com/watch?v=Xu47pPpXLFA. Accessed May 12, 2018.

Theses and Dissertations

Buchholtz, C. W. "The Historical Dichotomy of Use and Preservation in Glacier National Park." Master's thesis, University of Montana, Missoula, 1969. https://

scholarworks.umt.edu/cgi/viewcontent.cgi?article=3566&context=etd. Accessed May 27, 2018.

Dickey, Sonia. "Sacrilege in Dinétah: Native Encounters with Glen Canyon Dam." PhD diss., University of New Mexico, 2011.

Mayo, Dwight Eugene. "Arizona and the Colorado River Compact." Master's thesis, Arizona State University, 1964.

Neel, Susan Rhoades. "Irreconcilable Differences: Reclamation, Preservation, and the Origins of the Echo Park Dam Controversy." PhD diss., University of California, Los Angeles, 1990.

Oppedahl, R. James. "Conflicts Between Resource Development and Preservation at Glacier National Park." Master's thesis, University of Montana, 1976. https://scholarworks.umt.edu/cgi/viewcontent.cgi?article=9671&context=etd. Accessed May 27, 2018.

Pearson, Byron E. "People above Scenery: The Struggle over the Grand Canyon Dams, 1963–1968." PhD diss., University of Arizona, 1998.

Schilling, Ron K. "Indians and Eagles: The Struggle Against Orme Dam." Master's thesis, Prescott College, 1998.

Senecah, Susan Louise. "The Environmental Discourse of David Brower: Using Advocacy Advertising to Save the Grand Canyon." PhD diss., University of Minnesota, 1992.

Stack, Garrett. "The Sierra Club and the Rhetorical Sublime." PhD diss., Carnegie Mellon University, 2017.

United States Government Documents, Publications, and Reports

Congressional Quarterly. 1964–1966.

Congressional Record. 1919, 1960–1968.

Ives, Joseph C. *Report Upon the Colorado River of the West*. Washington, DC: Government Printing Office, 1861.

LaRue, E. C. *Colorado River and Its Utilization: Water-Supply Paper 395*. Washington, DC: Government Printing Office, 1916.

LaRue, E. C. *Water Power and Flood Control of Colorado River Below Green River Utah: Water-Supply Paper 556*. Washington, DC: Government Printing Office, 1925.

Leopold, Luna. *USGS Circular 410: Probability Analysis Applied to a Water Problem*. Washington, DC: Government Printing Office, 1958.

National Academy of Sciences. *Water and Choice in the Colorado Basin: An Example of Alternatives in Water Management*. Washington, DC: Printing and Publishing Office, National Academy of Sciences, 1968.

Public Law 90-537, title III sec. 303 (a). Colorado River Basin Project 890. https://www.gpo.gov/fdsys/pkg/STATUTE-82/pdf/STATUTE-82-Pg885-3.pdf#page=1. Accessed July 5, 2018.

US Congress, House. Committee on Interior and Insular Affairs. *Central Arizona Project: Hearings before the Committee on Interior and Insular Affairs*. 82nd Cong. 1st sess. 1951.

US Congress, House. Committee on Interior and Insular Affairs. *Colorado River Basin Project*. 90th Cong. 2nd sess. 1968. Report No. 1312.

US Congress, House. Subcommittee on Irrigation and Reclamation of the Committee on Interior and Insular Affairs. *Central Arizona Project: Hearings before the Subcommittee on Irrigation and Reclamation of the Committee on Interior and Insular Affairs*. 81st Cong. 1st sess. 1949.

US Congress, House. Subcommittee on Irrigation and Reclamation of the Committee on Interior and Insular Affairs. *Lower Colorado Basin Project: Hearings before the Subcommittee on Irrigation and Reclamation of the Committee on Interior and Insular Affairs*. 89th Cong. 1st sess. 1965.

US Congress, House. Subcommittee on Irrigation and Reclamation of the Committee on Interior and Insular Affairs. *Lower Colorado Basin Project: Hearings before the Subcommittee on Irrigation and Reclamation of the Committee on Interior and Insular Affairs*. 89th Cong. 2nd sess. 1966.

US Congress, House. Subcommittee on Irrigation and Reclamation of the Committee on Interior and Insular Affairs. *Lower Colorado Basin Project: Hearings before the Subcommittee on Irrigation and Reclamation of the Committee on Interior and Insular Affairs*. 90th Cong. 1st sess. 1967.

US Congress, Senate. S. 75. *A Bill Authorizing the Construction, Operation and Maintenance of a Dam and Incidental Works in the Main Stream of the Colorado River at Bridge Canyon, together with Certain Appurtenant Dams and Canals, and for other Purposes*. 82nd Cong., 1st sess. 1951.

US Congress, Senate. Subcommittee on Irrigation and Reclamation of the Committee on Interior and Insular Affairs. *Colorado River Storage Project: Hearings before the Subcommittee on Irrigation and Reclamation of the Committee on Interior and Insular Affairs*. 84th Cong. 1st sess. 1955.

US Congress, Senate. Subcommittee on Public Lands of the Committee on Interior and Insular Affairs. *Bridge Canyon Dam and Central Arizona Project: Hearings before the Subcommittee on Public Lands of the Committee on Interior and Insular Affairs*. 80th Cong. 1st sess. 1947.

US Department of the Interior. *Lake Powell: Jewel of the Colorado*. Washington, DC: Government Printing Office, 1965.

US Department of the Interior. "National Park Service Appendix to Pacific Southwest Water Plan." August 1963.

US Department of the Interior. "Pacific Southwest Water Plan Report." January 1964.

US Department of the Interior, Bureau of Reclamation. "Bridge and Marble Canyon Dams and Their Relationship to Grand Canyon National Park and Monument." 1964.

US Department of the Interior, Bureau of Reclamation. *The Colorado River: A Natural Menace Becomes a National Resource: A Comprehensive Report on the Development of the Water Resources of the Colorado River Basin for Irrigation, Power Production, and Other Beneficial Uses in Arizona, California, Colorado, Nevada, New Mexico, Utah, and Wyoming*. March 1946.

US Department of the Interior, Bureau of Reclamation. "Memorandum Report on Reconnaissance Studies, Marble Canyon–Kanab Creek Power Development." Boulder City, NV, October 1961.

US Department of the Interior, Bureau of Reclamation. "Preliminary Report on Colorado River–Phoenix Diversion Project, Arizona." March 1944.

US Department of the Interior, Bureau of Reclamation. "United Western Investigation, Interim Report on Reconnaissance." Salt Lake City, UT, 1951.

US Department of the Interior, Information Service. "Mathematics Applied to United States Water Supply Problems." July 19, 1959.

US Department of the Interior. National Park Service. "Final Wilderness Recommendation Update: 2010 (DRAFT) Grand Canyon National Park Arizona." https://www.nps.gov/grca/learn/management/upload/Draft_2010Final_Wilderness_Rec. pdf. Accessed July 6, 2018.

US Environmental Protection Agency. *Laws and Regulations*. "Summary of the Clean Air Act." https://www.epa.gov/laws-regulations/summary-clean-air-act. Accessed July 8, 2018.

Unpublished Sources

Brower, Barbara. Correspondence with author. December 19, 1997; January 9, 1998.

Harvey, Mark. "Paying the Taxpayer: The Internal Revenue Service and the Environmental Movement." Paper delivered at the biannual conference of the American Society for Environmental History, Baltimore, MD, March 6, 1997.

Harza Engineering Company. "Preliminary Planning Report: Colorado River Development within the State of Arizona: Colorado River Projects." Chicago, IL, December 15, 1958.

Jett, Stephen. Correspondence with author. December 28, 1997; February 6, 1998; January 16, 2015; April 24, May 2, August 8, 11, 2018.

———. "The Grand Canyon Dams Fight." n.d. Unpublished manuscript.

———. "Navajos Enter Fight Against Grand Canyon Dams." August 1966. Unpublished manuscript.

Index

Aandahl, Fred, 82
Adams, Ansel, 146, 219, 304n45
Akimel, O'odham Tribe, 205, 209
Albright, Horace, 29, 31, 36, 60, 141–42, 174, 218
Aldo Leopold Foundation, 308n18
Alexander, Les, 185–86, 232
Allott, Gordon, 243
"America the Bureautiful" (song), 195–96
American Planning and Civic Association, 58, 62, 73
American Public Power Association, 177
Anderson, Clinton, 75, 197, 238
Anderson, Harry, 185
Antiquities Act (1906), 120
"Appreciations" (Brower, K.), 251
Arizona, 32, 42; and CAP (see Central Arizona Project); Colorado River Compact and, 21–22, 25, 34; and Colorado River dams, 5, 7, 11, 22, 81–84, 86; and CRSP, 77–78; and LCRBP, 207, 227, 234; and PSWP, 131, 148–49; water rights, 33–34, 46, 115–17, 253–54
Arizona Council of Conservationists, 139
Arizona Daily Star, 223
Arizona Game and Fish Department (AZGF), 139
Arizona Game Protective Association (AGPA), 139, 188, 196, 198
Arizona Highline Canal, 22, 23, 24, 34
Arizona Interstate Stream Commission (AISC), 76, 91, 185

Arizona Power Authority (APA), 83–86, 90–91, 95, 126, 184, 248
Arizona Republic, 77–78, 121, 195, 223, 224
Arizona State Engineering Commission, 22
Arizona v. California (1963), 93, 96, 116, 254
Arizona Women's Club, 223
Ashurst, Henry, 14–15, 17, 33
Aspinall, Wayne, xvii, 88, 102–3, 112, 179, 253; and Bridge Canyon/ Hualapai Dam, 136, 255; and CAP, 67, 98, 127, 132, 168, 171, 238, 240, 242, 244–45, 254, 257, 258; environmentalists and, 173, 208, 212, 216; and LCRBP, 157, 165, 197, 200, 202, 207, 225–27, 231, 232, 234, 237
Atlantic Monthly, 160, 176, 180, 210
Atomic Energy Commission, 101, 149, 201
Audubon Magazine, 177, 186, 187
Audubon Society, 168, 172, 177, 186–87

Babbitt, David, 7
Baggley, George F., 54, 55
"Battle Ads" (Sierra Club), xviii, 211, 214–18, 215, 227, 229, 230, 240–41, 258, 301n5, 302n25
Baum, Frank, 13, 15, 17, 18
Beal, Merrill, 123, 222
Beard, Dan, xi
Bears Ears National Monument, 269
Berry, Philip, 89–90
Bible, Alan, 85
Big Thompson Project, 26, 306n65

Biophilist (newsletter), 195

Birdseye, Claude, 23

Black Canyon, 22, 26

Black Mesa, 271

Boulder Canyon, 23

Boulder Canyon Act (1928), 33, 34

Boulder Dam, 6, 25–27, 28, 115. *See also* Hoover Dam

Bradley, David, 146, 160, 186

Bradley, Harold, 146, 191

Bradley, Richard, 74, *191*; and dams in Grand Canyon, 146–48, 149, 159–60, 176–77, 179–80, 186, 210, 227, 259, 262; El Tovar symposium and, 192–93, 194; and *Reader's Digest* article, 187–88, 189

Bradley, William, 176

Brandenburg v. Ohio (1969), 154

Bridge and Marble Canyon Dams and Their Relationship to Grand Canyon NP and NM (Interior Department), 149

Bridge Canyon Dam, *ii, xx*, 23, *32*, 43, *44*, 51–53, *55*, 68–69, *206*; Arizona plan and, 31, 81–83, 91; CAP and, 116, 118, 132, 240–42, 257; and Grand Canyon NP and NM, 28–31, 35, 39–41, 47–49, 77, 103–4, 110–11, 141, 158, 174–75, 178, 193, 216–18, 233, 258, 260; Hualapai Nation and, 54, 61, 84–85, 105, 172–73, 183–86, 192, 203; LCRBP and, 161–62, 198, 200; opposition to, 57–58, 61–62, 147; PSWP and, 121–23, 134–39, 144–45, 255; Sierra Club and, 49, 51, 58–60, 64, 76, 98. *See also* Hualapai Dam

Brookhart, Smith, 95

Brower, David, xi, xvii, 11, 35, 94, *107*, 136, 154, *197*, 209, 247; and "Battle Ads," xviii, 211, 216–18, 249–50; and Bridge Canyon/Hualapai Dam, 59, 76, 209, 240; and dams in Grand Canyon, 120, 139, 170, 176, 186, 212, 214, 260, 269; and Dinosaur

controversy, 73–74, 79; El Tovar symposium and, 189–91, 194; and Glen Canyon Dam, 78, 106–8; lobbying by 89–90

Brower, Kenneth, xiii, 251

Brown, Edmund "Pat," 119, 126, 131, 143, 150

Brown, Keith, 119

Brown v. Board of Education (1954), 38, 153

Bryant, Harold, 39, 54

Burns, Hilda, 190, 196

Burton, Laurence J., 204

Bush, Nellie T., 27, *28*

Butcher, Devereaux, 57, 177

Cadillac Desert (movie), 251

Cadillac Desert (Reisner, book), 221, 251

Calhoun, John C., Jr., 149

California, 10, 42, 103; and CAP (*see* Central Arizona Project); Colorado River Compact and, 21–22; and Colorado River dams, 5, 19, 22, 26; and Columbia River diversion/importation, 46–47; and LCRBP, 226–27, 233–34; and MCKC, 90–91; and PSWP, 126, 142, 150–51; water rights, 21, 46, 115–16, 143, 156, 233, 245, 253

Callison, Charles, 168, 172

Cameron, Ralph, xv, 8, *9*, *12*, 13, 15, 17, 18

Cammerer, Arno, 36, 60

Cape Disappointment, WA, 225

Carlin, Alan, 160–61, 169, 198, 201–2, 259, 261–62

Carr, James, 93, 126

Carson, Rachel, 36, 151, 154–55

Carver, John, 124, 135

Cataract Canyon, 13

Caulfield, Henry, 139

Celebrating the Grand Canyon (Ingram, blog), 251–52

Central Arizona Project (CAP), xi,

253–58, Arizona-California relationship and, xv, xviii, 27, 46–47, 52, 66–67, 92–93, 103, 116–20, 128, 152, 156, 232–34; Arizona plan and, 84, 89, 90–91, 97–98; Congress and, 33, 63, 65–68, 126–27, 132, 143–44, 156, 165, 182–83, 207, 224–27, 231–32, 237–38, 242–45, 247, 306n85; hearings on, 41, 46–47, 52, 61, 75–78, 140–41, 167–73, 198–201; Hualapai Nation and, 202–4, 208–9, 260, 270–71; Navajo Nation and, 192, 205, 260, 270–71; opposition to, 62, 81–82, 160, 171–72; Stewart Udall and, 98–99, 102–3, 131, 155, 239–40, 256–58

Central Arizona Project Association, 76, 91, 148, 160, 177, 194–95

Central Valley Project, 26, 32

Chaffey, George, 5

Chandler, A. J., 7

Chandler, Otis, 150

Chapman, Oscar, 54, 65, 72–73

Chicago Daily News, 68

Christian Science Monitor, 188

civil rights, 37–38, 153; Native Americans and, 86–87, 105, 172–73, 184–86, 223

Clean Air Act (1970), 272

Clemons, Phil, 188

Coconino Dam, 43, 44, 134

Cohen, Sheldon, 219, 220

Cold War, 46, 63, 72, 110, 153

Colorado, 5, 19, 21–22, 62, 98, 142, 230

Colorado Mountain Club, 188

Colorado Open Space Coordinating Council (COSCC), 173, 176, 188, 210, 227

Colorado River, xx, 5; and dams in Grand Canyon, xv, 13, 17–18, 42, 57, 62, 160; hydroelectric potential of, xii, xiv, 6–8, 45, 47, 83, 137; within Grand Canyon, 19, 50, 95, 170, 214, 216, 248, 261

Colorado River, a Natural Menace

Becomes a Natural Resource, The (USBR), 42–43, 50–51

Colorado River Basin, 6, 19, 20, 41–43, 47, 99, 171; Colorado River Compact and, 21–22, 71, 98, 103, 253; lower basin states, xii, xv, 25, 115–16, 143; upper basin states, 62, 73, 165, 237, 254. *See also* water rights

Colorado River Basin Project, 247, 248, 263

Colorado River Commission, 31

Colorado River Compact (1922), 21–22, 25, 34, 73, 103, 115, 165, 253

Colorado River Storage Project (CRSP), 62, 71, 72–79, 95, 102

Colorado River Storage Project Act (1956), 94

Colorado-Verde Project, 22, 23–24, 24, 34, 41, 43

Colter, Fred, 21, 22, 34

Columbia Basin Project, 26

Columbia River, 32; water diversion/importation from, xvii, 46–47, 133–34, 149–50, 152, 162, 165, 167–68, 171, 182, 199, 225, 236–37, 243, 255, 256. *See also* Pacific Northwest

Congressional Record, 204, 223

conservation(ists), xix–xx, 9–10; and dams in Grand Canyon, 48, 51, 58, 61–62, 68, 69, 75, 120, 137; IRS and, 79, 82, 89, 104, 111, 148, 219, 253; lobbying by, 74, 80–81; political power of, 76–77, 98, 104; pro-dam, 52–53, 139–40, 188; and Progressive Conservation, 10, 212, 238; and Rainbow Bridge, 94–95. *See also* environmentalists; preservation(ists)

Conservation Law Society, 137

"Dam Foolishness" (article), 68

Davis, Arthur Powell, 6

Davis, John, 222

Davis Dam, 118, 200–201

Deadbeat Dams (Beard), xi

Debler, E. B., 31, 41
Democratic National Convention, 87
Denver Post, 147, 188
DeVoto, Bernard, 65
Diamond Creek, 22
Dingell, John, 196, 224
Dinosaur National Monument: dams in, xviii, 11, 36–37, 60, 62, 260; and dams controversy, 71–75, 76, 78, 79, 82, 91, 106
Dobyns, Henry, 203–4, 205, 260
Dominy, Floyd, xvii, 35, 92, 132, 147, 157–58, 219; and Bridge Canyon/ Hualapai Dam, 70, 97–98, 174, 242; and David Brower, xi, 217; and CAP, 131–33, 156, 167–68, 187–88, 194; and LCRBP, 198–99; and Marble Canyon Dam, 97, 238; and Rainbow Bridge, 94–95, 179
Doty, Dale, 93
Douglas, William O., 210
Downey, Sheridan, 46
Dreyfus, Daniel, 274
Drury, Newton, 36–38, 37, 72, 136, 247–48, 282n6; and dams in Grand Canyon, 39–41, 45, 47–55, 57, 60–61, 213
Dyer, Pauline, 114

Echo Park: dams in, 36, 62, 65, 73, 74, 78, 108, 204. *See also* Dinosaur National Monument
Eisenhower, Dwight D., 68, 78, 87, 257
Elson, Roy, 197, 219–20
El Tovar symposium, 189–94, 259
Ely, Northcutt "Mike," xvii, 117, 143, 166, 189, 190–92, 229–34, 256
Emergency Committee on Natural Resources, 73
Encounters with the Archdruid (McPhee), 251
Ensign, Jean, 194
environmental historians, xvi, 16, 71, 152, 231, 238, 249–51, 252, 263

environmentalists, xix–xx, 19, 70, 72–73, 212–14, 273; activism of, xxii, 175–77, 186–87; Congress and, 168–70, 252, 256, 272; and dams in Grand Canyon, xvi, 18, 45–46, 138–40, 173–74, 178–80, 196, 227, 250, 263–64; El Tovar symposium and, 189–94; and Glen Canyon Dam, 71, 78–79, 108; Native Americans and, 202–4, 208, 228, 270; Stewart Udall and, 88–89, 127, 239. *See also* conservation(ists); preservation(ists)
Escalante National Monument, 71

Fannin, Paul, 91, 131, 243, 245
Federal Power Acts (1920, 1921, 1935), 11, 81, 82, 85, 138, 178
Federal Power Commission (FPC), 81, 89, 120, 128; and Bridge Canyon/ Hualapai Dam, 29, 31, 171, 183; MCKC hearings, 90–91, 93, 95–97, 99, 289n56
Federal Regulation of Lobbying Act (1946), 79, 80, 111, 172, 220, 222
Ferris Water-Power bill, 11, 15
Fierce Green Fire, A (film), 251, 265–68
Fish and Wildlife Coordination Act (1934), 273
Flaming Gorge, 62
Flathead River, 41
Flood Control Act (1944), 122
Foley, Thomas, 167–68, 177, 199, 207, 224, 226
Fortune (magazine), 159
Four Corners Power Plant, 271–72
Fox, Stephen, 14, 79
Francis, Sharon, 88, 235
Freeman, Mander & Gossage, 211
Fryingpan–Arkansas Mountain Diversion Project, 244

Gabrielson, Ira, 57–58, 73, 249
Garrison, Lemuel, 64–65

General Federation of Women's Clubs, 223
General Grant National Park, 279n19
Gila River, 116
Glacier National Park, 41, 60, 62
Glacier View Dam, 41, 45, 50, 53
Glen Canyon Dam, xi, xii, xx, 23, 62, 71–72, 89, 90, 158, 159, 236; environmentalists and, 74, 78, 106–8, 120, 170, 263
Goddard, Sam, 122, 189
Goldwater, Barry, 119, 208, 216; and CAP, 116, 121, 126, 168; El Tovar symposium and, 189, 192, 193
Good Fight: The Martin Litton Story, The (film), 251
Gordon, Kermit, 149
Gorman, Howard, 228
Goss, Floyd, 241–42
Gossage, Howard, 211, 229
Grand Canyon, The Ever-Changing Giant (movie), 223
Grand Canyon Electric Power Company, 7
Grand Canyoneers, 210
Grand Canyon National Park and National Monument, xi, xiii, xv, 8, 13–14, 17–19, 30, 31, 44, 178, 246; national park enlargement, 40, 114, 120, 196, 238, 240, 242, 244; hydroelectric potential in, xii, xiv, 23, 42, 83
Grand Canyon National Park Enlargement Act (1975), 247–48
Grand Canyon National Park Establishment Act (1919), 18, 178
Grand Canyon of the Living Colorado (Nash), 249–50
Grand Canyon Task Force, 145, 146, 160, 176, 210
Grand Coulee Dam, 26
Grand Staircase–Escalante National Monument, 269
Grand Wash Cliffs, 17, 120, 247
Grant, Ulysses, III, 73–74, 76

Graves, Henry S., xv, 14–17, *16*, 18, 19
Green Fire, Aldo Leopold and a Land Ethic for Our Time (film), 308n18
Green River, xx, 36, 62, 71, 72
Griffin, Frank, 175

Hanna, Bert, 194
Harper's (magazine), 65, 180, 302n25
Hartzog, George, 134–36, 174–75, 222
Harvey, Mark, 36
Harza Engineering Company, 83–84
Havasu Creek, 13, 40
Havasupai Falls, 13
Havasupai Tribe, 61, 241
Hayden, Carl, xvii, 87, 101–2, 115, 122, 220, 242, *245*; and CAP, xv, 33, 46, 52, 65, 68–69, 97, 116–19, 126, 130, 131, 140, 143–44, 156, 238, 244, 247, 306n85; and dams in Grand Canyon, 13, 17–18, 124, 135, 136, 161, 242–43
Hetch Hetchy Valley, xi, xv, 9–11, 14, 108, 146, 218; precedent of, 15, 16, 29, 38–39, 60, 71
Highline Reclamation Association, 22
Hildebrand, Alex, 51
Hobbs, Joseph, 95
Hoehn, William, 201–2
Holifield, Chet, 150
Holum, Kenneth, 149–150, 161, 199
Hoover, Herbert, 21, 28, 67
Hoover Dam, xii, 103, 109, 110, 118, 200–201. *See also* Boulder Dam
Hopi Tribe, 205
Hosmer, Craig, 156, 170, 200, 201, 202, 220, 226
Houston, Charles, 38
Hualapai Dam, *ii*, 171, 184, *203*, 206, 209, 217, 223, 241, 243, 248, 260. *See also* Bridge Canyon Dam
Hualapai Nation, 196, 202–4, 270, 271; and Bridge Canyon/Hualapai Dam, 54, 61, 84–85, 105, 170–71, 172–73, 183–86, 192, 203, 209, 223, 241, 248
Hunt, George W. P., 21, 22

hydroelectric power, 6, 22, 62; alternatives to, 112, 147, 149–50, 168–69, 174, 186, 202, 237; dams and, xii, 109, 110, 121, 132, 178. *See also* Colorado River

Ickes, Harold, 27, 31, 41, 71
Imperial Valley, 5, 19
Indian Reorganization Act (1934), 85, 86
Ingram, Jeff, 161, 251–52, 269; El Tovar symposium and, 189–90, 194; and LCRBP, 198, 200–201, 261
Internal Revenue Service (IRS): and conservationists, 82, 89, 111, 172, 253; lobbying regulations, 79–80; and Sierra Club, xviii–xix, 90, 125, 219–22, 241, 262, 264
Ives, Joseph Christmas, 1, 8
Izaak Walton League, xviii, 68–69, 138–39, 168

Jackson, Henry, xvii, 242, 275; and CAP, xviii, 177, 238, 242–43, 258; and Columbia River diversion/importation, 143, 150, 156, 165, 224–25, 256, 273; and NEPA, 162–64, 274–75; and PSWP, 133–34, 151
James, Harlean, 57–58, 62
Jasperson, Robert, 137–38
Jensen, Joe, 150
Jett, Stephen, xiii, 192, 204–5, 228, 241, 260
Johnson, Lady Bird, 154, 235–36, 245, 247
Johnson, Lyndon, 38, 87, 88, 129–30, 153, 245; and CAP, 142–43, 152, 234–35, 238, 244, 247
Johnson, Rich, 126, 156, 194, 197, 209, 260
Jones, Paul, 97
Judd, Ashley, 265
J. Walter Thompson Company, 189–90, 196

Kaibab National Forest, 196, 198
Kanab Creek, 3, 7, 42, 43, 92, 187
Kanab Creek Power Development Project, 42, 43. *See also* Marble Canyon–Kanab Creek Project
Kennedy, John F., 87, 110, 119, 120, 128–29, 153
Kimball, Thomas L., 139–40, 198, 260
Kings Canyon National Park, 50, 51
Kitchell, Mark, 265
Knight, Bruce, 169
Kolb, Emery, 23
Krech, Shepard, 270
Krug, Julius, 46, 47–48, 52, 57, 58, 92
Kuchel, Thomas, 119, 126, 143, 156–57, 221

Lake Havasu, 41
Lake Mead, xii, 33, 40, 107, 248
Lake Mead National Recreation Area, 84, 247
Lake Powell, 94, 107, 112, 157–58, 179, 201, 227, 241, 248
Lake Powell: Jewel of the Colorado (Interior Dept.), 157–58, 194
Lamm, Richard, 173–74, 176, 186
Lane, Franklin, 13, 15
La Rue, E. C., 19, 22–23, 39
Lava Falls, 149, 193
Lazarus, Arthur, 85
Lee Ferry, 20, 21, 280n41
Lee's Ferry, 17, 20, 23, 71, 120, 244, 247, 280n41, 281n45
Leonard, Richard, 49, 58–59, 63–64, 80–81, 89–90
Leopold, Aldo, 35, 276
Leopold, Luna, 120, 145, 147, 149, 237
Leopold, Madelyn, 169
Leydet, François, 145
Life (magazine), 159, 180, 187, 195
Light, Kenneth, 210
Littell, Norman, 228
Little Colorado River, 24, 43, 44, 58–59, 84, 134

Litton, Martin, xvii, 38, 113–14, *114*, 125, 145, 193, 265, 276

Living Wilderness (magazine), 147

Los Angeles Times, 150, 301n5

Lower Colorado River Basin Project (LCRBP), 161–62, 188; Congress and, 143, 157, 207–8, 224–27, 229–34, 236–37, 273; hearings on, 197–204, 207

Luten, Daniel, 188

Mahon, George, 199

Mammoth Cave National Park, 62

Mandell, Jeff, 210

Mander, Jerry, 211, 214–16, 217, 229, 265, 267

Marble Canyon Dam, xx, 23, 54–55, *56*, 83, 161, *166*, 183, *206*; CAP and, 93, 118, 148, 240; and Grand Canyon NP and NM, 43, 90, 103–4, 149, 158, 238; National Park Service and, 91–92, 95; LCRBP and, 198, 200–202, 207; Navajo Nation and, 84–86, 184–85, 192, 205; opposition to, 120, 147, 186; PSWP and, 121–22, 144, 151, 255; Sierra Club and, 91, 97, 113, 269

Marble Canyon–Kanab Creek Project (MCKC), 43, *44*, 47–48, 54–56, 92–93, 104, 137; Los Angeles plan and, 81, 90–91; opposition to, 45, 46, 48–49, 57, 93, 95, 123, 145

Marble Canyon National Monument, 247

March, Frederic, 178

Marks, Royal, 85, 170–71, 172, 183, 185

Marsh, Edward, 95

Marshall, Thurgood, 38

Martin, Calvin, 270

McFarland, Ernest, 33, 34, 41, 46, 52, 61, 65, 130

McKay, Douglas, 73

McKee, Edwin, 39–40

McLaughlin, John, 81–82, 134–35

McPhee, John, 251

Mead, Elwood, 29, 36, 141–42, 174

Merriam, John, 40

Metropolitan Water District of Southern California (MWD), 27, 150, 177

Mexico, 21, 33

Moeur, Benjamin B., 27, 233

Montana, 41

Montana Power Company, 50

Mooney Falls, 13

Moss, Frank, 143, 179

Moss, Laurence, 161, 198, 202, 259, 261–62

Mount Olympus National Monument, 13

Moyers, Bill, 131

Muir, John, 9–11, 108, 212, 214–15, 229

Murdock, John, 45, 52, 65, 66–67, 68, 103

Muskie, Edmund, 273

Myers, Harold, 134

Nash, Roderick, 14, 250–51, 269

National Congress of American Indians, 84

National Environmental Policy Act (NEPA) (1970), xi, xvi, xix, 164, 252, 274–75

National Parks (magazine), 82, 96, 124, 139

National Parks Association (NPA), xviii, 73, 104; and Bridge Canyon/Hualapai Dam, 57, 61–62, 82; and dams in Grand Canyon, 76, 96, 127, 168, 178, 250; and MCKC, 57, 93, 95; and PWSP, 124–25, 138, 140, 144–45

National Park Service (NPS), 62, 189, 213; and Bridge Canyon/Hualapai Dam, 48, 81, 123, 134–35, 175, 222; Bureau of Reclamation and, 29, 31, 35, 36–37, 39–41, 47, 54; and Marble Canyon Dam, 91–92, 95; and MCKC, 81, 92, 123, 137; preservationists and, 11, 17, 135

National Park System: dams in, 41, 60, 62, 74–75, 76, 78, 174, 178; protection of, 71–72, 80–81, 127, 173, 276

National Reclamation Association, 164

National Review, 302n25

National Wildlife Federation (NWF), 138, 139–40, 188, 198, 213, 260

Native Americans, 54, 84–87, 90, 205; and environmentalists, 202–4, 208, 270; and civil rights, 105, 172–73, 184–86, 223. *See also specific tribes*

Natural Resources Council, 51

Navajo Generating Plant, 271–72

Navajo Nation, 270–72; and CAP, 192, 204–5, 207; and Marble Canyon Dam, 84–86, 95, 97, 184–85, 228

Navajo Wildlands (Jett), 241

Neal, Phil, 89–90

Nevada, 21–22, 25, 66, 73, 91, 115, 116, 121

Newlands Reclamation Act (1902), 6

New Mexico, 21–22, 75, 92, 121, 197

New Mexico Wildlife and Conservation Association, 188

Newsweek, 195, 217

New Yorker, 251

New York Times, 122, 159, 180, 186, 188, 221; and "Battle Ads," 211, 214–16, 215, 227

New York Times Co. v. United States (1971), 154

Nicholson, Marjorie, 187

Nixon, Richard, 87, 119

Oakes, John, 122, 159, 211

Olmsted, Frederick Law, Jr., 39–40, 50–51, 53, 57

O'Mahoney, Joseph, 75

Oregon, 47

Outdoor Life (magazine), 195

Outdoor Recreation Resources Review Commission, 88

Owens River, 19

Pacific Northwest, 26, 32, 133, 151, 156, 158, 171, 262. *See also* Columbia River

Pacific Southwest Water Plan (PSWP), 121–24, 122, 130, 134, 150–51; alternatives to, 139, 144–45, 146–48, 149; and Bridge Canyon/Hualapai Dam, 134–39, 255; Bureau of the Budget and, 142, 161–62; conservationists and, 137, 139–40; opposition to, 138, 178; Stewart Udall and, 126, 155, 244

Packard, Fred, 48, 57, 61–63, 73, 75, 76

Paria River, 21, 43, 44, 134, 201

Parker, Rupert, 241

Parker Dam, 26–27, 103, 109, 110, 118, 200–201

Peabody Coal Company, 228

Pierce, Caroline, 223

Pima Tribe. *See* Akimel O'odham Tribe

Pinchot, Gifford, 9, 10, 13–14

Place No One Knew, The (Porter), 112–13, 120

Plato, 268

Plessy v. Ferguson (1896), 38

Pomeroy, F. I., 27

Pope, Carl, 251

Porter, Eliot, 112

Poulson, Norris, 46

Powell, John Wesley, 1–2, 3–4, 4, 21

Power for the Nation (film), 178

preservation(ists), xix–xx, 13–14, 17, 65; as elitist, 88, 158–59, 170, 212, 259; and dams in Grand Canyon, 15–16, 49, 67, 135, 195, 214, 218, 235, 258; and LCRBP, 199–202, 204–5, 207; versus conservation, 9–11. *See also* conservation(ists); environmentalists

Preston, Porter, 22

Project Rescue symposium, 160

Prospect Canyon Dam, 83–84

Pulliam, Eugene, 121

Quiet Crisis, The (Udall, S.), 88, 100, 131, 154, 212, 235

Rainbow Bridge National Monument, 78–79, 89, 94–95, 108, 179, 263
Raker Act (1913), 10
Ramparts (magazine), 302n25
Ramsing, F. C., 241
RAND Corporation, 160
Raushenbush, Stephen, 144–45
Rayburn, Sam, 87
Reader's Digest, 36, 187–88, 189, 259; El Tovar symposium and, 189–94, 195
Redford, Robert, 265, 266, 267
Redwood National Park, 211
Reisner, Marc, 27, 221, 251
Report on the Lands of the Arid Region of the US, (Powell), 3
Republic (Plato), 268
Rhodes, John, xvii, *203, 245;* and CAP, 77, 99, 116, 148, 165, 171, 172, 218, 224, 240; and Hualapai Nation, 183–84, 185; and LCRBP, 162, 199, 208, 229–33, 236
Rifkind, Simon H., 89, 254
Riggins, J. A., 117
Robinson, Bestor, 48, 51, 52–53, 58–59, 68, 89, 113–14, 269
Rocha, George, 170–71, 172, 202–4, *203,* 209, 223
Rockwood, Charles, 5
Rogers, Walter, 224
Roosevelt, Franklin Delano, 26, 36, 37, 71, 130, 131
Roosevelt, Theodore, xv, 1, 2, 2–3, 10, 131, 188
"Ruin for the Grand Canyon" (Bradley, R.), 186–87, 259

Salt Lake City Tribune, 7
Salton Sea/Sink, 5
Salt River Project, 6
Salt River Valley, 24

San Carlos Apache Nation, 205, 209
San Francisco Chronicle, 229, 301n5
Saturday Evening Post, 65, 187
Saturday Review, 302n25
Saylor, John, 147, 196, *245;* and CAP, 66, 238, 257; and LCRBP, 200, 201, 202, 224–25, 226–27, 229, 231–34
Scenic Hudson Preservation Conference v. FPC (a.k.a. Storm King decision; 1965), 97, 272
Science (magazine), 210
Scientific American (magazine), 23, 302n25
Scott, Doug, 265, 266
Seaborg, Glen, 100
Seabach, Susan, 217–18
Senner, George, 116, 183, 199, 223, 238
Sequoia National Park, 279n19
"Shall We Let Them Ruin Our National Parks" (DeVoto), 65
Sheppard, Harry R., 46
Sierra Club, xvi–xvii, xviii, 9–11, 71, 73–74; activism of, 80–82, 83, 108, 159, 175–76, 261–64, 276; "Battle Ads," xviii, 211, 214–18, *215,* 227, 229, 230, 240–41, 258, 301n5, 302n25; and Bridge Canyon/ Hualapai Dam, 49, 51, 58–60, 76, 98; and CAP, 168, 169–70, 240; and dams in Grand Canyon, 63–64, 70, 112–15, 127, 145–46, 159, 210, 212, 222, 250–53, 255–56, 260; in *A Fierce Green Fire,* 265–68; IRS and, xviii, 219–21, 241; lobbying by, 74, 79–81, 89–90, 96, 125–26; and Marble Canyon Dam, 91, 97, 113, 169–70, 269; and PSWP, 124–25, 138, 140
Sierra Club Bulletin, 89, 125, 147, 160, 175, 227
Sierra Club Foundation, 89–90
Silent Spring (Carson), 151, 154–55
Siri, William, 220
Skelton, Helen, 228

Smith, Anthony Wayne, 61, 93, 95, 96, 104, 178; on alternative energy sources, 139, 145, 149, 168–69

Southern California Edison, 22

Southern Pacific Railroad, 5

Southern Ute Tribe, 209

Southwest Progress Committee, 223

Soviet Union, 46, 100, 109–10, 119

Sparks, Felix, 209

Split Mountain Dam, 62, 73, 74, 78. *See also* Dinosaur National Monument

Spurr, Stephen, 191

Staats, Elmer, 142, 161

Stafford, William Henry, 18

Stanton, Robert Brewster, 2, 7

Stebbins, Robert C., 64–65

Steck, George, 191

Stegner, Wallace, 88, 176, 288n39

Steiger, Sam, 240, 245

Still the Wild River Runs (Pearson), xix

Storm King decision, 97, 272

Straus, Michael, 42, 49, 52, 54–55, 55, 57, 65

Streep, Meryl, 265

Tapeats Creek, 58, 92

Theodore Roosevelt Dam, 6

This Is Dinosaur (Sierra Club), 74

Tillotson, M. R., 31, 55, 64–65

Time (magazine), 180

Time and the River Flowing (Leydet), 145–46, 159, 169–70, 174, 175

Toll, Roger, 29

Toroweap Point, 188, 191, 193

Truman, Harry, 67, 73

Trustees for Conservation, 80, 89

Turner, Tom, 265

Tusayan National Forest, 86

Two Yosemites (film), 146

Udall, Morris, xvii, 94, 97–98, 122, 174, 191, 203, 297n2; and "Battle Ads," 216–17, 218; and CAP, 116, 165, 168, 169–72, 177, 182, 238, 240; El Tovar symposium and, 189, 190–92, 193, 194; and Hualapai Nation, 172–73, 183–84, 185; and IRS, 219–21; and LCRBP, 198–99, 200, 204, 208, 226–27, 229–33, 236

Udall, Stewart, xiii, xvii, 35, 122, 129, 219, 245, 253; and Bridge Canyon/ Hualapai Dam, 141–42; and CAP, xviii, 75–78, 81, 98–99, 117, 118–20, 131, 140, 156, 167–68, 237, 239–40, 242, 256–58; and dams in Grand Canyon, 243–44, 250–51; and Glen Canyon Dam, 106–7; as Interior secretary, 87–89, 92–94, 101, 105–6, 221–22, 238–39, 262; on Lyndon Johnson, 129–30, 143, 234; and PSWP, 121–22, 126, 134, 137, 150–51, 155, 244; *The Quiet Crisis*, 88, 100, 131, 154, 212, 235; and Rainbow Bridge, 94–95; and regional water plan, 101–4, 108–12, 157, 254–55

United States v. Harriss (1954), 94, 96, 111, 125, 255; Sierra Club and, 80–81, 83, 219

Upper Colorado River Commission, 209

US Army Corps of Engineers, 41, 67, 73, 93, 142

US Bureau of Reclamation (USBR), xvi, 23, 25, 67; and Bridge Canyon/ Hualapai Dam, 28, 39, 53, 59, 110–11, 184; and CAP, 47, 141, 165; and Colorado River dams, 26, 41–43, 84; and CRSP, 62, 72; cost-benefit analyses, 160, 174, 251; and dams in Grand Canyon, 29, 31, 136–37, 177, 248, 266; El Tovar symposium and, 189–90; feasibility studies, 34, 92, 163–64, 274; and Marble Canyon Dam, 54–55, 201; and MCKC, 43, 45, 54–55, 92, 95, 123, 137; National Park Service and, 29, 31, 35, 36–37, 39–41, 47, 54

US Bureau of the Budget, 142, 161–62, 171, 183, 234, 235

US Congress, xvi, 13, 29, 33, 242; and Bureau of Reclamation, 163–64; and CAP, 52, 61, 63, 65–68, 126–27, 140–42, 148, 165, 167–73, 182–83, 240–43, 244–45, 247; and CRSP, 72–73, 74–77; and LCRBP, 143, 157, 197–204, 207–8, 210–11, 224–27, 229–34, 236–37, 273

US Department of the Interior, 11, 15, 18, 34, 101, 109, 110, 148, 221, 235; and Bridge Canyon/Hualapai Dam, 48, 49, 63–64; and CAP, 51–52, 126, 172, 184, 242; and CRSP, 60, 72; and dams in Grand Canyon, 37, 58, 113, 124, 237, 248; intra-agency relations, 28–29, 36, 45, 54–55, 60, 93, 216, 222; *Lake Powell, Jewel of the Colorado*, 157–58, 194; and LCRBP, 161, 163, 199; and PSWP, 121–22, 135, 139, 142. *See also specific agencies*

US Forest Service, xv, 9, 13–14, 16–17, 19, 43

US Geological Survey (USGS), 3, 19, 22, 23, 120, 145, 237

US Reclamation Service, 6, 23

US Supreme Court, 17, 27, 38, 80, 84–85; and water rights, xv, xviii, 21, 46, 52, 66, 69, 81, 89, 105, 115–16. *See also specific decisions*

US War Department: and dams in Grand Canyon, 46

Utah, 7, 21–22, 25, 73, 121

Ute Mountain Ute Tribe, 209

Van Ness, Bill, xvii, 274, 275

Venture (magazine), 244

Verde River, 24, 241

Voight, William, 68

von Neumann, John, 100

Vosburgh, John, 177

Wall Street Journal, 229

Warner, Tucker & Company, 8

Warren, Earl, 116

Washington, 47, 50, 152, 168, 225

Washington Post, 219, 223, 301n5

Water Quality Act (1965), 274

water rights: and lower Colorado River Basin, 25, 46, 52, 69, 81, 97, 105, 115–16, 143, 253–55; per Colorado River Compact; 21–22, 103; prior appropriation doctrine, 3, 21, 22, 33, 115, 116, 117, 233; riparian, 21

Wauneka, Annie, 228

Wayburn, Edgar, 219

"We Can Only Mar It" (Pope), 251

Weiner, Eugene, 176, 204

Weiner, Ruth, 176

Western Federation of Outdoor Clubs, 64, 138

White Mountain Apache Nation, 205, 209

Whitsit, Lyle A., 17

wilderness, xx; preservation of, 40, 70, 88, 108, 111, 113

Wilderness Act (1964), xx, 89, 151, 154, 235

Wilderness and the American Mind (Nash), 250

Wilderness Society, xviii, 58, 76, 140, 148, 168, 260

Wildlife Management Institute, 57–58

Wilson, Woodrow, 10, 13

Winter, Bill, 188, 198

Wirth, Conrad, 81–82, 91–92, 93, 95, 123–24

World War II, 26, 31, 35, 41, 42

Wupatki National Monument, 43, 44, 59, 84, 134

Wyoming, 21–22, 62

Yampa River, 36, 62, 72

Yosemite National Park, 9, 11, 16, 57, 124, 212, 279n19

Zahniser, Howard, 62, 76, 80, 146

Acknowledgments

While camping at Soap Creek rapid on the Colorado River more than thirty years ago, I tried to figure out where the high-water mark of the Marble Canyon reservoir would have been on the scarlet cliffs far above my head. I have been thinking and writing about the Grand Canyon dams ever since. Many people have played important roles along the way and deserve my gratitude. I appreciate the many friends and colleagues who have encouraged me to keep going when life, funding, or teaching loads got in the way. I'd also like to thank the people who have been critical of my previous publications about the Grand Canyon dams. Your criticism has forced me to reexamine my interpretations, dig deeper for new sources and reinforce my conclusions, add nuances I had not considered previously, or draw new conclusions altogether. Ultimately our interpretations may differ, but our hearts are in the same place.

Although many people have been part of this journey, I'd like to thank several in particular. Justin Race and Alrica Goldstein at the University of Nevada Press have been models of encouragement and patience. The late G. Lynn Nelson, my first English professor at Arizona State University recognized that I had potential and administered well-earned doses of tough love when I tried to skate by on talent alone. Douglas Weiner and Katherine Morrissey of the University of Arizona History Department and George Lubick of the Northern Arizona University History Department have been part of this research since the very beginning. I appreciate Stephen Jett's willingness to correspond with me about his involvement in these events during the last twenty years and to review parts of the manuscript for accuracy. I am also indebted to Jerry Mander who graciously gave me permission to use his Grand Canyon Battle Ads despite our differing interpretations of these events, and to Howie Usher who drew upon his forty years as a Grand Canyon river guide to help me pinpoint the exact locations of several of the stunning photographs that appear in the book.

The dedicated archival staffs who assisted me at the following repositories also deserve mention: Arizona Historical Society, University of Arizona Special Collections; National Archives in College Park, Maryland; Houghton Library at Harvard University; Conservation Collection at the Denver Public Library; Denver Federal Records Center; Indiana University of Pennsylvania; Arizona State University; Northern Arizona University; American Heritage Center, University of Wyoming; Clemson University; Bancroft Library at University of California, Berkeley; University of Washington; and the Grand Canyon National Park Research Library and Museum collection. Nathaniel Douglass of <ndcartography.com> added important context to the story with his beautiful maps and is the living embodiment of patience.

Closer to home, I'd like to thank the West Texas A&M University administration for giving me course reassign-time and monetary support so I could continue my research, and the staff at the West Texas A&M University Cornette Library, especially the interlibrary loan department, for obtaining obscure and hard-to-find materials quickly. I'd like to give research librarian Steve Ely a special acknowledgement for his online sorcery in finding and gaining access to sources when my own efforts proved futile.

As a faculty member in the history department at West Texas A&M University for the past twenty years, I have had the privilege of working with the most wonderful colleagues anyone could ever have. I have spent innumerable hours with Bruce Brasington, Jean Stuntz, and Tim Bowman discussing research and teaching over coffee, dark beer, and bourbon. I admire their dedication to scholarship and for refusing to compromise the standards of our discipline in spite of their heavy teaching loads. Likewise, Bryan Vizzini, one of the finest teachers I have ever known, has interceded at key moments with my own tendencies towards melancholia, and as a Latin Americanist he has forced me to see far beyond America's borders.

I have also been blessed with a wonderful family without whom none of this would have been possible. My parents, the late Kathryn and Ben C. Pearson, always gave me steadfast encouragement and support. My children, Nathaniel, Cameron, Joshua, and Cassandra, keep me grounded with their unconditional love.

Being married to a historian is wonderful and occasionally intimidating, especially when she is also an editor. Kim Engel-Pearson, whom I knew in graduate school and was finally smart enough to marry a decade ago, challenges me intellectually with her pointed questioning, stellar editing, elegant writing, and her high expectations. Thank you, K, for encouraging me to hone the "art" versus the "craft," for being relentless in pursuing the "discipline of the discipline," for choosing the hard over the easy, and for everything else.

These and many other people have helped me research and write this book. However, I am responsible for assessing and presenting the evidence upon which my conclusions are based. The responsibility for any and all inadequacies and omissions of argument, style, and interpretation rests with me.